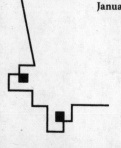

HAJIME KOMOTO

Thank you very much for buying volume 6. Look at how awe-inspiring my eyes have become. That's because this is number 6…

Hajime Komoto made his manga debut with the hit series *Mashle: Magic and Muscles,* which began serialization in *Weekly Shonen Jump* in January 2020.

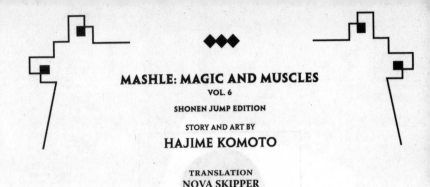

MASHLE: MAGIC AND MUSCLES

VOL. 6

SHONEN JUMP EDITION

STORY AND ART BY

HAJIME KOMOTO

TRANSLATION
NOVA SKIPPER

SHONEN JUMP SERIES LETTERING
EVE GRANDT

GRAPHIC NOVEL TOUCH-UP ART & LETTERING
RINA MAPA

DESIGN
JIMMY PRESLER

EDITOR
KARLA CLARK

Printed in the U.S.A.

Published by VIZ Media, LLC
P.O. Box 77010
San Francisco, CA 94107

10 9 8 7 6 5 4 3 2 1
First printing, May 2022

VIZ MEDIA　**SHONEN JUMP**

viz.com

MASHLE

MAGIC AND MUSCLES

STORY AND ART BY

HAJIME KOMOTO

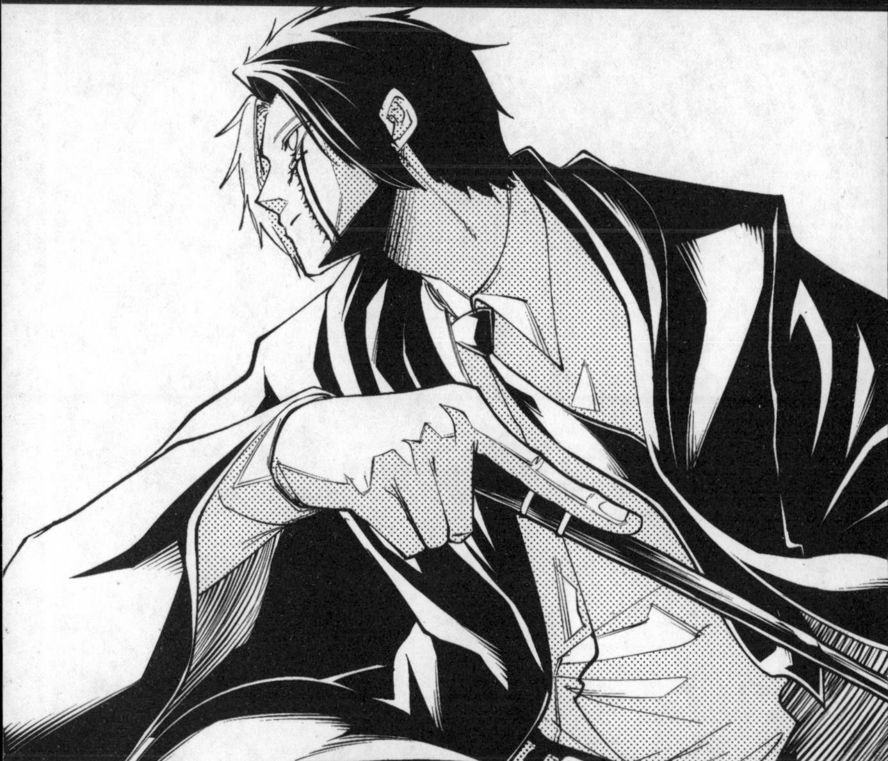

6

FINN AMES
AND THE FRIEND

CHARACTERS

MASH BURNEDEAD

An unusual boy incapable of using magic. With his finely honed muscles, he's able to punch his way through any spell, but it's not so easy to fight off his ignorance of the world. He values his family and friends and loves cream puffs, and he can't tell if a door is pushable or pullable.

LANCE CROWN

A powerful pretty boy who ranked first in the entrance exams. Loves his sister a little too much.

FINN AMES

Mash's roommate. Comedic foil and Mash's very first friend.

LEMON IRVINE

Fell in love with Mash after he saved her during the entrance exams.

DOT BARRETT

A loud, impulsive, unpopular guy who has a boundless hatred of pretty boys.

RAYNE AMES

Adler's top student and this year's Divine Visionary. Finn's older brother.

HEADMASTER WAHLBERG

Headmaster of the magic academy. Has high expectations for Mash.

MARGARETTE MACARON

Prefect of Orca Dorm. An aesthete who prefers stimulation to coins.

ORTER MADL

"The Desert Cane." The Divine Visionary in charge of the Magical Power Administration.

STORY

In the magic realm, everyone is capable of magic, and your skill at it (or lack thereof) determines everything. Deep in the forest lives a boy named Mash. Daily training has turned him into a god of physical fitness, but he has a secret—he can't use magic! In the magic realm, that's cause for extermination. To keep his secret under wraps, Mash enters magic school with the goal of earning the title "Divine Visionary"—one chosen by the gods. Luckily, his exceptional strength helps him hide his lack of magic from the world and aids him in gathering the coins he needs to achieve his goal.

Mash and friends' celebration of their victory over the coin-hoarding students of Lang Dorm is quickly interrupted by the appearance of the mysterious organization Innocent Zero. While Mash is pinned down, a counterattack from Abel, leader of the Magia Lupus, helps turn the tide. Time for a bigger and better victory party! Unfortunately, this incident makes Mash's lack of magic known throughout the school, and he's called to an emergency council! Mash is given one chance at leniency—if he helps bring down Innocent Zero! Then another adversary appears on the eve of the Divine Visionary selection exam...

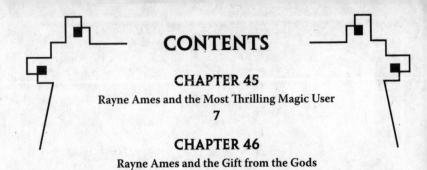

CONTENTS

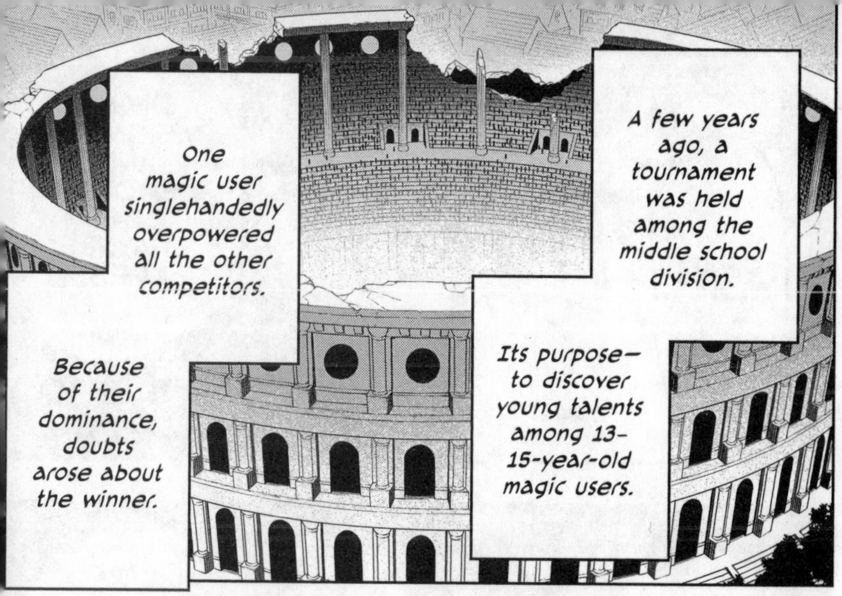
A few years ago, a tournament was held among the middle school division.
Its purpose— to discover young talents among 13-15-year-old magic users.
One magic user singlehandedly overpowered all the other competitors.
Because of their dominance, doubts arose about the winner.

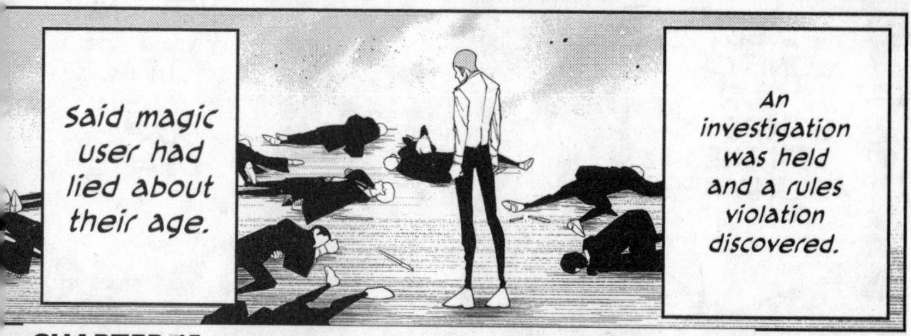
An investigation was held and a rules violation discovered.
Said magic user had lied about their age.

CHAPTER 45: RAYNE AMES AND THE MOST THRILLING MAGIC USER

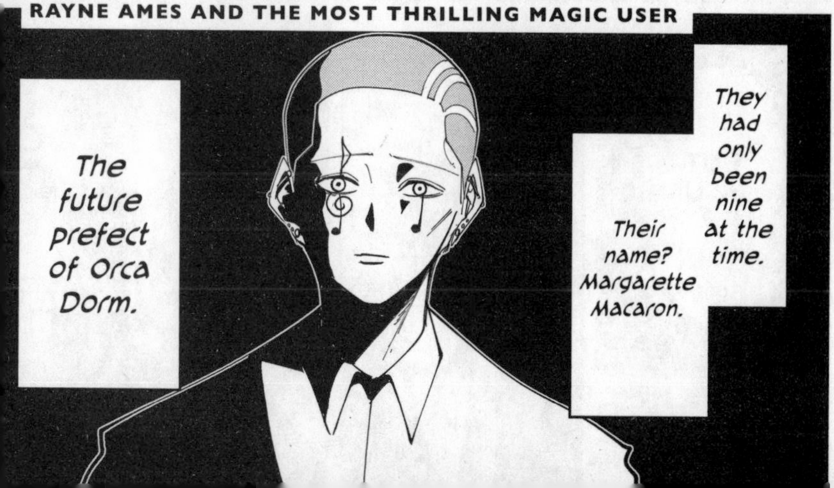
They had only been nine at the time.
Their name? Margarette Macaron.
The future prefect of Orca Dorm.

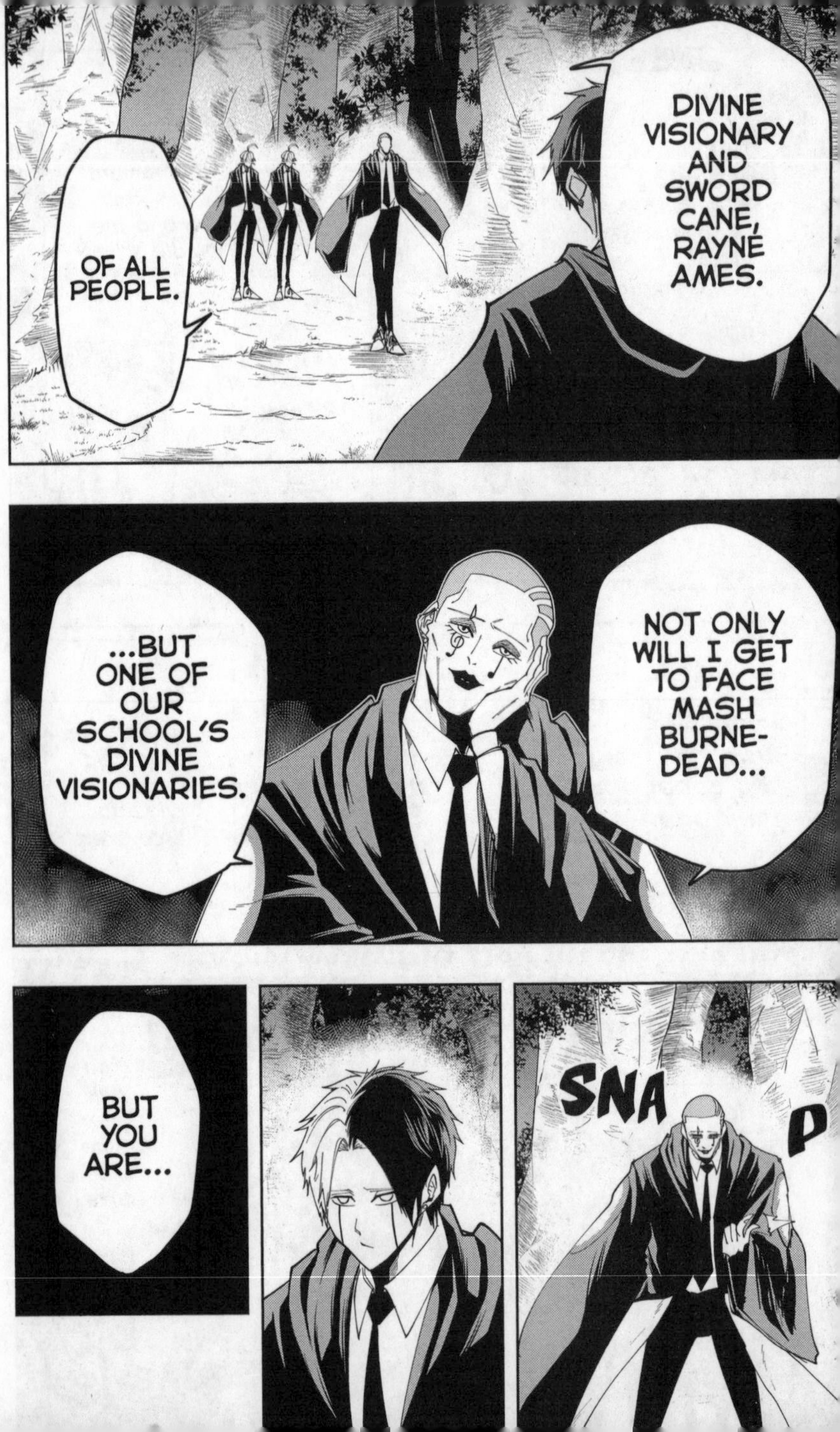
DIVINE VISIONARY AND SWORD CANE, RAYNE AMES.
OF ALL PEOPLE.
NOT ONLY WILL I GET TO FACE MASH BURNE-DEAD...
...BUT ONE OF OUR SCHOOL'S DIVINE VISIONARIES.
SNAP
BUT YOU ARE...

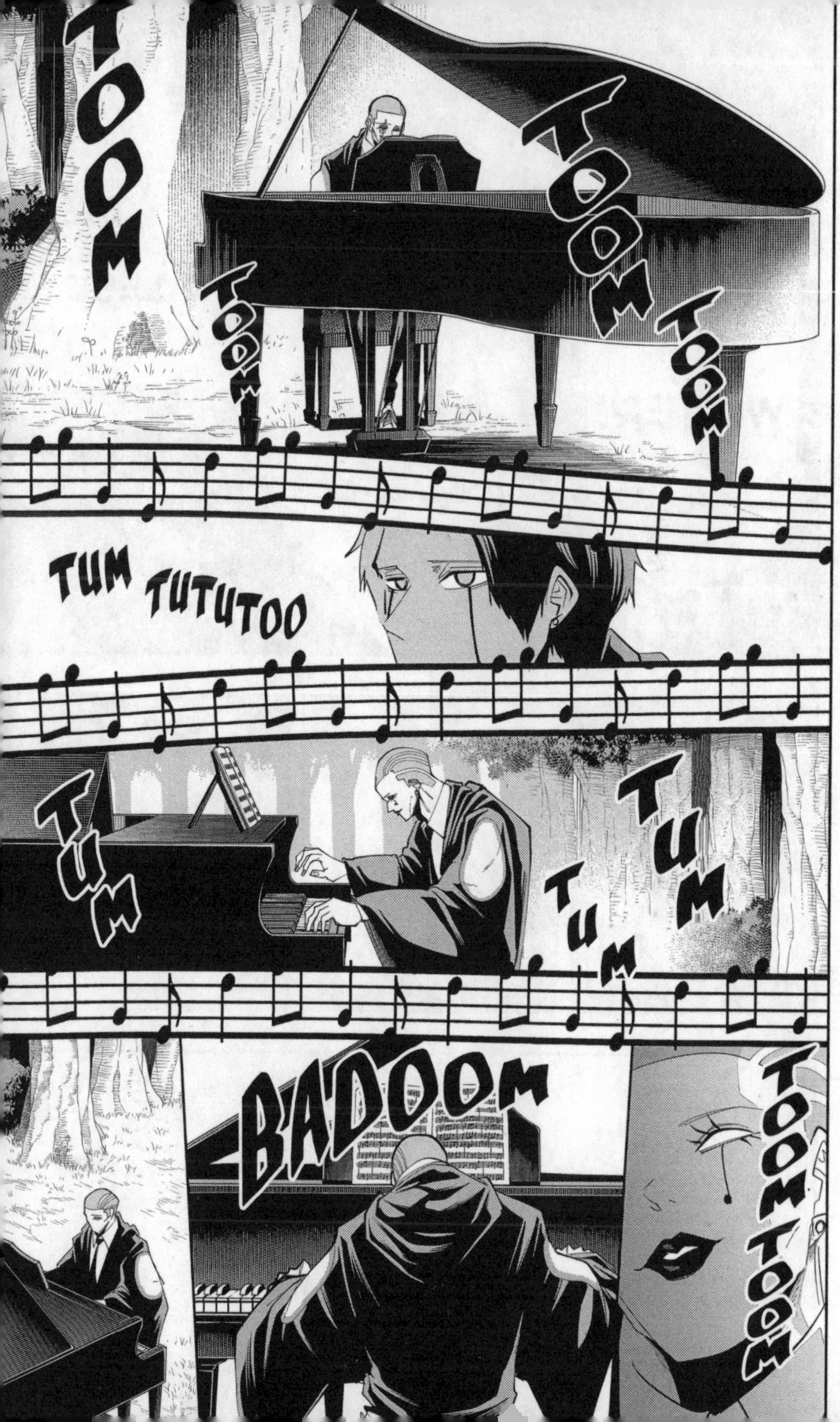
TOOM
TOOM
TOOM
TOOM
TOOM
TUM TUTUTOO
TUM
TUM
TUM
TOOM TOOM
BADOOM

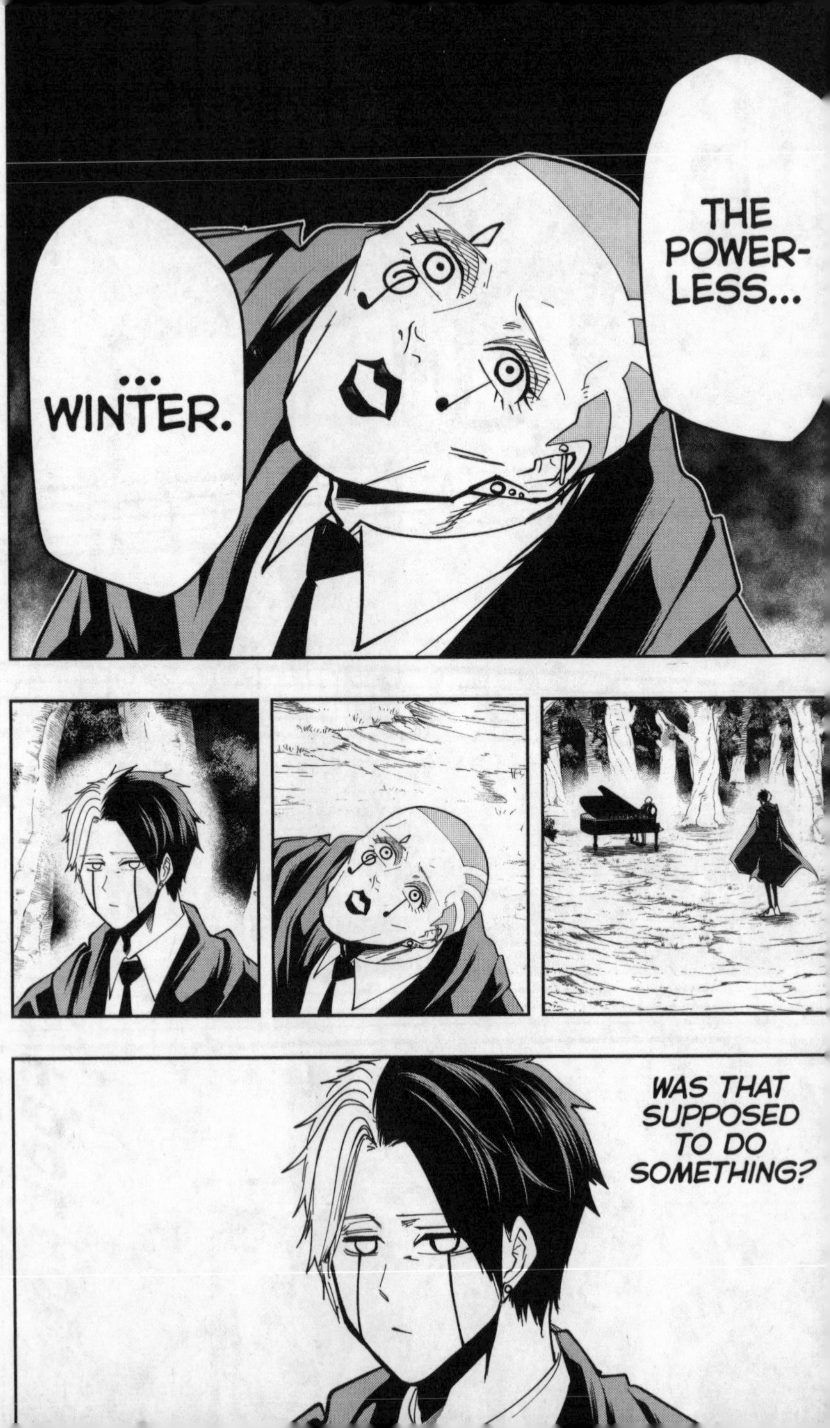
THE POWER-LESS...
... WINTER.
WAS THAT SUPPOSED TO DO SOMETHING?

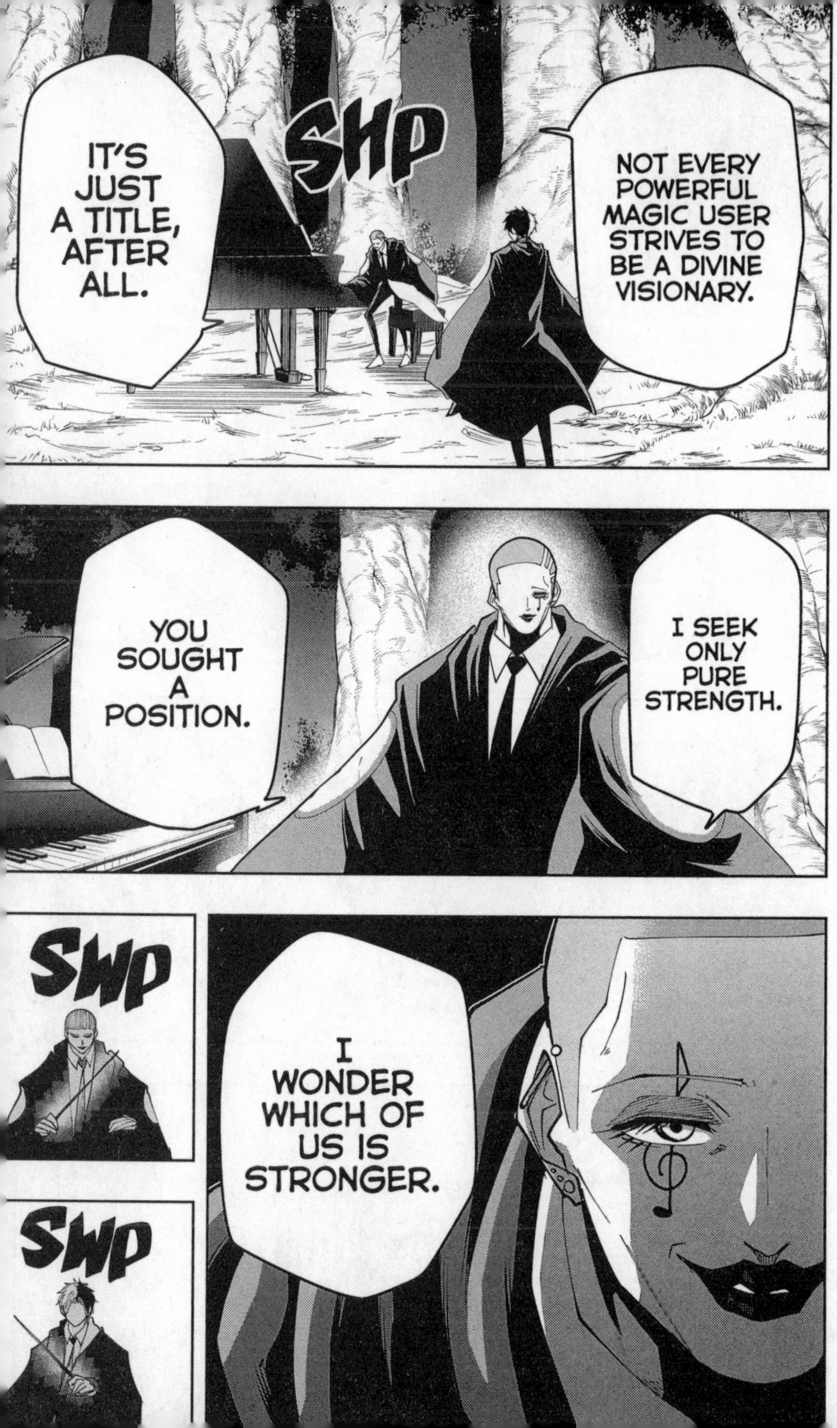
NOT EVERY POWERFUL MAGIC USER STRIVES TO BE A DIVINE VISIONARY.
SHP
IT'S JUST A TITLE, AFTER ALL.
I SEEK ONLY PURE STRENGTH.
YOU SOUGHT A POSITION.
I WONDER WHICH OF US IS STRONGER.
SWP
SWP

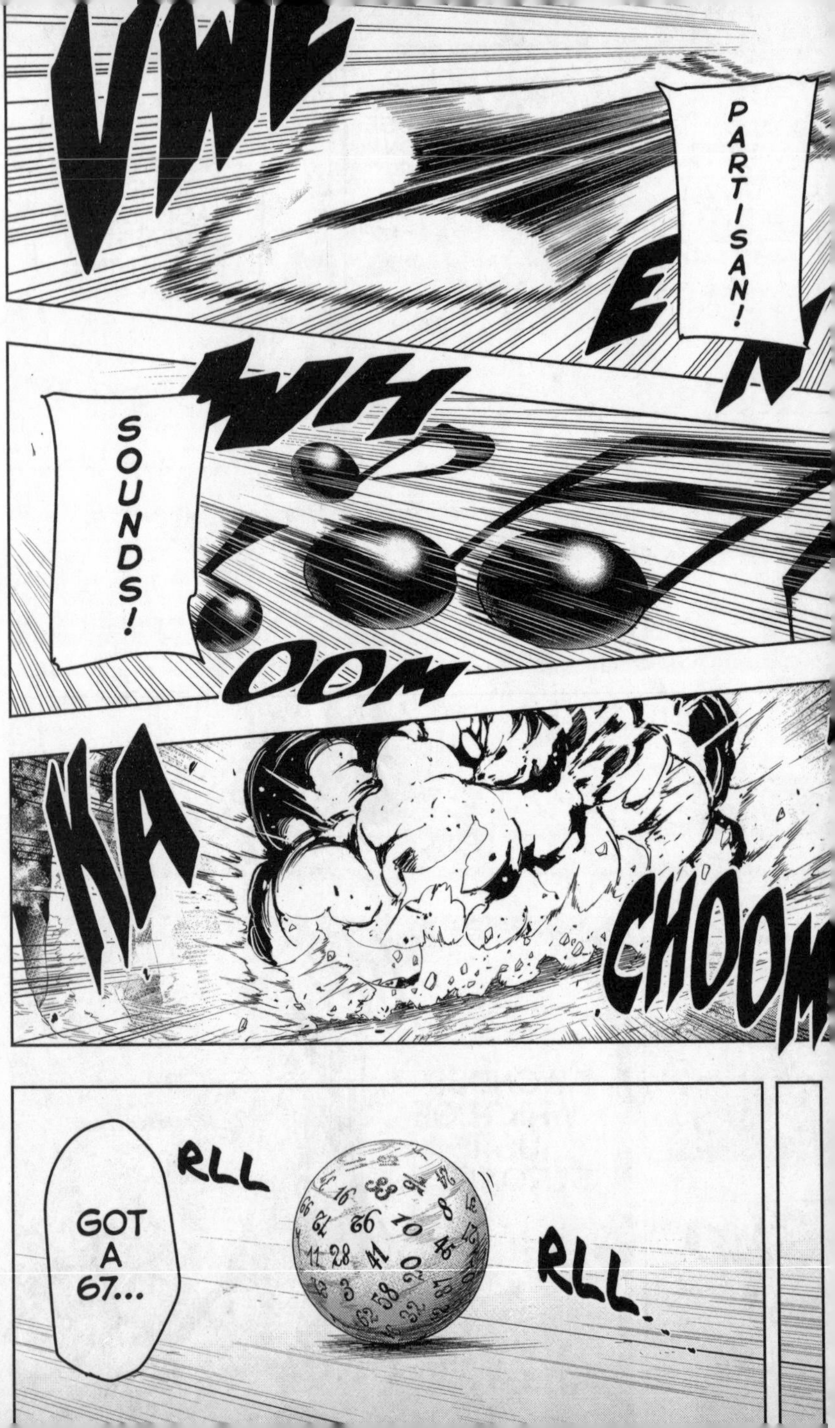
PARTISAN!
SOUNDS!
WHOOM
KA
CHOOM
RLL
RLL...
GOT A 67...

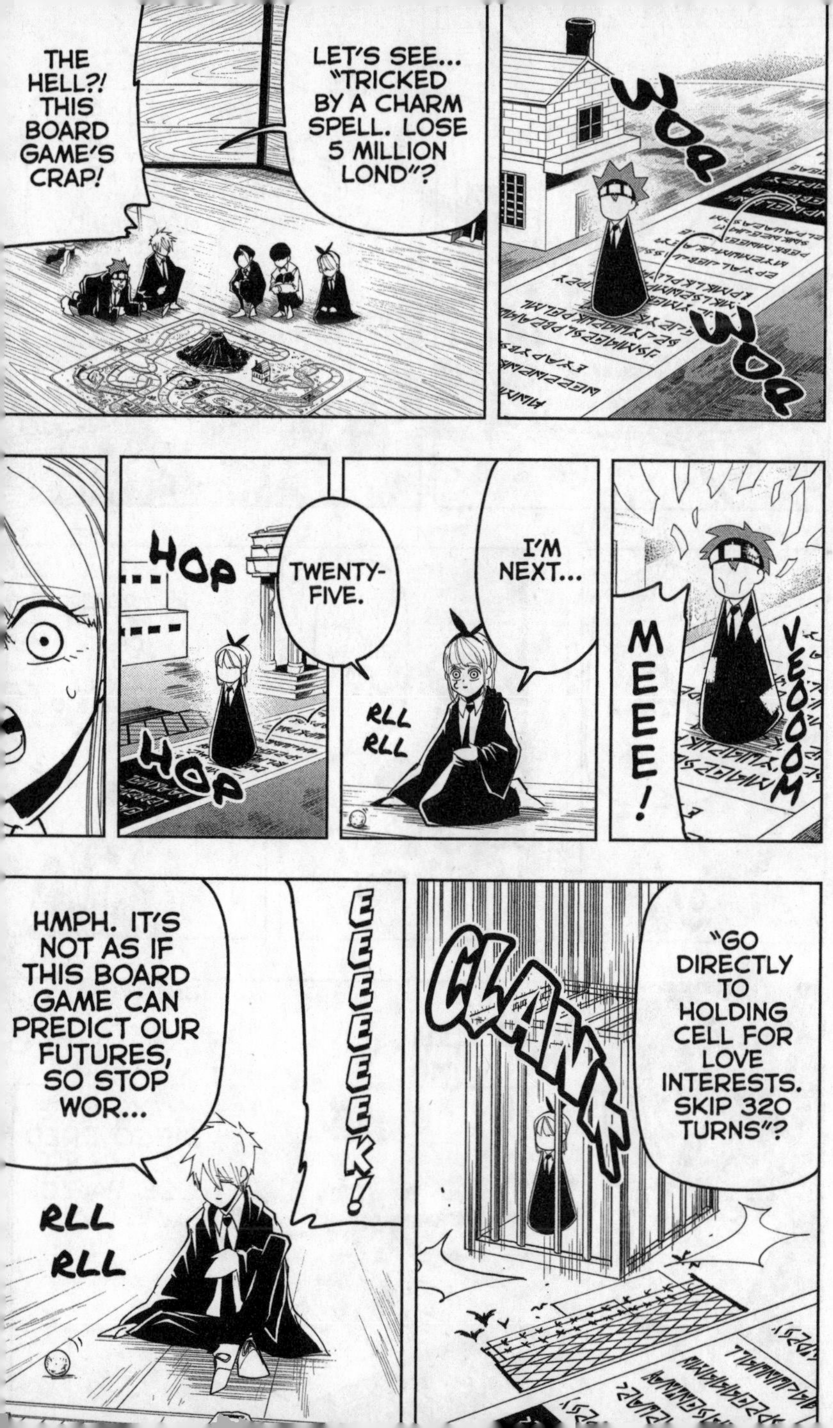
WOP
WOP
LET'S SEE... "TRICKED BY A CHARM SPELL. LOSE 5 MILLION LOND"?
THE HELL?! THIS BOARD GAME'S CRAP!
MEEE!
VEOOOOM
I'M NEXT...
RLL RLL
TWENTY-FIVE.
...HOP
HOP
"GO DIRECTLY TO HOLDING CELL FOR LOVE INTERESTS. SKIP 320 TURNS"?
CLANK
EEEEEEK!
HMPH. IT'S NOT AS IF THIS BOARD GAME CAN PREDICT OUR FUTURES, SO STOP WOR...
RLL RLL

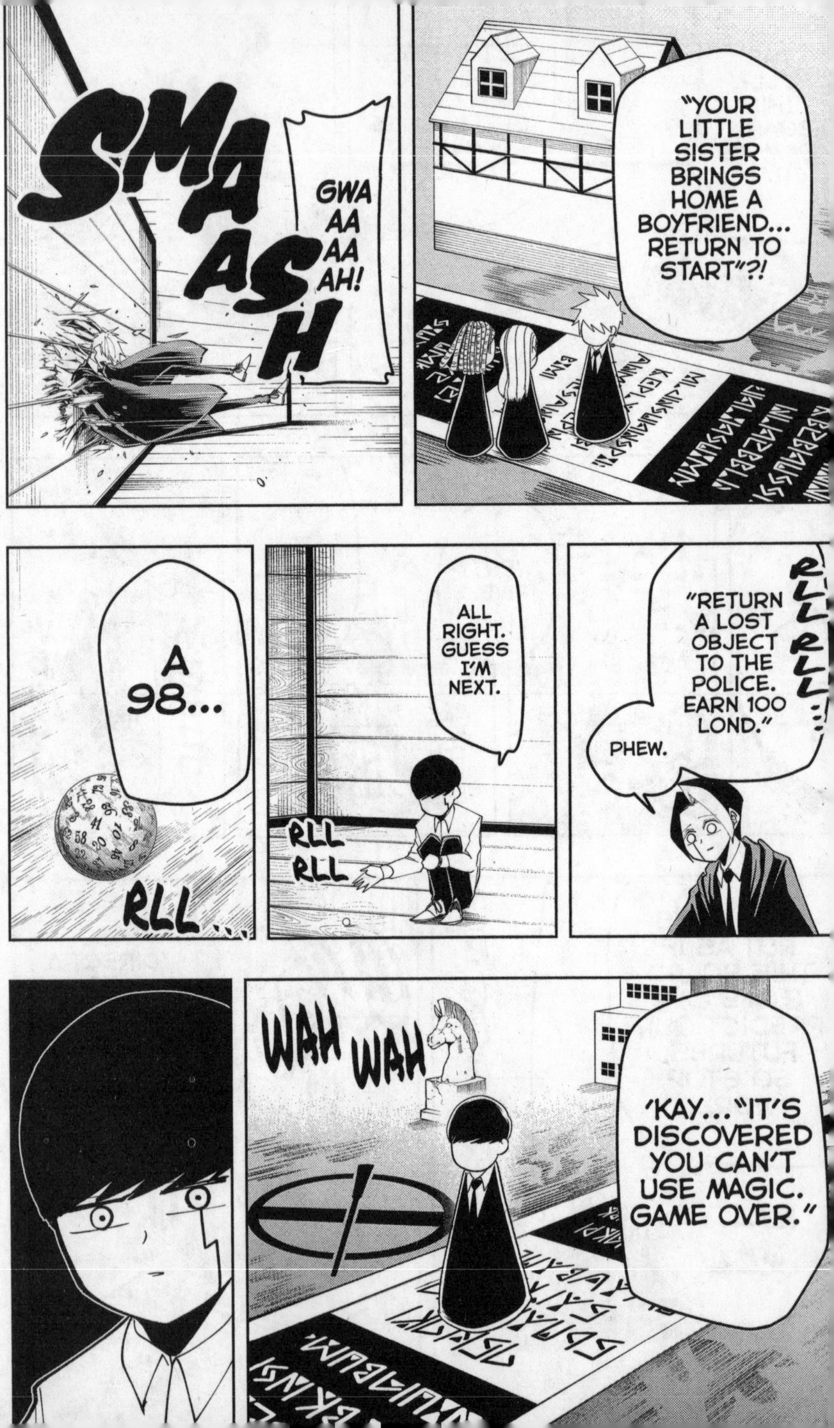
"YOUR LITTLE SISTER BRINGS HOME A BOYFRIEND... RETURN TO START"?!
GWAAAAAAAH!
SMAASH
"RETURN A LOST OBJECT TO THE POLICE. EARN 100 LOND."
RLL RLL...
PHEW.
ALL RIGHT. GUESS I'M NEXT.
RLL RLL
A 98...
RLL...
WAH WAH
'KAY... "IT'S DISCOVERED YOU CAN'T USE MAGIC. GAME OVER."

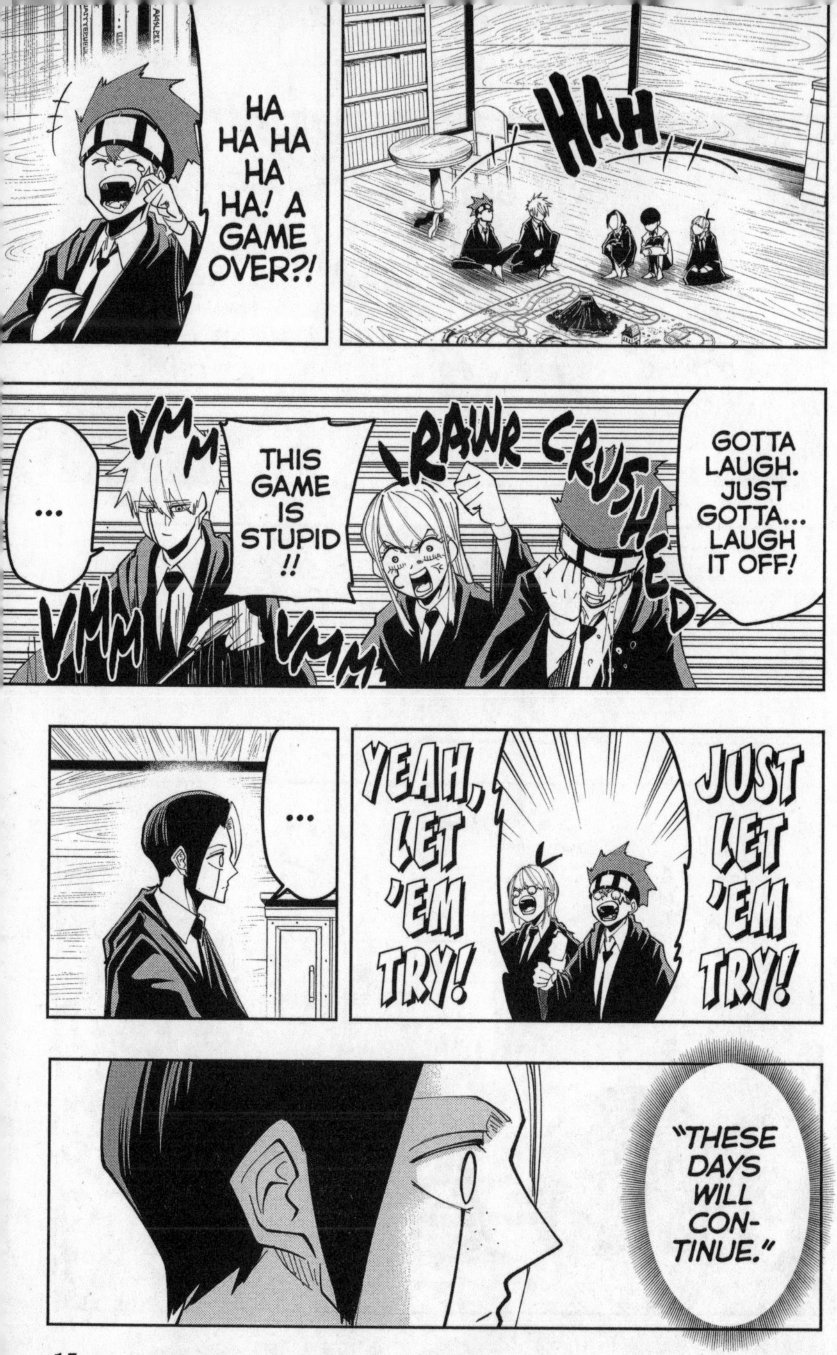
HAH
HA HA HA HA HA! A GAME OVER?!
GOTTA LAUGH. JUST GOTTA... LAUGH IT OFF!
CRUSHED
RAWR
THIS GAME IS STUPID!!
VMM
...
VMM
VMM
JUST LET 'EM TRY!
YEAH, LET 'EM TRY!
...
"THESE DAYS WILL CON-TINUE."

"WORDS ONLY HAVE MEANING WHEN PAIRED WITH ACTION."
"IF YOU CAN'T ACT, IT'S THE SAME AS NOT SAYING ANYTHING AT ALL."
I'LL KEEP THEM GOING...

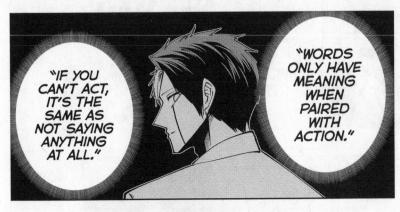

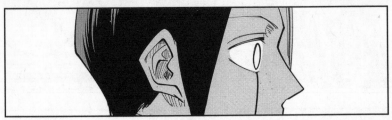

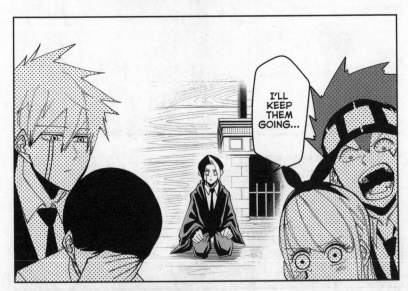

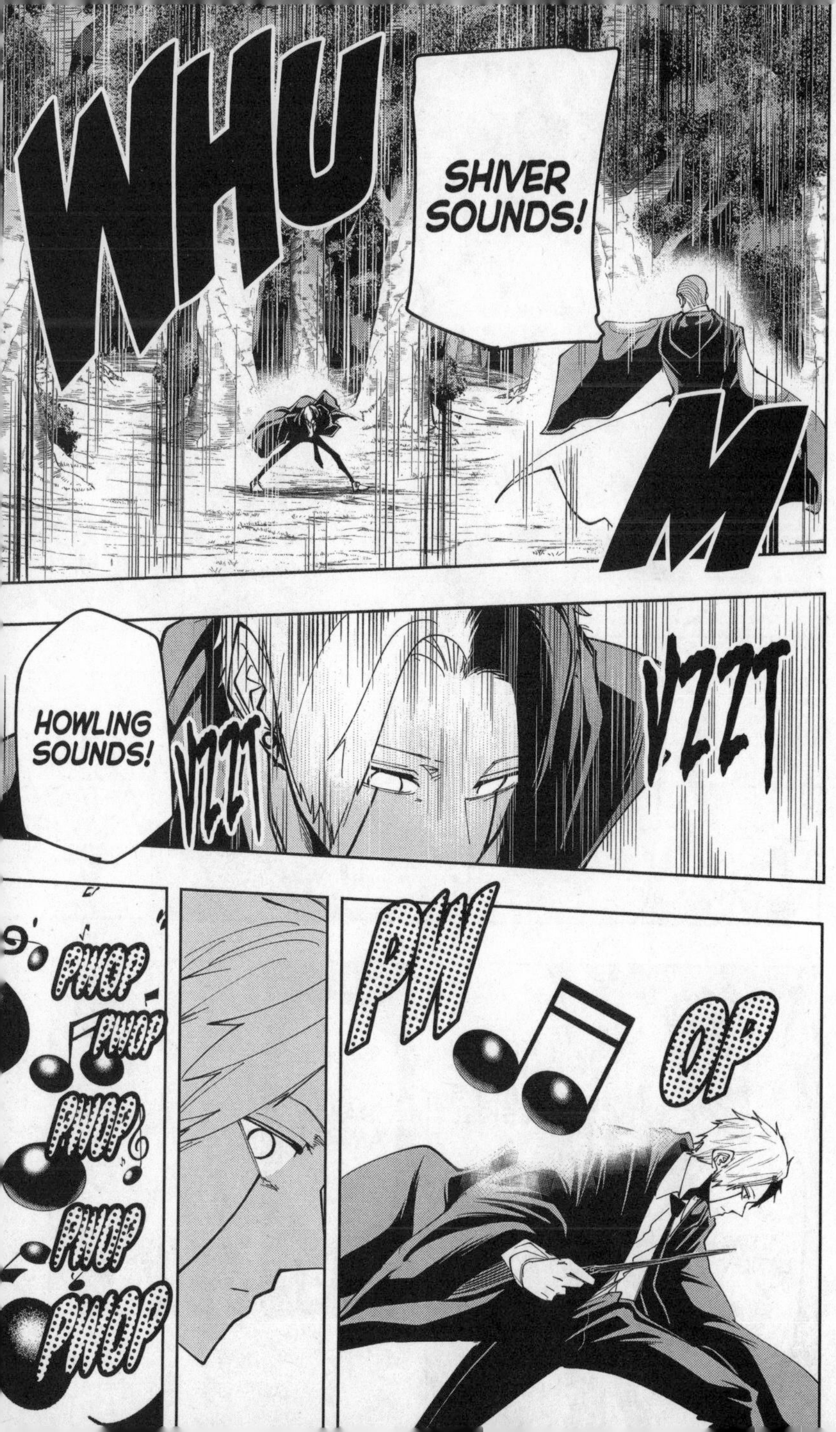
SHIVER SOUNDS!
WHU
M
VZZT
VZZT
HOWLING SOUNDS!
PW
OP
PWOP
PWOP
PWOP
PWOP
PWOP

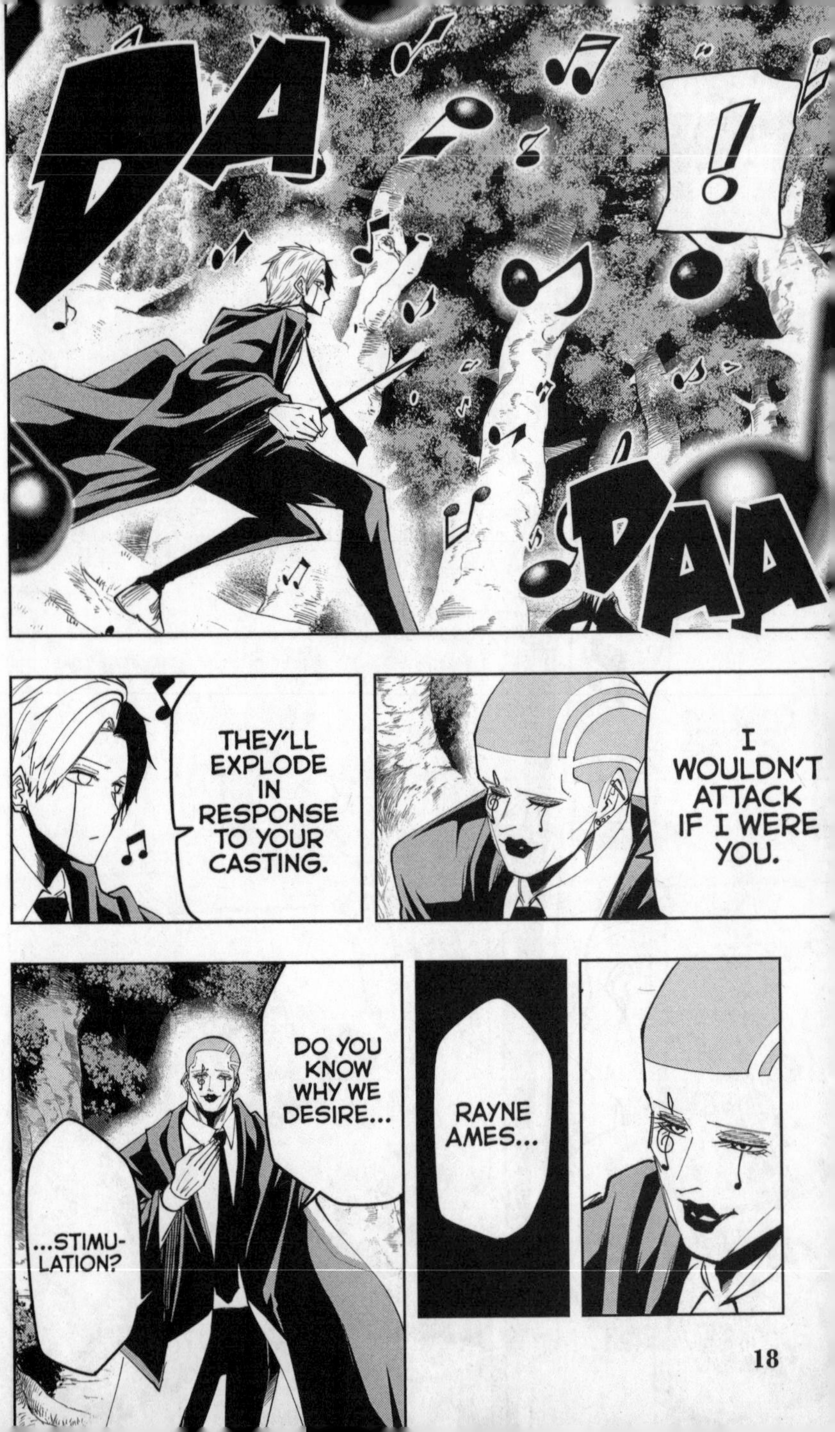
!
DA
DAA
I WOULDN'T ATTACK IF I WERE YOU.
THEY'LL EXPLODE IN RESPONSE TO YOUR CASTING.
RAYNE AMES...
DO YOU KNOW WHY WE DESIRE...
...STIMULATION?

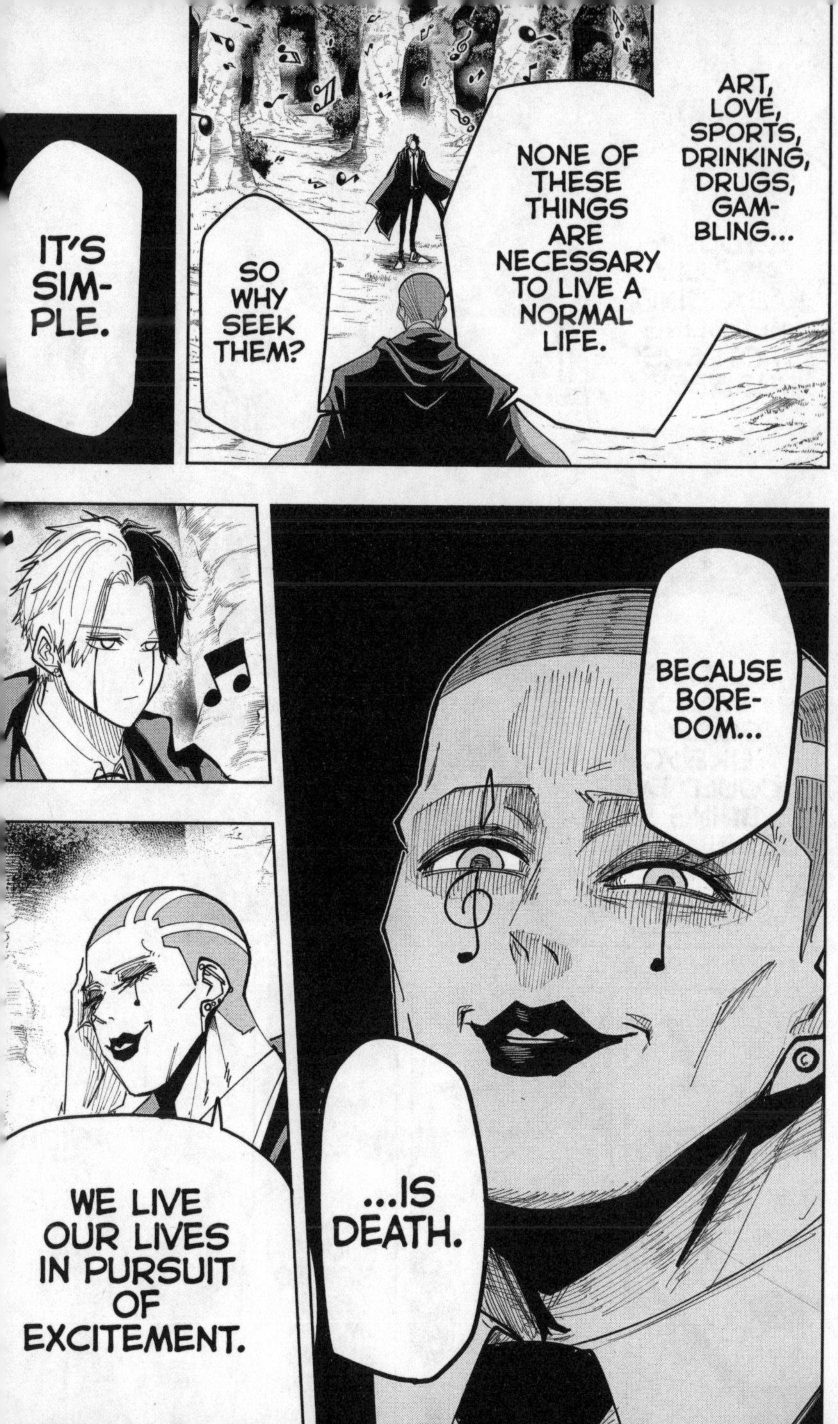
ART, LOVE, SPORTS, DRINKING, DRUGS, GAMBLING...
NONE OF THESE THINGS ARE NECESSARY TO LIVE A NORMAL LIFE.
SO WHY SEEK THEM?
IT'S SIMPLE.
BECAUSE BOREDOM...
...IS DEATH.
WE LIVE OUR LIVES IN PURSUIT OF EXCITEMENT.

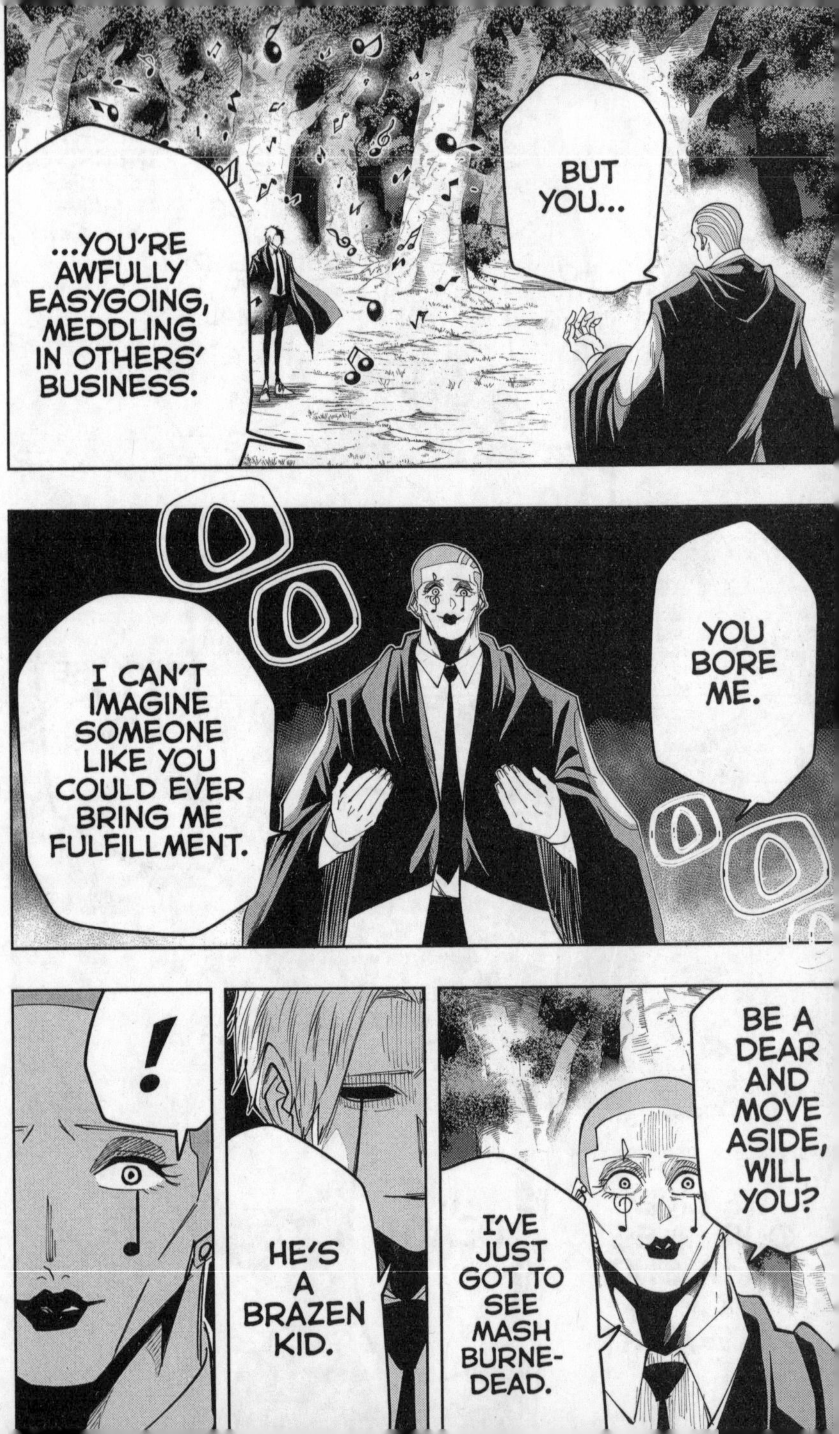
BUT YOU...
...YOU'RE AWFULLY EASYGOING, MEDDLING IN OTHERS' BUSINESS.
YOU BORE ME.
I CAN'T IMAGINE SOMEONE LIKE YOU COULD EVER BRING ME FULFILLMENT.
BE A DEAR AND MOVE ASIDE, WILL YOU?
I'VE JUST GOT TO SEE MASH BURNEDEAD.
HE'S A BRAZEN KID.
!

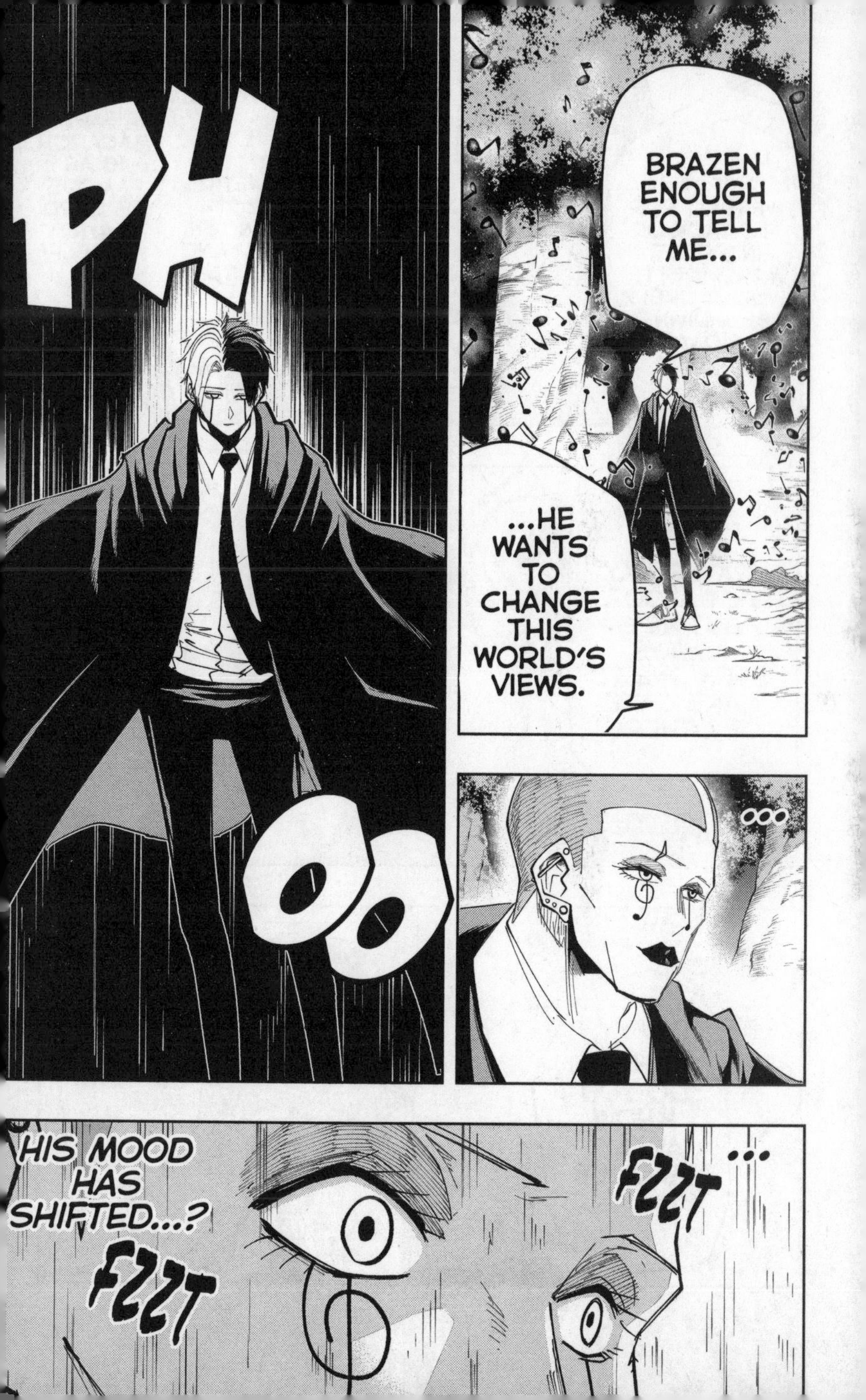
BRAZEN ENOUGH TO TELL ME...
...HE WANTS TO CHANGE THIS WORLD'S VIEWS.
OOO
PH
OO
FZZT ...
HIS MOOD HAS SHIFTED...?
FZZT

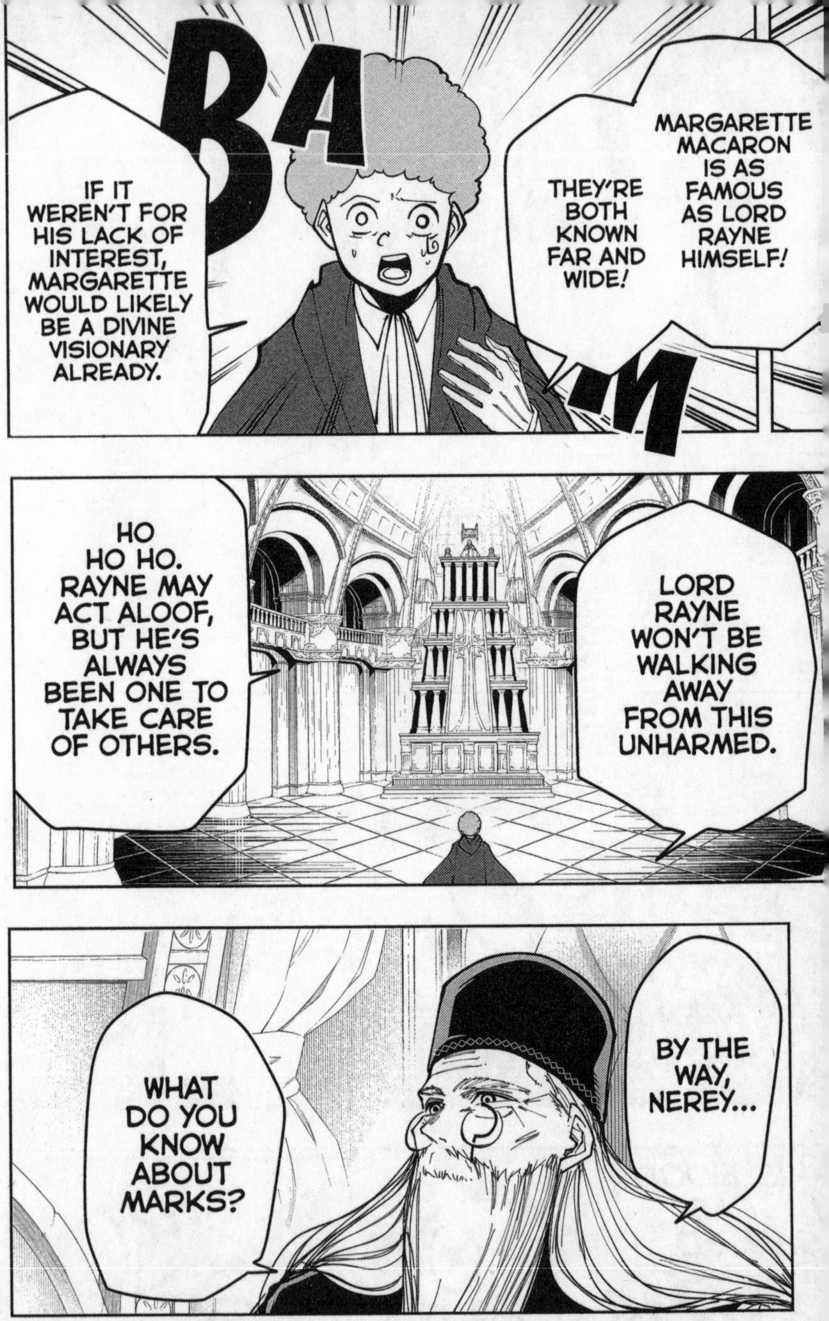
MARGARETTE MACARON IS AS FAMOUS AS LORD RAYNE HIMSELF!
THEY'RE BOTH KNOWN FAR AND WIDE!
BAM
IF IT WEREN'T FOR HIS LACK OF INTEREST, MARGARETTE WOULD LIKELY BE A DIVINE VISIONARY ALREADY.
LORD RAYNE WON'T BE WALKING AWAY FROM THIS UNHARMED.
HO HO HO. RAYNE MAY ACT ALOOF, BUT HE'S ALWAYS BEEN ONE TO TAKE CARE OF OTHERS.
BY THE WAY, NEREY...
WHAT DO YOU KNOW ABOUT MARKS?

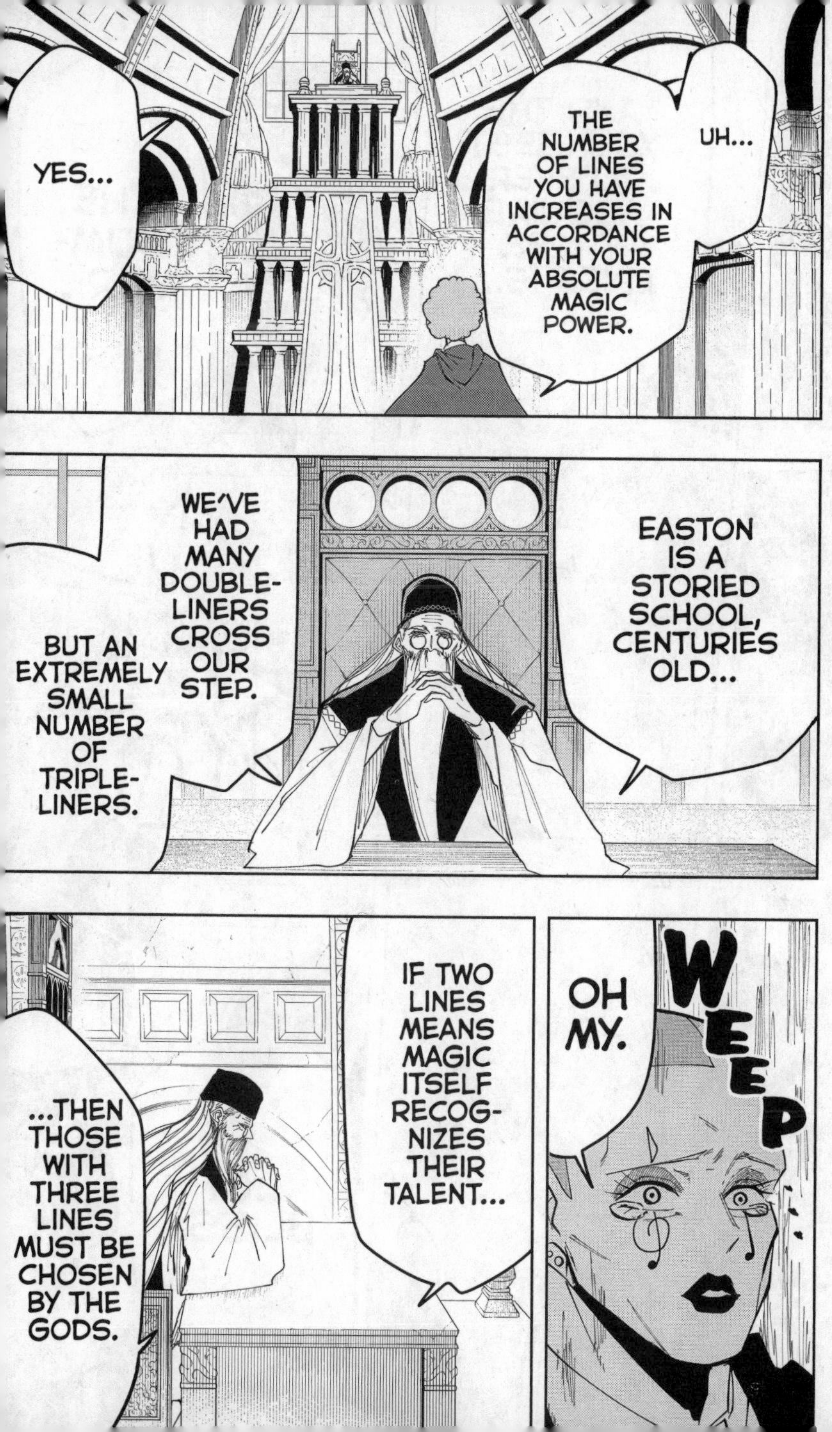
UH...
THE NUMBER OF LINES YOU HAVE INCREASES IN ACCORDANCE WITH YOUR ABSOLUTE MAGIC POWER.
YES...
EASTON IS A STORIED SCHOOL, CENTURIES OLD...
WE'VE HAD MANY DOUBLE-LINERS CROSS OUR STEP.
BUT AN EXTREMELY SMALL NUMBER OF TRIPLE-LINERS.
WEEP
OH MY.
IF TWO LINES MEANS MAGIC ITSELF RECOGNIZES THEIR TALENT...
...THEN THOSE WITH THREE LINES MUST BE CHOSEN BY THE GODS.

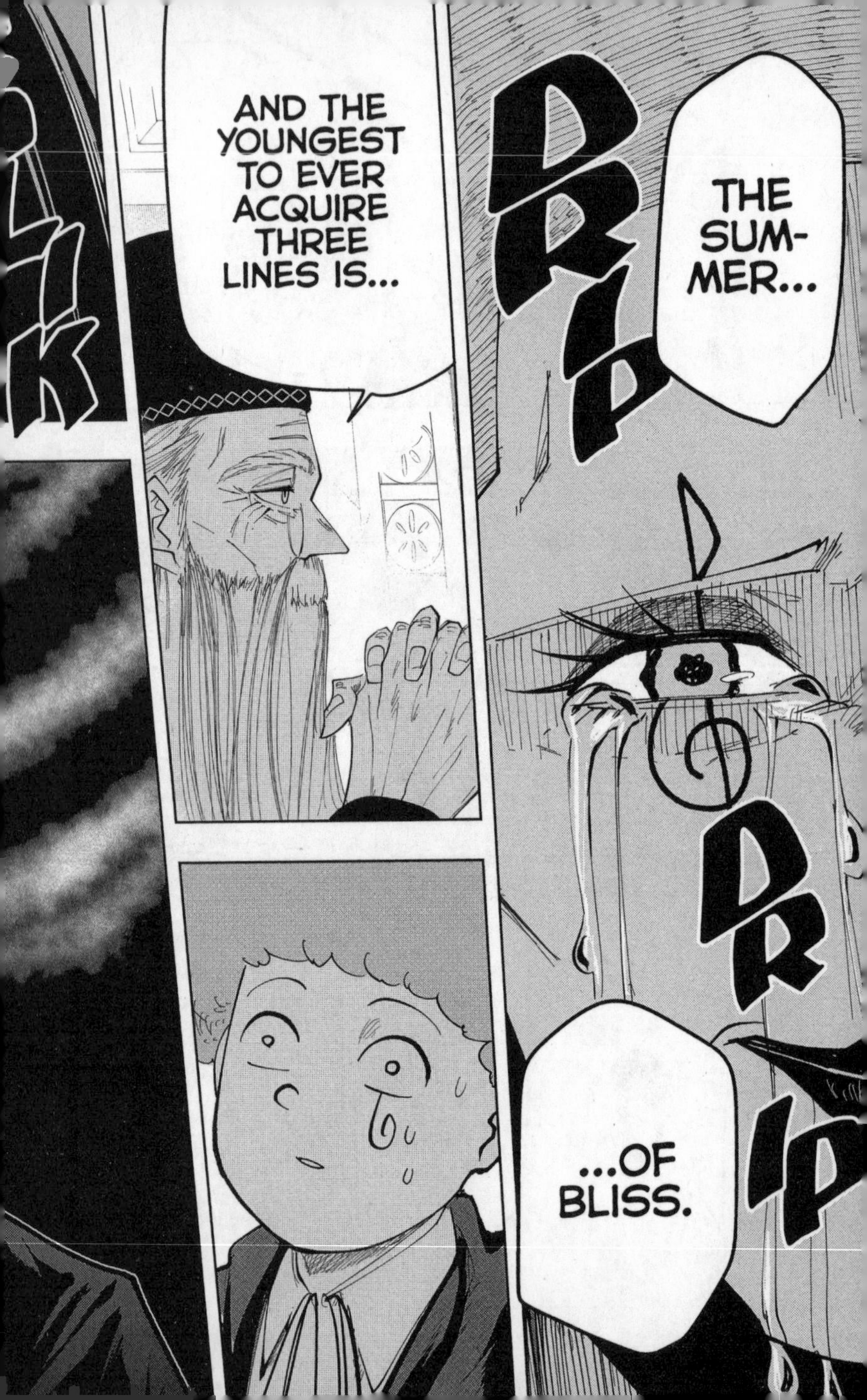
THE SUM-MER...
DRIP
DRIP
...OF BLISS.
AND THE YOUNGEST TO EVER ACQUIRE THREE LINES IS...

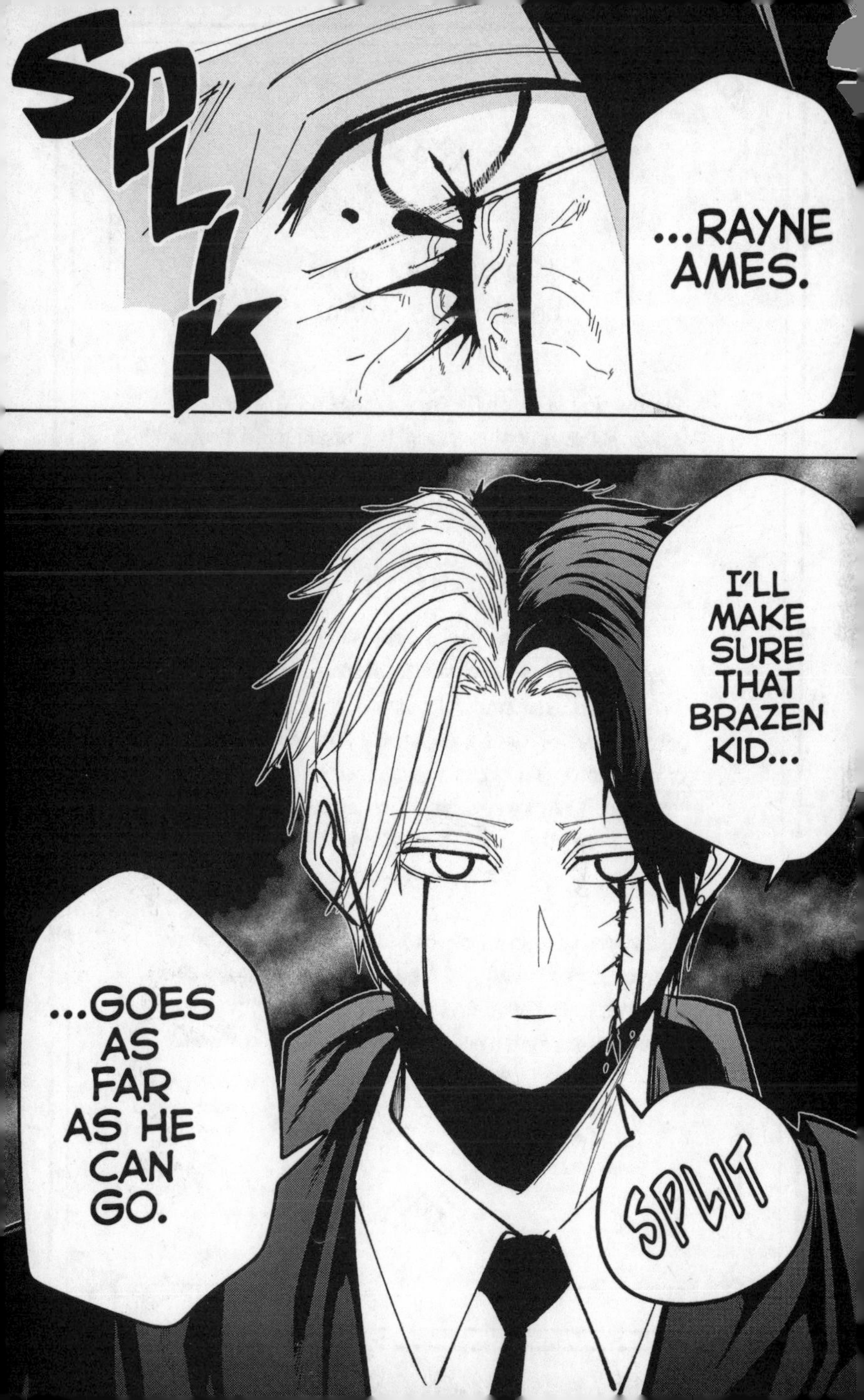
SPLIK
...RAYNE AMES.
I'LL MAKE SURE THAT BRAZEN KID...
...GOES AS FAR AS HE CAN GO.
SPLIT

To everyone who bought this volume...

Thank you very much for purchasing volume 6 of Mashle: Magic and Muscles. In the beginning, I thought this might go for five volumes, maybe. So here I am, surprised as a sunfish...

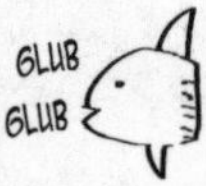
GLUB
GLUB

It hasn't even been a year since volume 1, and we're on volume 6... To all the good children out there...remember to watch your purchases! Don't go out of your way, really! Too much spending is bad. Don't feel pressured to spend money on this manga. That's right, just relax... Here, have some buckwheat tea! Drink buckwheat tea and put in a hard day's work!!

P.S. Thank you so much for sending in gifts for the characters' birthdays. I'll hop on a broom and make sure they get them! And thanks for the fan letters too! Hearing that this story cheers you up makes me...really happy!!

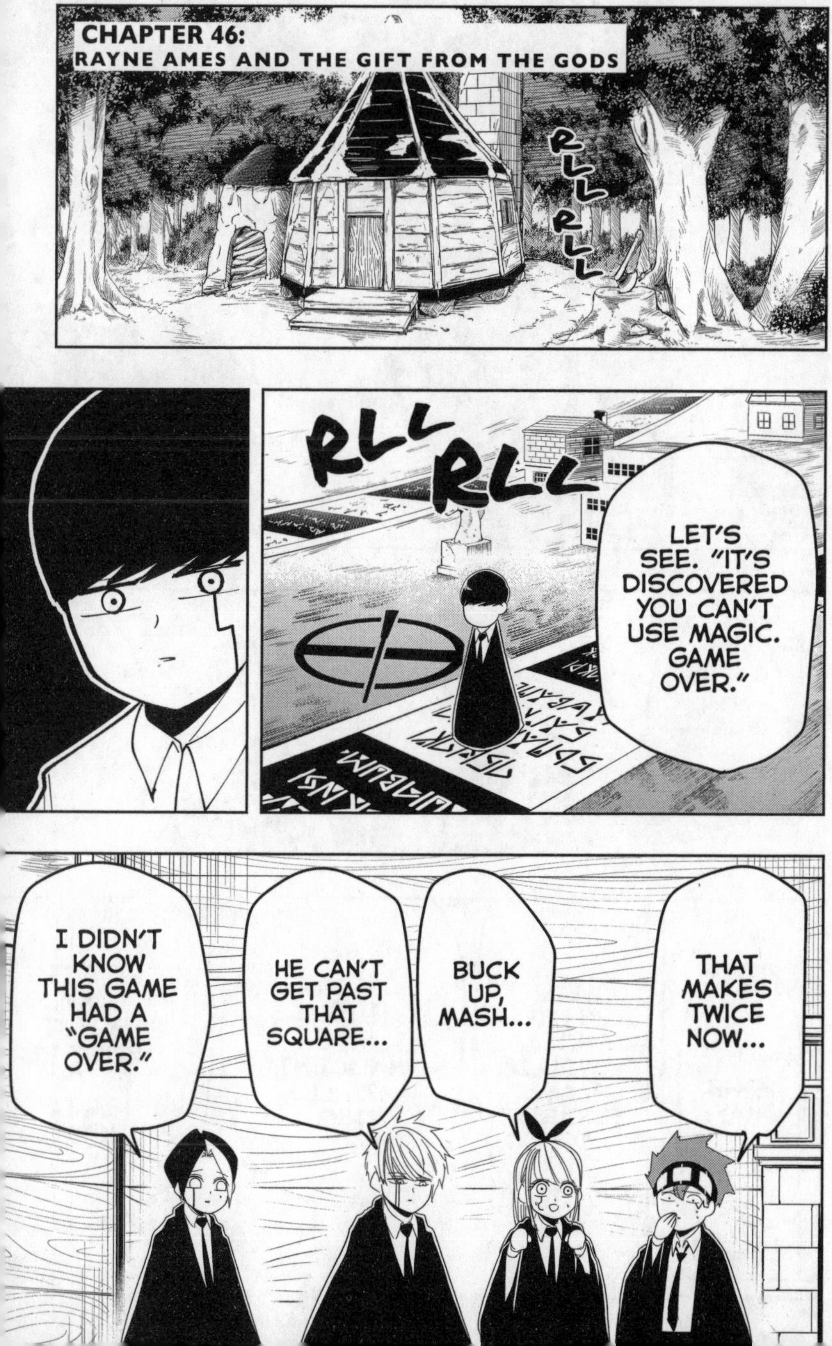
CHAPTER 46:
RAYNE AMES AND THE GIFT FROM THE GODS
RLL RLL
RLL RLL
LET'S SEE. "IT'S DISCOVERED YOU CAN'T USE MAGIC. GAME OVER."
THAT MAKES TWICE NOW...
BUCK UP, MASH...
HE CAN'T GET PAST THAT SQUARE...
I DIDN'T KNOW THIS GAME HAD A "GAME OVER."

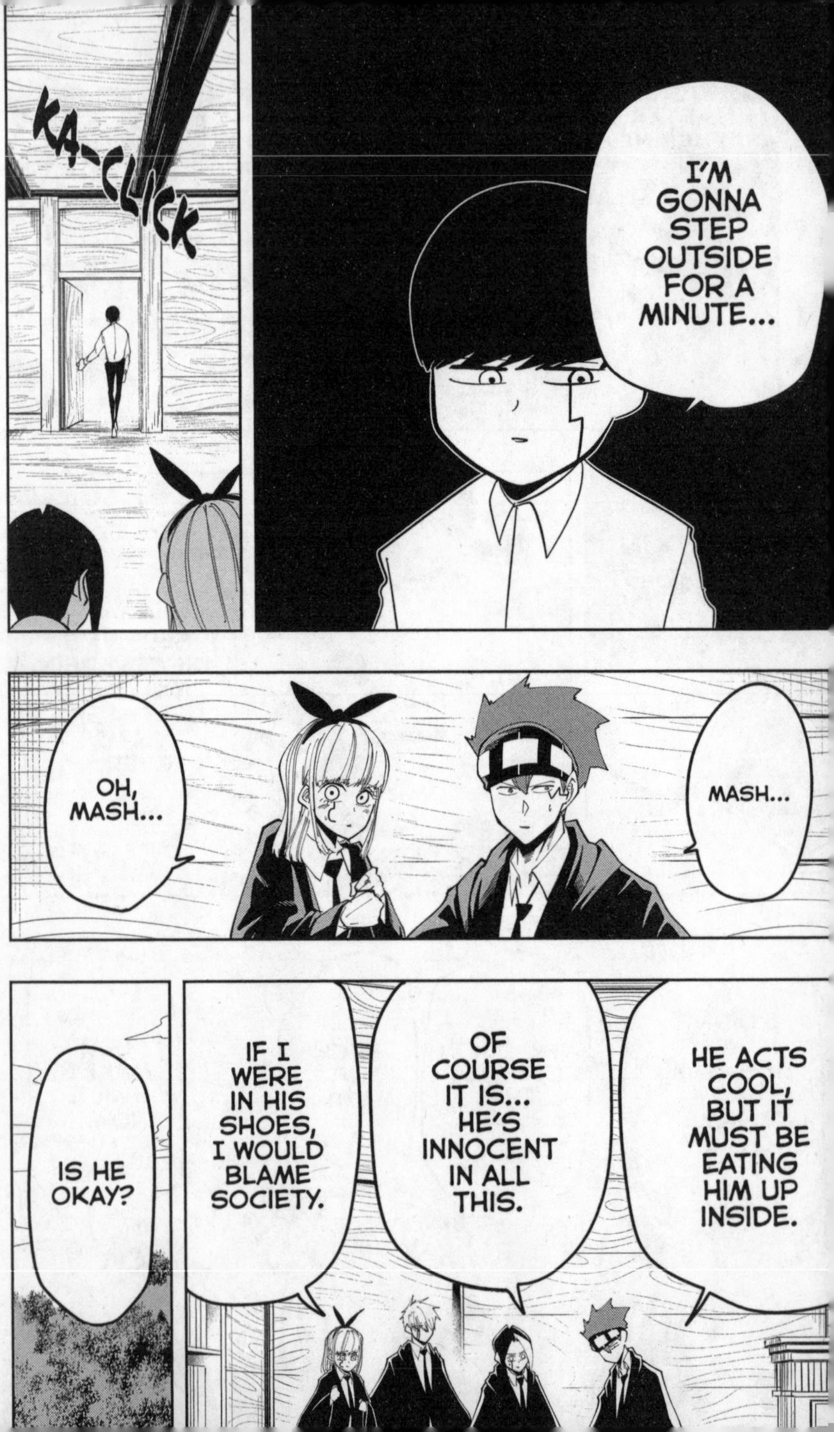
I'M GONNA STEP OUTSIDE FOR A MINUTE...
KA-CLICK
MASH...
OH, MASH...
HE ACTS COOL, BUT IT MUST BE EATING HIM UP INSIDE.
OF COURSE IT IS... HE'S INNOCENT IN ALL THIS.
IF I WERE IN HIS SHOES, I WOULD BLAME SOCIETY.
IS HE OKAY?

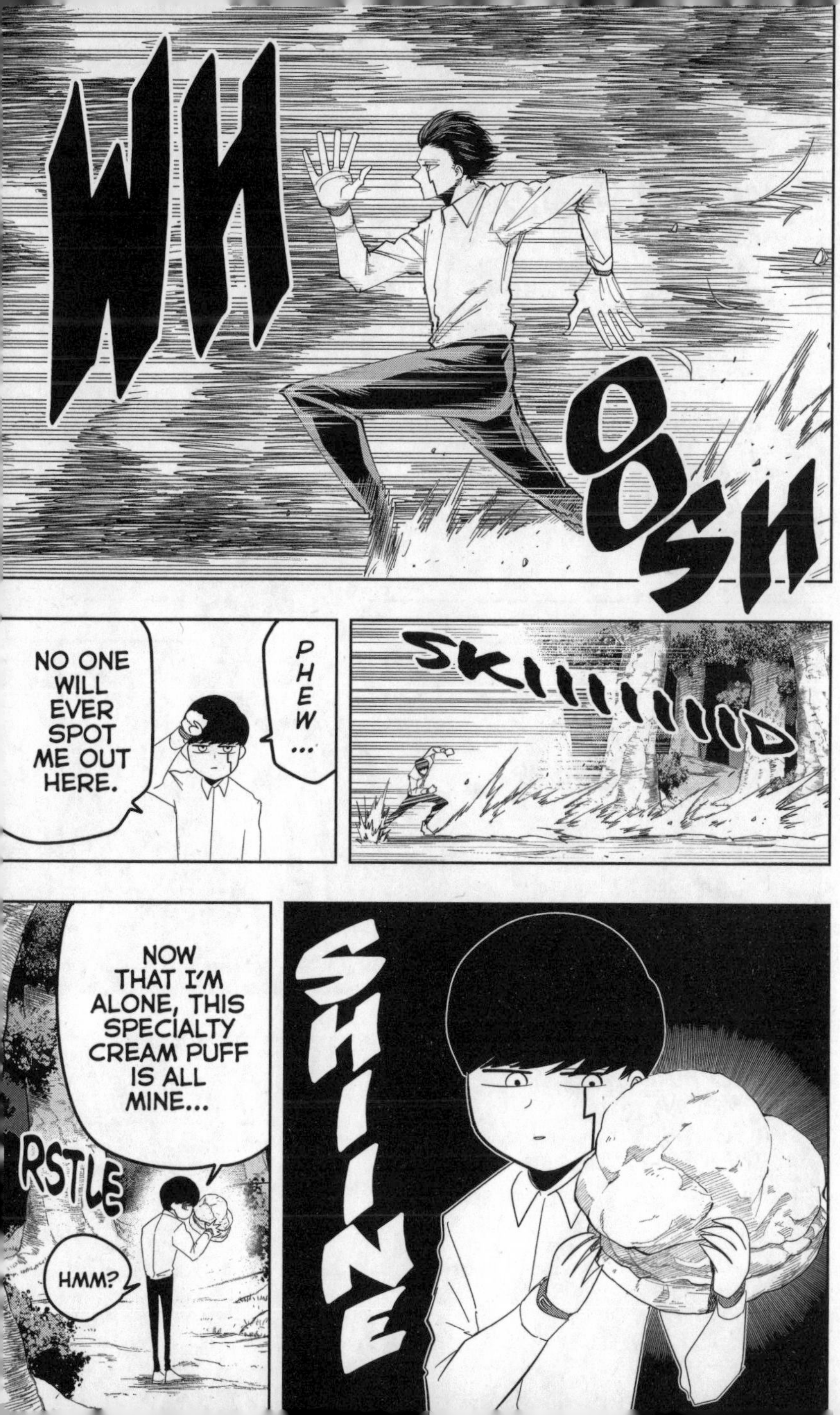
WHOOSH
SKIIIIIIIID
PHEW...
NO ONE WILL EVER SPOT ME OUT HERE.
SHINE
NOW THAT I'M ALONE, THIS SPECIALTY CREAM PUFF IS ALL MINE...
RSTLE
HMM?

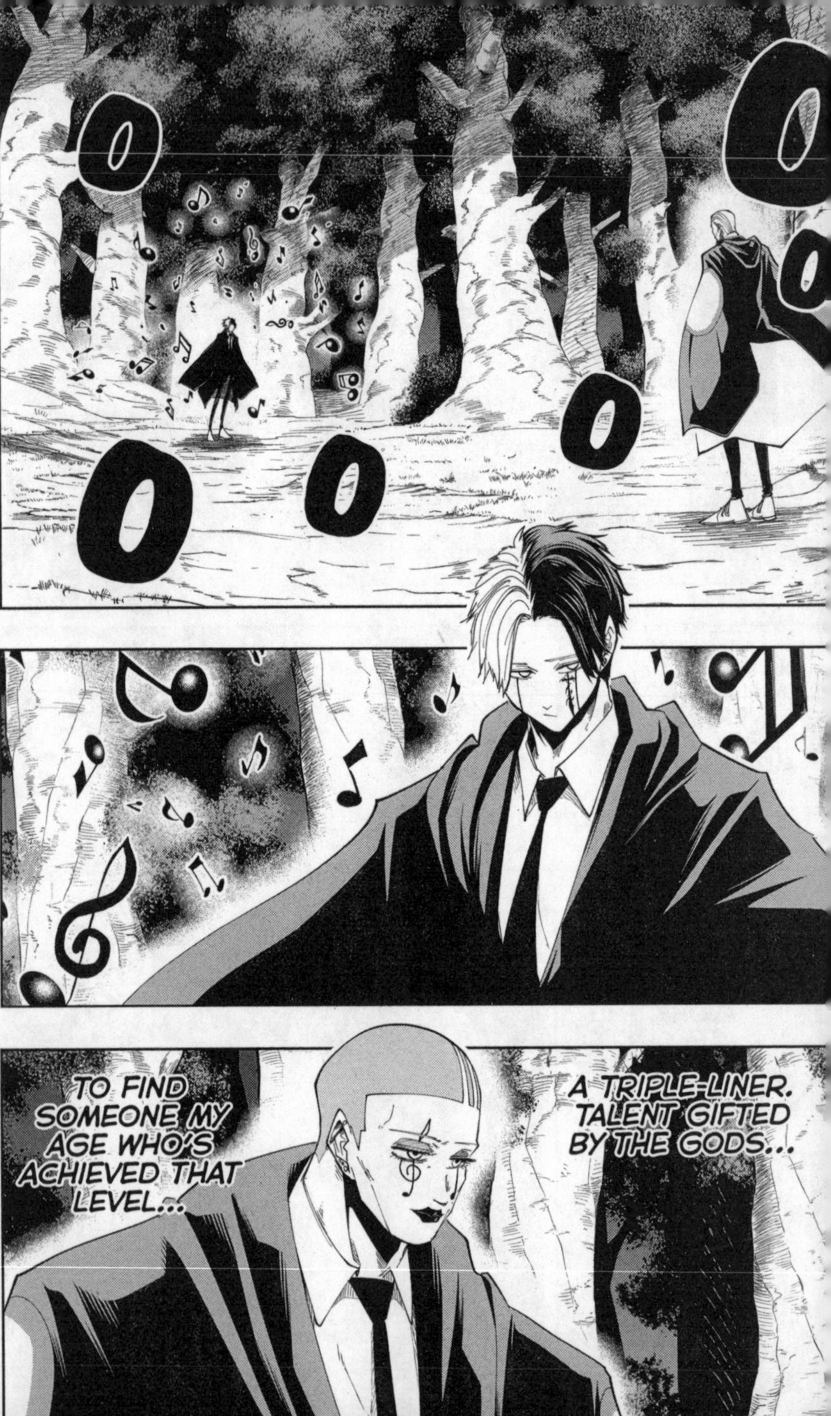
A TRIPLE-LINER. TALENT GIFTED BY THE GODS...
TO FIND SOMEONE MY AGE WHO'S ACHIEVED THAT LEVEL...

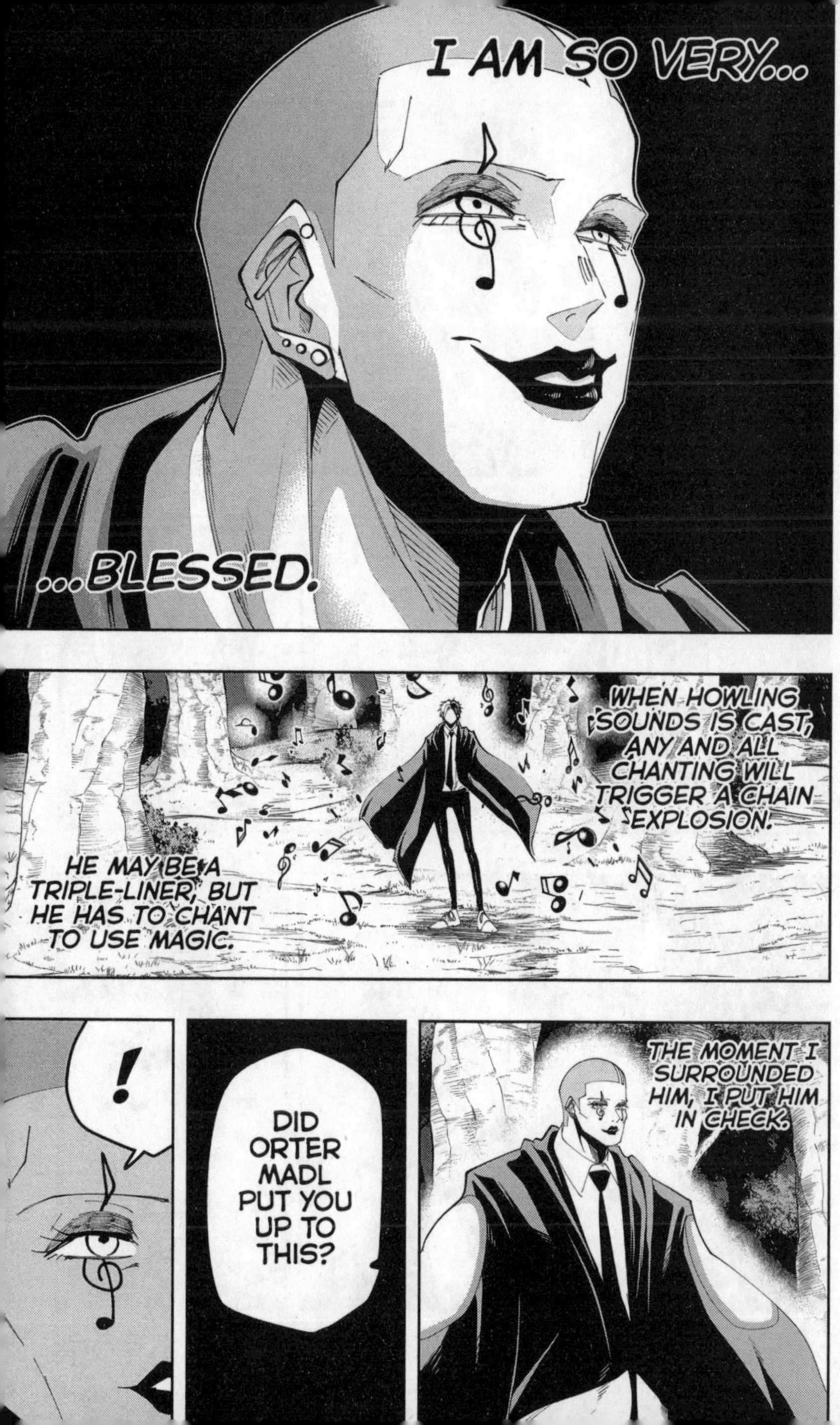
I AM SO VERY...
...BLESSED.
WHEN HOWLING SOUNDS IS CAST, ANY AND ALL CHANTING WILL TRIGGER A CHAIN EXPLOSION.
HE MAY BE A TRIPLE-LINER, BUT HE HAS TO CHANT TO USE MAGIC.
THE MOMENT I SURROUNDED HIM, I PUT HIM IN CHECK.
DID ORTER MADL PUT YOU UP TO THIS?
!

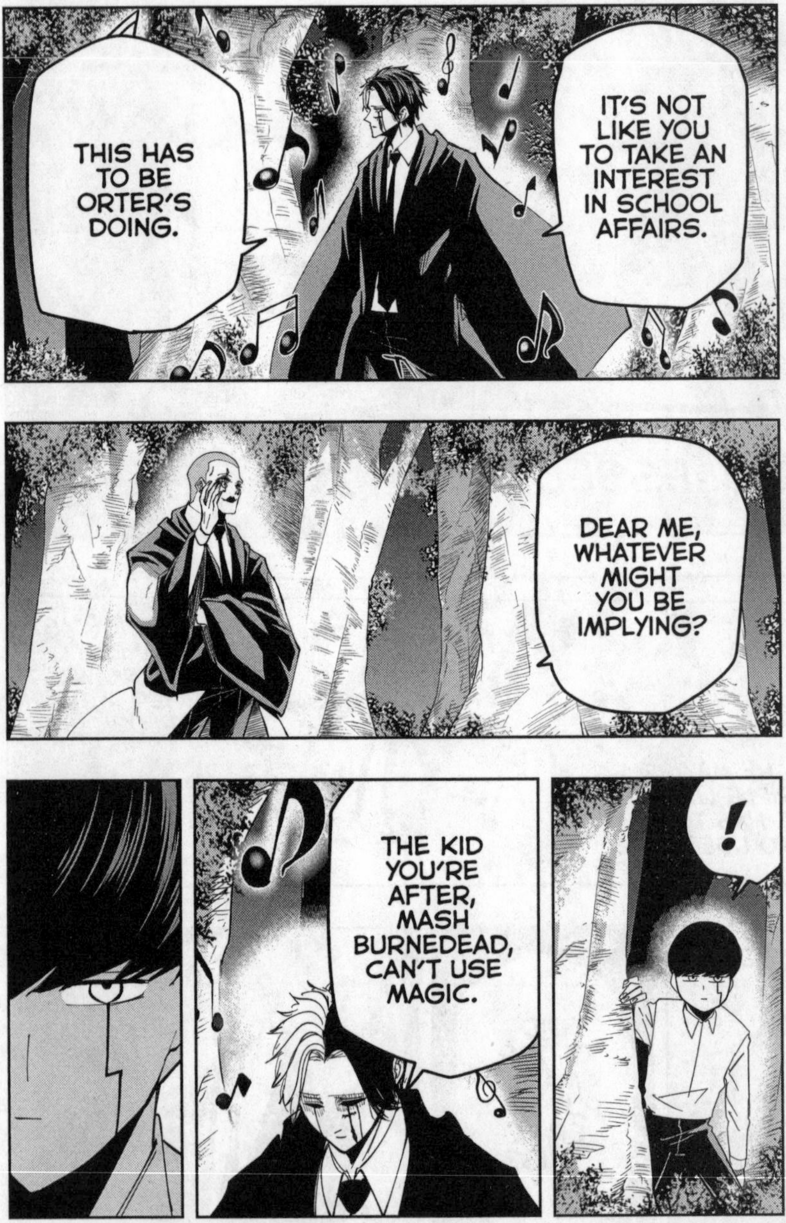
IT'S NOT LIKE YOU TO TAKE AN INTEREST IN SCHOOL AFFAIRS.
THIS HAS TO BE ORTER'S DOING.
DEAR ME, WHATEVER MIGHT YOU BE IMPLYING?
!
THE KID YOU'RE AFTER, MASH BURNEDEAD, CAN'T USE MAGIC.

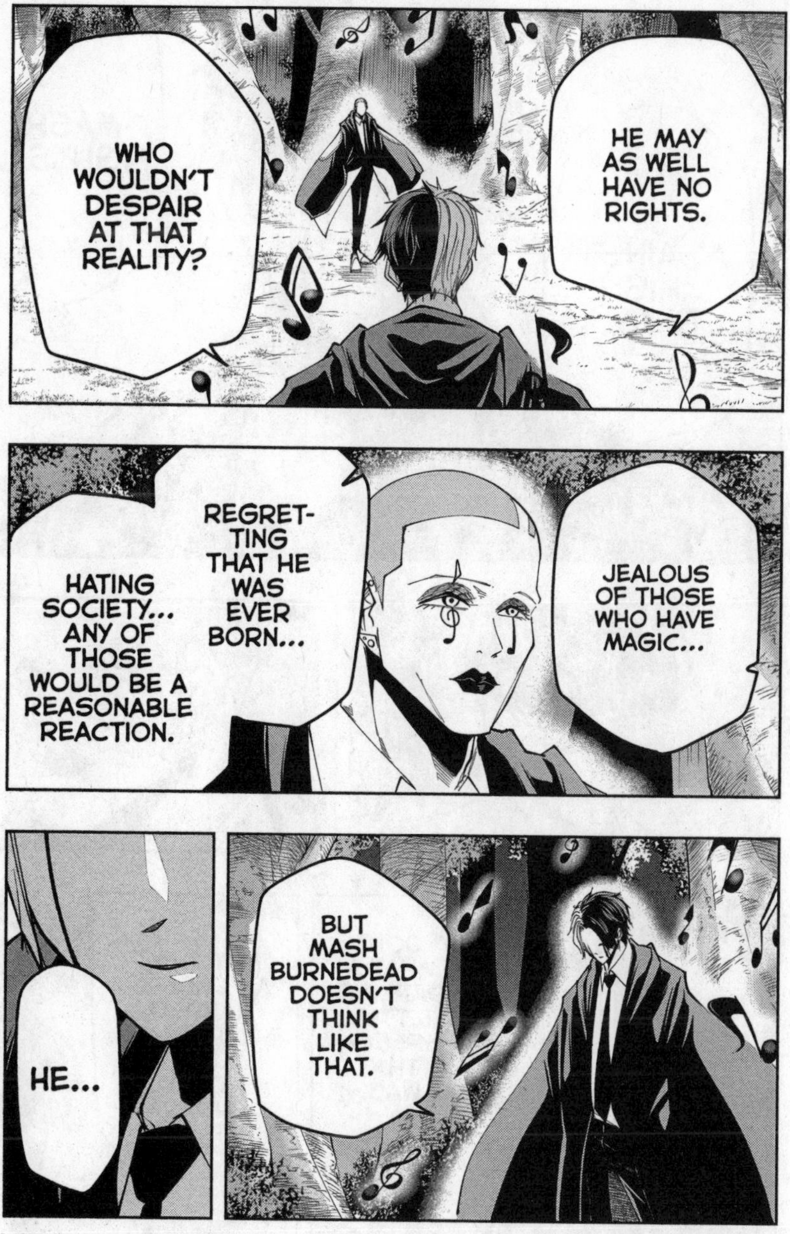
HE MAY AS WELL HAVE NO RIGHTS.
WHO WOULDN'T DESPAIR AT THAT REALITY?
JEALOUS OF THOSE WHO HAVE MAGIC...
REGRET-TING THAT HE WAS EVER BORN...
HATING SOCIETY... ANY OF THOSE WOULD BE A REASONABLE REACTION.
BUT MASH BURNEDEAD DOESN'T THINK LIKE THAT.
HE...

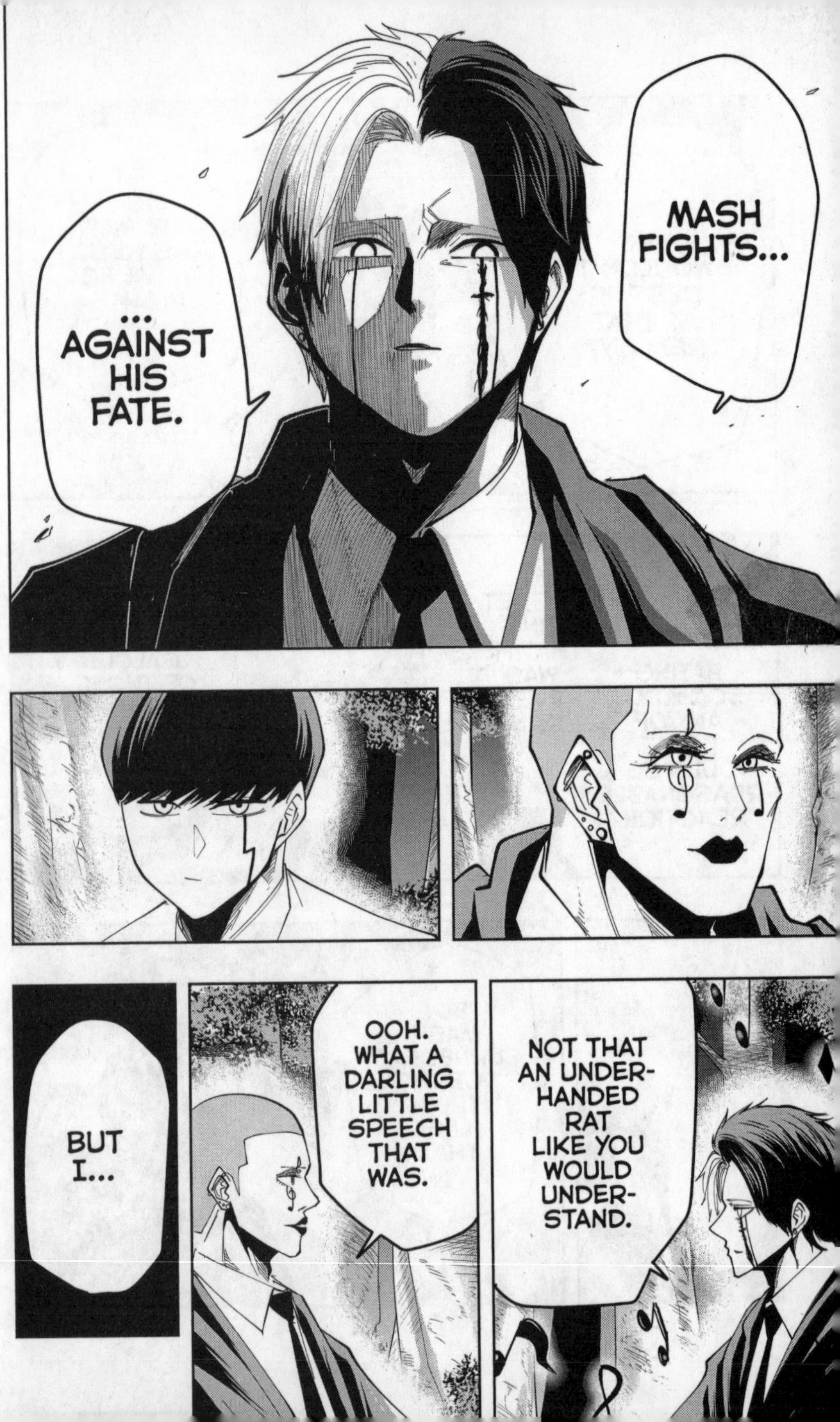
MASH FIGHTS...
...AGAINST HIS FATE.
NOT THAT AN UNDER-HANDED RAT LIKE YOU WOULD UNDER-STAND.
OOH. WHAT A DARLING LITTLE SPEECH THAT WAS.
BUT I...

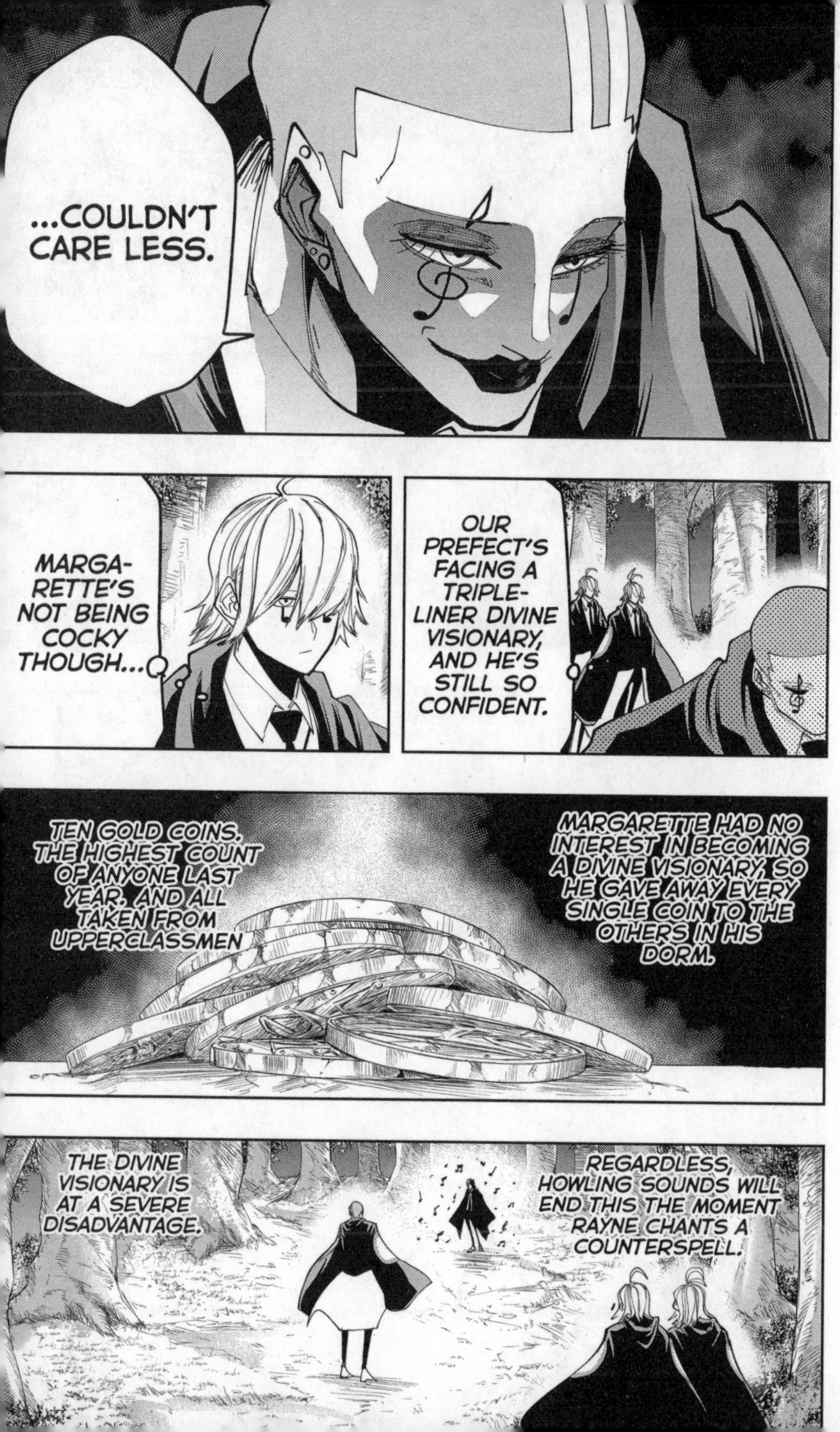
...COULDN'T CARE LESS.
OUR PREFECT'S FACING A TRIPLE-LINER DIVINE VISIONARY, AND HE'S STILL SO CONFIDENT.
MARGARETTE'S NOT BEING COCKY THOUGH...
MARGARETTE HAD NO INTEREST IN BECOMING A DIVINE VISIONARY, SO HE GAVE AWAY EVERY SINGLE COIN TO THE OTHERS IN HIS DORM.
TEN GOLD COINS. THE HIGHEST COUNT OF ANYONE LAST YEAR. AND ALL TAKEN FROM UPPERCLASSMEN
REGARDLESS, HOWLING SOUNDS WILL END THIS THE MOMENT RAYNE CHANTS A COUNTERSPELL.
THE DIVINE VISIONARY IS AT A SEVERE DISADVANTAGE.

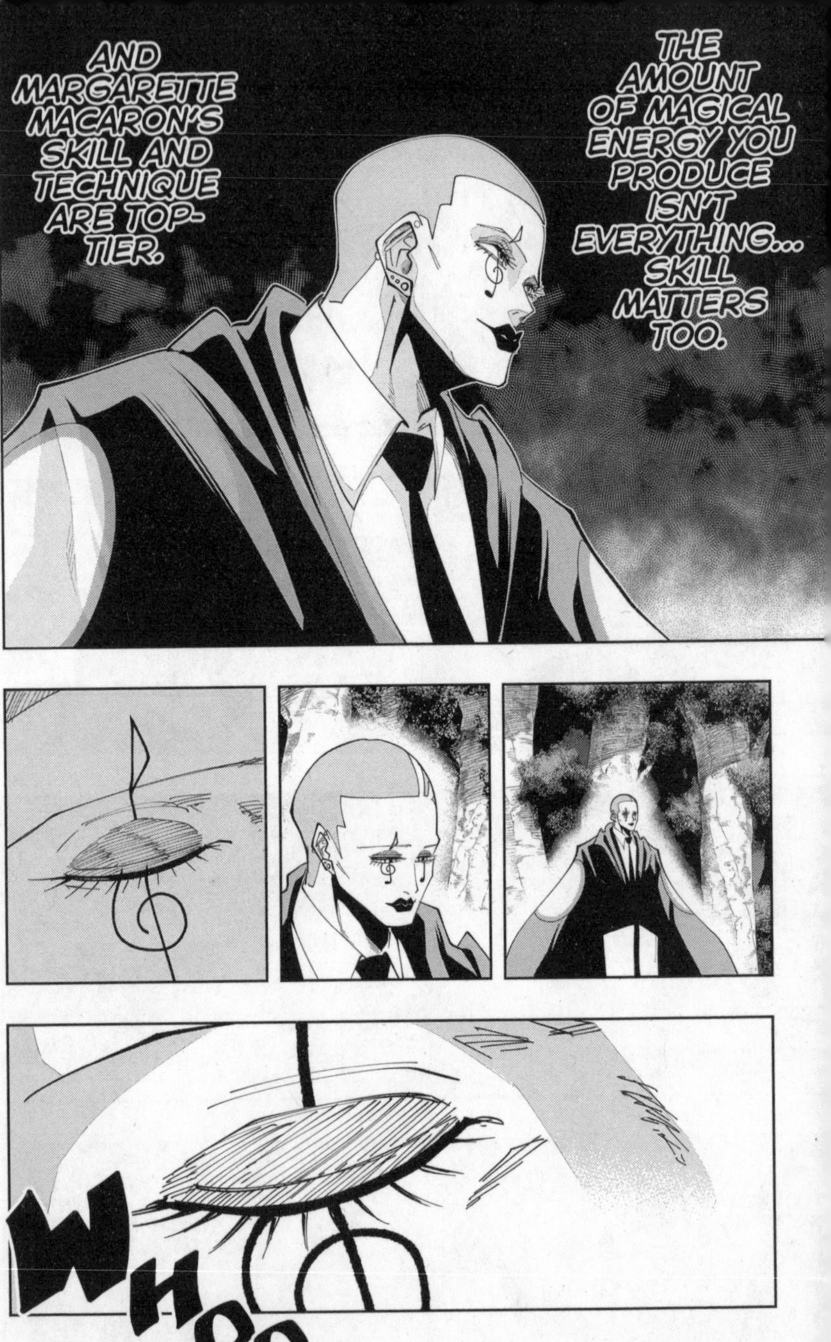
THE AMOUNT OF MAGICAL ENERGY YOU PRODUCE ISN'T EVERYTHING... SKILL MATTERS TOO.
AND MARGARETTE MACARON'S SKILL AND TECHNIQUE ARE TOP-TIER.
WHOOO

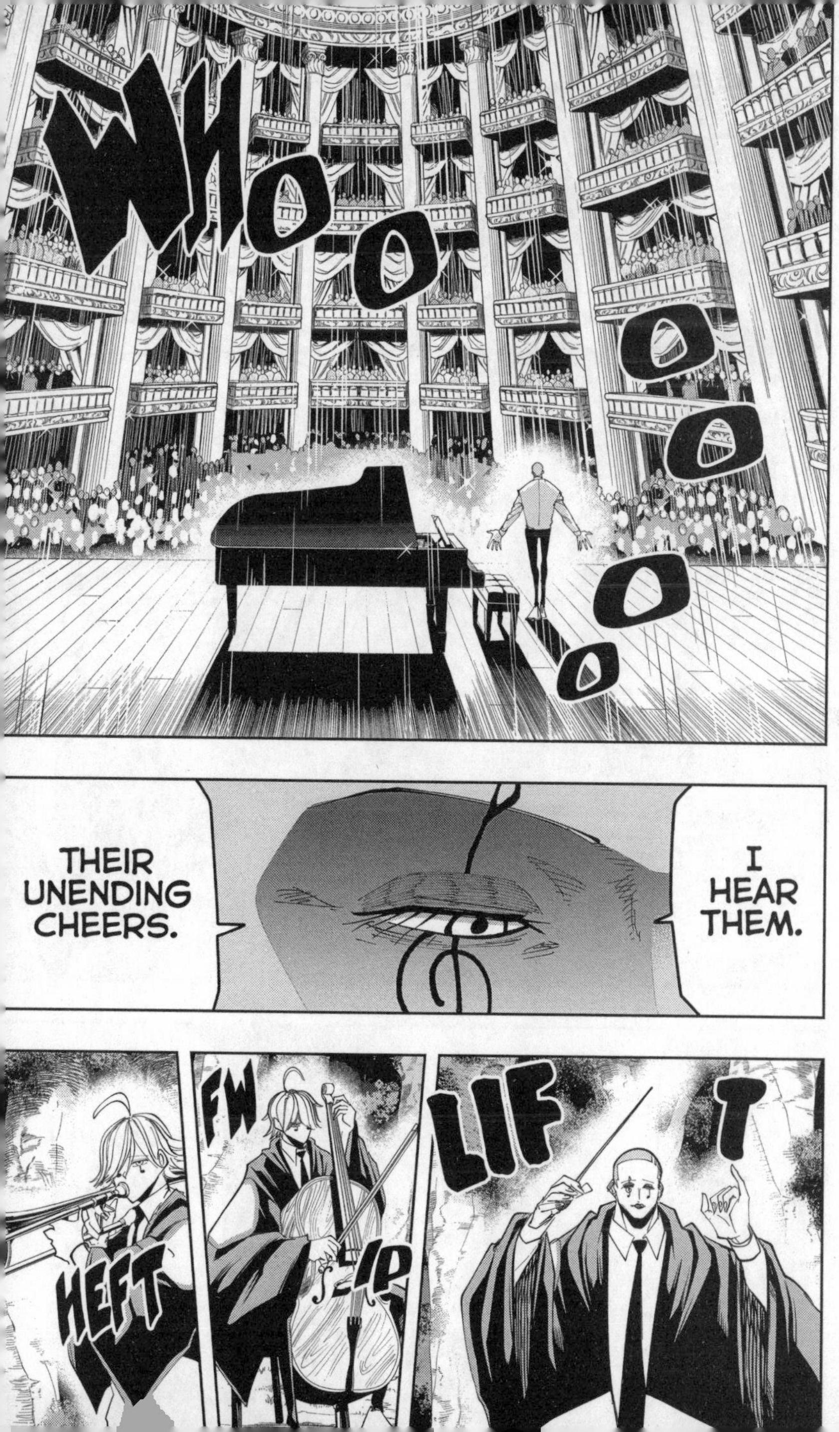

WHOOOOOO
I HEAR THEM.
THEIR UNENDING CHEERS.
LIFT
FWIP
HEFT

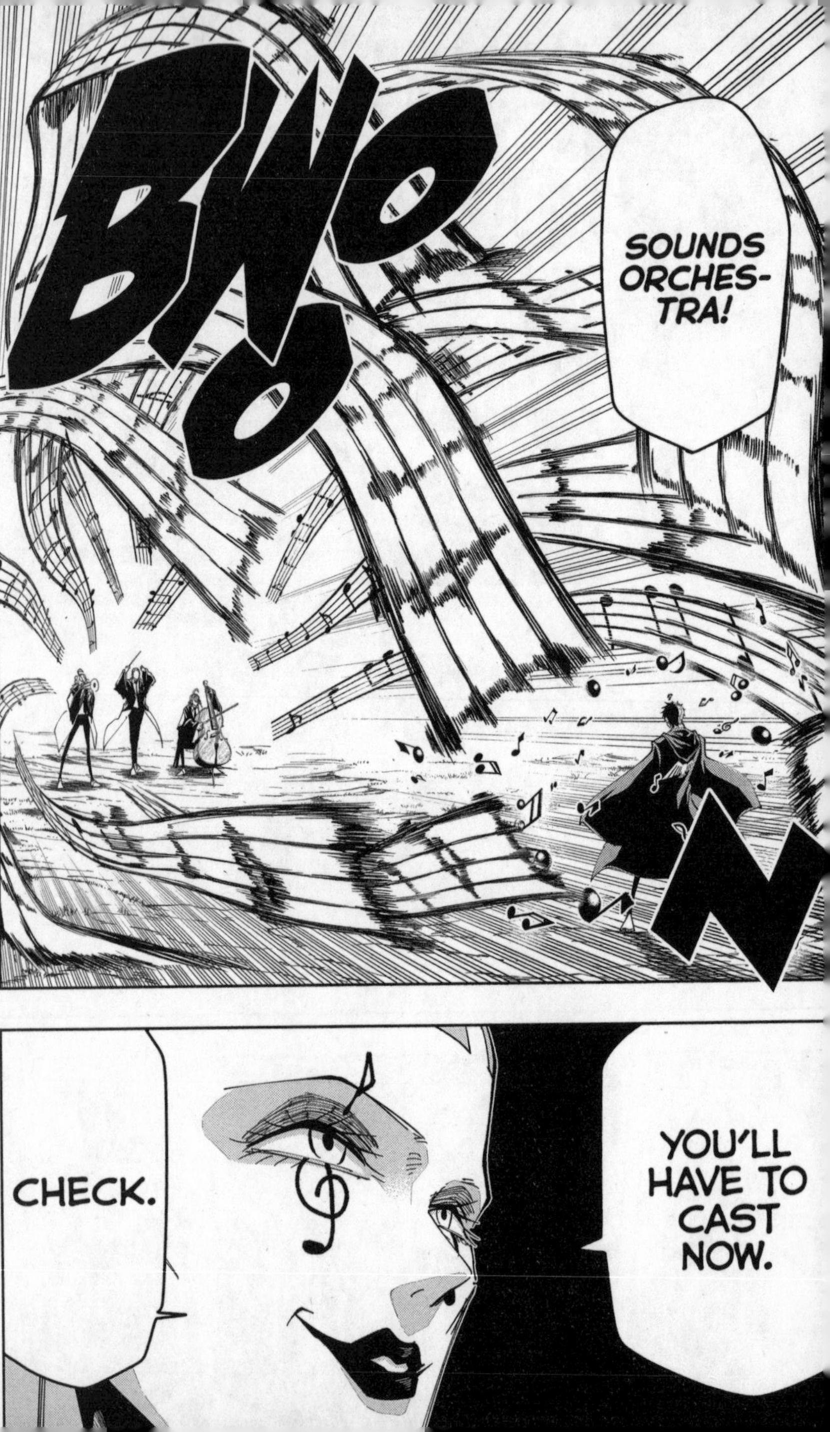
SOUNDS ORCHES-TRA!
BWOOON
YOU'LL HAVE TO CAST NOW.
CHECK.

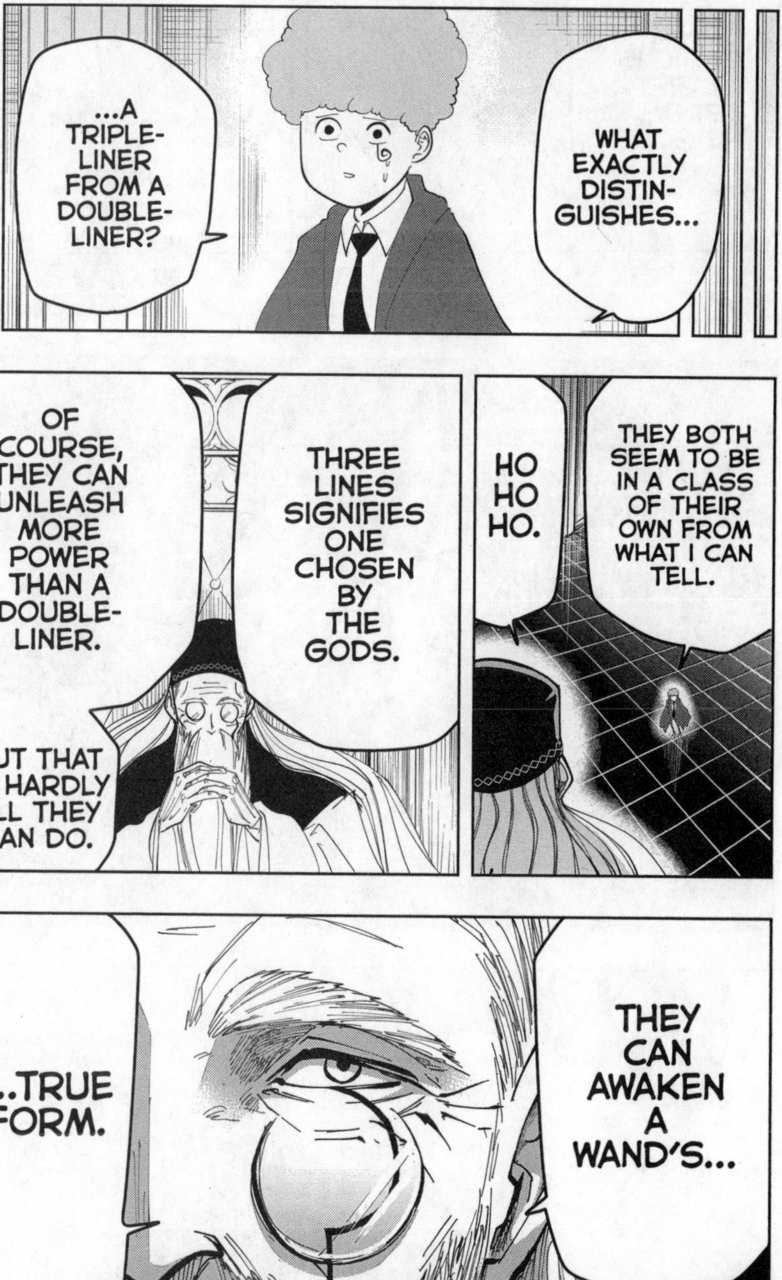
WHAT EXACTLY DISTINGUISHES...
...A TRIPLE-LINER FROM A DOUBLE-LINER?
THEY BOTH SEEM TO BE IN A CLASS OF THEIR OWN FROM WHAT I CAN TELL.
HO HO HO.
THREE LINES SIGNIFIES ONE CHOSEN BY THE GODS.
OF COURSE, THEY CAN UNLEASH MORE POWER THAN A DOUBLE-LINER.
BUT THAT IS HARDLY ALL THEY CAN DO.
THEY CAN AWAKEN A WAND'S...
...TRUE FORM.

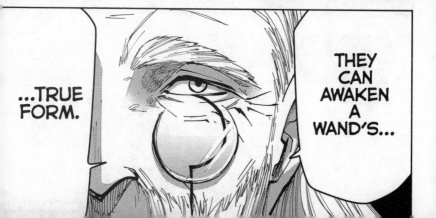

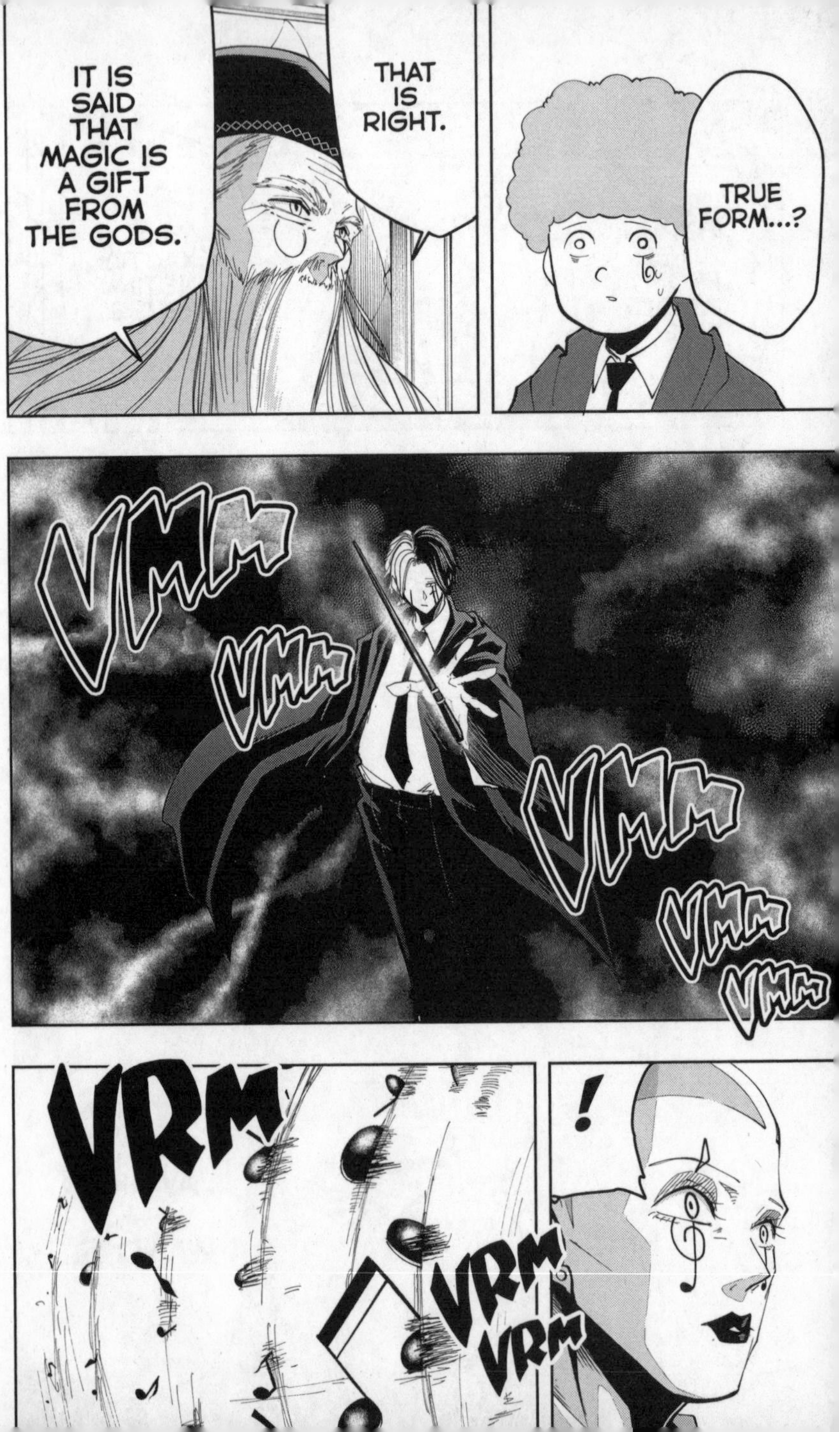
TRUE FORM...?
THAT IS RIGHT.
IT IS SAID THAT MAGIC IS A GIFT FROM THE GODS.
VMM
VMM
VMM
VMM
VMM
!
VRM
VRM
VRM

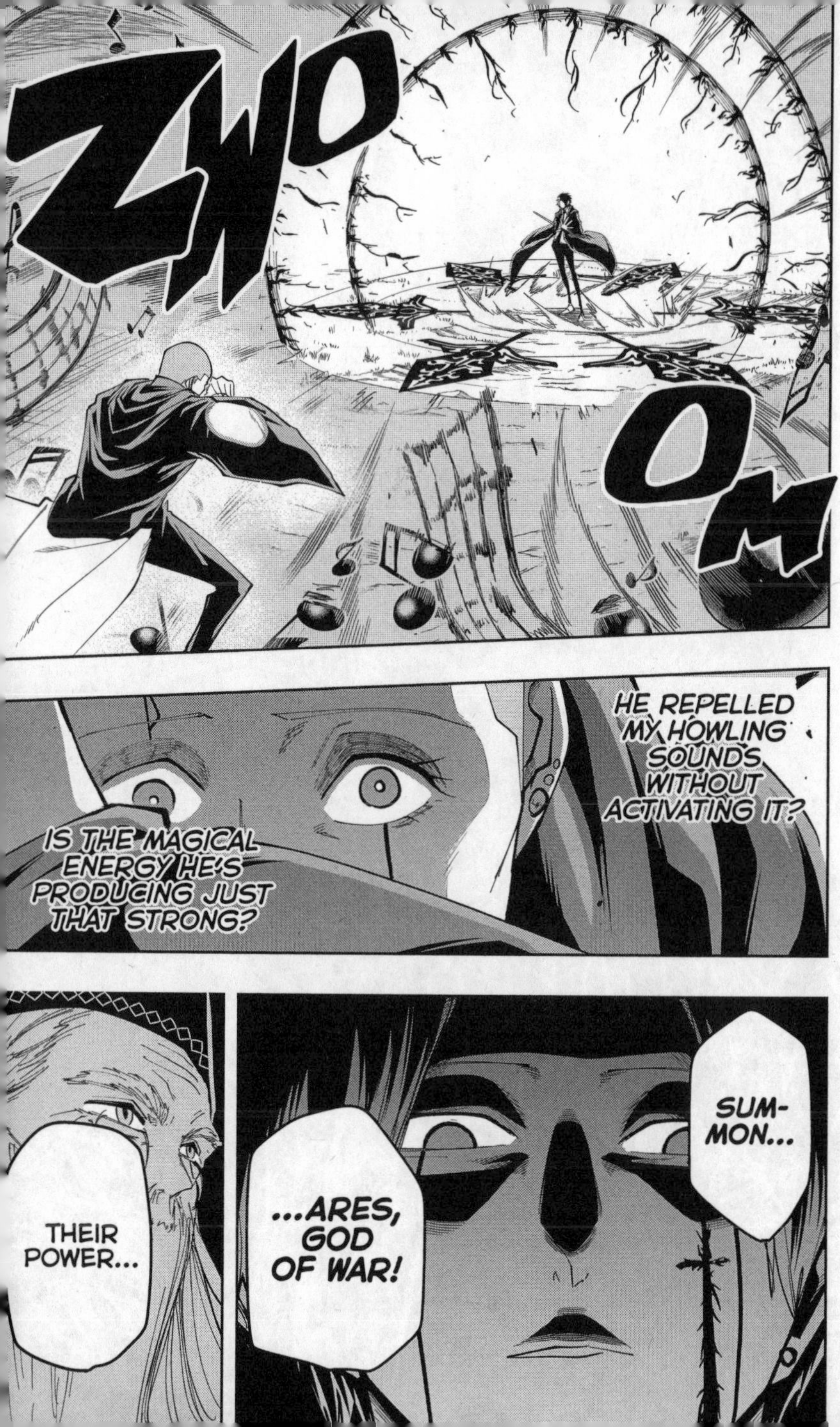
ZWO
OM
HE REPELLED MY HOWLING SOUNDS WITHOUT ACTIVATING IT?
IS THE MAGICAL ENERGY HE'S PRODUCING JUST THAT STRONG?
SUM-MON...
...ARES, GOD OF WAR!
THEIR POWER...

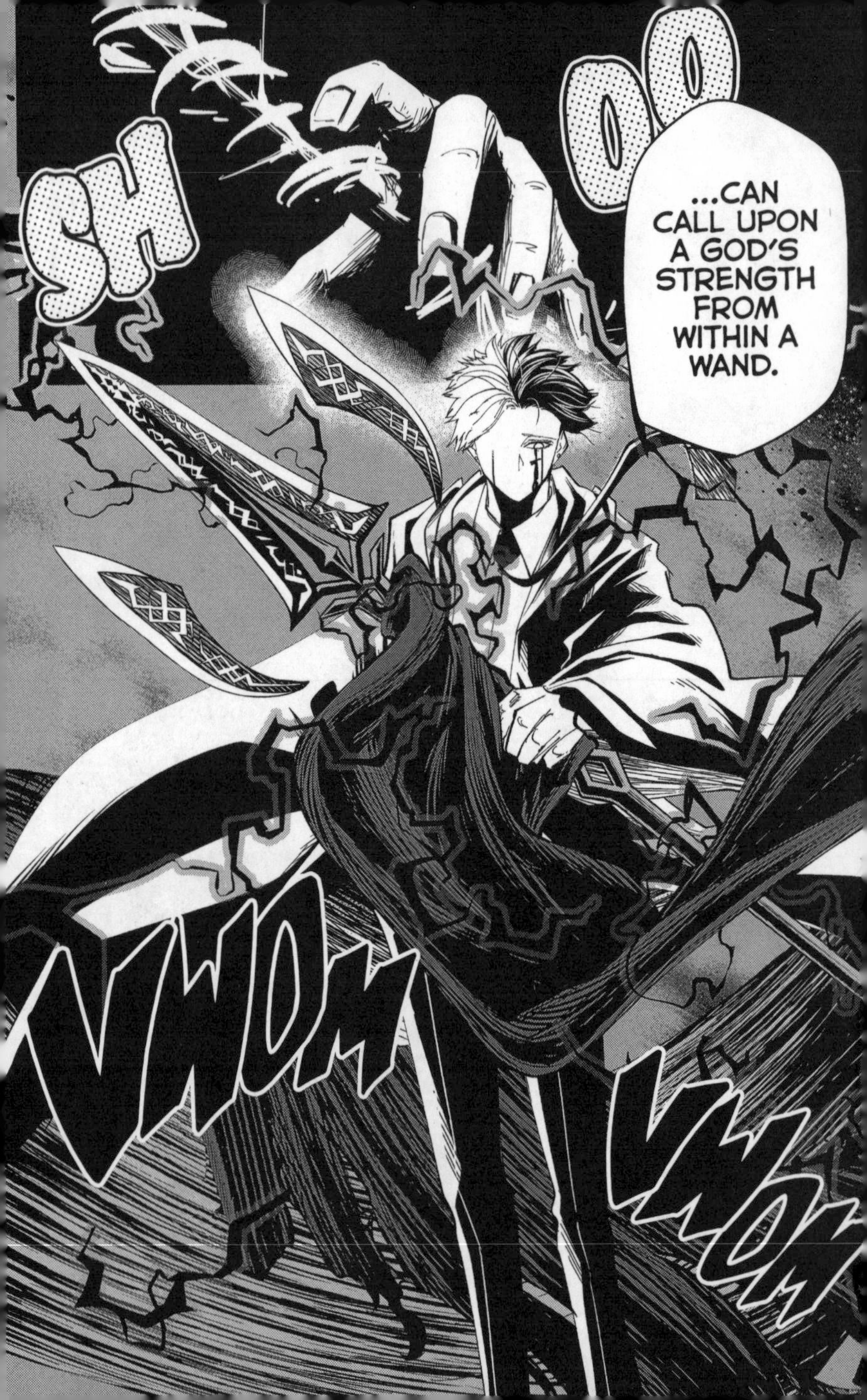
SHOOO
...CAN CALL UPON A GOD'S STRENGTH FROM WITHIN A WAND.
VWOM
VWOM

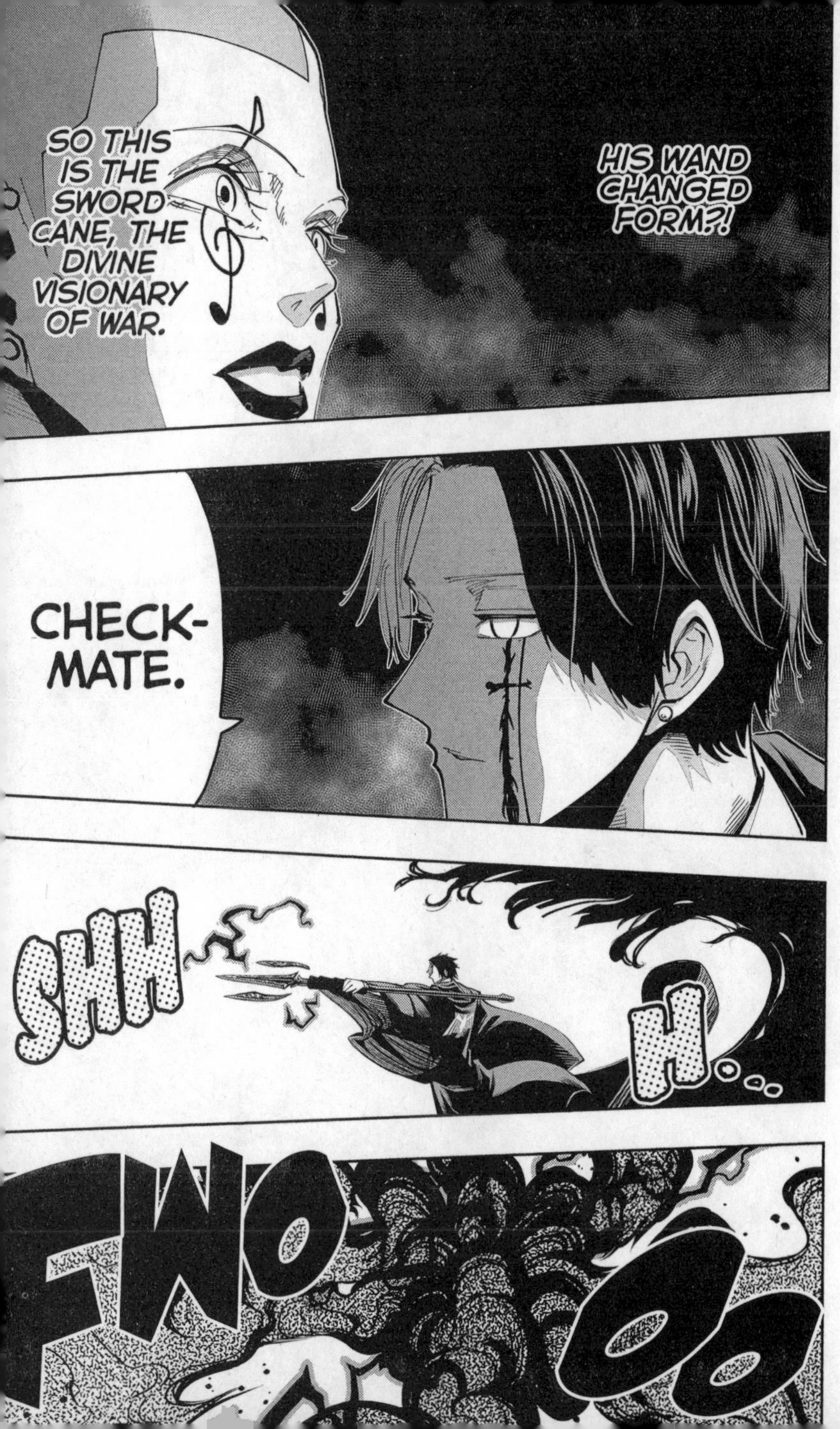

HIS WAND CHANGED FORM?!
SO THIS IS THE SWORD CANE, THE DIVINE VISIONARY OF WAR.
CHECK-MATE.
SHHH
FWOOO

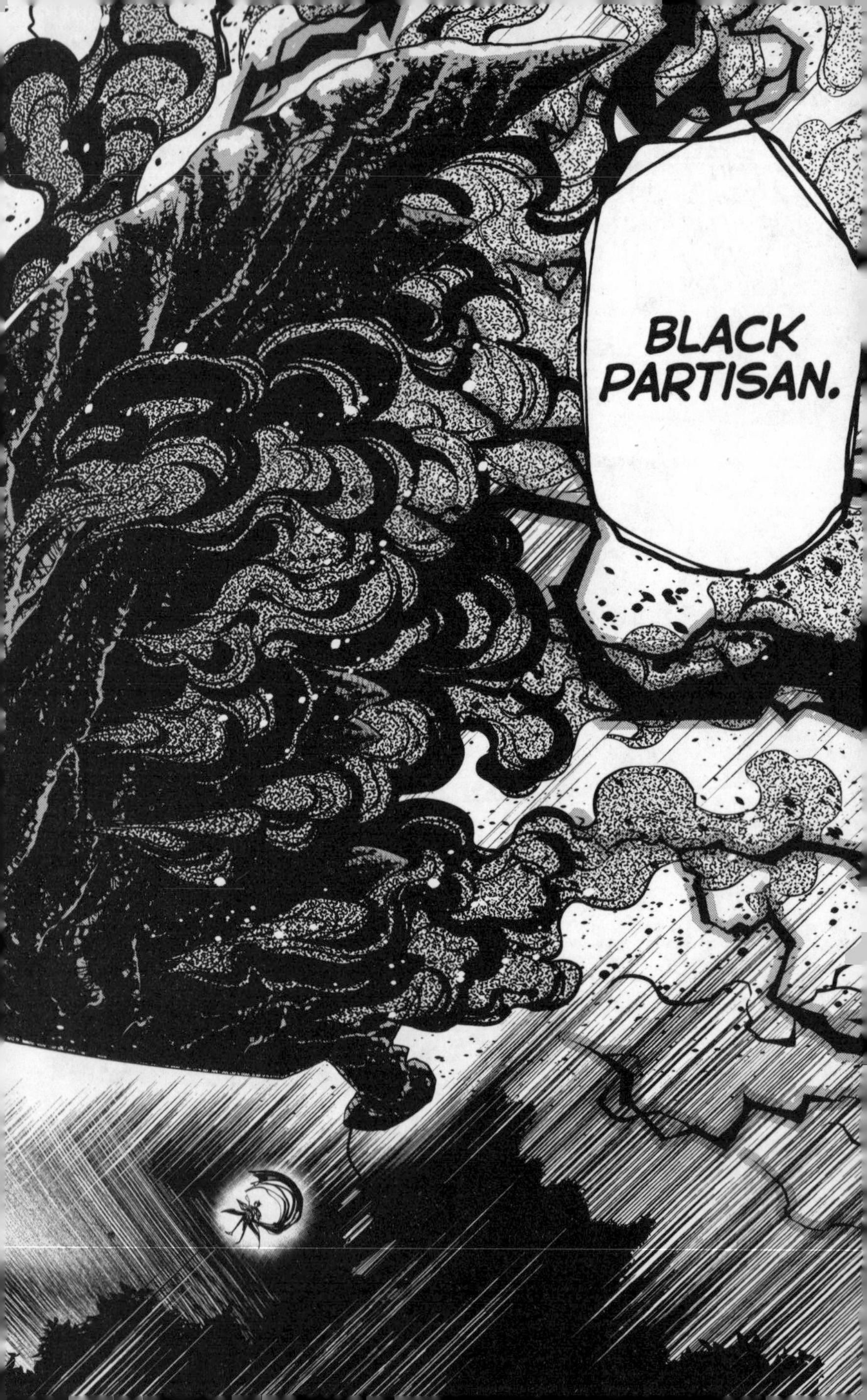
BLACK PARTISAN.

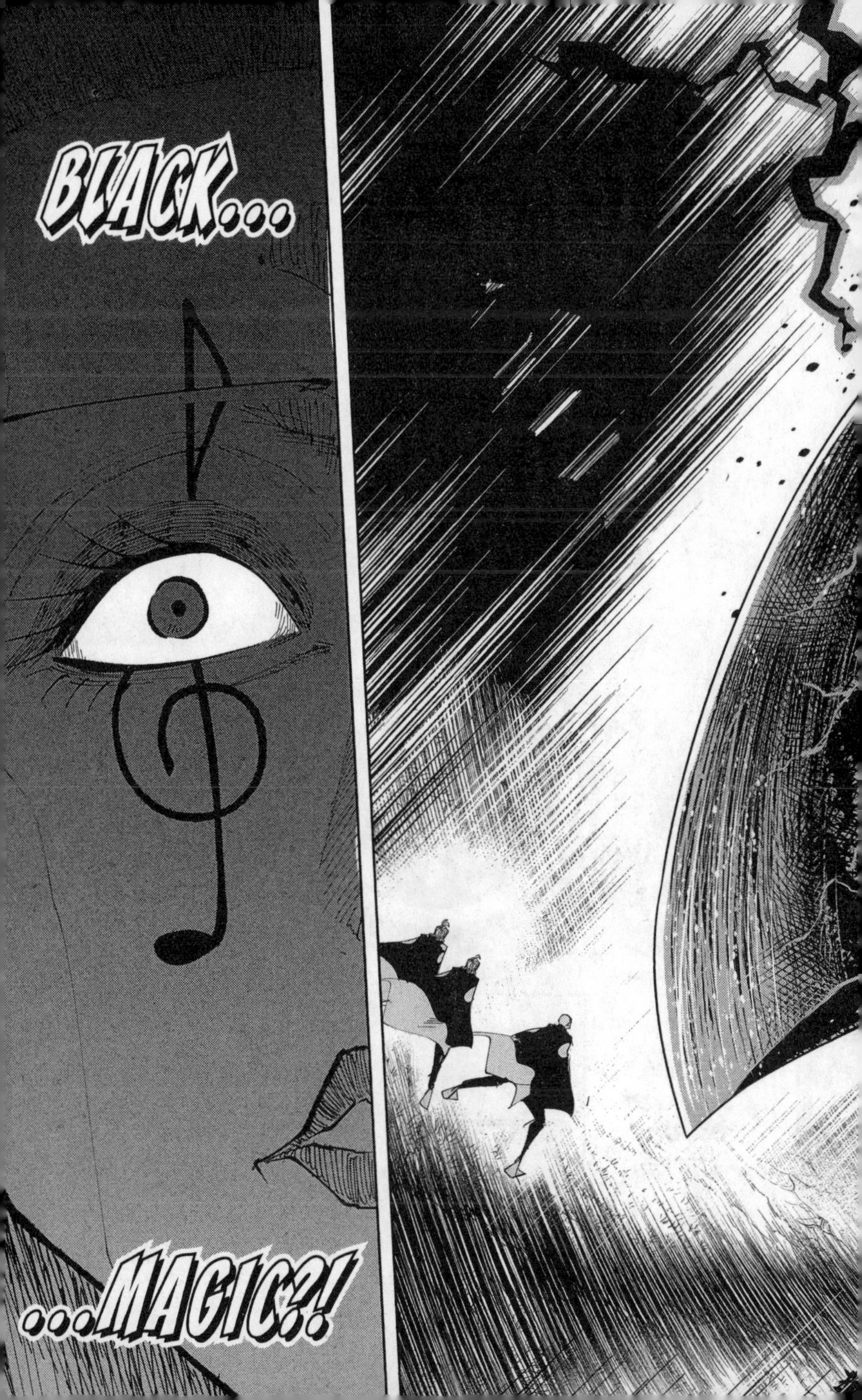
BLACK...
...MAGIC?!

Adler Dorm, Room 1106.

TAP TAP

The Youngest Divine Visionary, Rayne Ames.

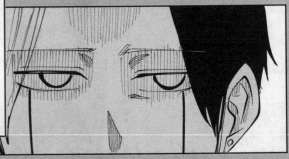

He has a secret no one knows.

CONTINUED ON PAGE 68

CHAPTER 47: MASH BURNEDEAD AND THE SELECTION EXAM

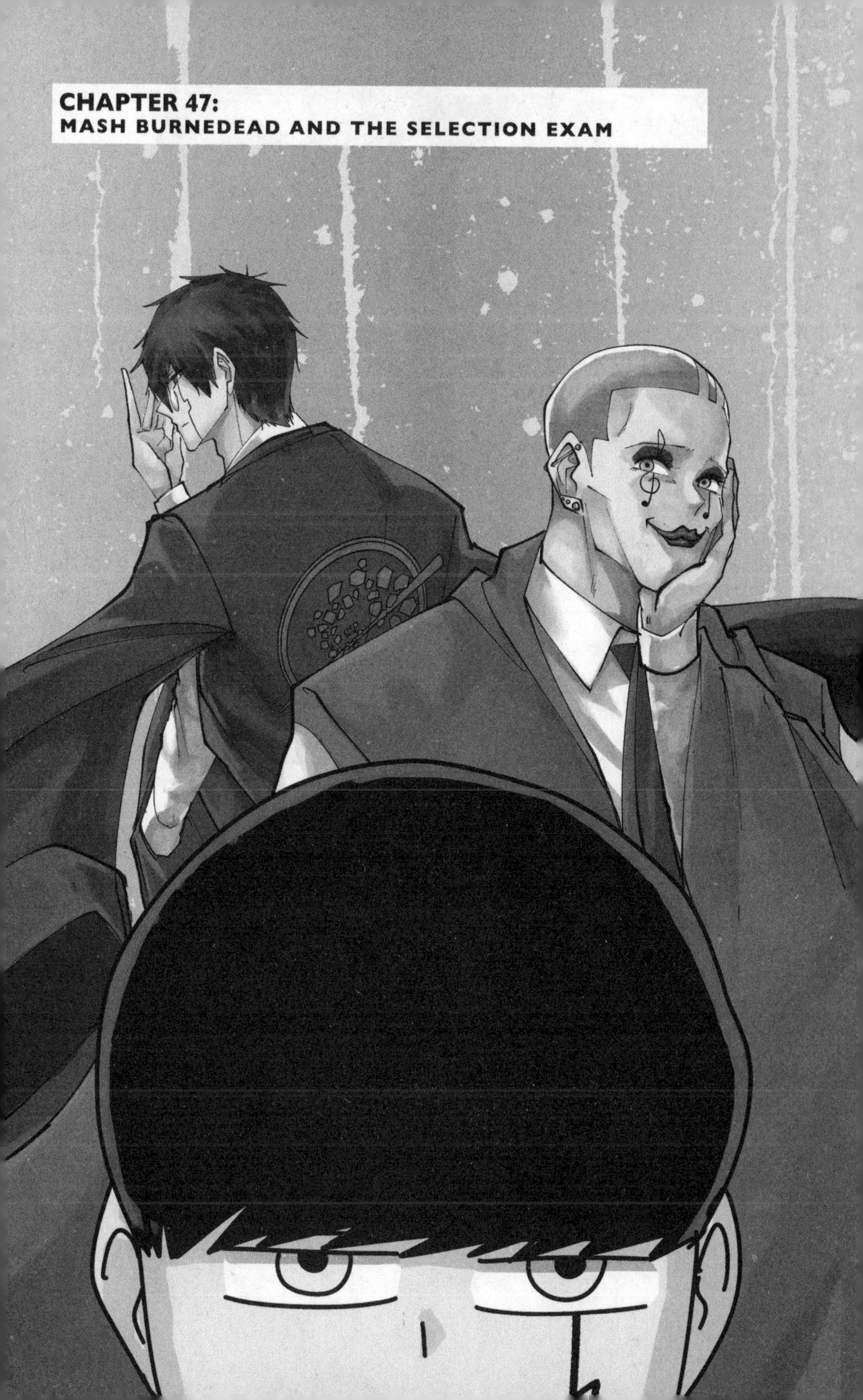

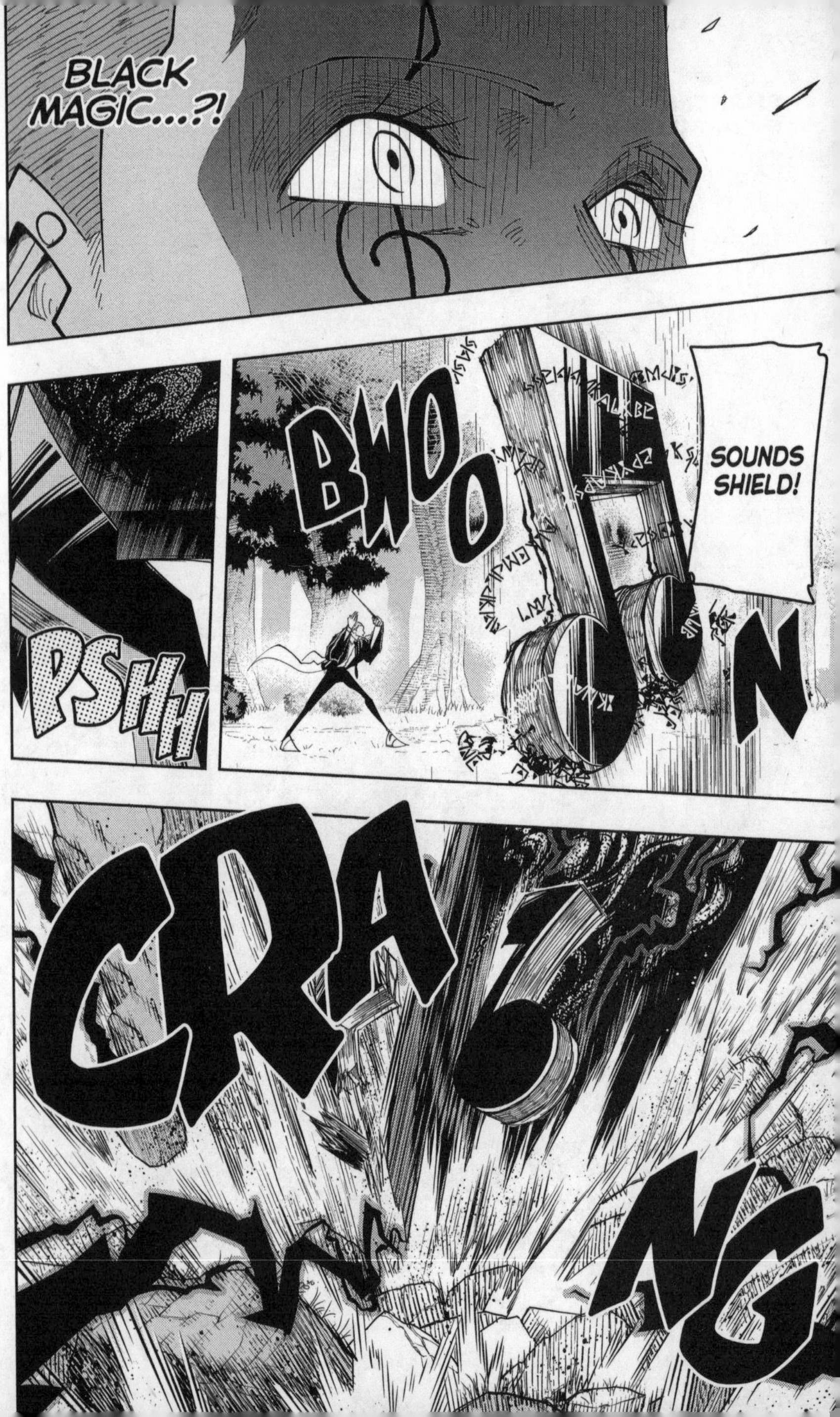
BLACK MAGIC...?!
BWOO
N
SOUNDS SHIELD!
PSHH
CRA
NG

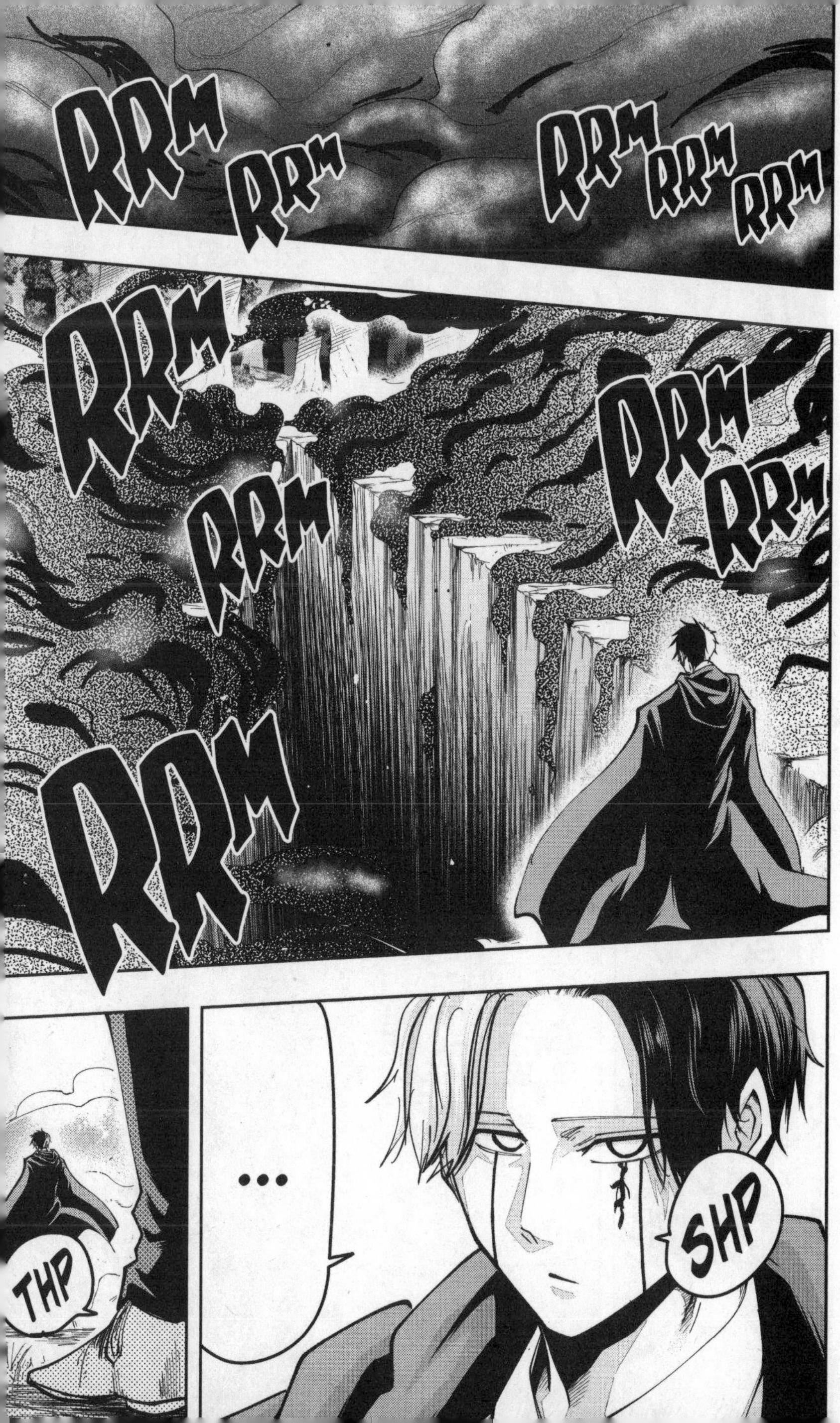

RRM
RRM
RRM
RRM
RRM
RRM
RRM
RRM
RRM
RRM
SHP
...
THP

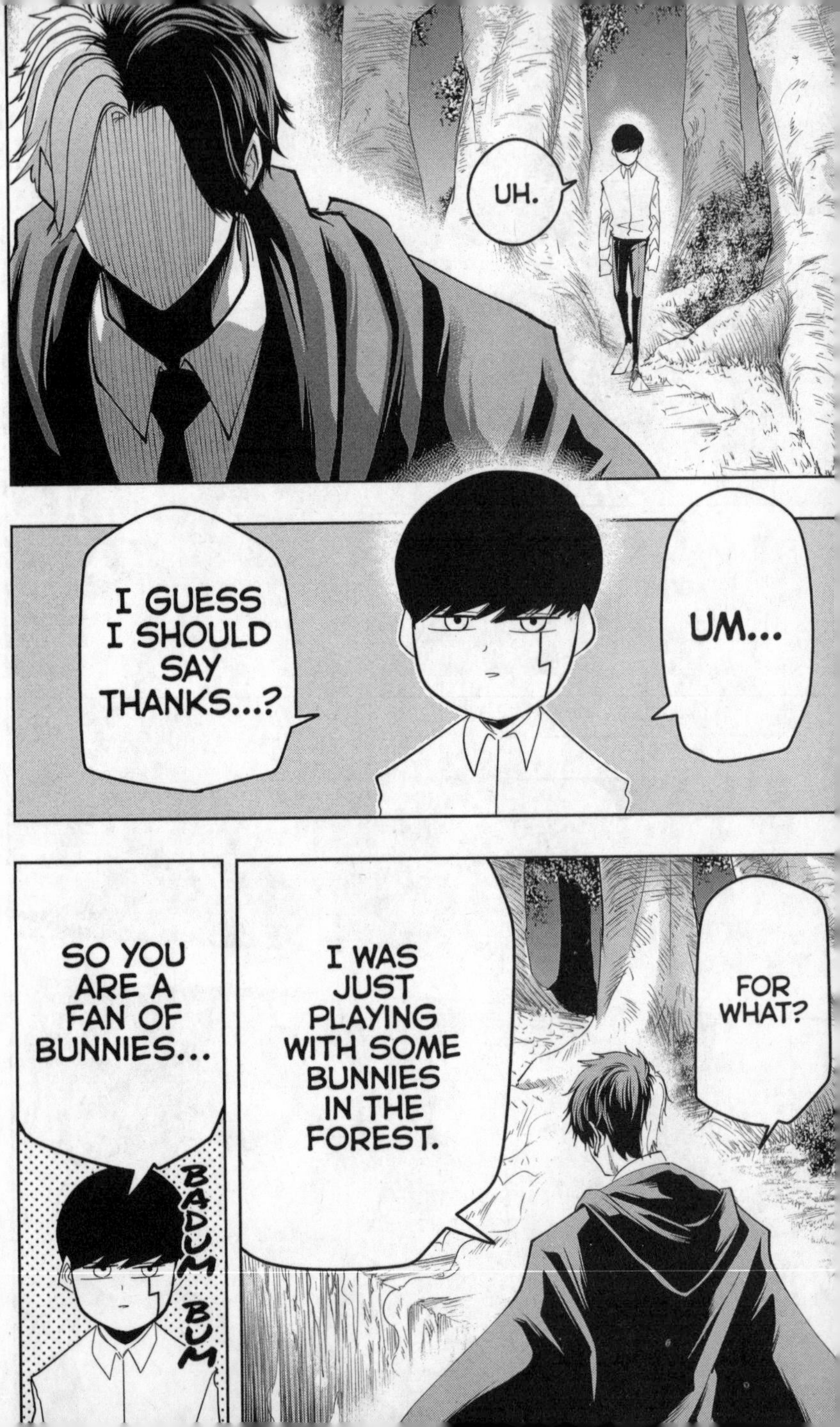
UH.
UM...
I GUESS I SHOULD SAY THANKS...?
FOR WHAT?
I WAS JUST PLAYING WITH SOME BUNNIES IN THE FOREST.
SO YOU ARE A FAN OF BUNNIES...
BADUM BUM

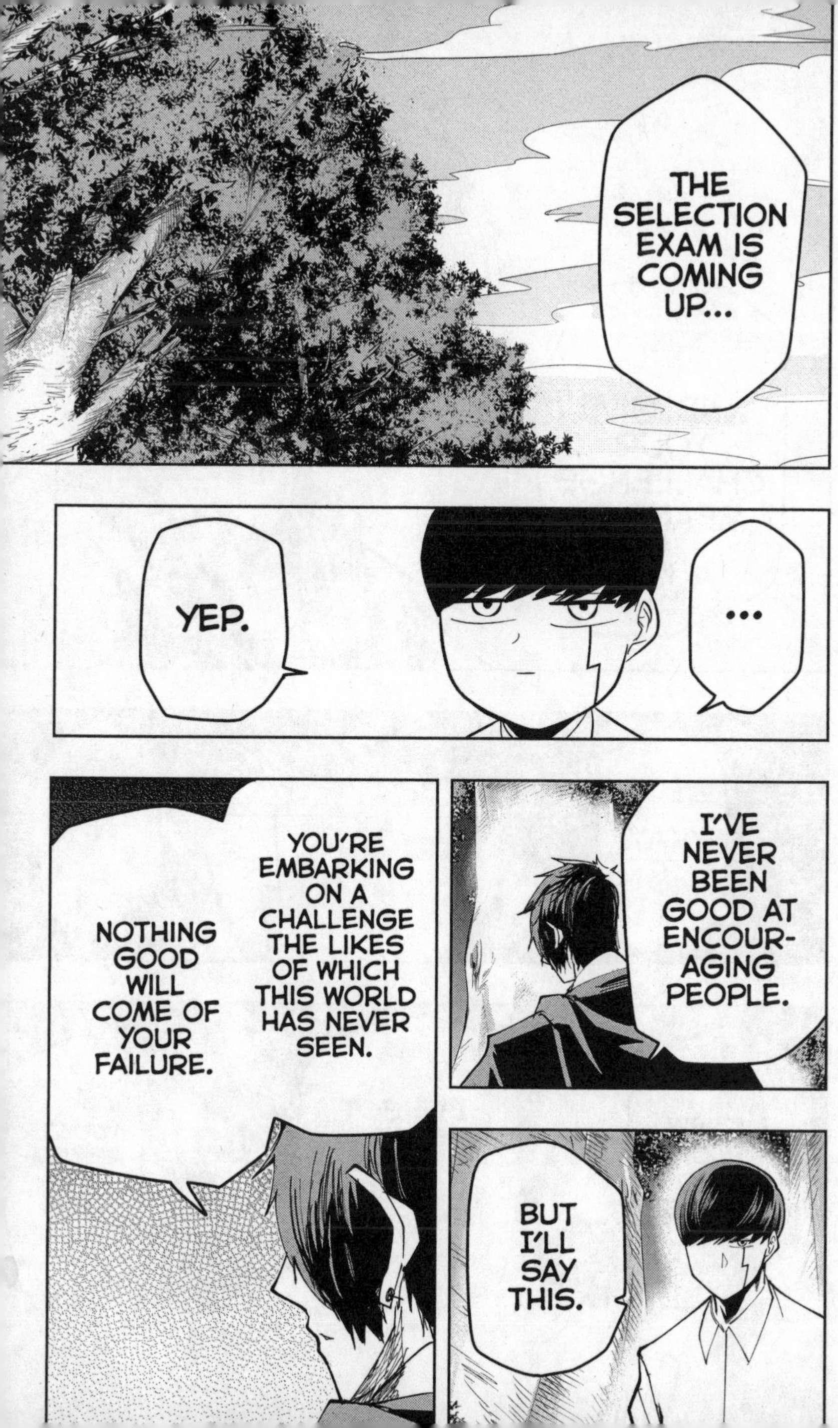
THE SELECTION EXAM IS COMING UP...
...
YEP.
I'VE NEVER BEEN GOOD AT ENCOUR-AGING PEOPLE.
BUT I'LL SAY THIS.
YOU'RE EMBARKING ON A CHALLENGE THE LIKES OF WHICH THIS WORLD HAS NEVER SEEN.
NOTHING GOOD WILL COME OF YOUR FAILURE.

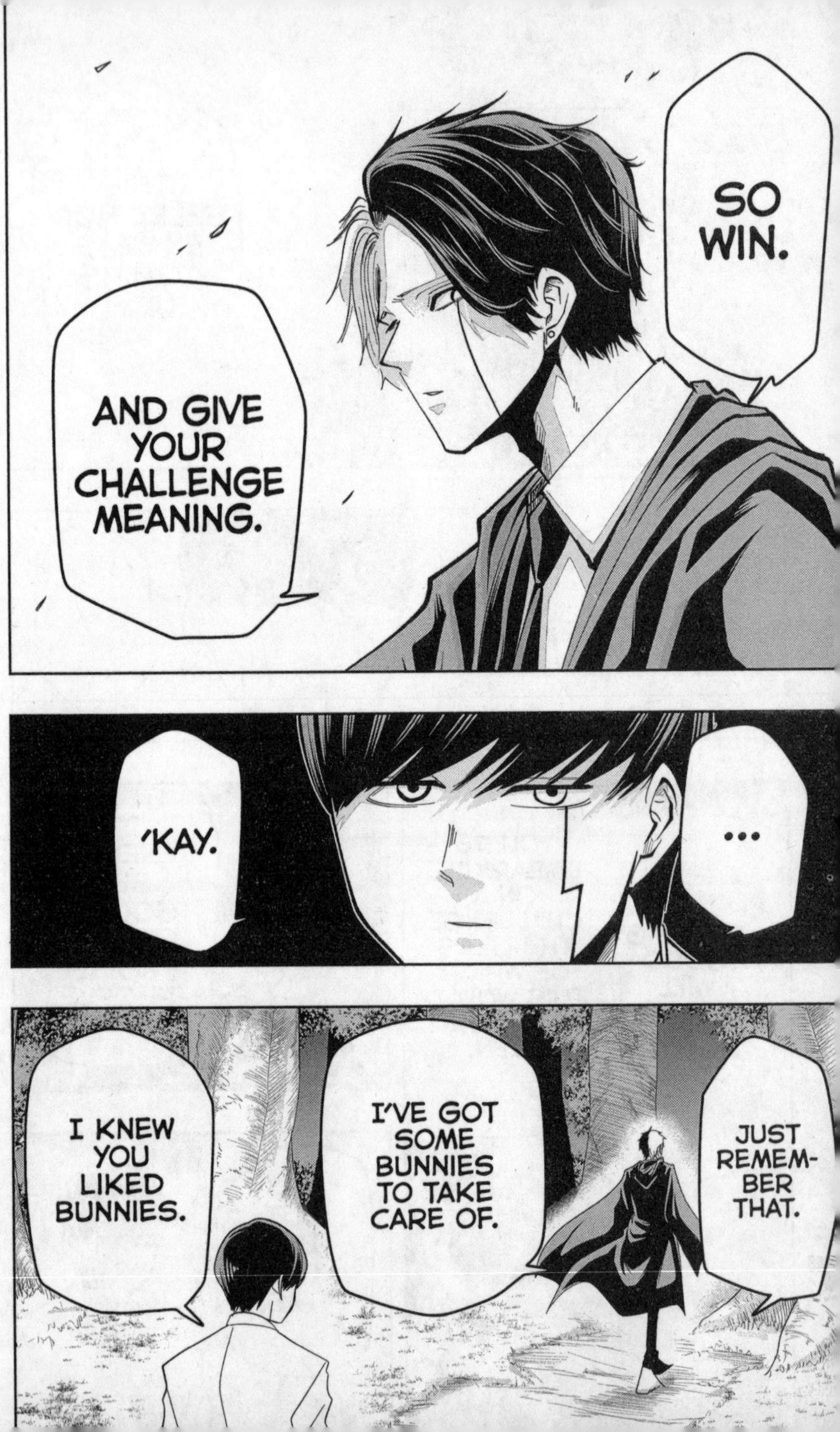
SO WIN.
AND GIVE YOUR CHALLENGE MEANING.
...
'KAY.
JUST REMEMBER THAT.
I'VE GOT SOME BUNNIES TO TAKE CARE OF.
I KNEW YOU LIKED BUNNIES.

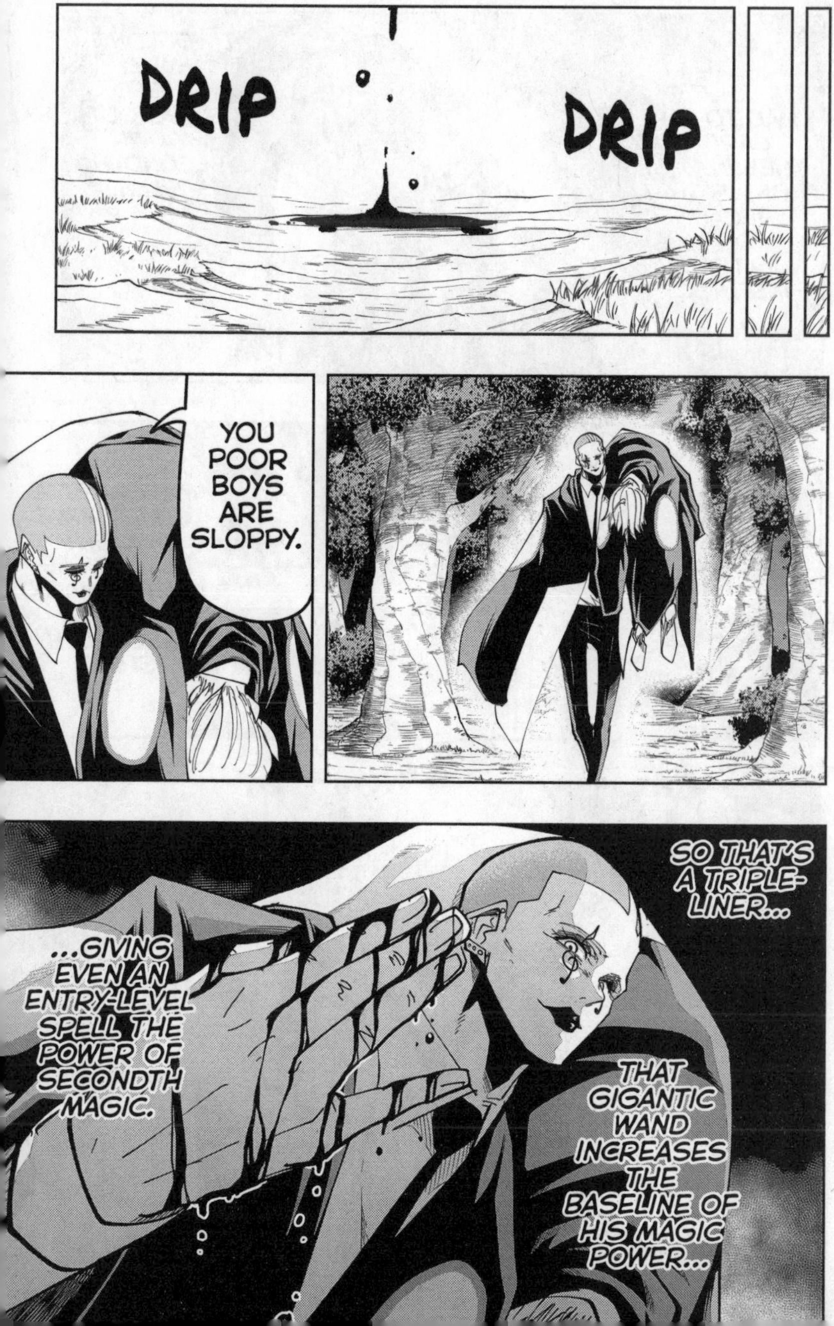
DRIP
DRIP
YOU POOR BOYS ARE SLOPPY.
SO THAT'S A TRIPLE-LINER...
THAT GIGANTIC WAND INCREASES THE BASELINE OF HIS MAGIC POWER...
...GIVING EVEN AN ENTRY-LEVEL SPELL THE POWER OF SECONDTH MAGIC.

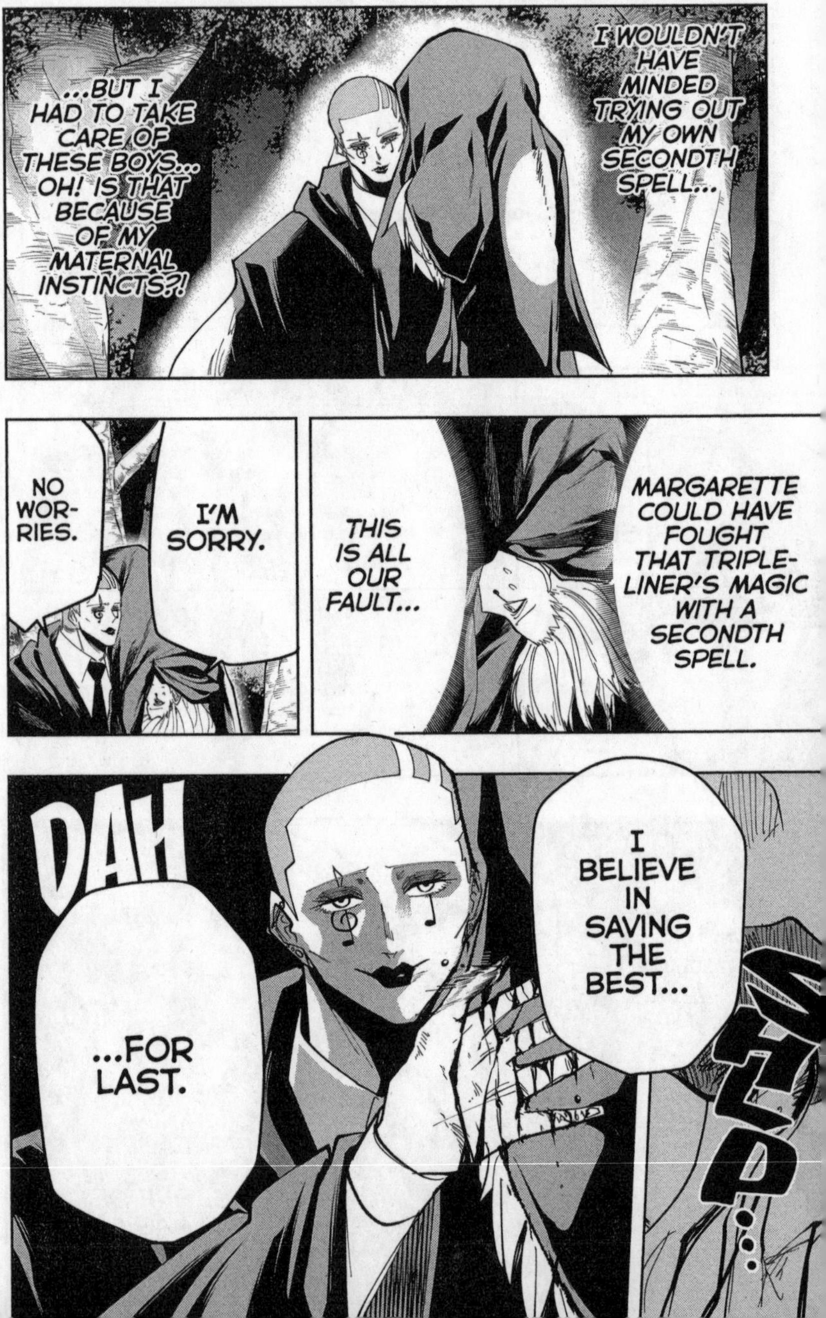
I WOULDN'T HAVE MINDED TRYING OUT MY OWN SECONDTH SPELL...
...BUT I HAD TO TAKE CARE OF THESE BOYS... OH! IS THAT BECAUSE OF MY MATERNAL INSTINCTS?!
MARGARETTE COULD HAVE FOUGHT THAT TRIPLE-LINER'S MAGIC WITH A SECONDTH SPELL.
THIS IS ALL OUR FAULT...
I'M SORRY.
NO WORRIES.
I BELIEVE IN SAVING THE BEST...
DAH
...FOR LAST.

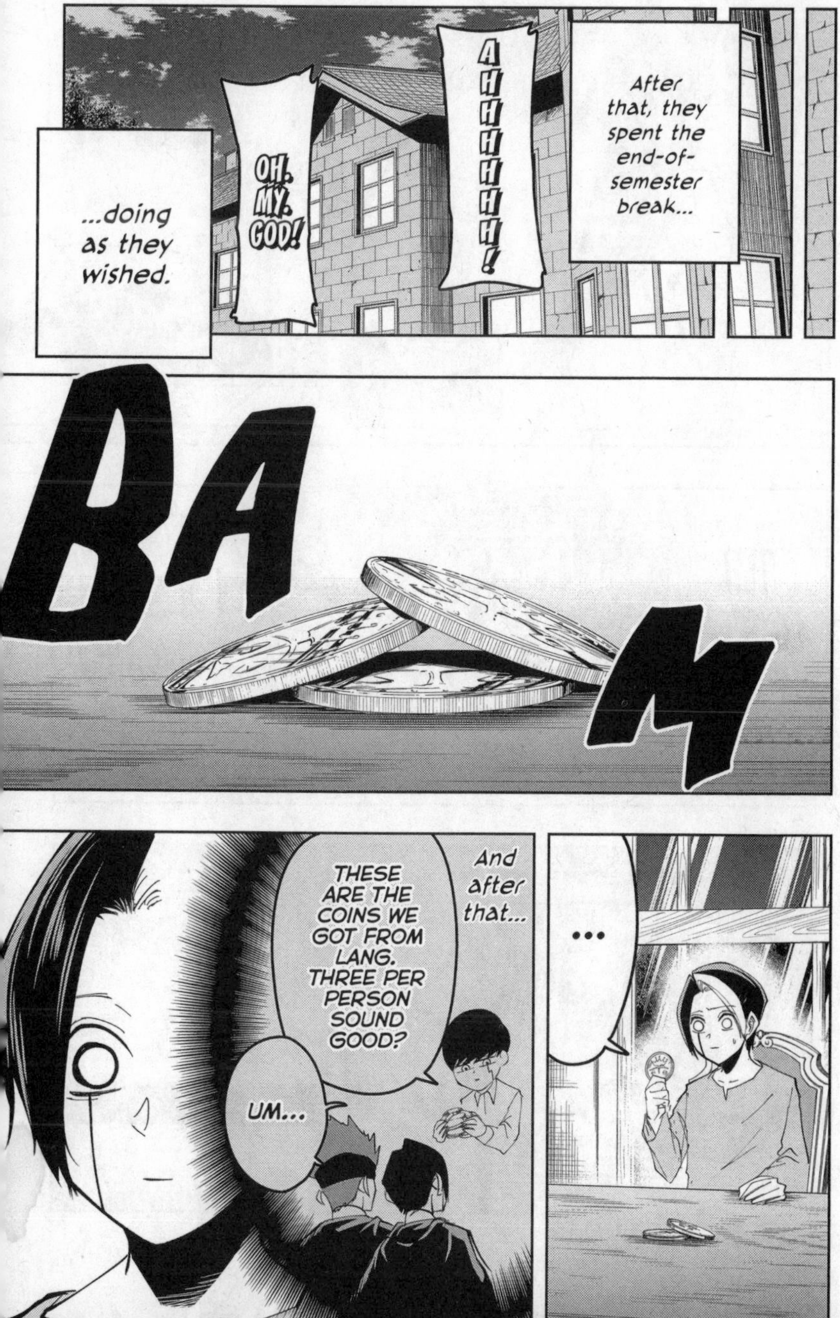
After that, they spent the end-of-semester break...
AHHHHHHH!
OH. MY. GOD!
...doing as they wished.
BAM
...
And after that...
THESE ARE THE COINS WE GOT FROM LANG. THREE PER PERSON SOUND GOOD?
UM...

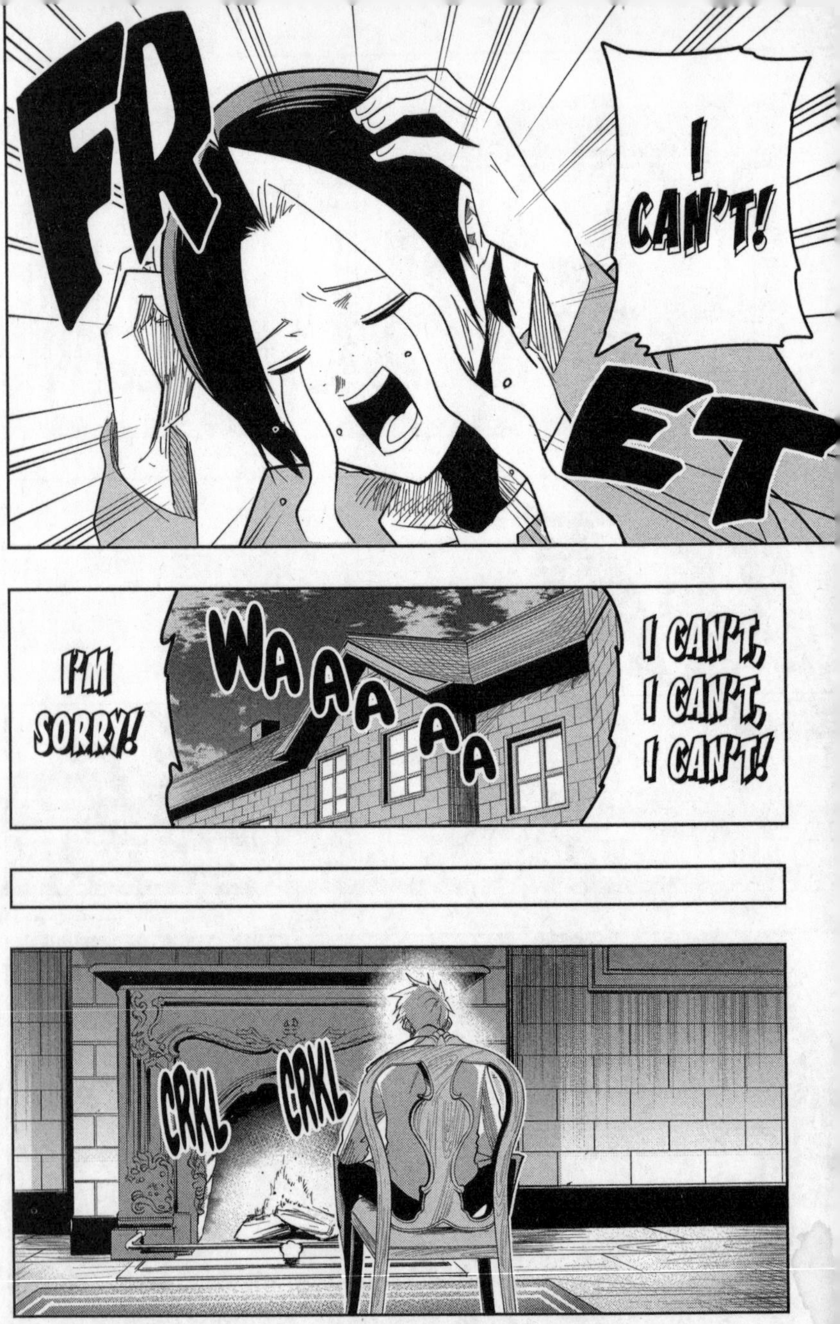
I CAN'T!
FRET
I CAN'T, I CAN'T, I CAN'T!
WAAAAAA
I'M SORRY!
CRKL
CRKL

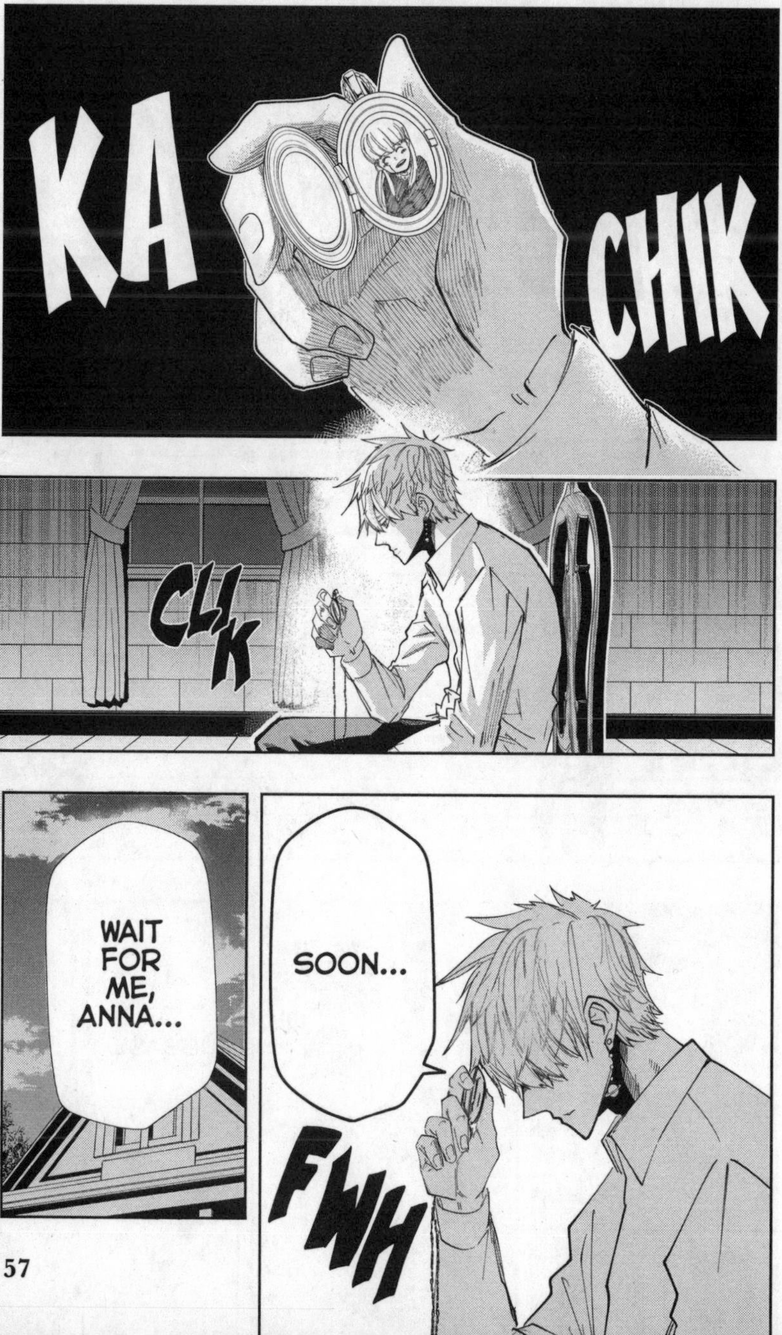
KA
CHIK
CLIK
SOON...
FWH
WAIT FOR ME, ANNA...

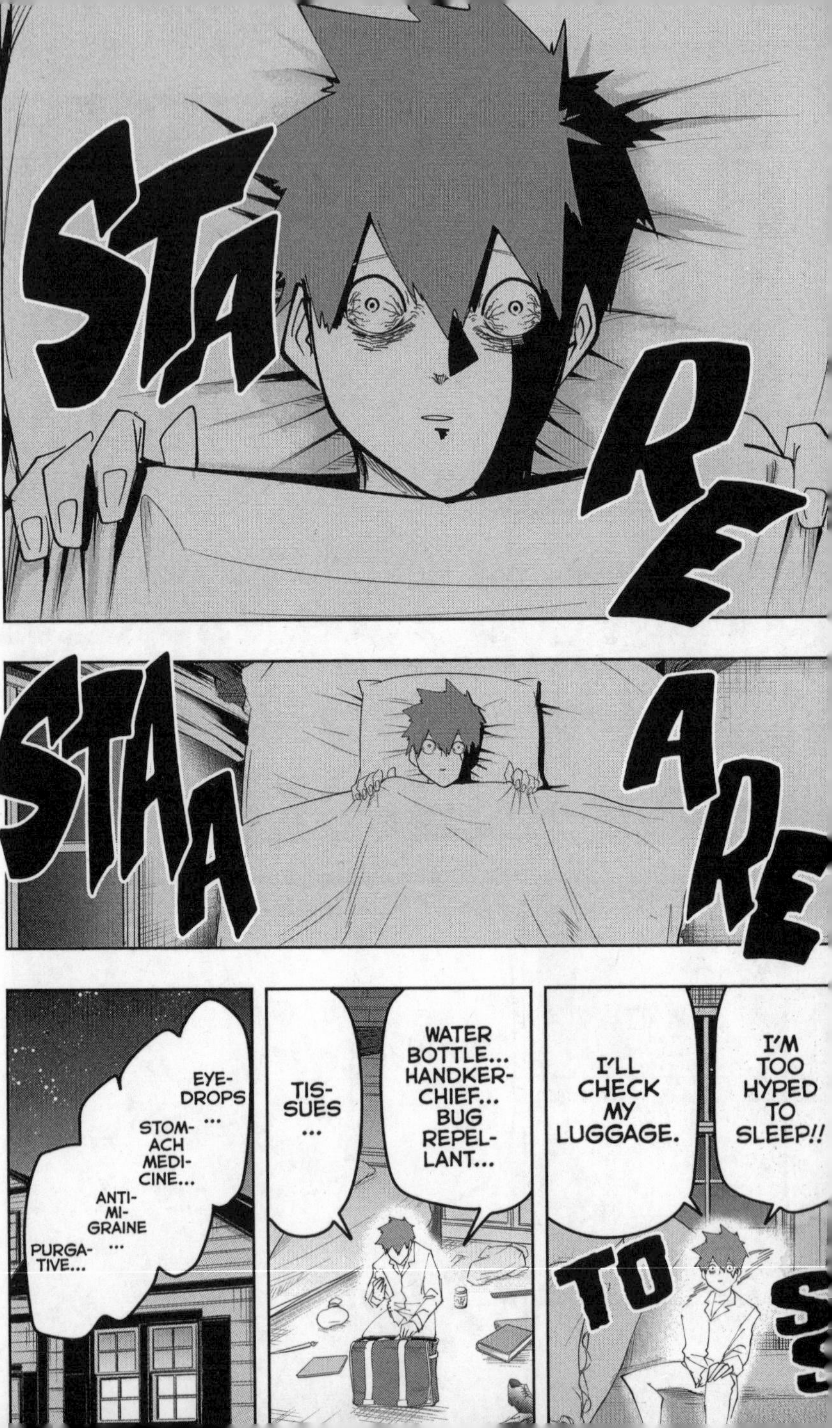

STARE
STAAARE
I'M TOO HYPED TO SLEEP!!
TO
I'LL CHECK MY LUGGAGE.
WATER BOTTLE... HANDKERCHIEF... BUG REPELLANT...
TISSUES...
EYEDROPS... STOMACH MEDICINE... ANTI-MIGRAINE... PURGATIVE...

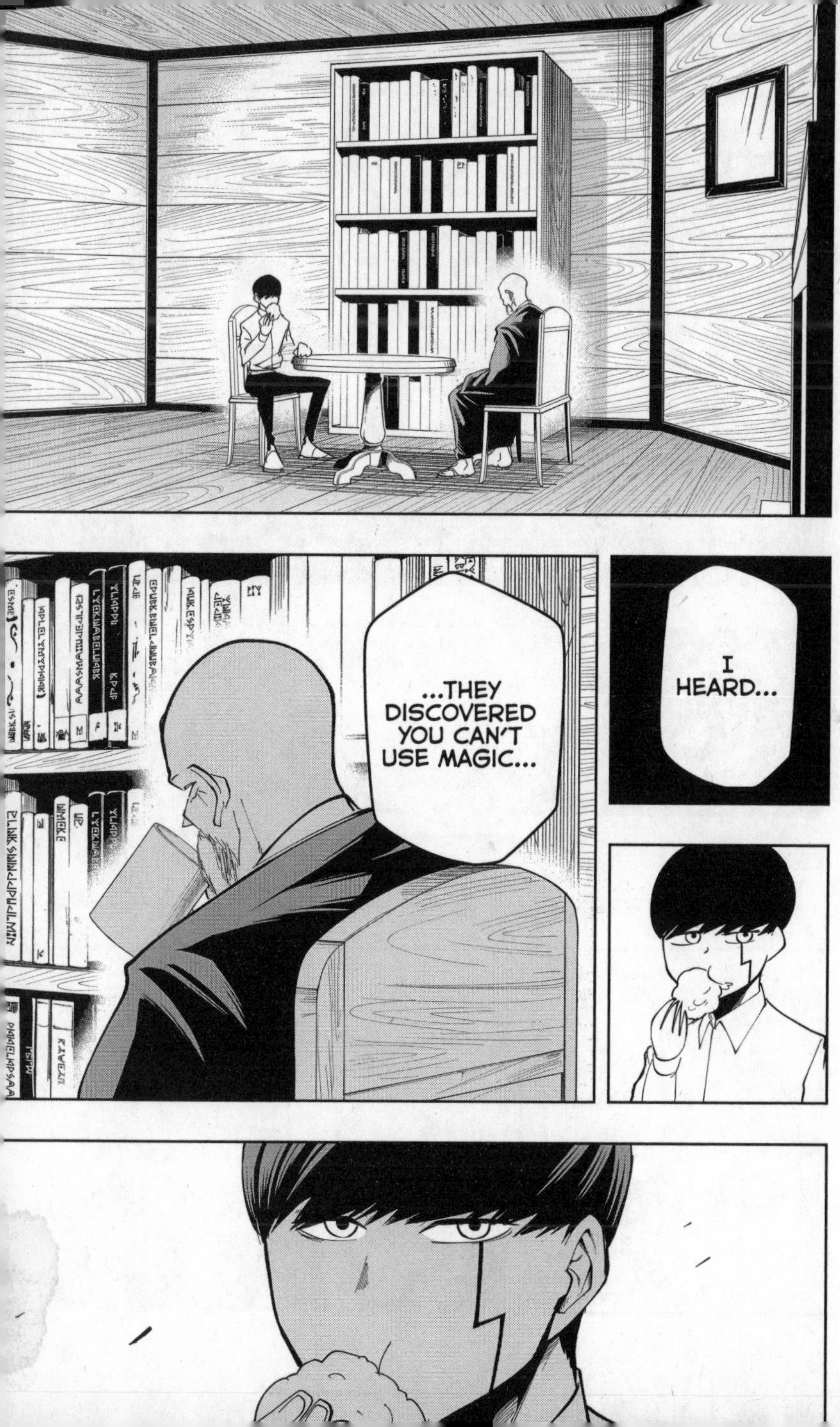
I HEARD...
...THEY DISCOVERED YOU CAN'T USE MAGIC...

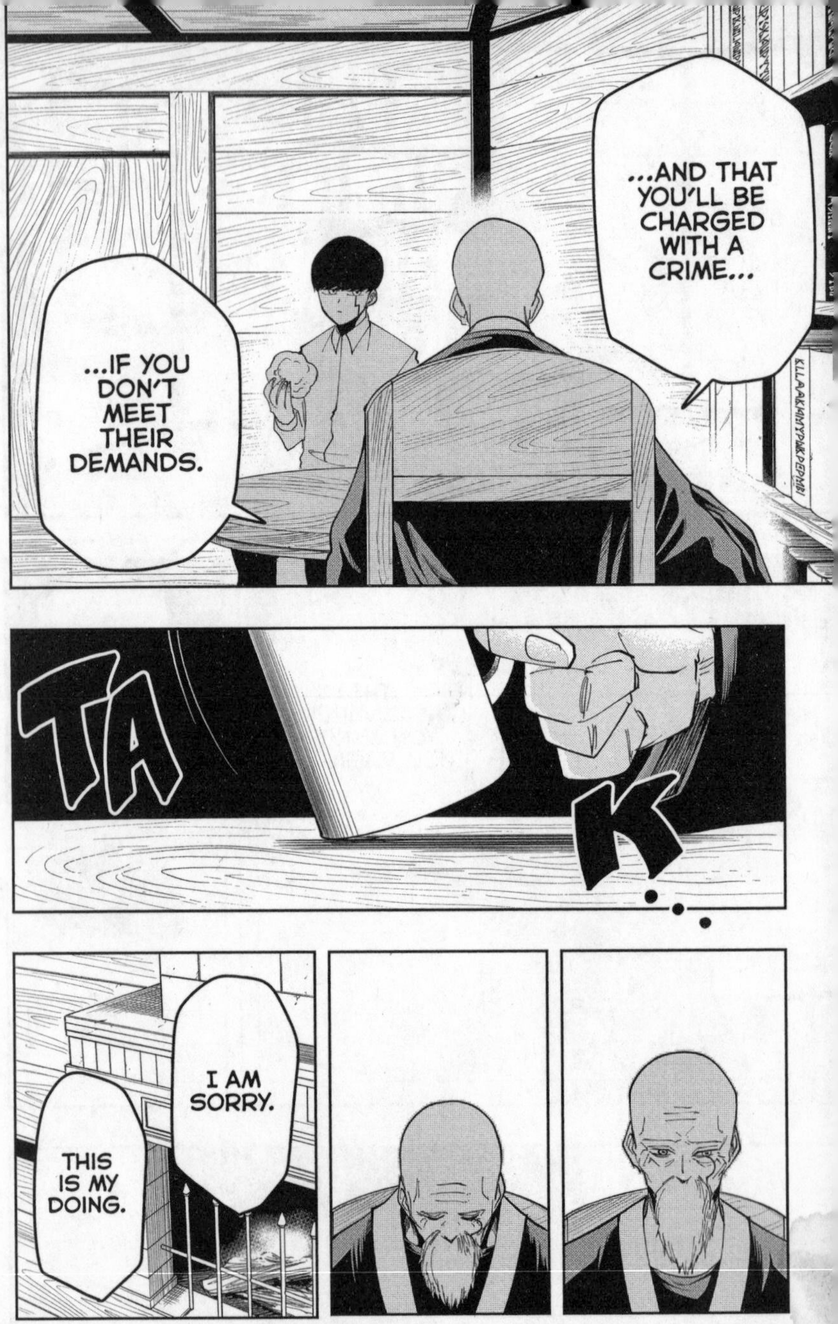
...AND THAT YOU'LL BE CHARGED WITH A CRIME...
...IF YOU DON'T MEET THEIR DEMANDS.
TAK
...
I AM SORRY.
THIS IS MY DOING.

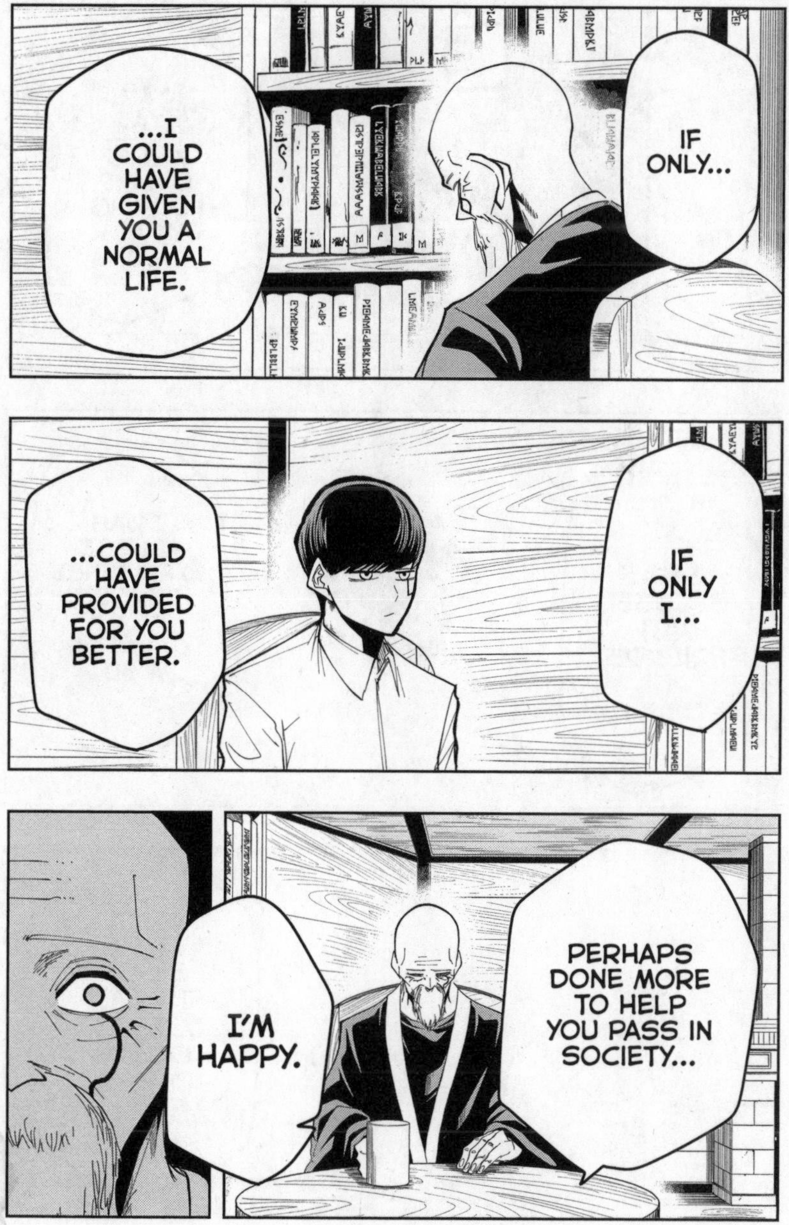
IF ONLY...
...I COULD HAVE GIVEN YOU A NORMAL LIFE.
IF ONLY I...
...COULD HAVE PROVIDED FOR YOU BETTER.
PERHAPS DONE MORE TO HELP YOU PASS IN SOCIETY...
I'M HAPPY.

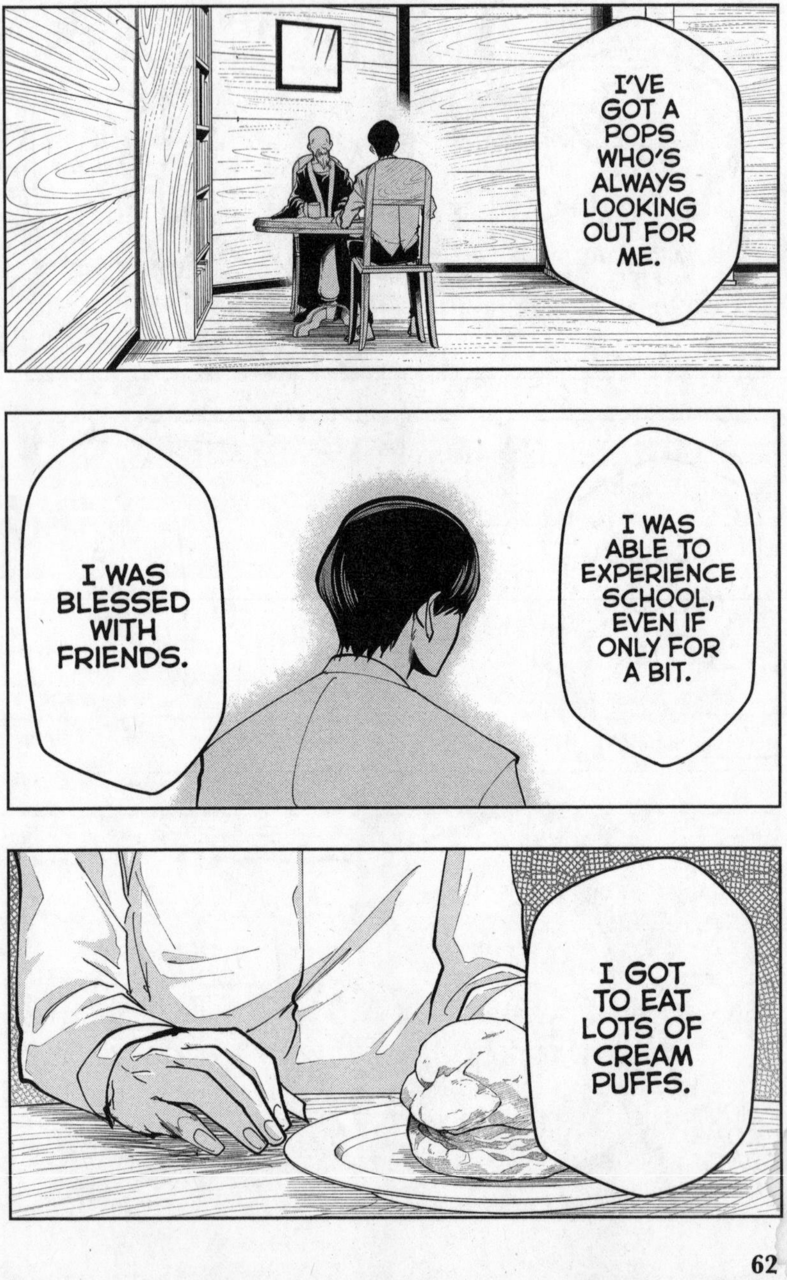
I'VE GOT A POPS WHO'S ALWAYS LOOKING OUT FOR ME.
I WAS ABLE TO EXPERIENCE SCHOOL, EVEN IF ONLY FOR A BIT.
I WAS BLESSED WITH FRIENDS.
I GOT TO EAT LOTS OF CREAM PUFFS.

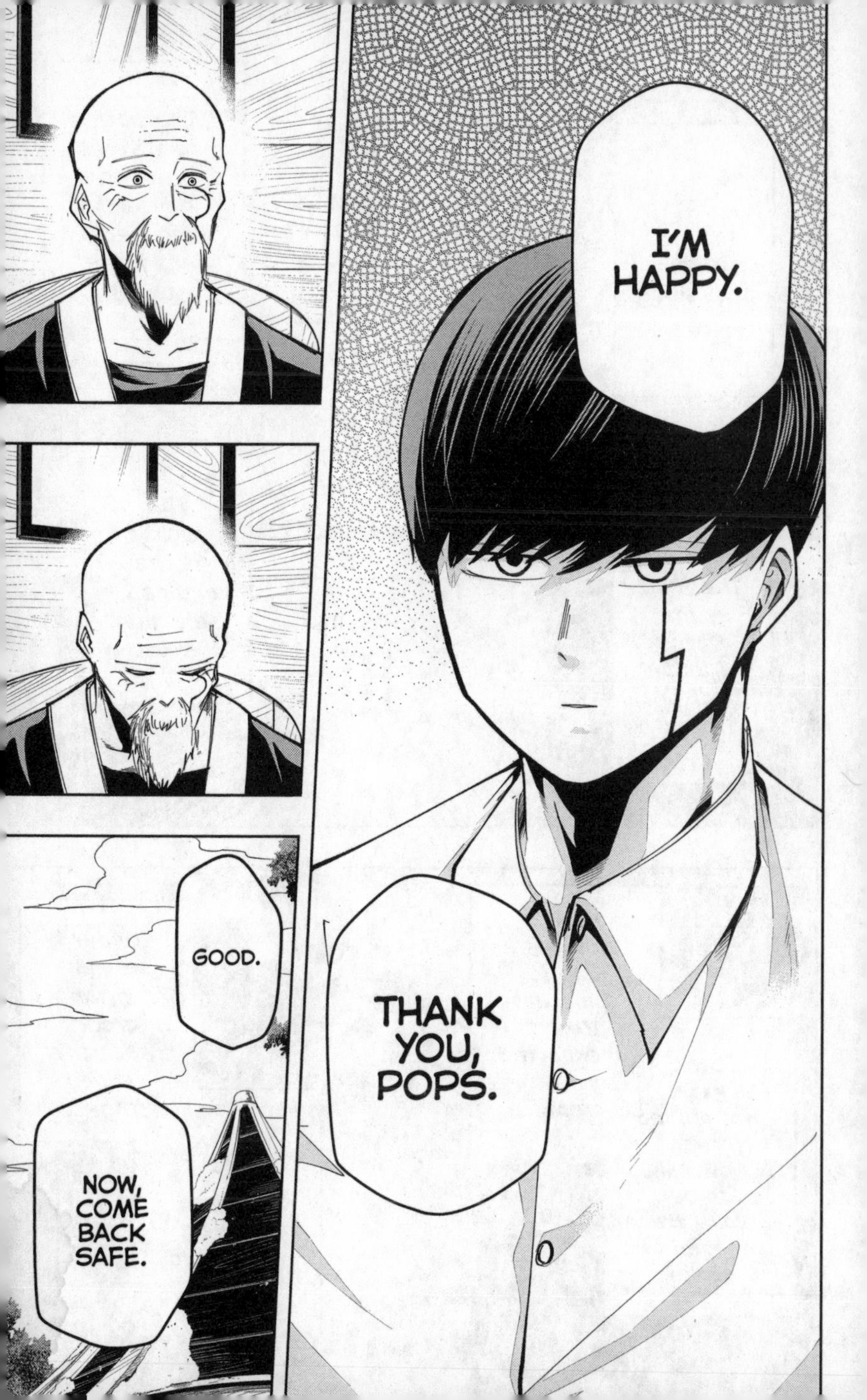
I'M HAPPY.
THANK YOU, POPS.
GOOD.
NOW, COME BACK SAFE.

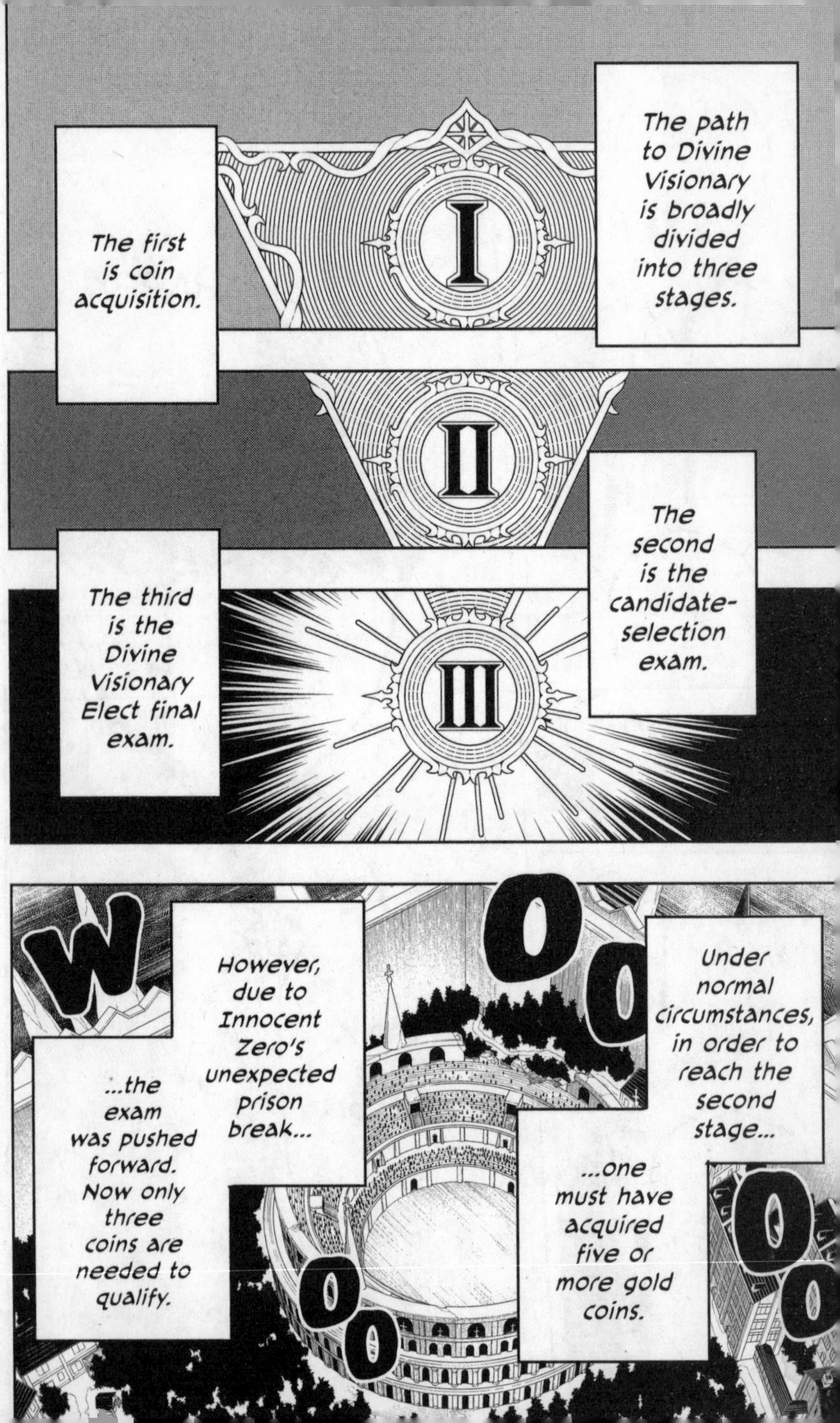
The path to Divine Visionary is broadly divided into three stages.
The first is coin acquisition.
I
II
The second is the candidate-selection exam.
III
The third is the Divine Visionary Elect final exam.
Under normal circumstances, in order to reach the second stage...
...one must have acquired five or more gold coins.
However, due to Innocent Zero's unexpected prison break...
...the exam was pushed forward. Now only three coins are needed to qualify.
WOOOOOO

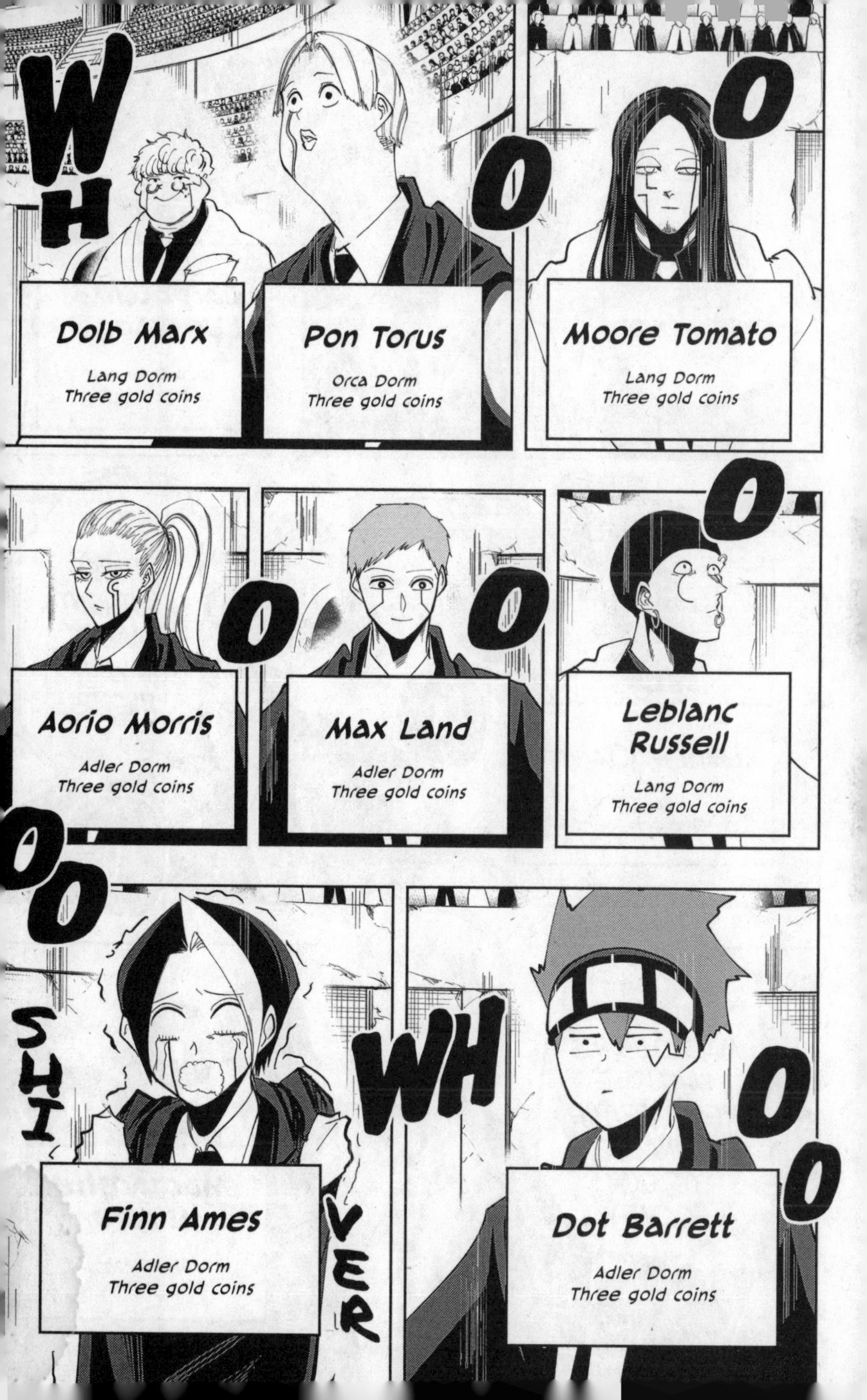
WHOOOO
Moore Tomato
Lang Dorm
Three gold coins
Pon Torus
Orca Dorm
Three gold coins
Dolb Marx
Lang Dorm
Three gold coins
OOOOO
Leblanc Russell
Lang Dorm
Three gold coins
Max Land
Adler Dorm
Three gold coins
Aorio Morris
Adler Dorm
Three gold coins
WHOOO
Dot Barrett
Adler Dorm
Three gold coins
SHIVER
Finn Ames
Adler Dorm
Three gold coins

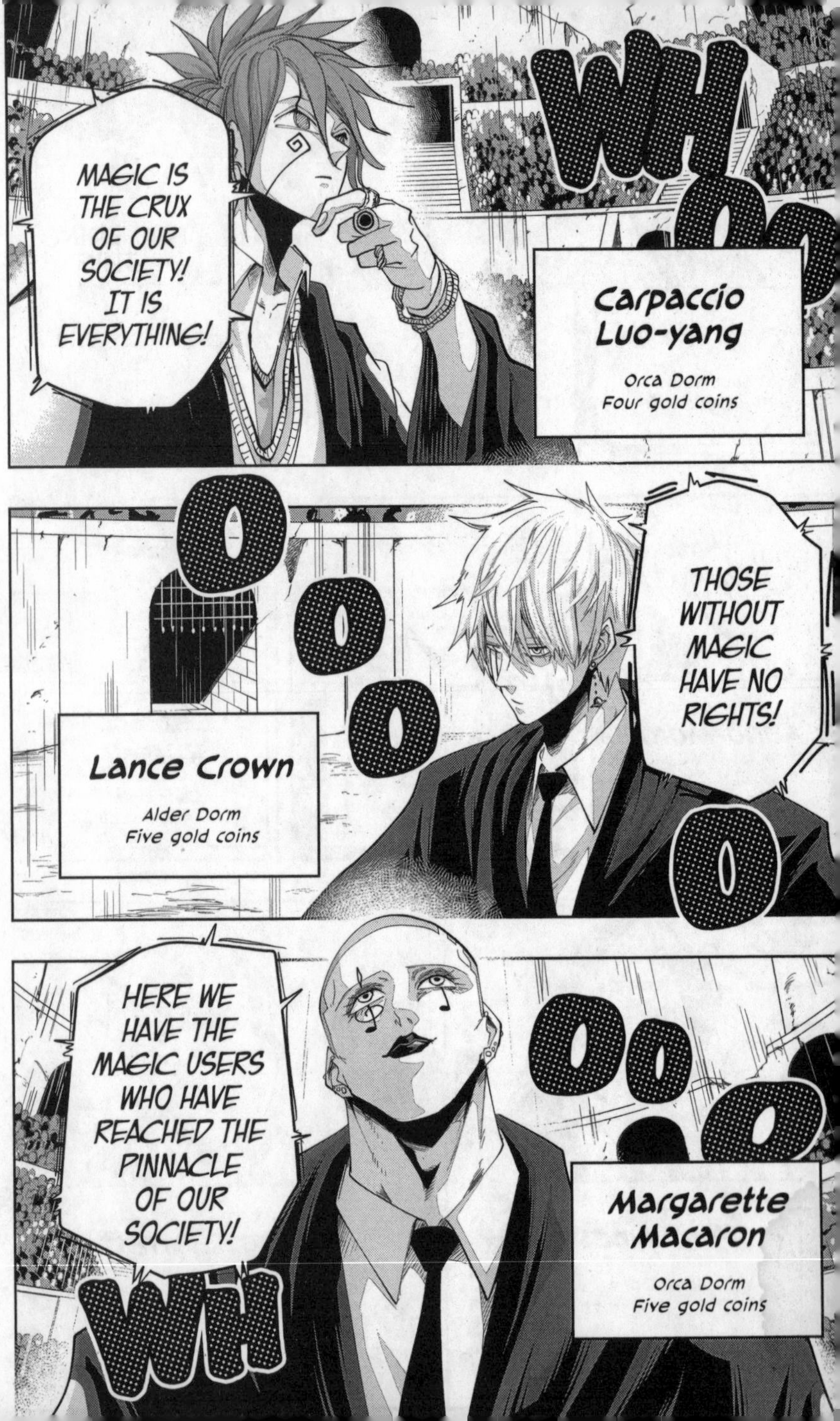
WHOO
MAGIC IS THE CRUX OF OUR SOCIETY! IT IS EVERYTHING!
Carpaccio Luo-yang
Orca Dorm
Four gold coins
THOSE WITHOUT MAGIC HAVE NO RIGHTS!
OOOO
Lance Crown
Alder Dorm
Five gold coins
OOOO
HERE WE HAVE THE MAGIC USERS WHO HAVE REACHED THE PINNACLE OF OUR SOCIETY!
Margarette Macaron
Orca Dorm
Five gold coins
WH

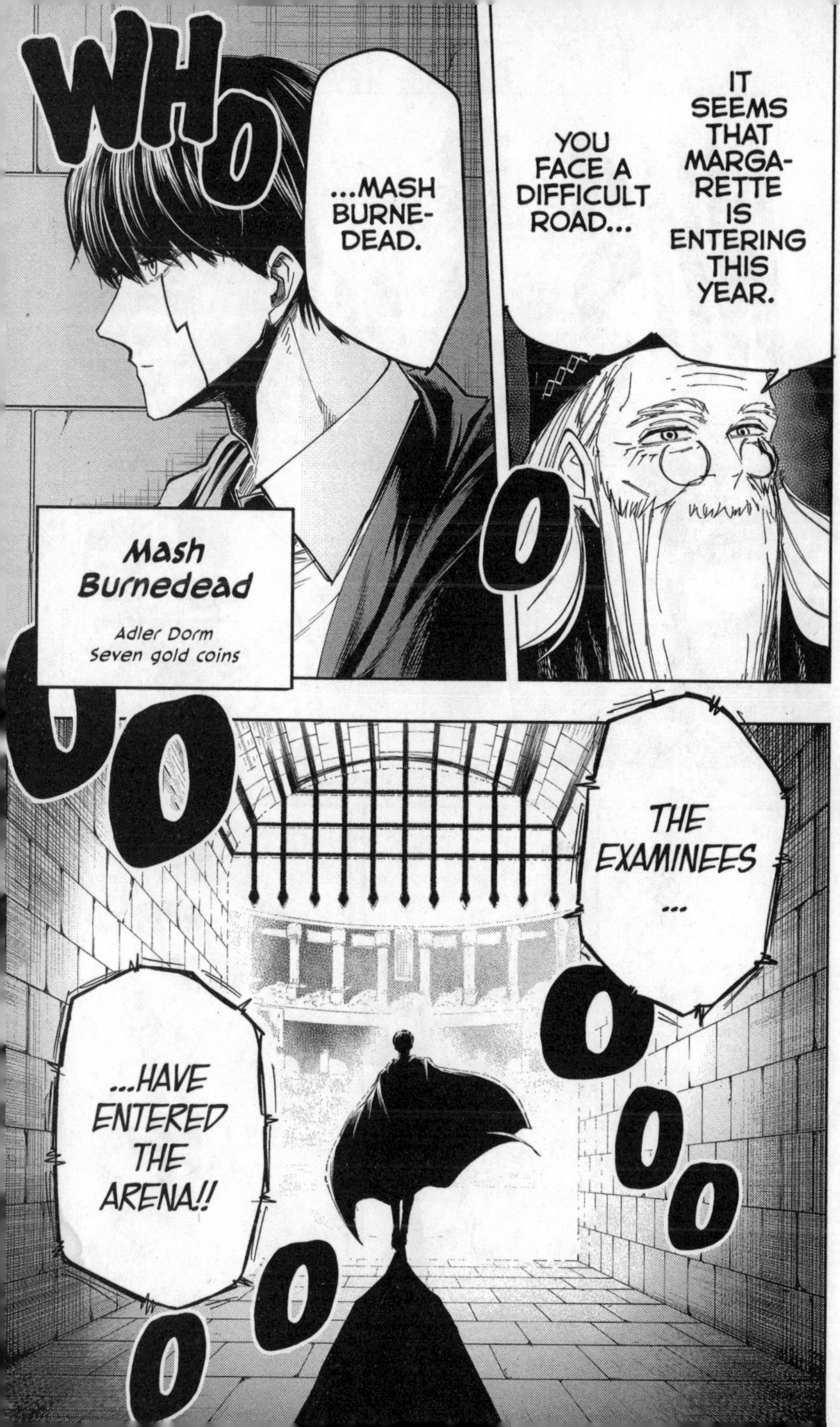
IT SEEMS THAT MARGA-RETTE IS ENTERING THIS YEAR.
YOU FACE A DIFFICULT ROAD...
...MASH BURNE-DEAD.
WHOOOOOOOOOO
Mash Burnedead
Adler Dorm
Seven gold coins
THE EXAMINEES ...
...HAVE ENTERED THE ARENA!!

BONUS, PART 2

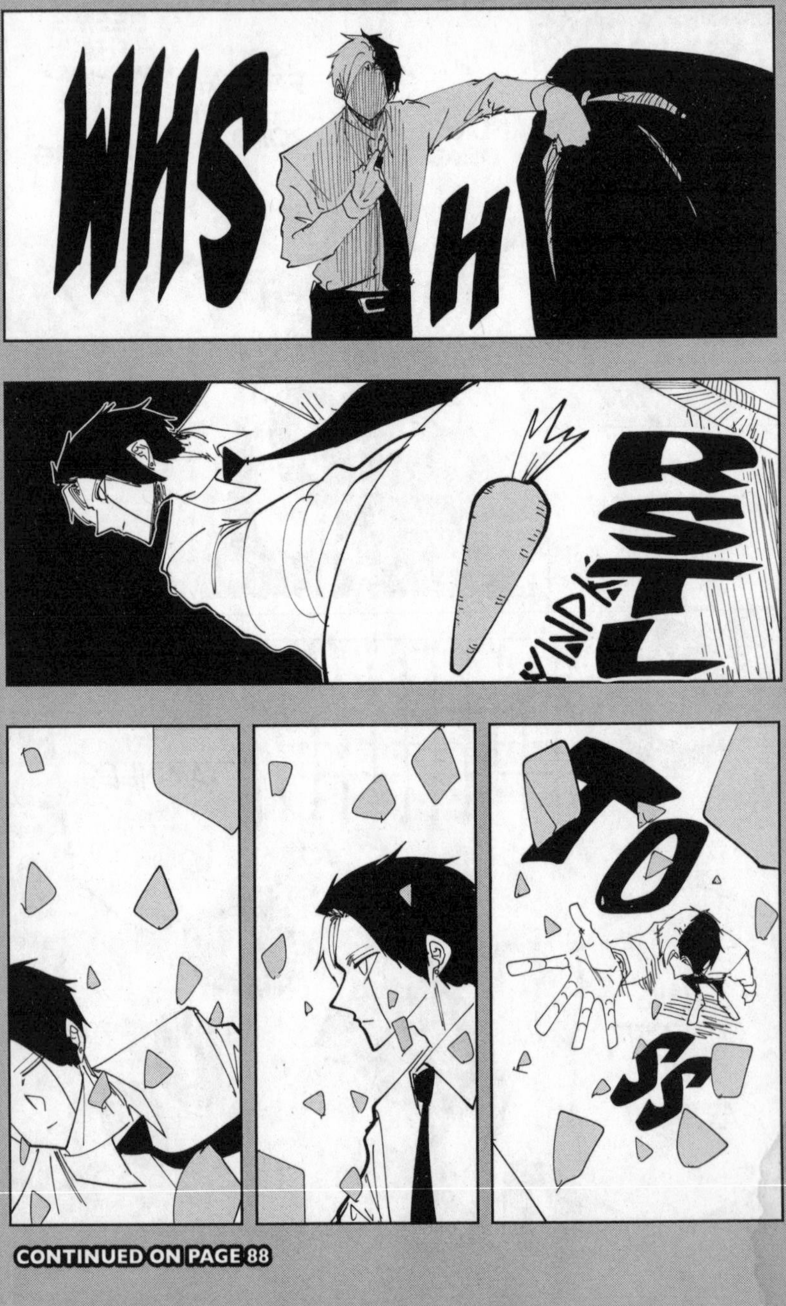
WHSH
RSTL
TOSS

CONTINUED ON PAGE 88

CHAPTER 48: MASH BURNEDEAD AND THE LAMBS TO THE SLAUGHTER

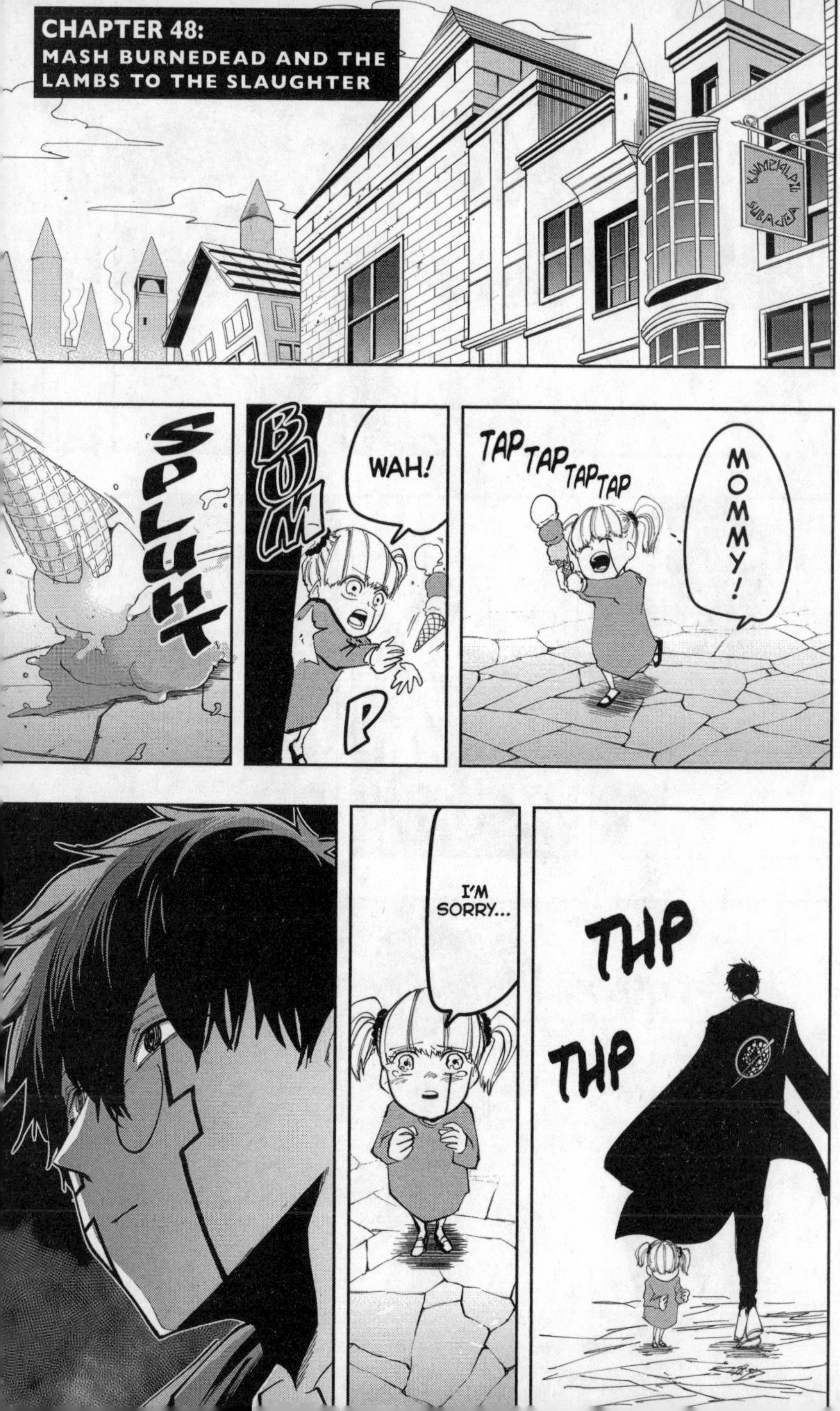
TAP TAP TAP TAP
MOMMY!
BUMP
WAH!
SPLUHT
THP
THP
I'M SORRY...

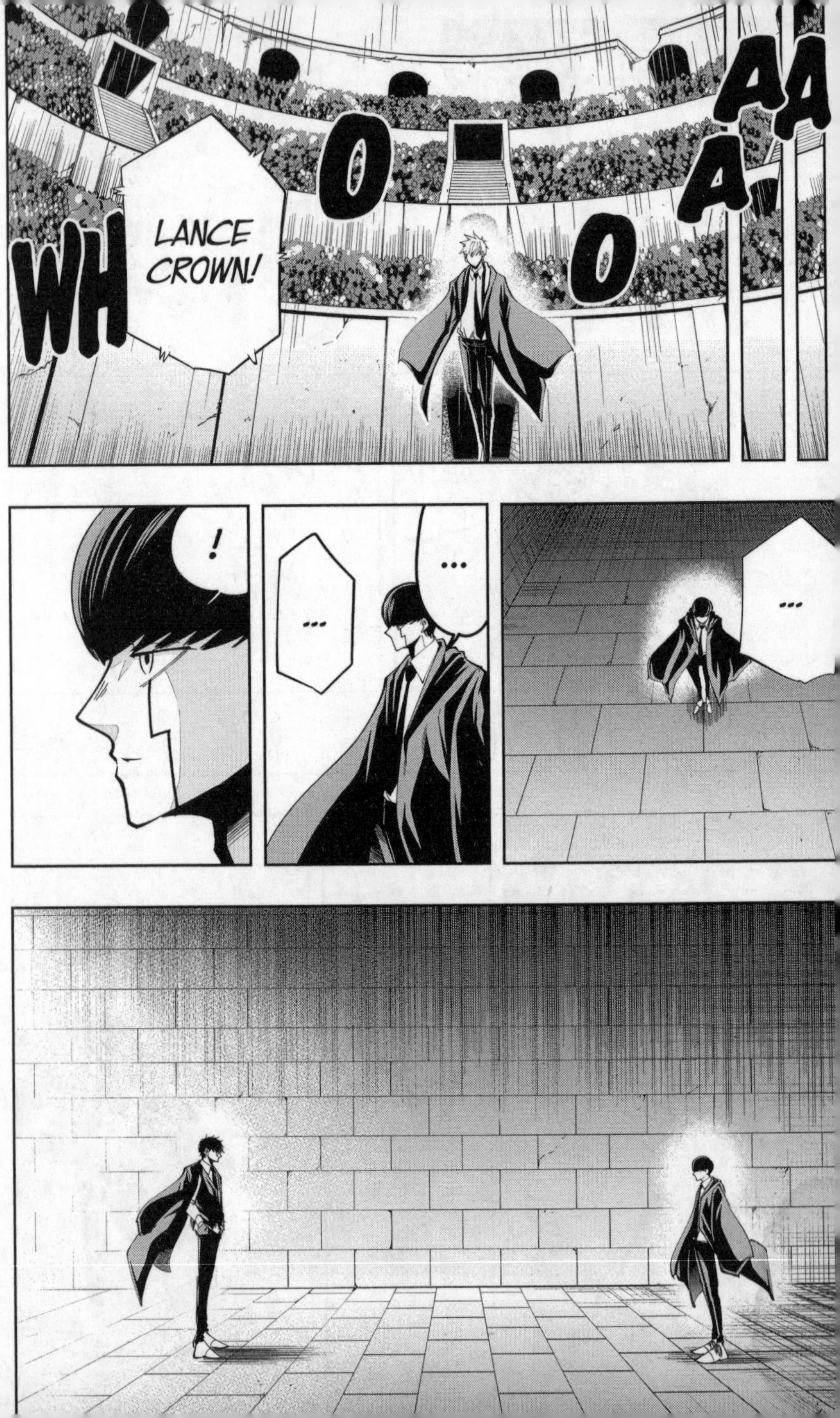

WHOOAAAA
LANCE CROWN!
...
...
...
!

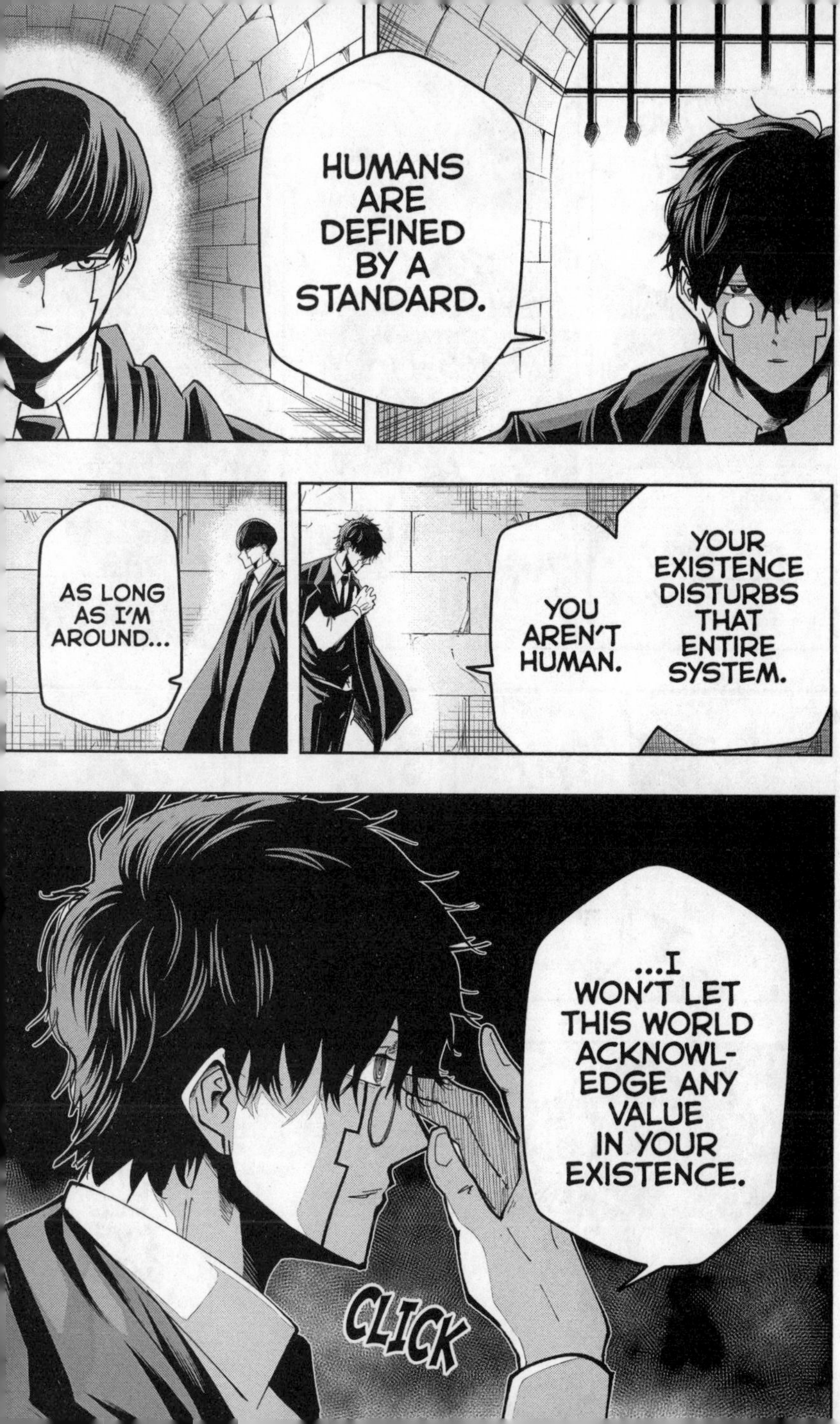
HUMANS ARE DEFINED BY A STANDARD.
YOUR EXISTENCE DISTURBS THAT ENTIRE SYSTEM.
YOU AREN'T HUMAN.
AS LONG AS I'M AROUND...
...I WON'T LET THIS WORLD ACKNOWL-EDGE ANY VALUE IN YOUR EXISTENCE.
CLICK

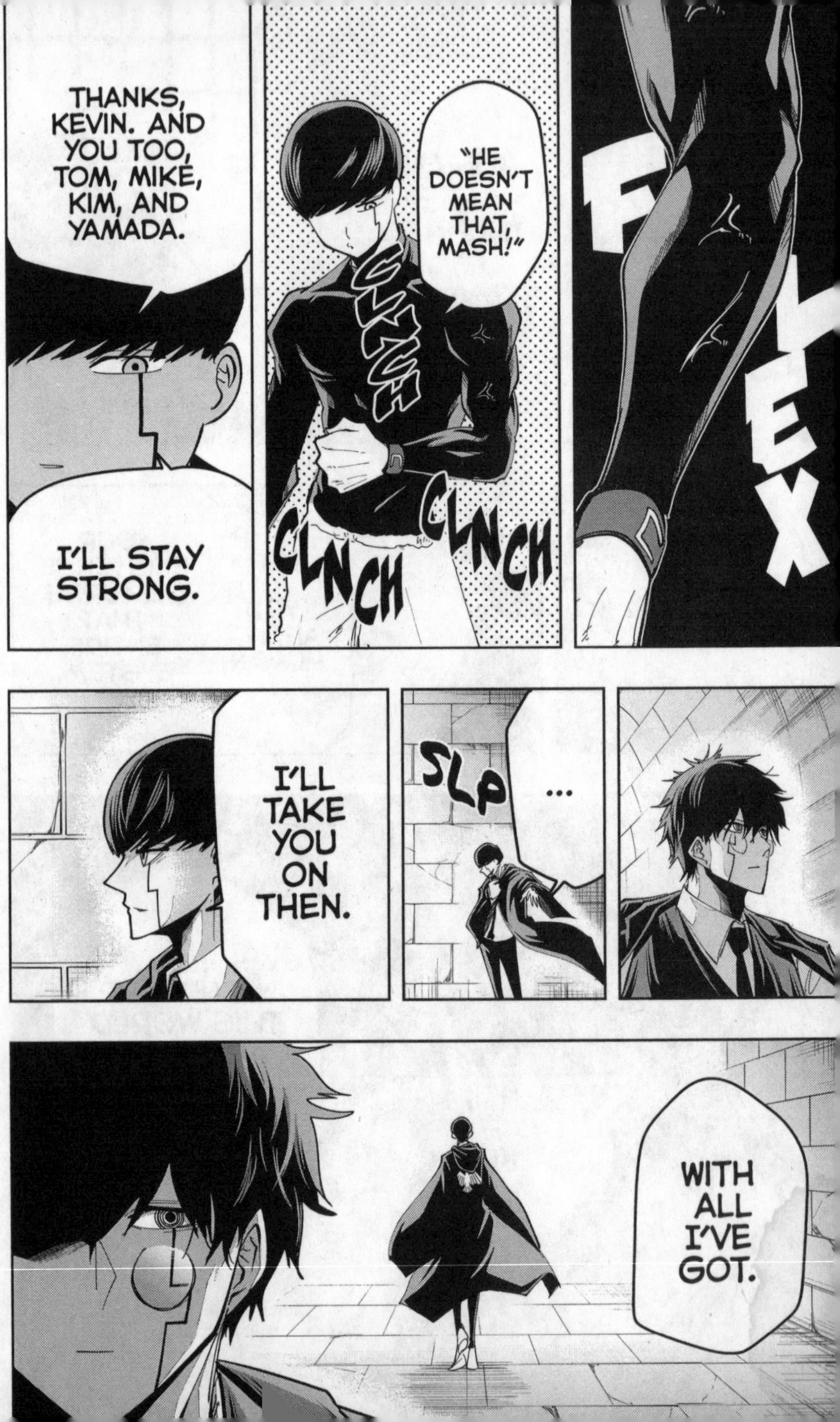
FLEX
"HE DOESN'T MEAN THAT, MASH!"
CLNCH
CLNCH
CLNCH
THANKS, KEVIN. AND YOU TOO, TOM, MIKE, KIM, AND YAMADA.
I'LL STAY STRONG.
SLP
...
I'LL TAKE YOU ON THEN.
WITH ALL I'VE GOT.

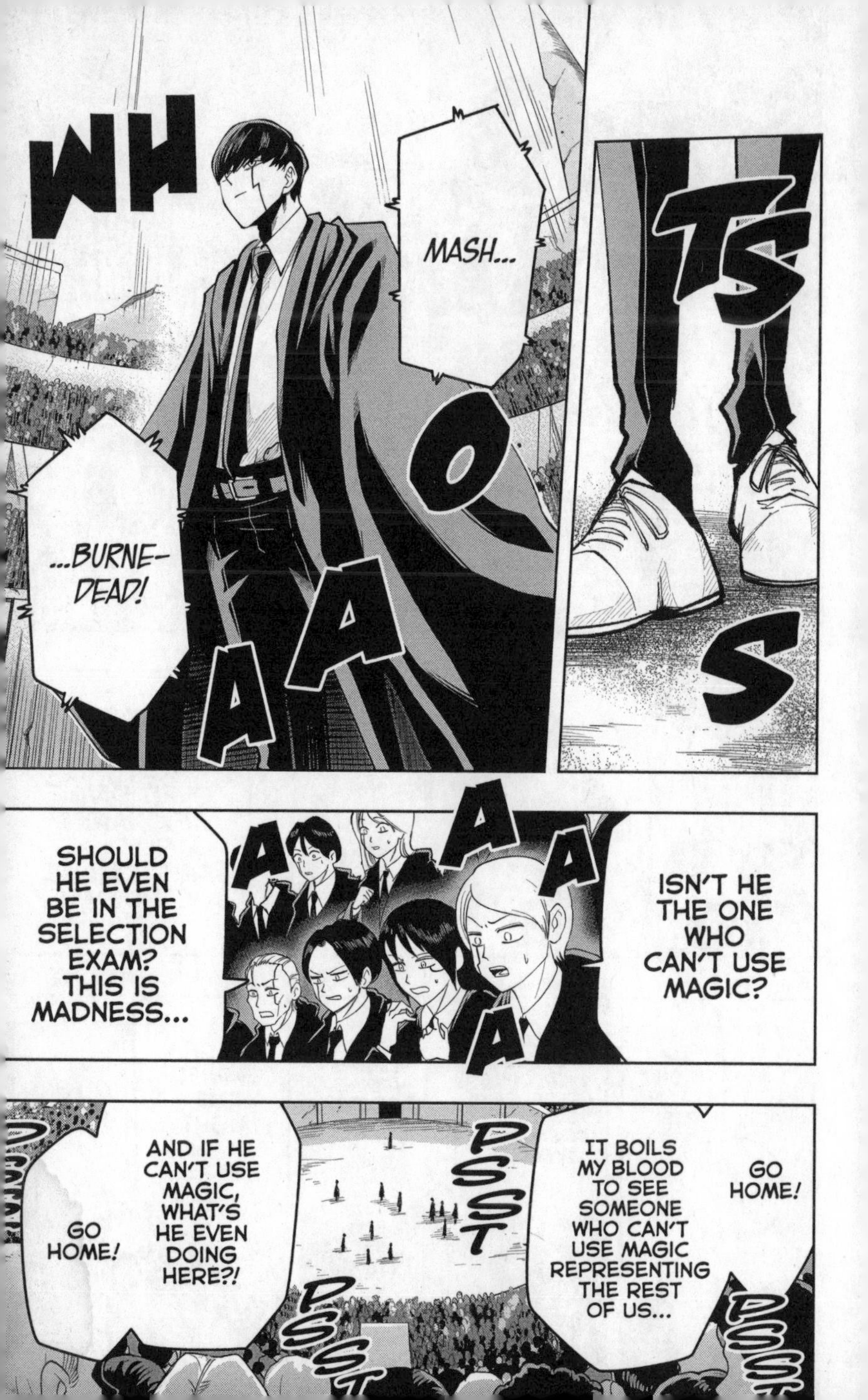
TS
S
MASH...
WH
O
...BURNE-DEAD!
A
A
ISN'T HE THE ONE WHO CAN'T USE MAGIC?
A
A
A
A
SHOULD HE EVEN BE IN THE SELECTION EXAM? THIS IS MADNESS...
GO HOME!
IT BOILS MY BLOOD TO SEE SOMEONE WHO CAN'T USE MAGIC REPRESENTING THE REST OF US...
PSST
AND IF HE CAN'T USE MAGIC, WHAT'S HE EVEN DOING HERE?!
GO HOME!

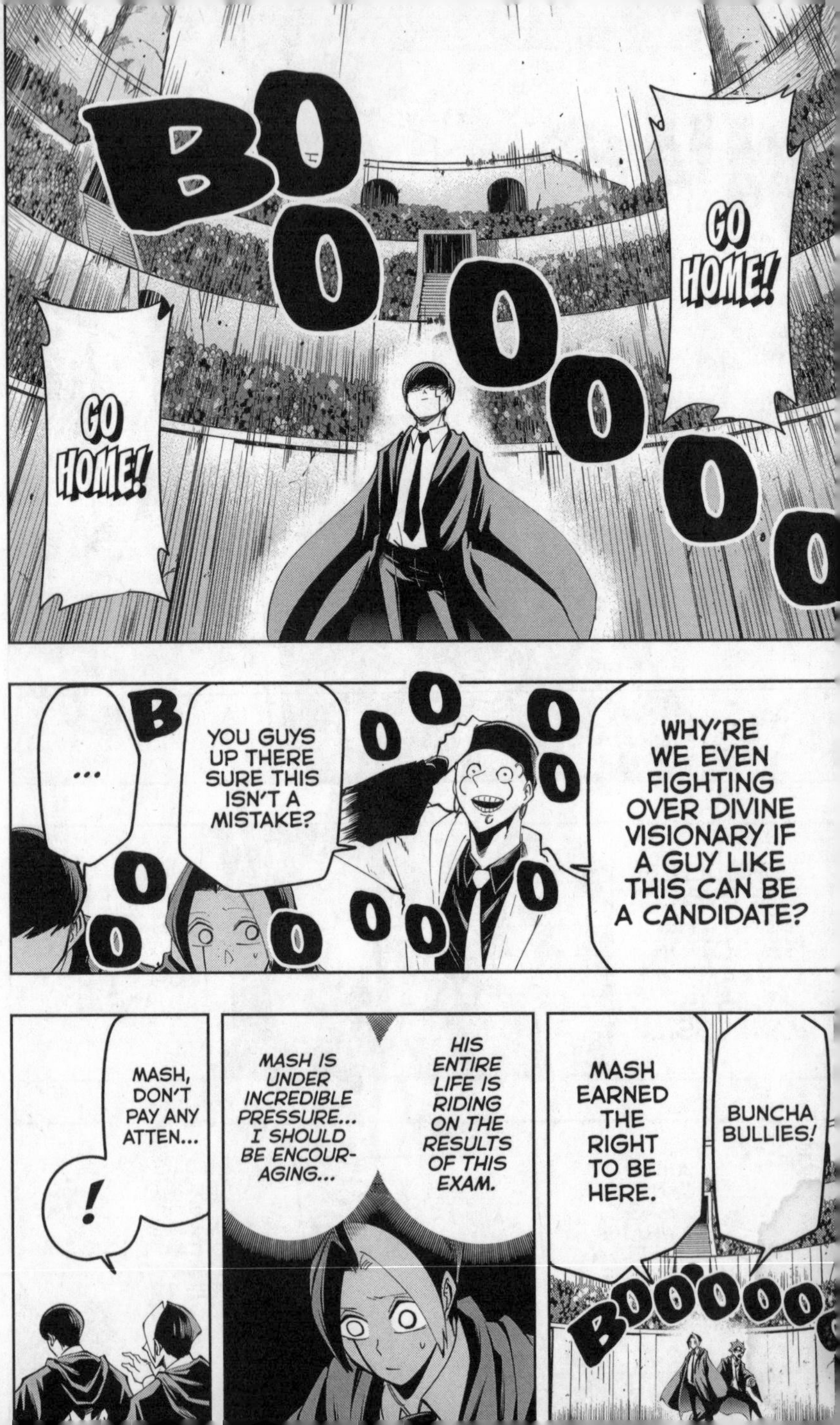
GO HOME!
BOOOOOOO
GO HOME!
WHY'RE WE EVEN FIGHTING OVER DIVINE VISIONARY IF A GUY LIKE THIS CAN BE A CANDIDATE?
BOOOOOOOOOOO
YOU GUYS UP THERE SURE THIS ISN'T A MISTAKE?
...
BUNCHA BULLIES!
MASH EARNED THE RIGHT TO BE HERE.
BOOOOOO
HIS ENTIRE LIFE IS RIDING ON THE RESULTS OF THIS EXAM.
MASH IS UNDER INCREDIBLE PRESSURE... I SHOULD BE ENCOUR-AGING...
MASH, DON'T PAY ANY ATTEN...
!

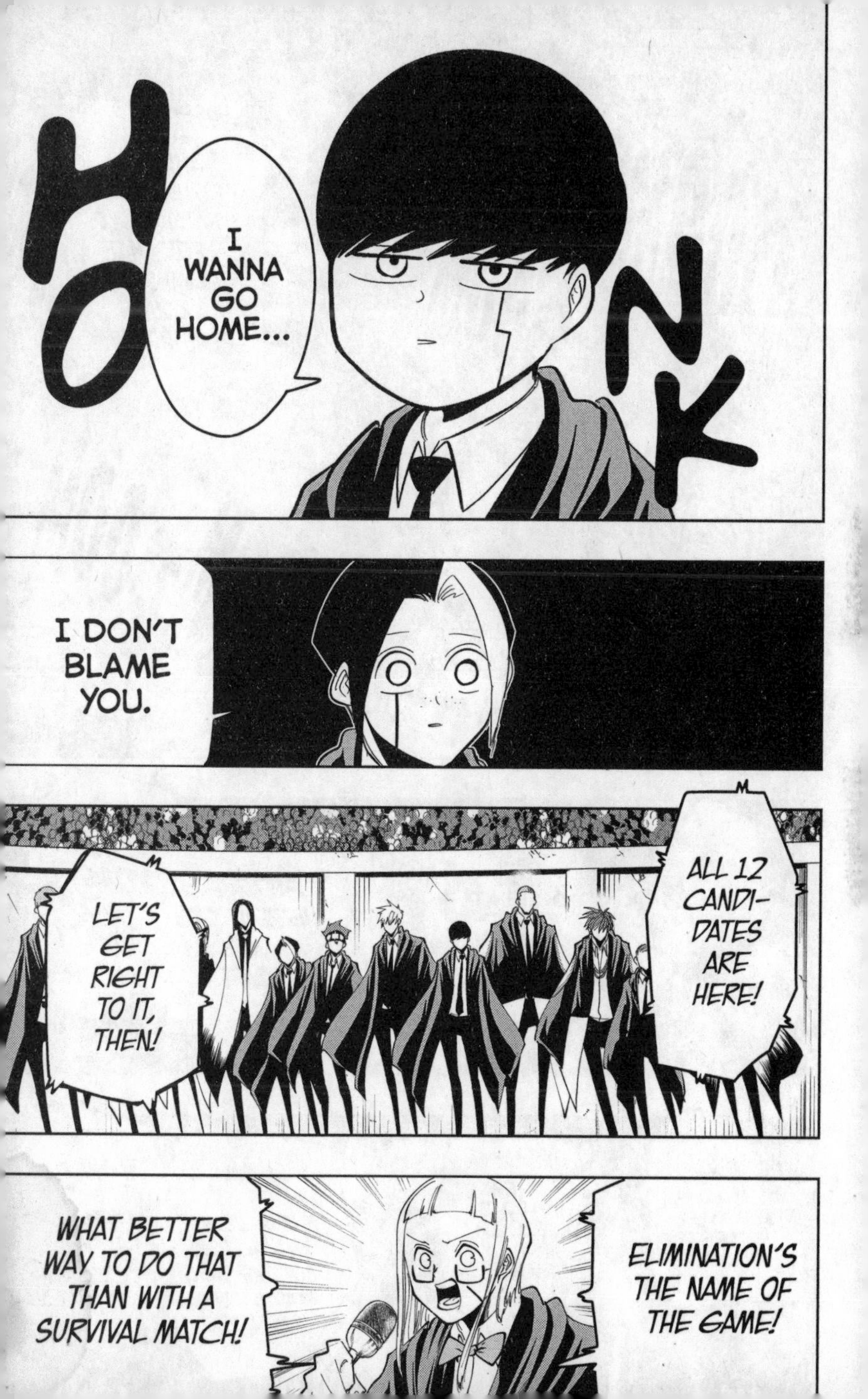
HONK
I WANNA GO HOME...
I DON'T BLAME YOU.
ALL 12 CANDI- DATES ARE HERE!
LET'S GET RIGHT TO IT, THEN!
ELIMINATION'S THE NAME OF THE GAME!
WHAT BETTER WAY TO DO THAT THAN WITH A SURVIVAL MATCH!

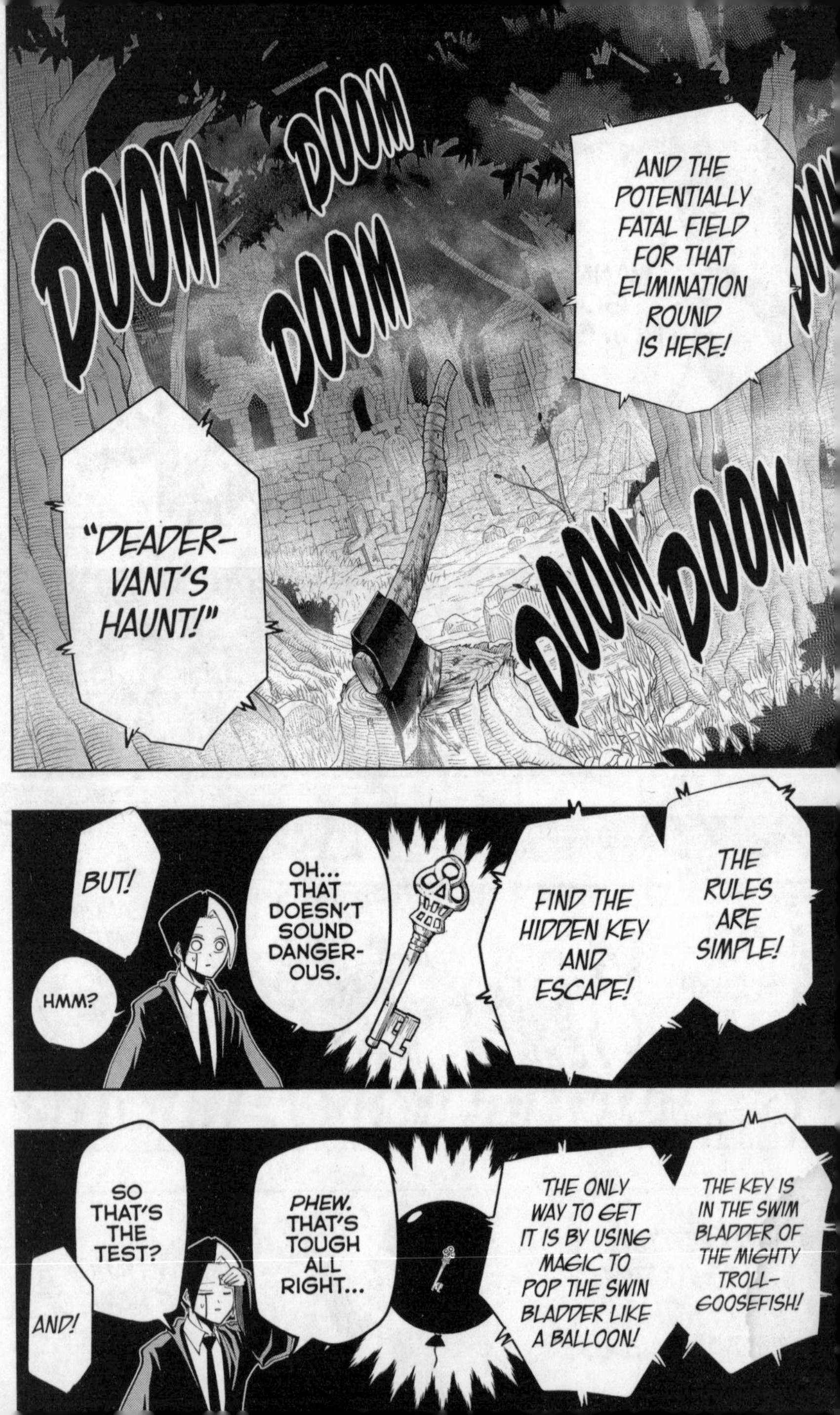
AND THE POTENTIALLY FATAL FIELD FOR THAT ELIMINATION ROUND IS HERE!
DOOM DOOM
DOOM DOOM
DOOM
"DEADER-VANT'S HAUNT!"
THE RULES ARE SIMPLE!
FIND THE HIDDEN KEY AND ESCAPE!
OH... THAT DOESN'T SOUND DANGER-OUS.
BUT!
HMM?
THE KEY IS IN THE SWIM BLADDER OF THE MIGHTY TROLL-GOOSEFISH!
THE ONLY WAY TO GET IT IS BY USING MAGIC TO POP THE SWIN BLADDER LIKE A BALLOON!
PHEW. THAT'S TOUGH ALL RIGHT...
SO THAT'S THE TEST?
AND!

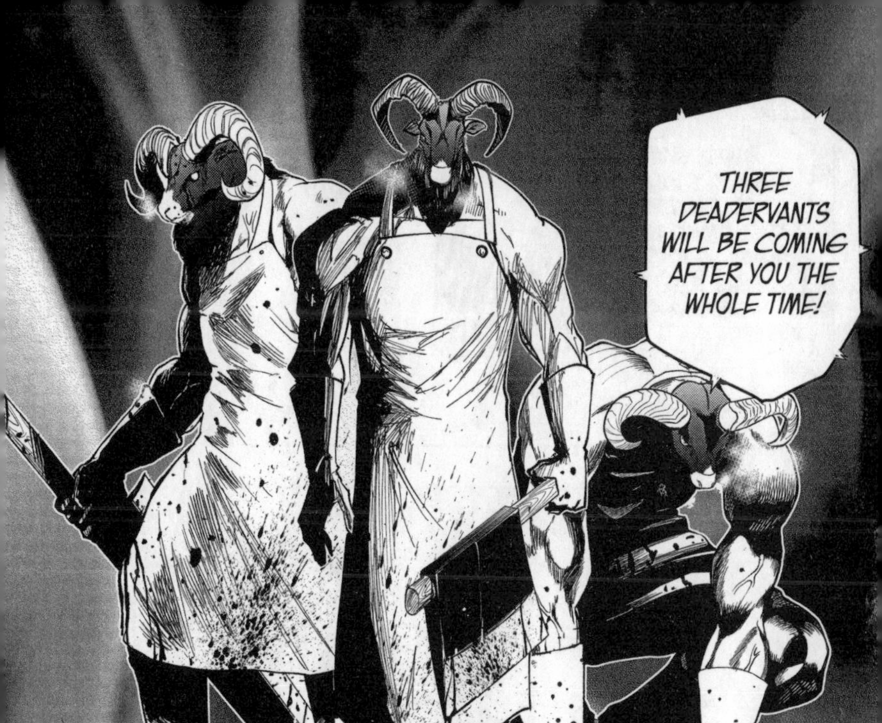
THREE DEADERVANTS WILL BE COMING AFTER YOU THE WHOLE TIME!

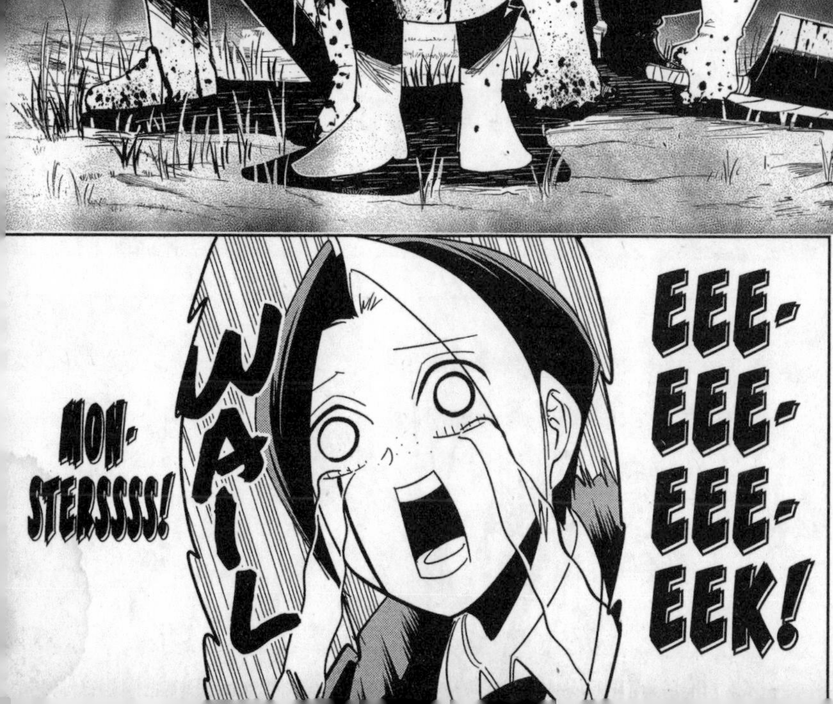
EEE-
EEE-
EEE-
EEK!
WAIL
MON-
STERSSSS!

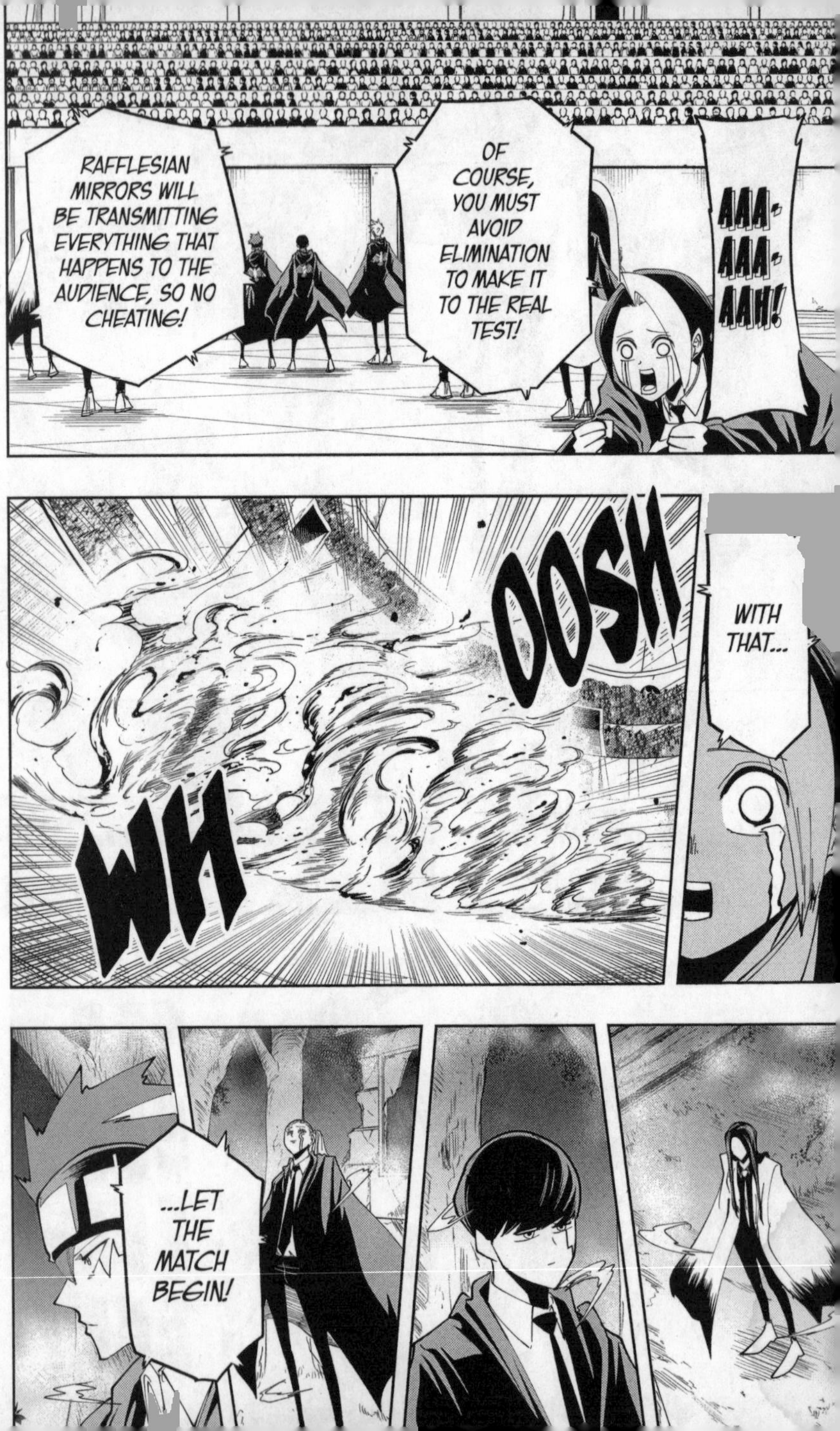
AAA-AAA-AAH!
OF COURSE, YOU MUST AVOID ELIMINATION TO MAKE IT TO THE REAL TEST!
RAFFLESIAN MIRRORS WILL BE TRANSMITTING EVERYTHING THAT HAPPENS TO THE AUDIENCE, SO NO CHEATING!
WITH THAT...
WHOOSH
...LET THE MATCH BEGIN!

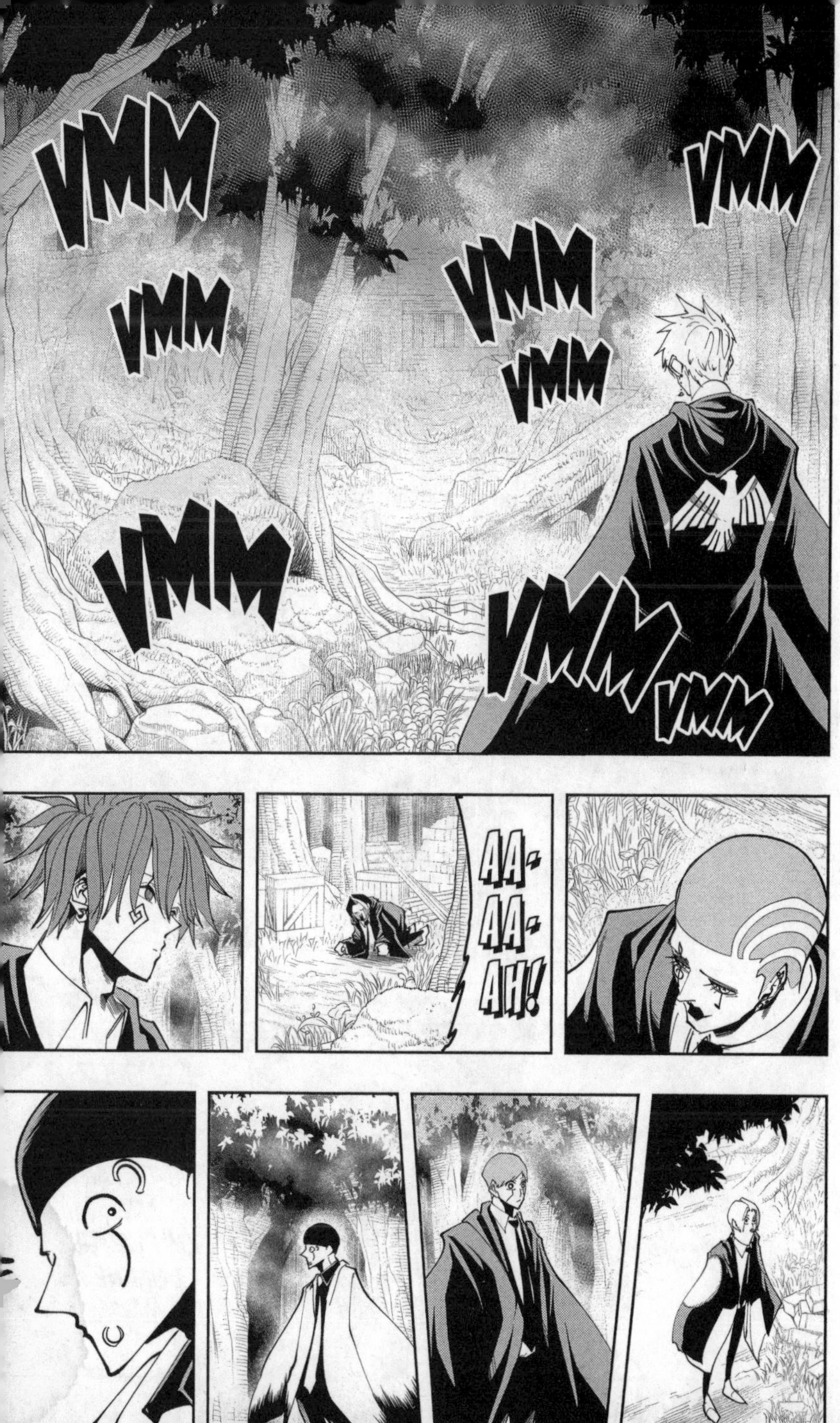
VMM
VMM
VMM
VMM
VMM
VMM
VMM
VMM
AA-AA-AH!

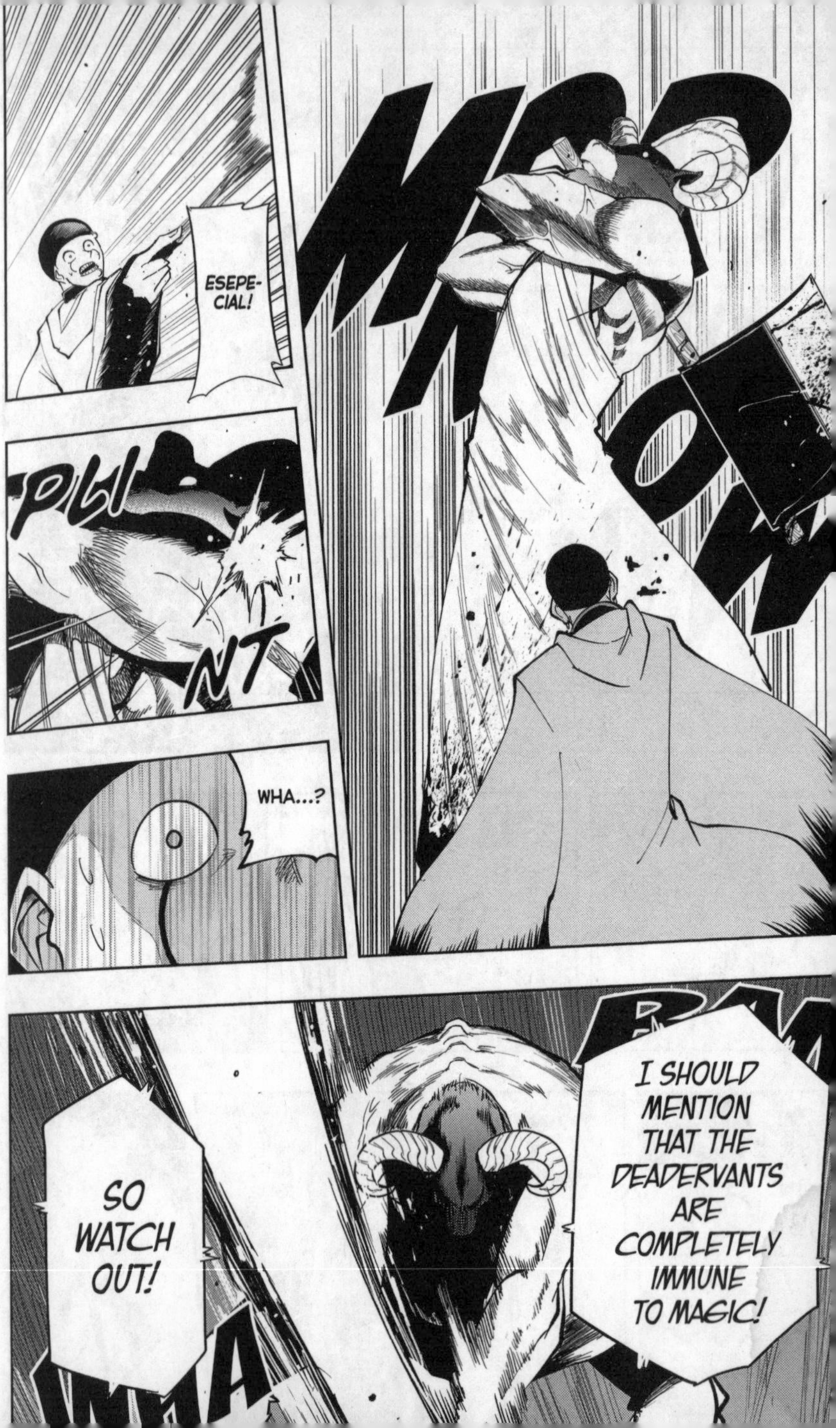
ESEPE-CIAL!
PWI NT
WHA...?
I SHOULD MENTION THAT THE DEADERVANTS ARE COMPLETELY IMMUNE TO MAGIC!
SO WATCH OUT!

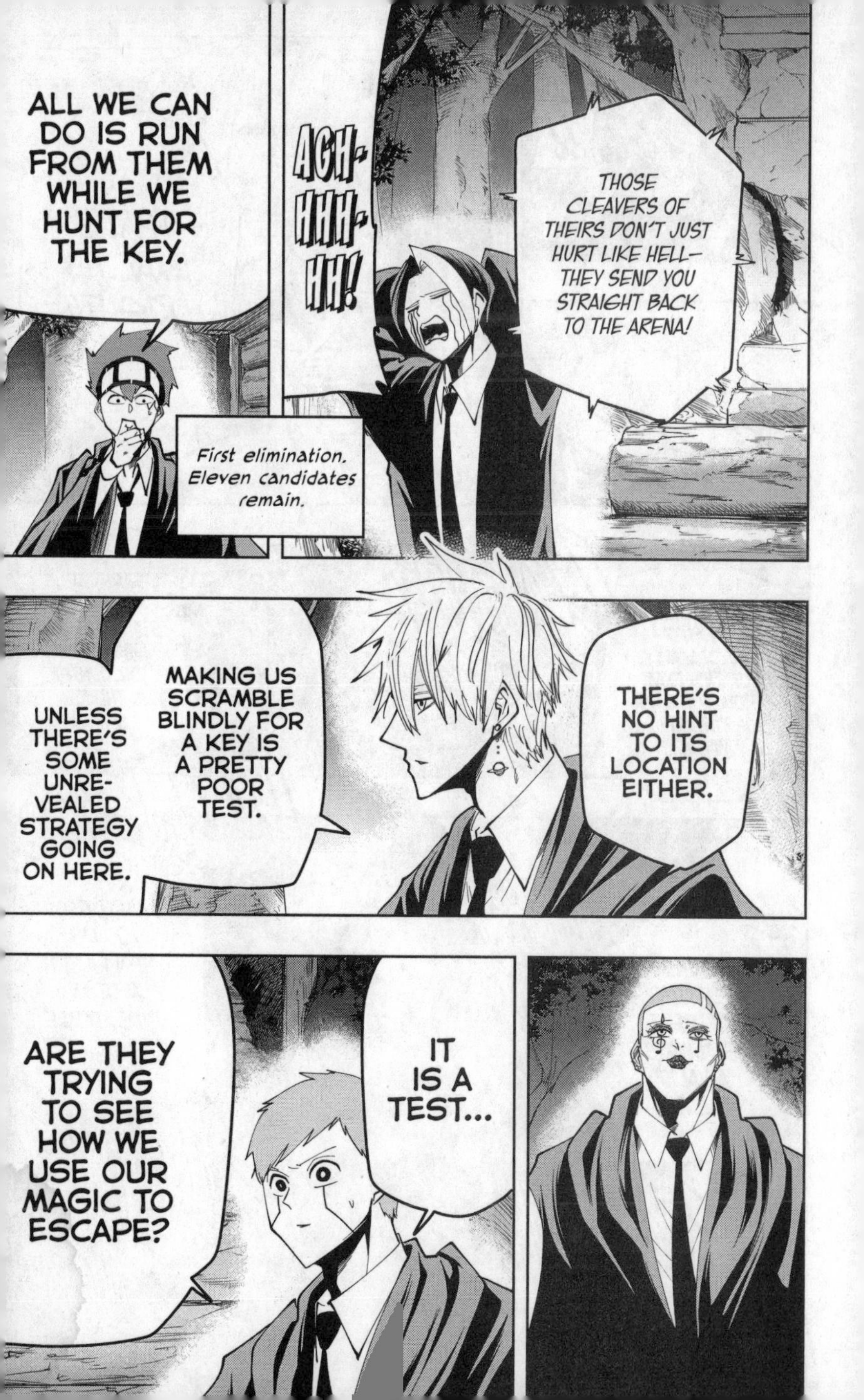
THOSE CLEAVERS OF THEIRS DON'T JUST HURT LIKE HELL— THEY SEND YOU STRAIGHT BACK TO THE ARENA!
AGH-HHH-HH!
ALL WE CAN DO IS RUN FROM THEM WHILE WE HUNT FOR THE KEY.
First elimination. Eleven candidates remain.
THERE'S NO HINT TO ITS LOCATION EITHER.
MAKING US SCRAMBLE BLINDLY FOR A KEY IS A PRETTY POOR TEST.
UNLESS THERE'S SOME UNRE-VEALED STRATEGY GOING ON HERE.
IT IS A TEST...
ARE THEY TRYING TO SEE HOW WE USE OUR MAGIC TO ESCAPE?

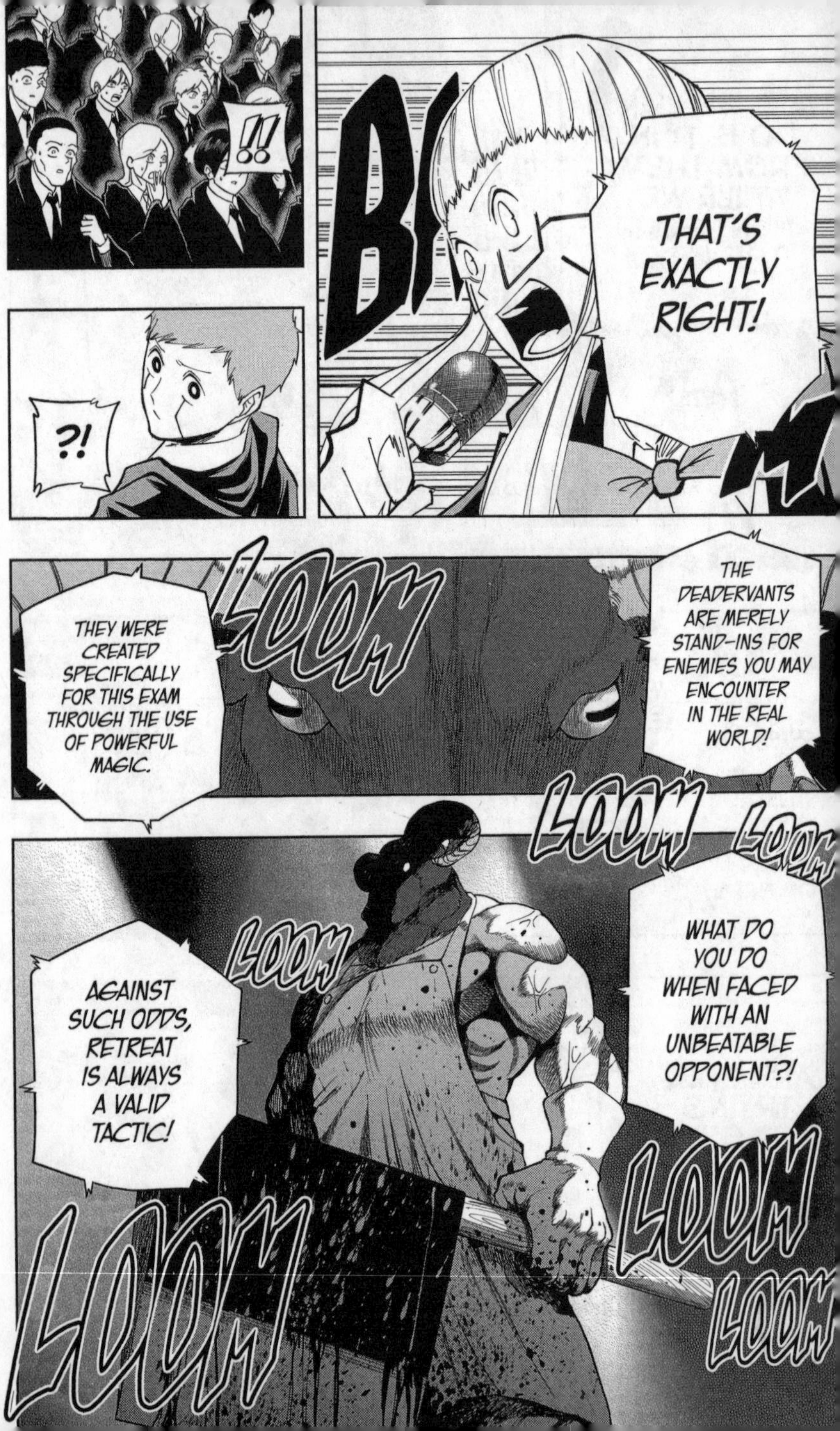
B
THAT'S EXACTLY RIGHT!
!!
?!
THE DEADERVANTS ARE MERELY STAND-INS FOR ENEMIES YOU MAY ENCOUNTER IN THE REAL WORLD!
LOOM
THEY WERE CREATED SPECIFICALLY FOR THIS EXAM THROUGH THE USE OF POWERFUL MAGIC.
LOOM
LOOM
WHAT DO YOU DO WHEN FACED WITH AN UNBEATABLE OPPONENT?!
LOOM
AGAINST SUCH ODDS, RETREAT IS ALWAYS A VALID TACTIC!
LOOM
LOOM
LOOM

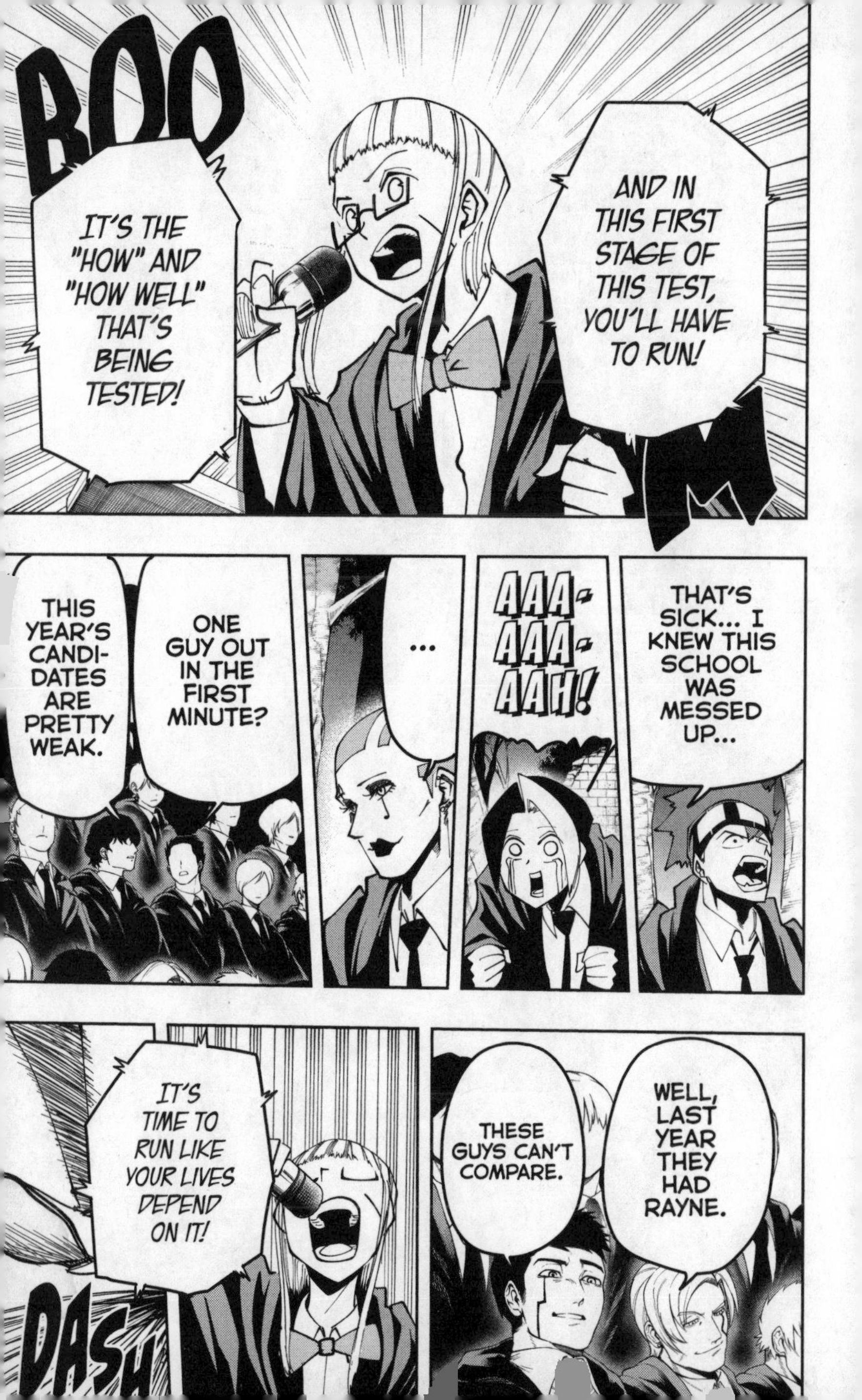
AND IN THIS FIRST STAGE OF THIS TEST, YOU'LL HAVE TO RUN!
BOO
IT'S THE "HOW" AND "HOW WELL" THAT'S BEING TESTED!
THAT'S SICK... I KNEW THIS SCHOOL WAS MESSED UP...
AAA-AAA-AAH!
...
ONE GUY OUT IN THE FIRST MINUTE?
THIS YEAR'S CANDI-DATES ARE PRETTY WEAK.
WELL, LAST YEAR THEY HAD RAYNE.
THESE GUYS CAN'T COMPARE.
IT'S TIME TO RUN LIKE YOUR LIVES DEPEND ON IT!
DASH

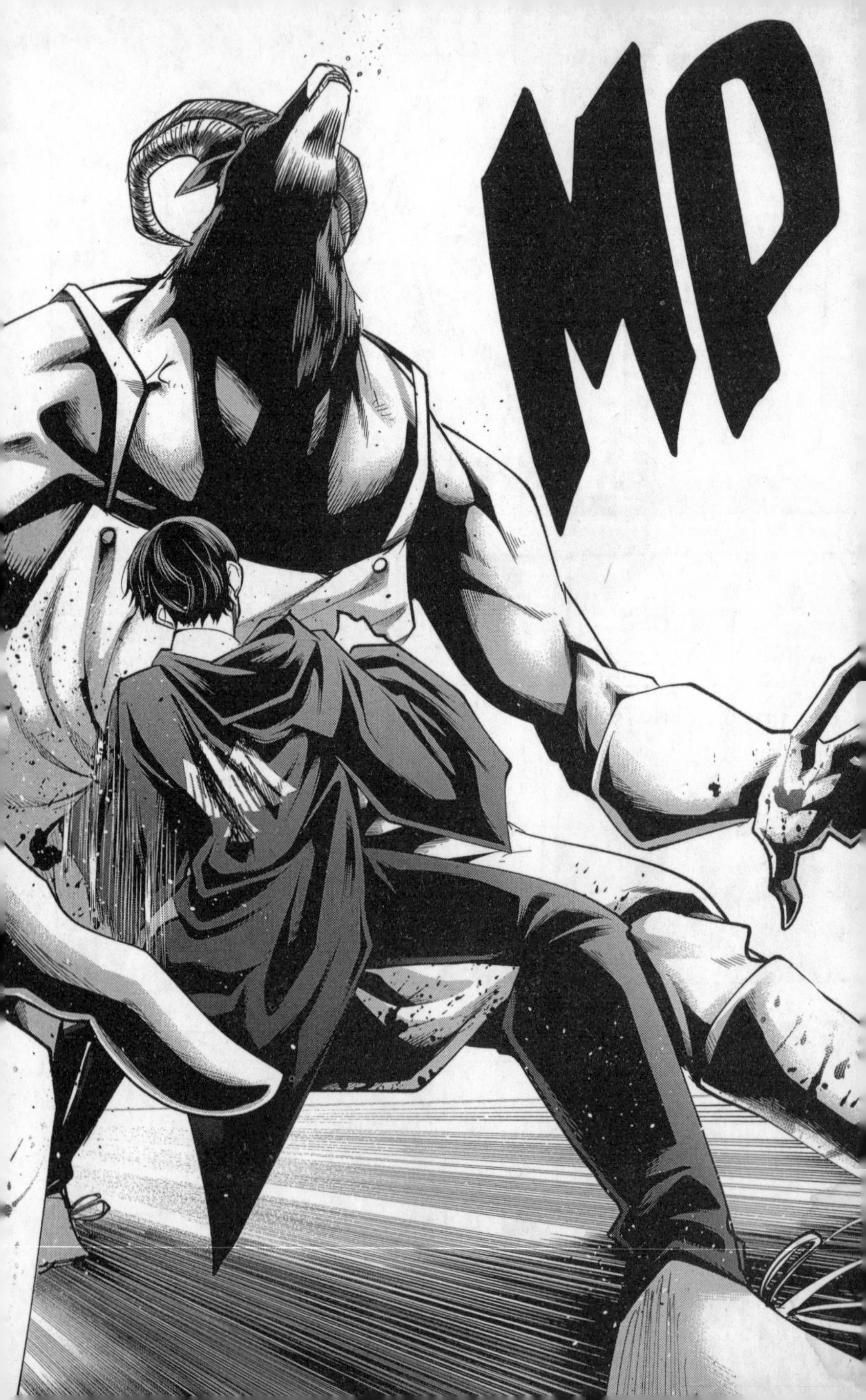
MP

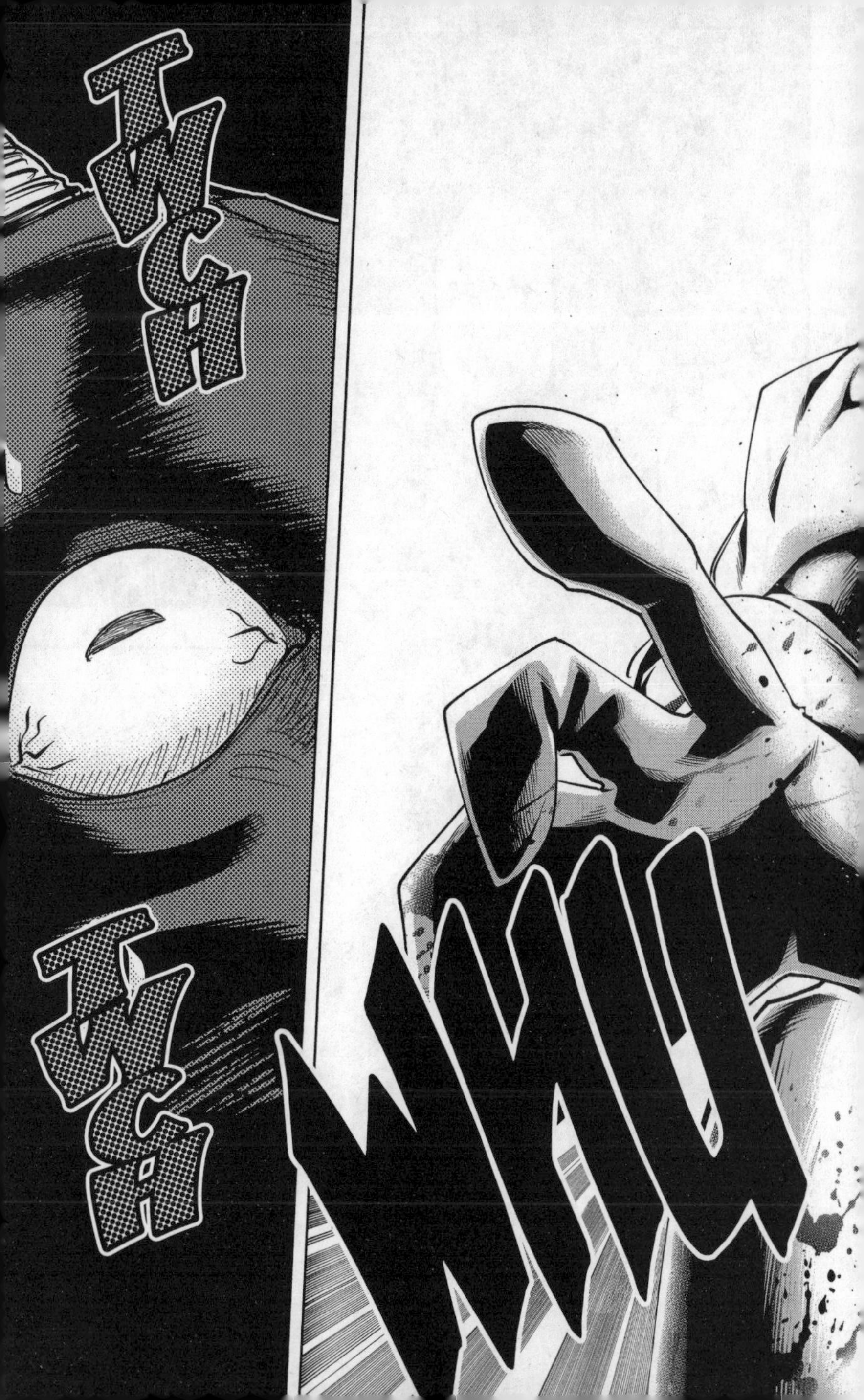
TWCH
TWCH

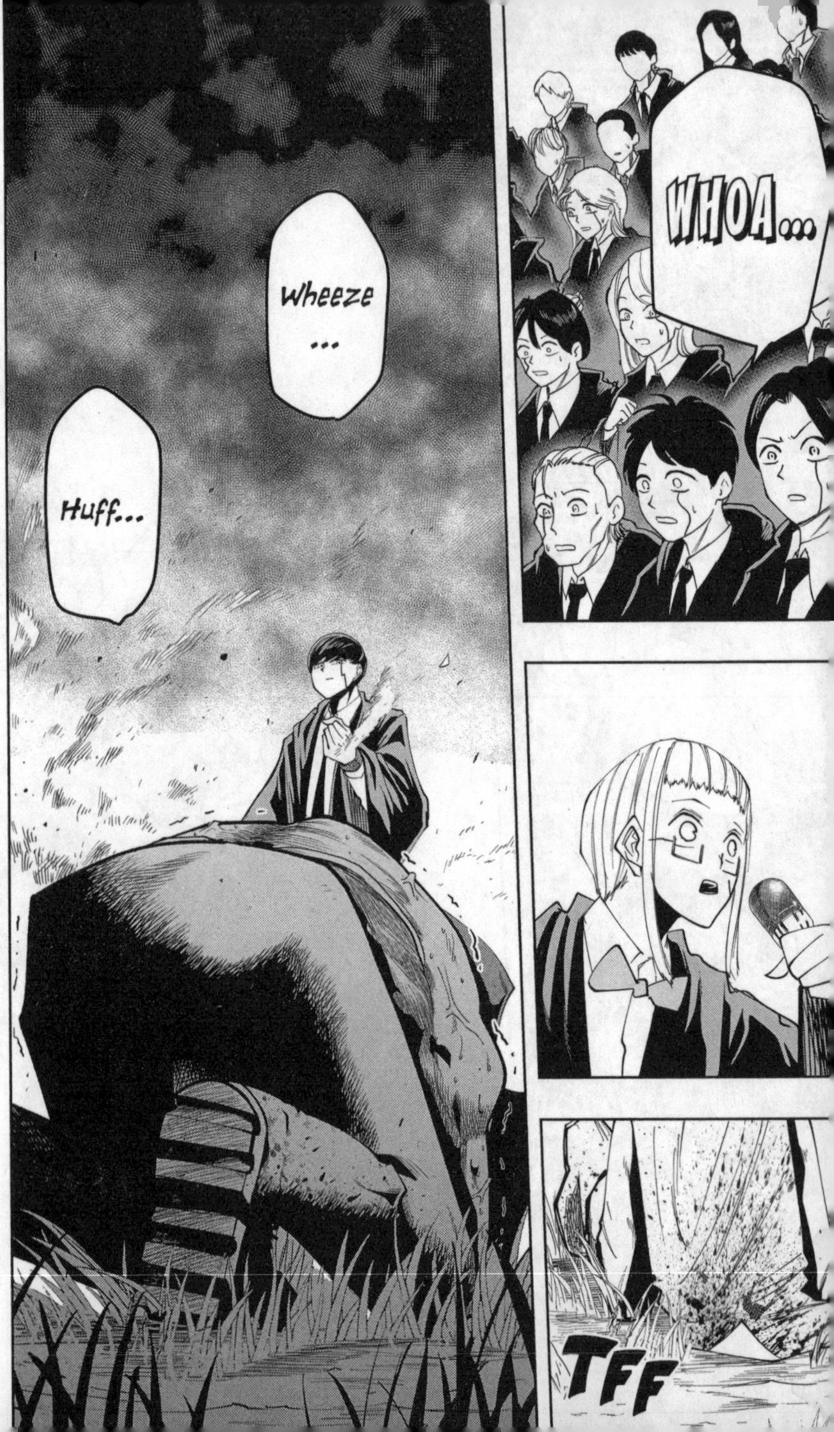
WHOA...
TFF
Wheeze ...
Huff...

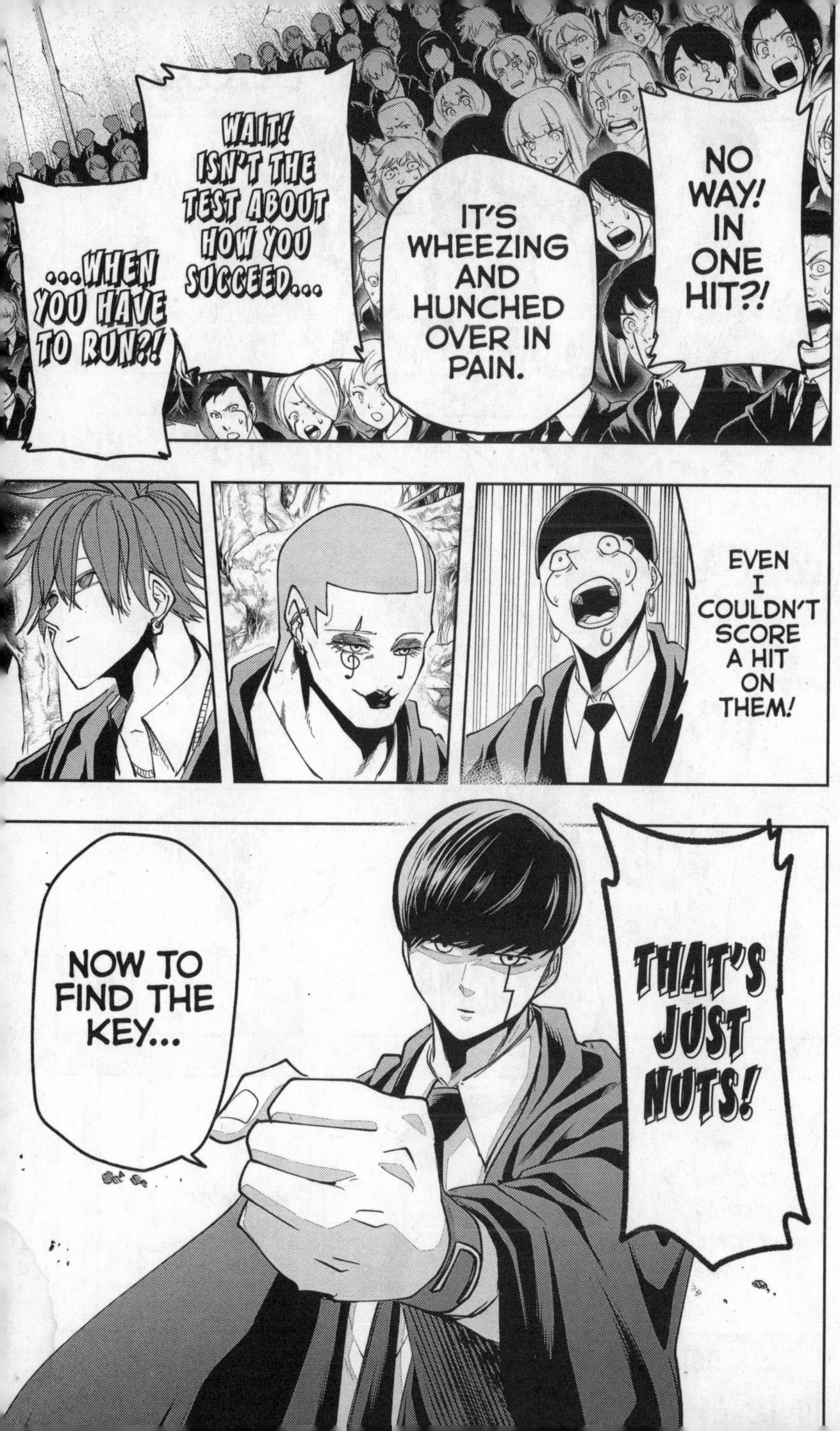
NO WAY! IN ONE HIT?!
IT'S WHEEZING AND HUNCHED OVER IN PAIN.
WAIT! ISN'T THE TEST ABOUT HOW YOU SUCCEED...
...WHEN YOU HAVE TO RUN?!
EVEN I COULDN'T SCORE A HIT ON THEM!
THAT'S JUST NUTS!
NOW TO FIND THE KEY...

BONUS, PART 2

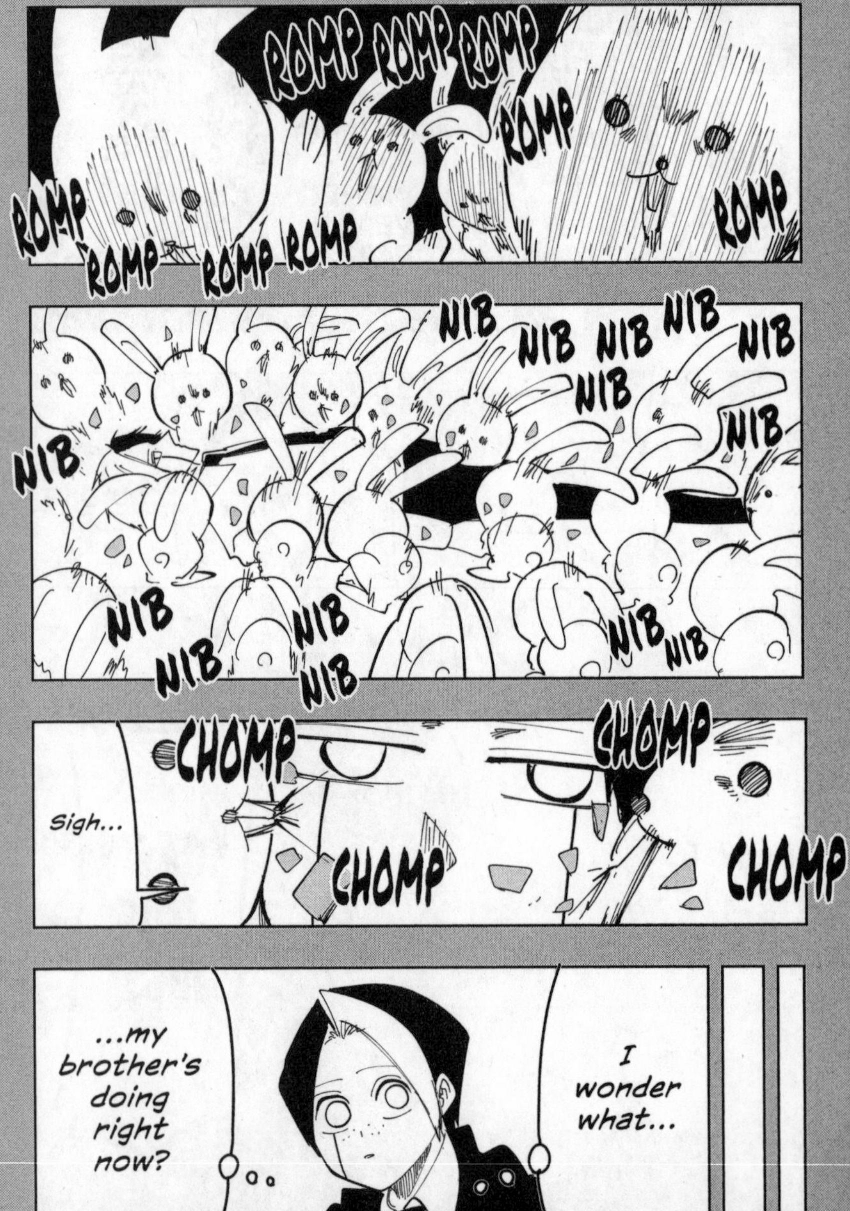
ROMP
ROMP
ROMP ROMP ROMP
ROMP ROMP
ROMP
ROMP
ROMP
NIB
NIB
NIB NIB NIB
NIB
NIB
NIB
NIB NIB
NIB NIB
NIB NIB
CHOMP
CHOMP
CHOMP
CHOMP
Sigh...
I wonder what...
...my brother's doing right now?

BONUS COMIC (END)

CHAPTER 49:
MASH BURNEDEAD AND THE BRAWNY BALLOON

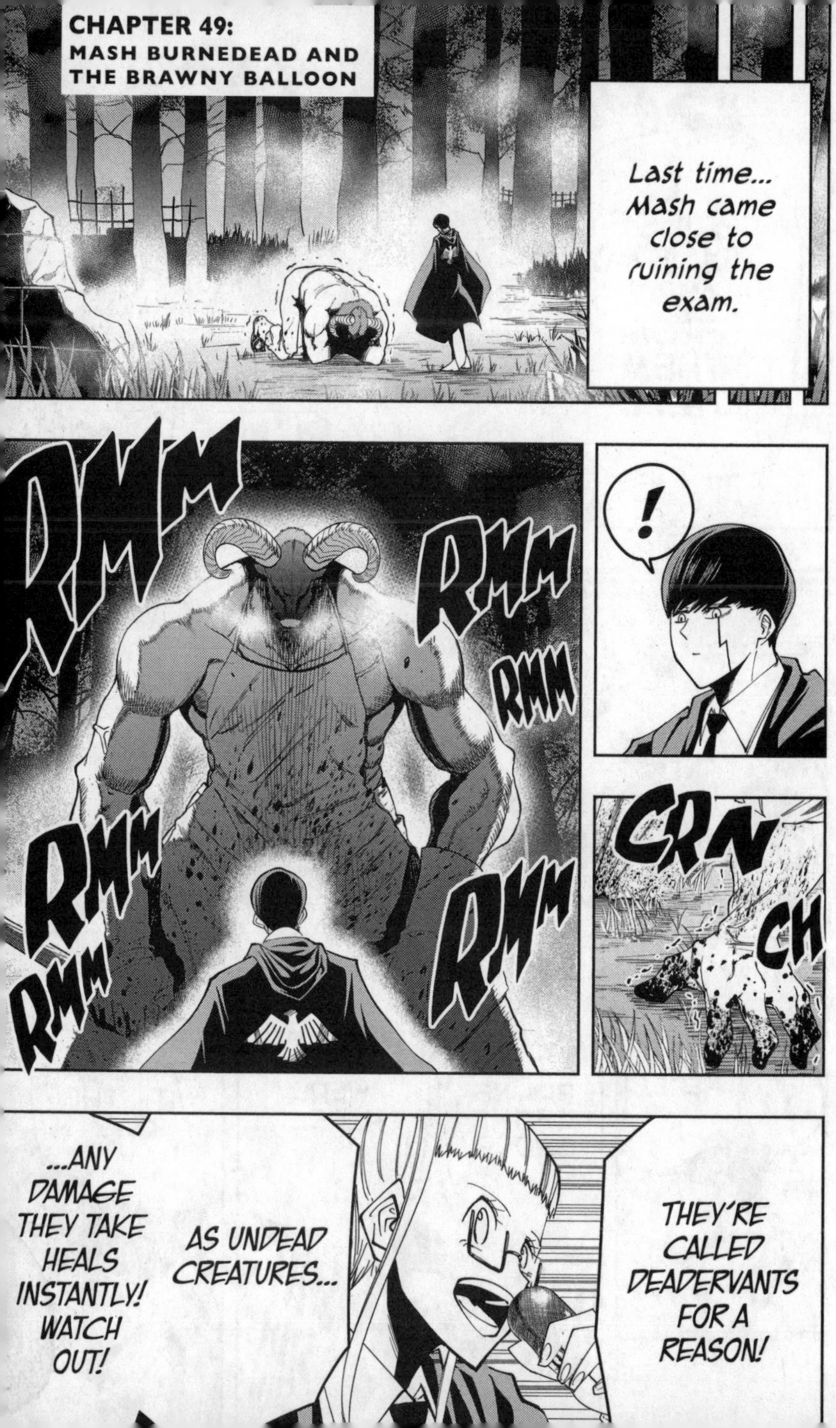

Last time... Mash came close to ruining the exam.
!
CRNCH
RMM
RMM
RMM
RMM
RMM
RMM
THEY'RE CALLED DEADERVANTS FOR A REASON!
AS UNDEAD CREATURES...
...ANY DAMAGE THEY TAKE HEALS INSTANTLY! WATCH OUT!

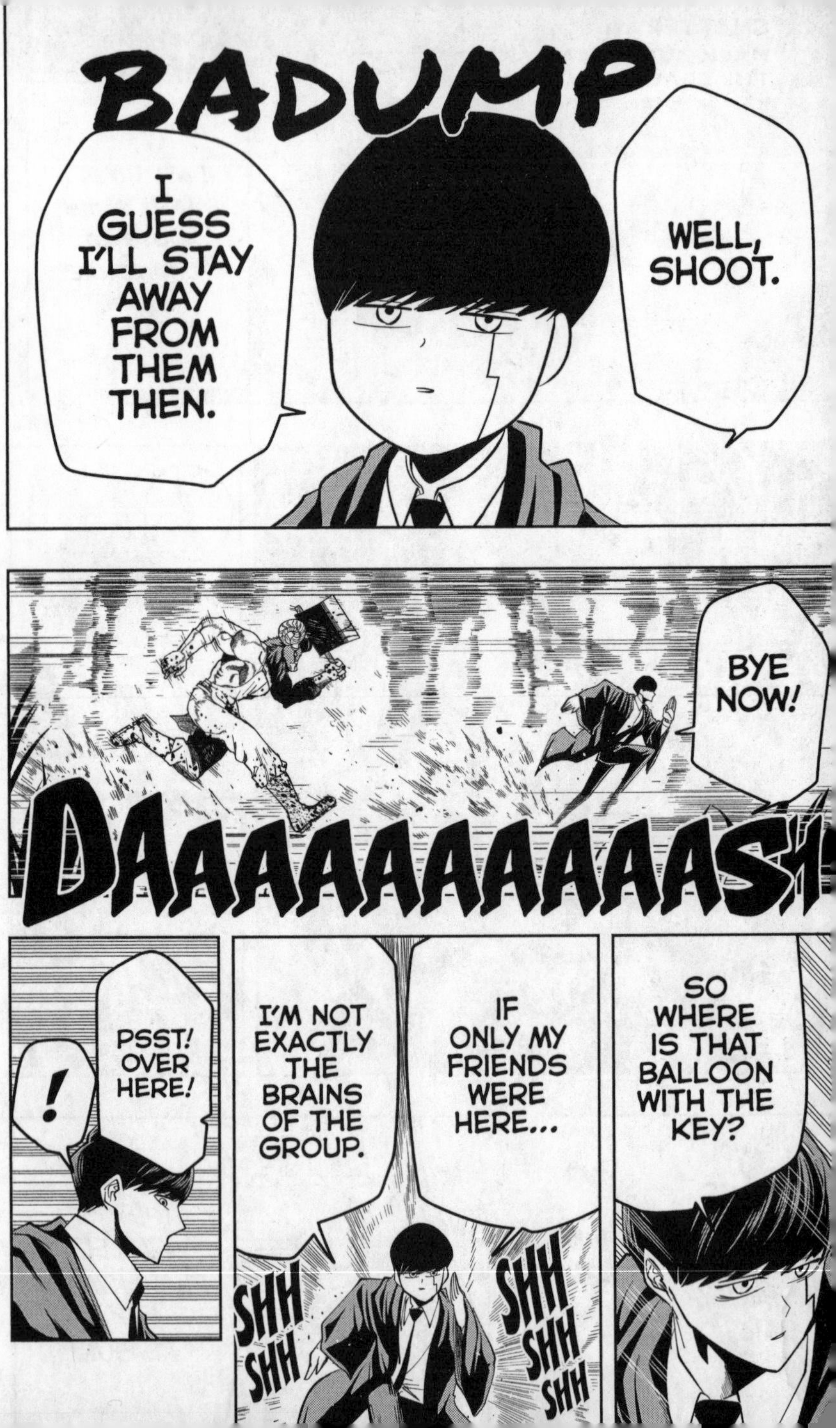
BADUMP
WELL, SHOOT.
I GUESS I'LL STAY AWAY FROM THEM THEN.
BYE NOW!
DAAAAAAAAAAS
SO WHERE IS THAT BALLOON WITH THE KEY?
IF ONLY MY FRIENDS WERE HERE...
I'M NOT EXACTLY THE BRAINS OF THE GROUP.
SHH SHH SHH SHH
SHH SHH
PSST! OVER HERE!
!

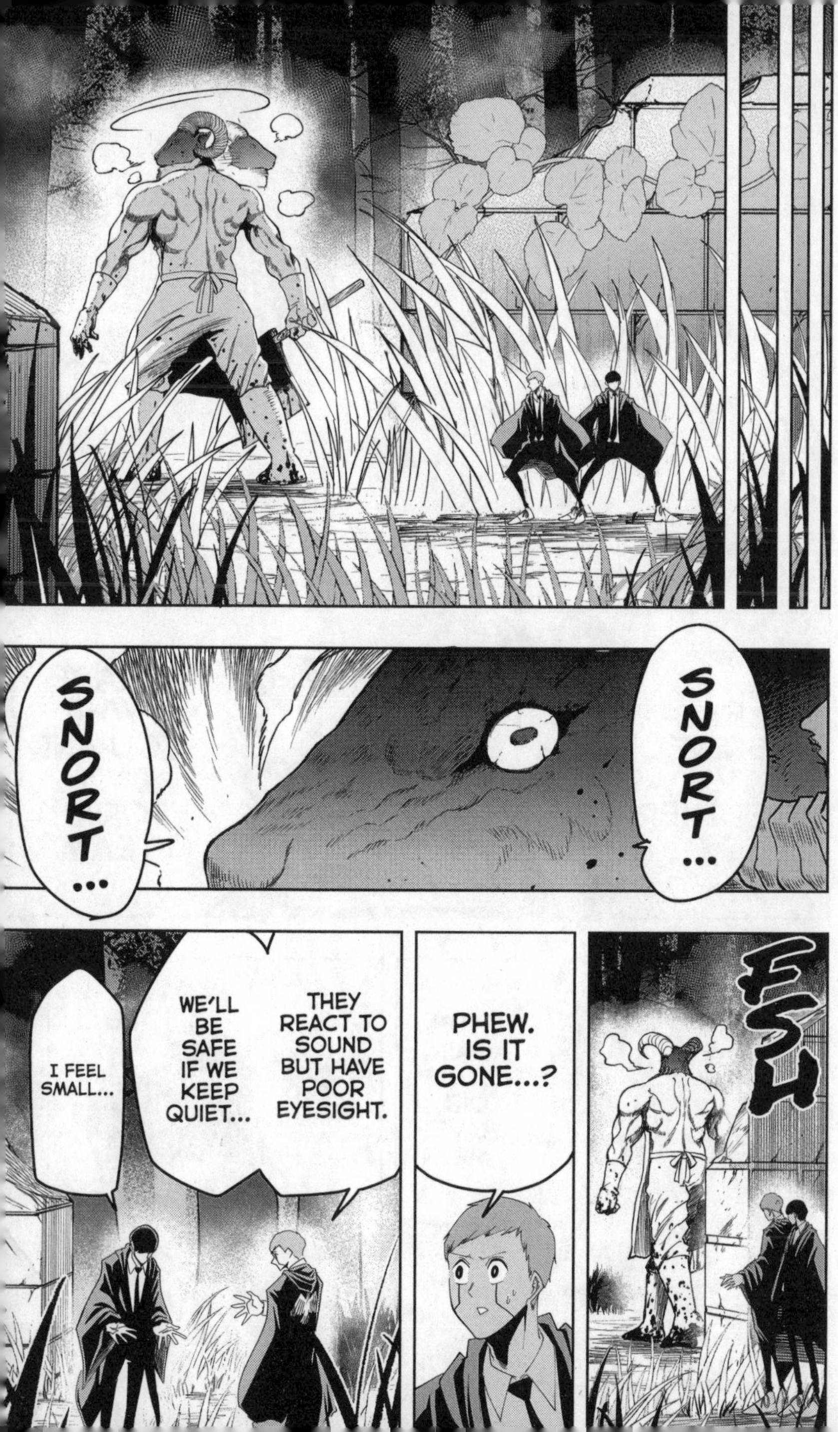
SNORT...
SNORT...
PHEW. IS IT GONE...?
THEY REACT TO SOUND BUT HAVE POOR EYESIGHT.
WE'LL BE SAFE IF WE KEEP QUIET...
I FEEL SMALL...

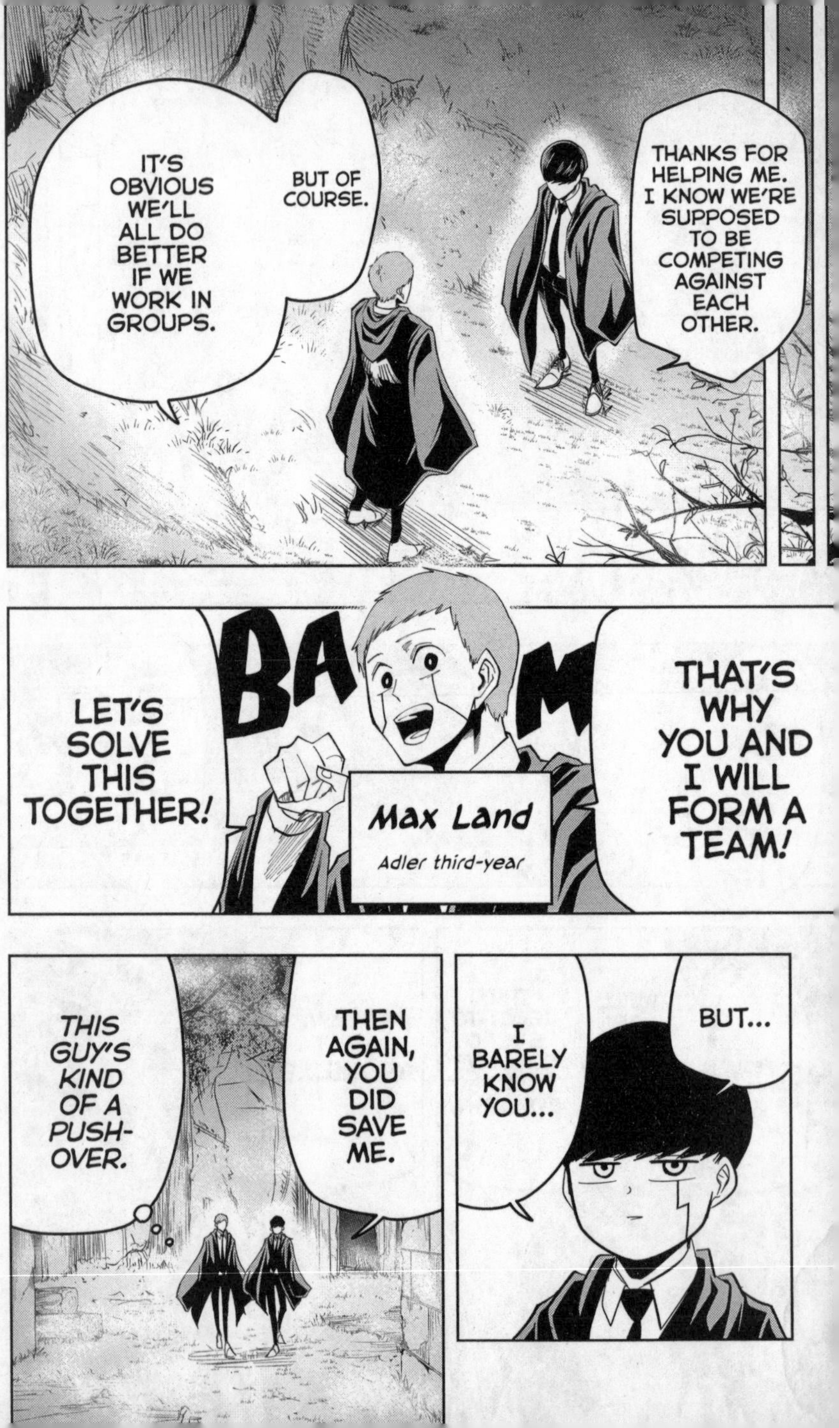
THANKS FOR HELPING ME. I KNOW WE'RE SUPPOSED TO BE COMPETING AGAINST EACH OTHER.
BUT OF COURSE.
IT'S OBVIOUS WE'LL ALL DO BETTER IF WE WORK IN GROUPS.
THAT'S WHY YOU AND I WILL FORM A TEAM!
BAM
Max Land
Adler third-year
LET'S SOLVE THIS TOGETHER!
BUT...
I BARELY KNOW YOU...
THEN AGAIN, YOU DID SAVE ME.
THIS GUY'S KIND OF A PUSH-OVER.

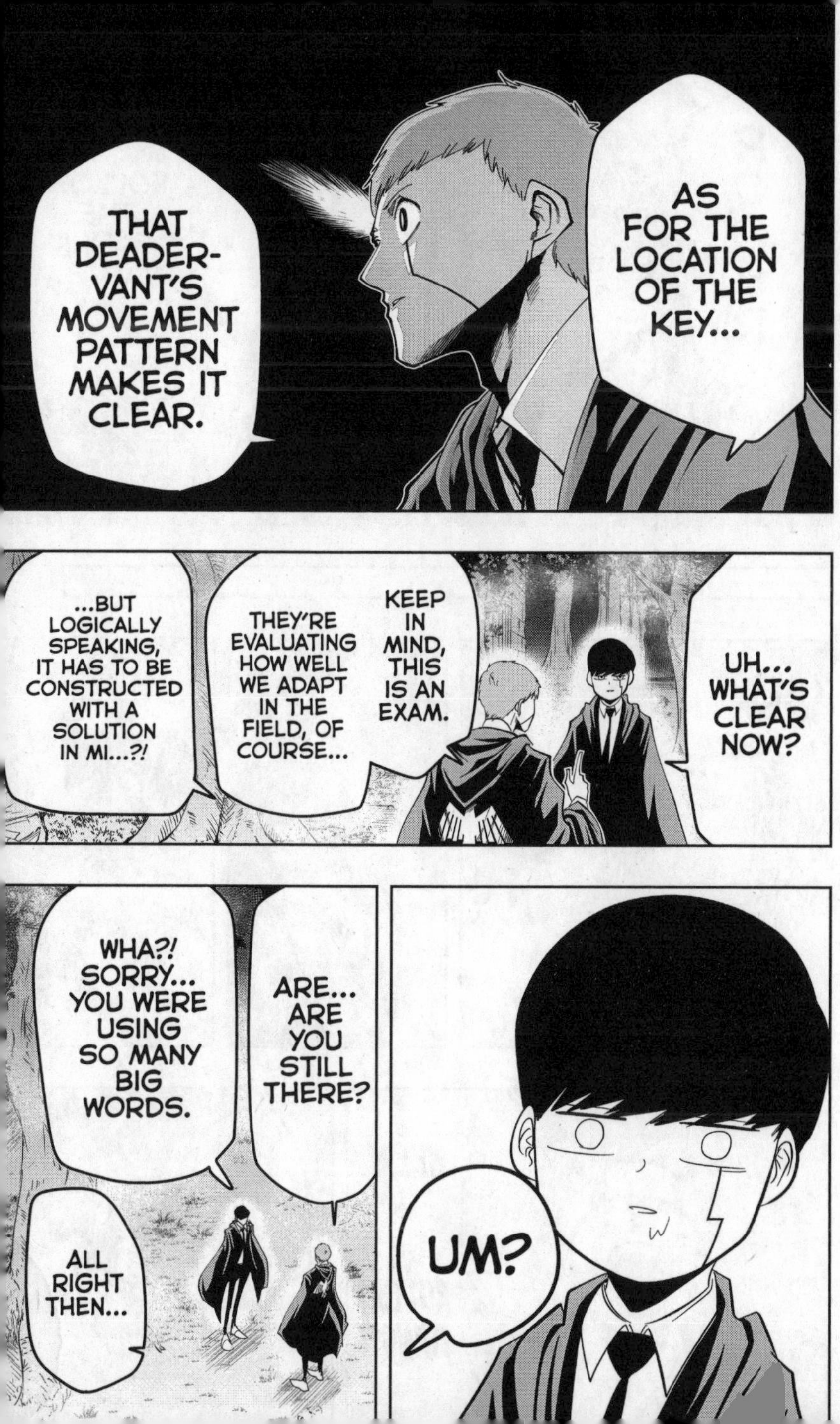
AS FOR THE LOCATION OF THE KEY...
THAT DEADER-VANT'S MOVEMENT PATTERN MAKES IT CLEAR.
UH... WHAT'S CLEAR NOW?
KEEP IN MIND, THIS IS AN EXAM.
THEY'RE EVALUATING HOW WELL WE ADAPT IN THE FIELD, OF COURSE...
...BUT LOGICALLY SPEAKING, IT HAS TO BE CONSTRUCTED WITH A SOLUTION IN MI...?!
UM?
ARE... ARE YOU STILL THERE?
WHA?! SORRY... YOU WERE USING SO MANY BIG WORDS.
ALL RIGHT THEN...

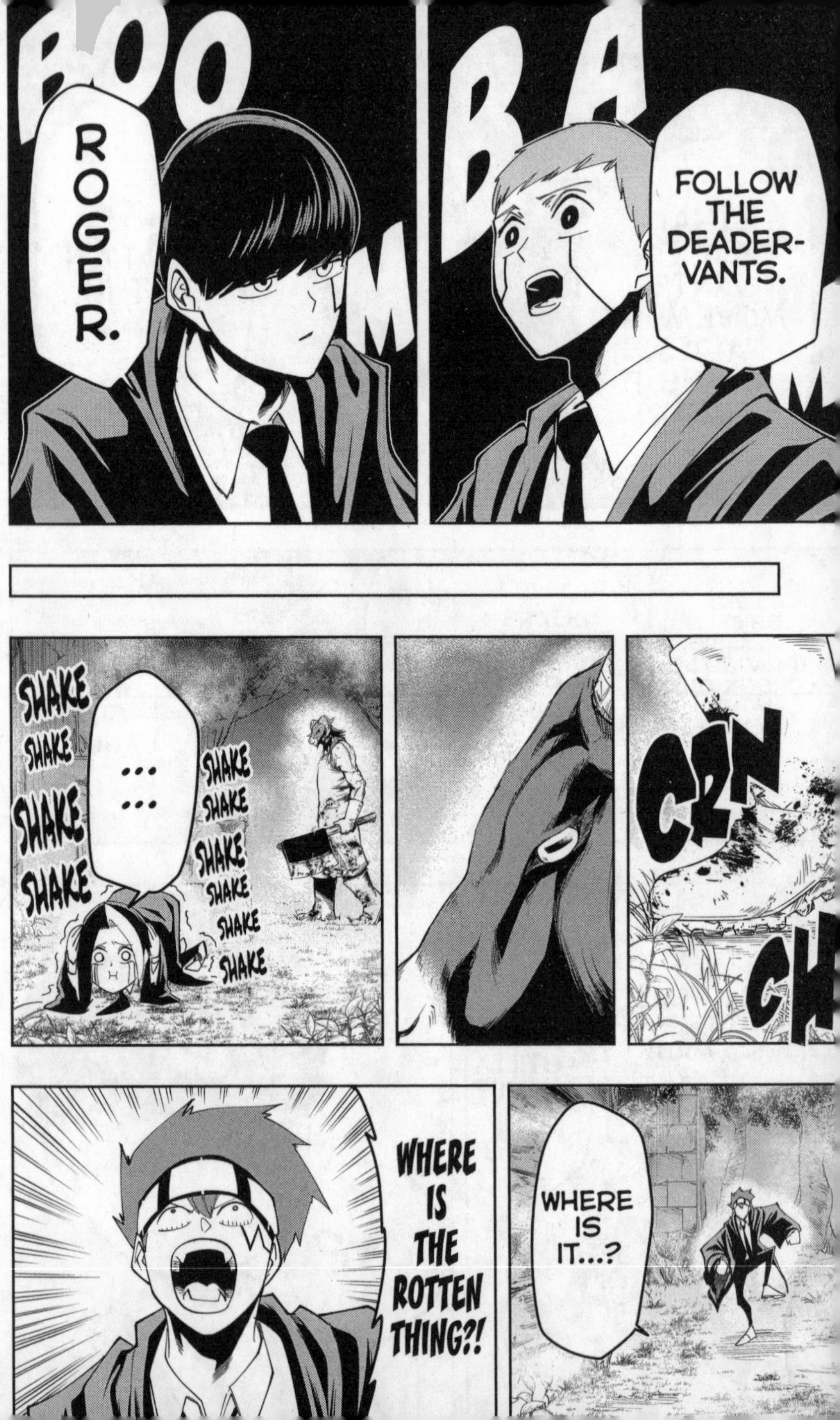
BA
M
FOLLOW THE DEADER-VANTS.
BOO
M
ROGER.
CRN
CH
SHAKE SHAKE SHAKE SHAKE
......
SHAKE SHAKE SHAKE SHAKE SHAKE SHAKE
WHERE IS IT...?
WHERE IS THE ROTTEN THING?!

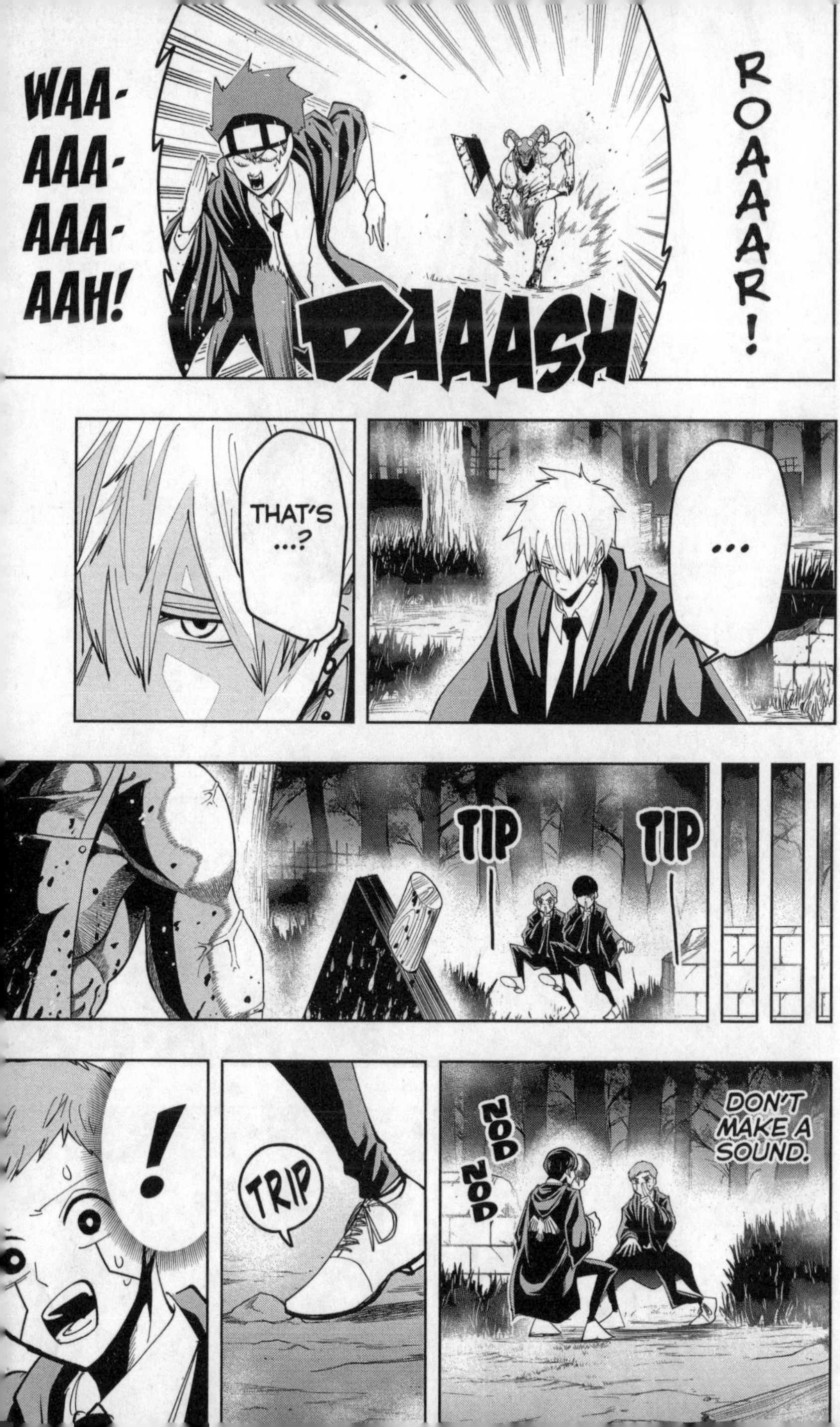
ROAAAR!
DAAASH
WAA-AAA-AAA-AAH!
...
THAT'S ...?
TIP
TIP
DON'T MAKE A SOUND.
NOD NOD
TRIP
!

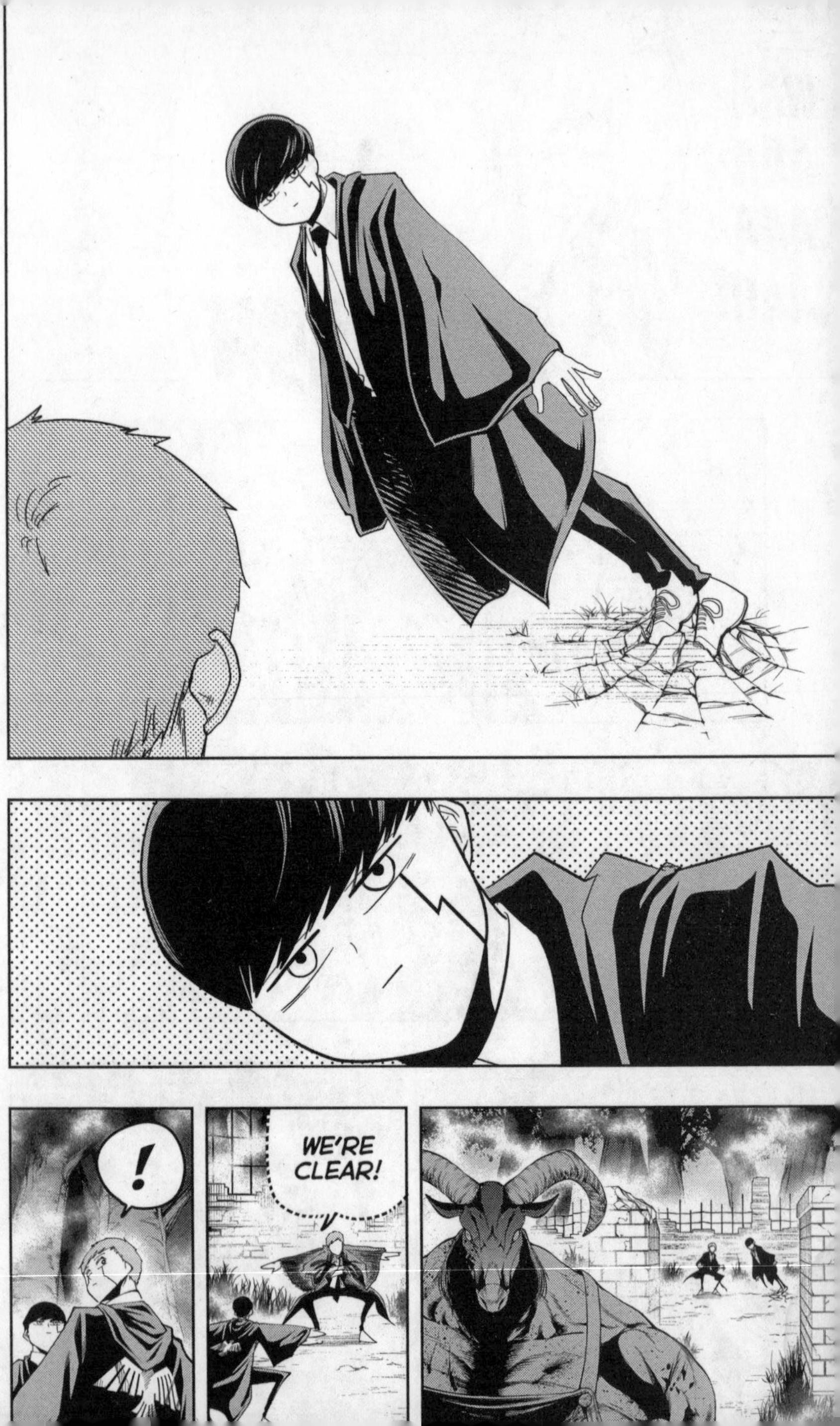
WE'RE CLEAR!
!

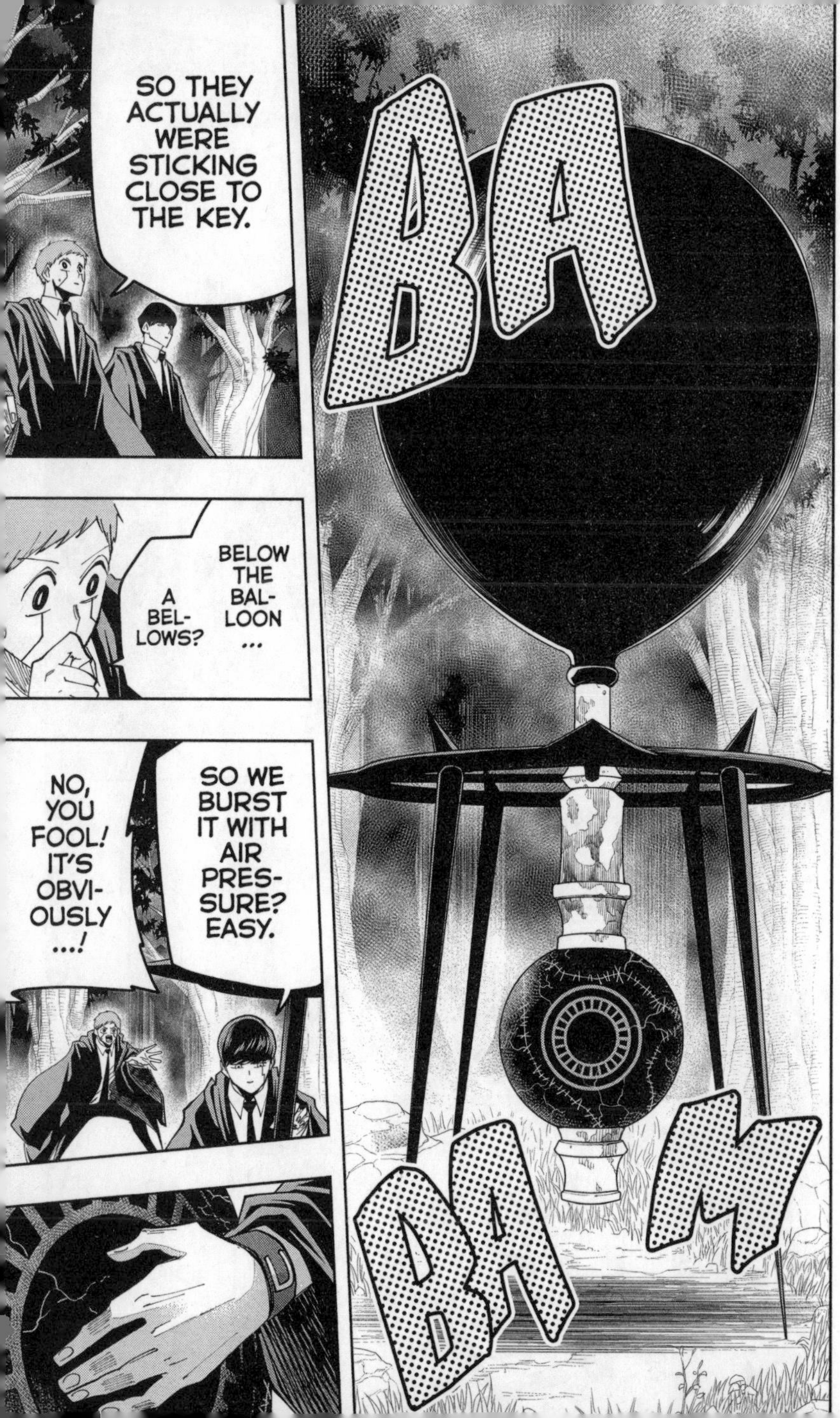
BA BAM
SO THEY ACTUALLY WERE STICKING CLOSE TO THE KEY.
BELOW THE BAL-LOON...
A BEL-LOWS?
SO WE BURST IT WITH AIR PRES-SURE? EASY.
NO, YOU FOOL! IT'S OBVI-OUSLY...!

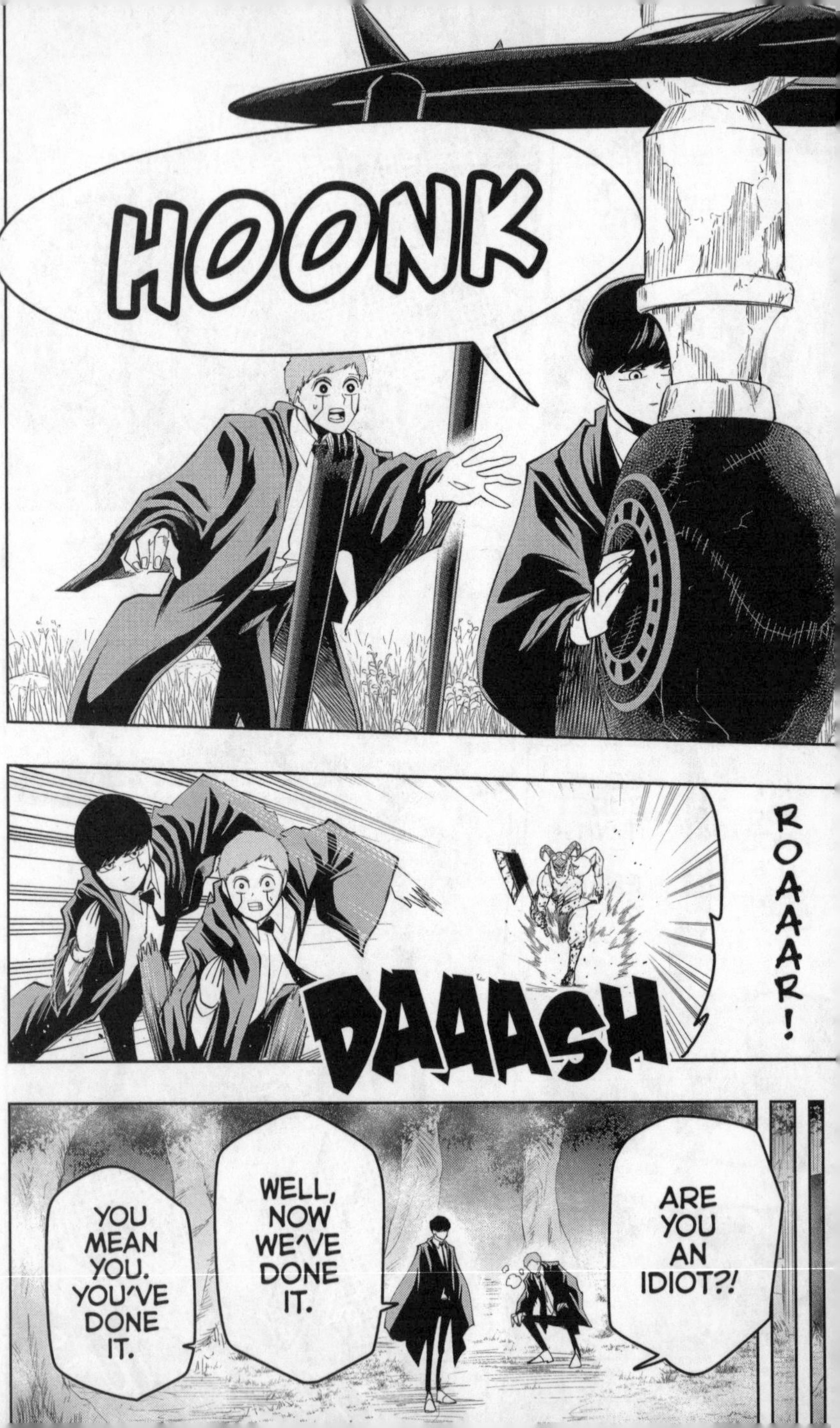
HOONK
ROAAAR!
DAAASH
ARE YOU AN IDIOT?!
WELL, NOW WE'VE DONE IT.
YOU MEAN YOU. YOU'VE DONE IT.

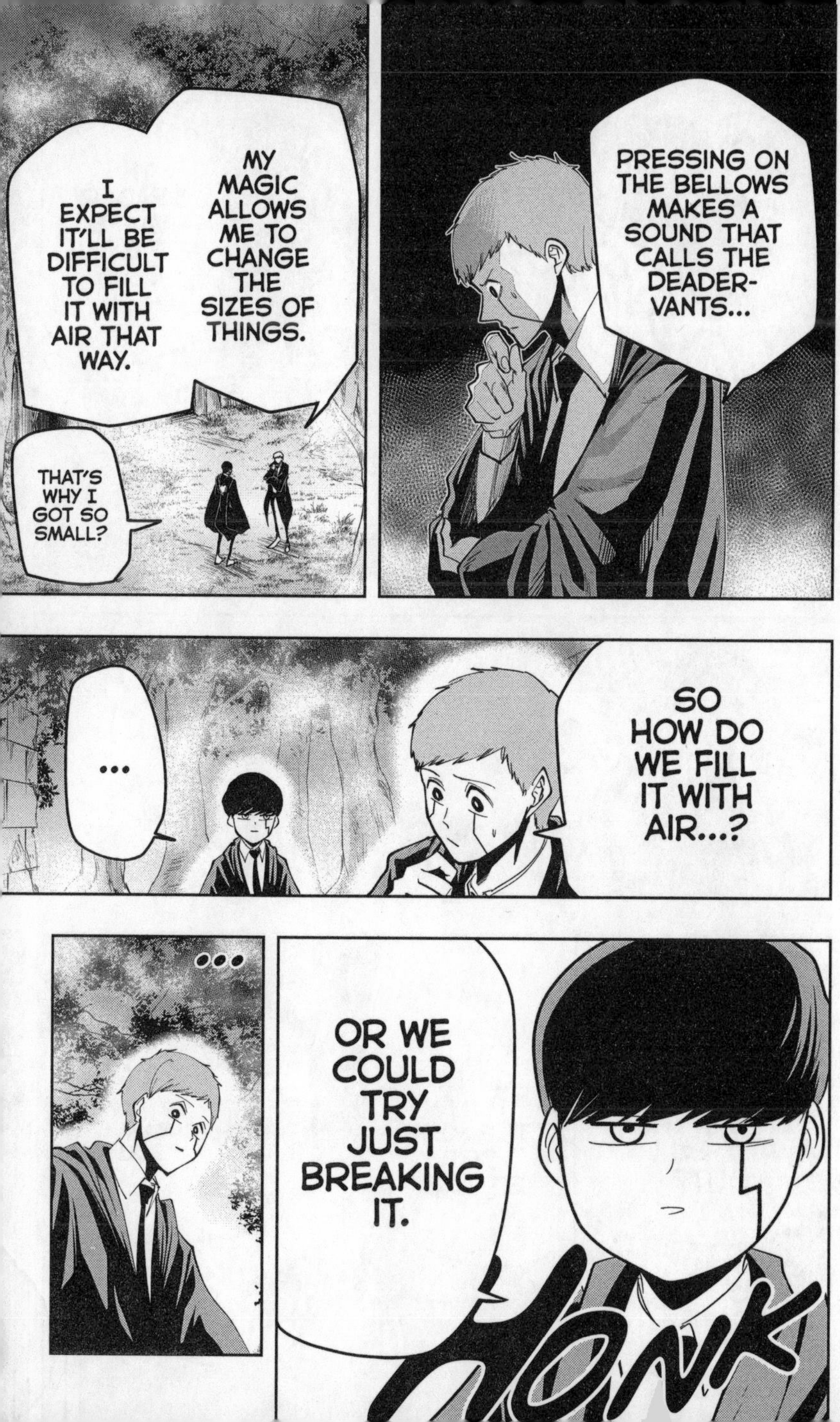
PRESSING ON THE BELLOWS MAKES A SOUND THAT CALLS THE DEADER-VANTS...
MY MAGIC ALLOWS ME TO CHANGE THE SIZES OF THINGS.
I EXPECT IT'LL BE DIFFICULT TO FILL IT WITH AIR THAT WAY.
THAT'S WHY I GOT SO SMALL?
SO HOW DO WE FILL IT WITH AIR...?
...
OR WE COULD TRY JUST BREAKING IT.
...

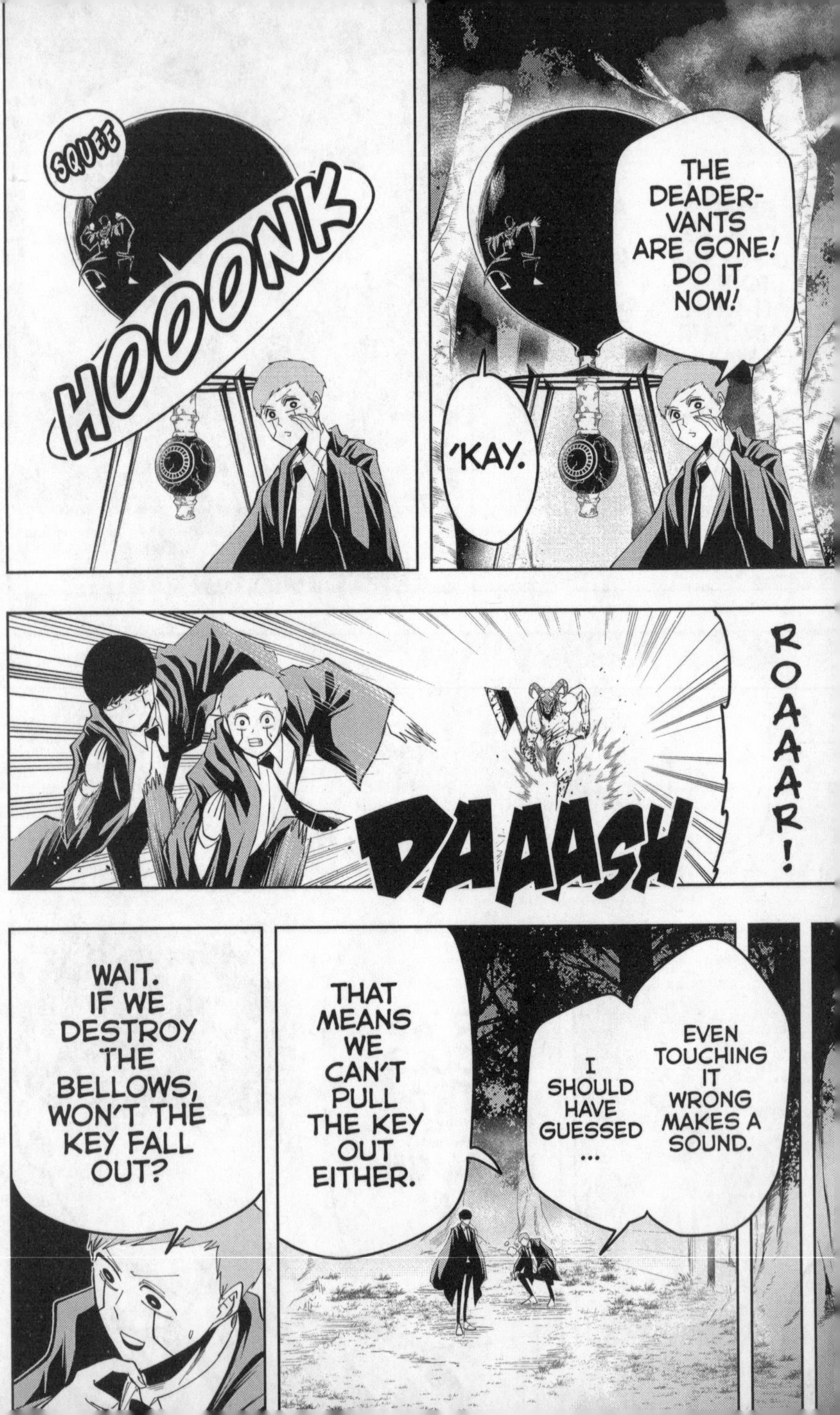
THE DEADER-VANTS ARE GONE! DO IT NOW!
'KAY.
SQUEE
HOOONK
ROAAAR!
DAAASH
EVEN TOUCHING IT WRONG MAKES A SOUND.
I SHOULD HAVE GUESSED...
THAT MEANS WE CAN'T PULL THE KEY OUT EITHER.
WAIT. IF WE DESTROY THE BELLOWS, WON'T THE KEY FALL OUT?

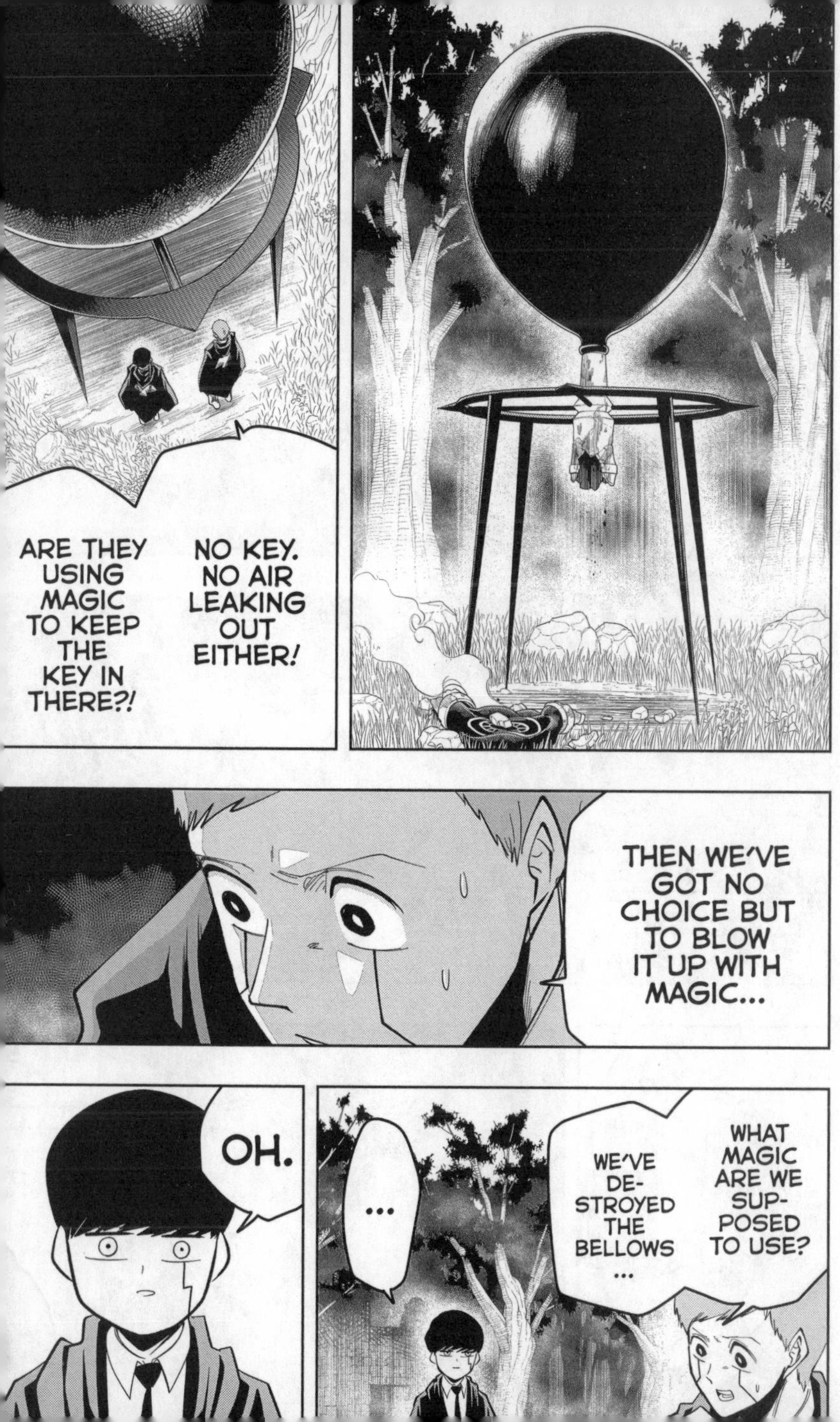
NO KEY. NO AIR LEAKING OUT EITHER!
ARE THEY USING MAGIC TO KEEP THE KEY IN THERE?!
THEN WE'VE GOT NO CHOICE BUT TO BLOW IT UP WITH MAGIC...
WHAT MAGIC ARE WE SUPPOSED TO USE?
WE'VE DESTROYED THE BELLOWS...
...
OH.

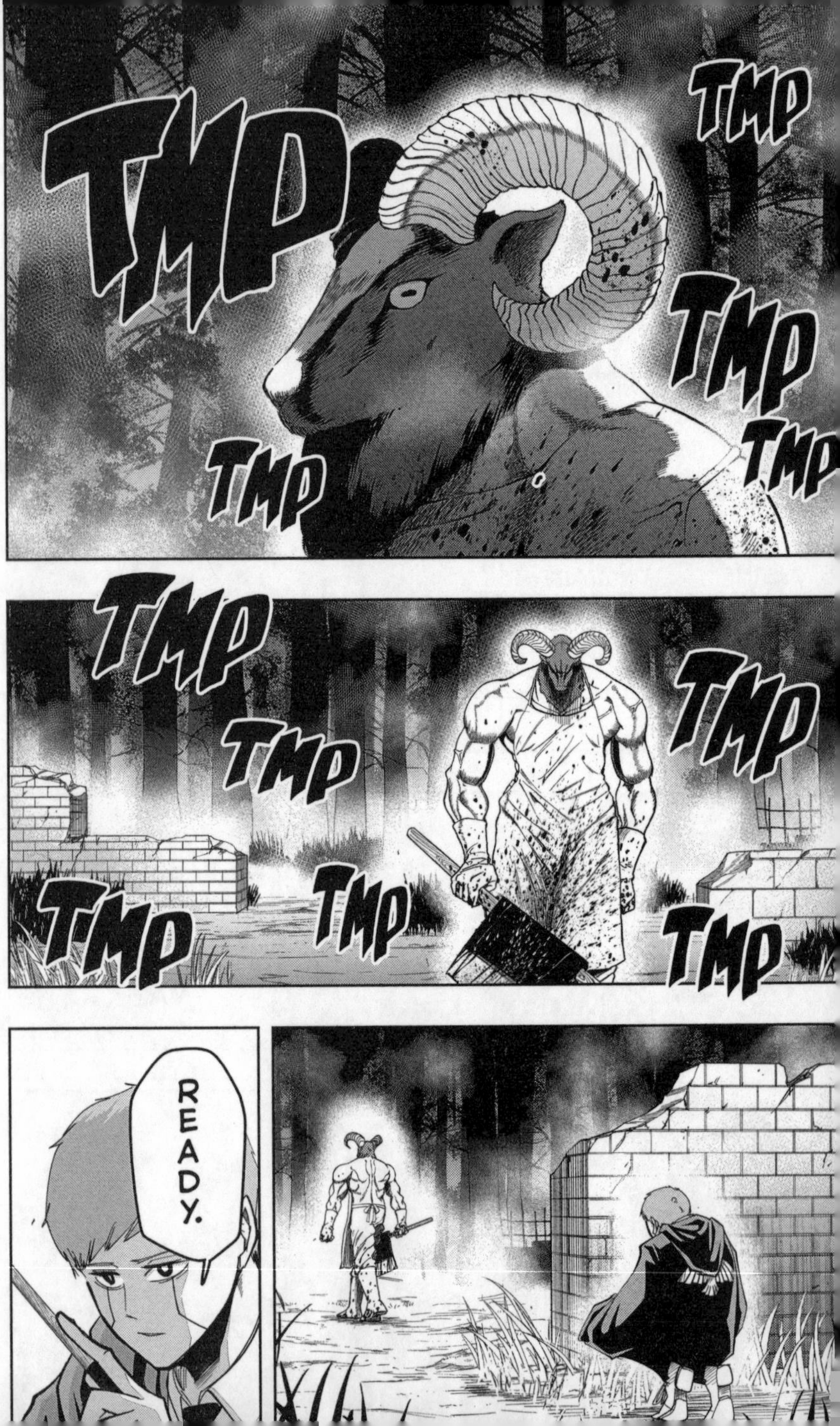
TMP
TMP
TMP
TMP
TMP
TMP
TMP
TMP
TMP
TMP
TMP
READY.

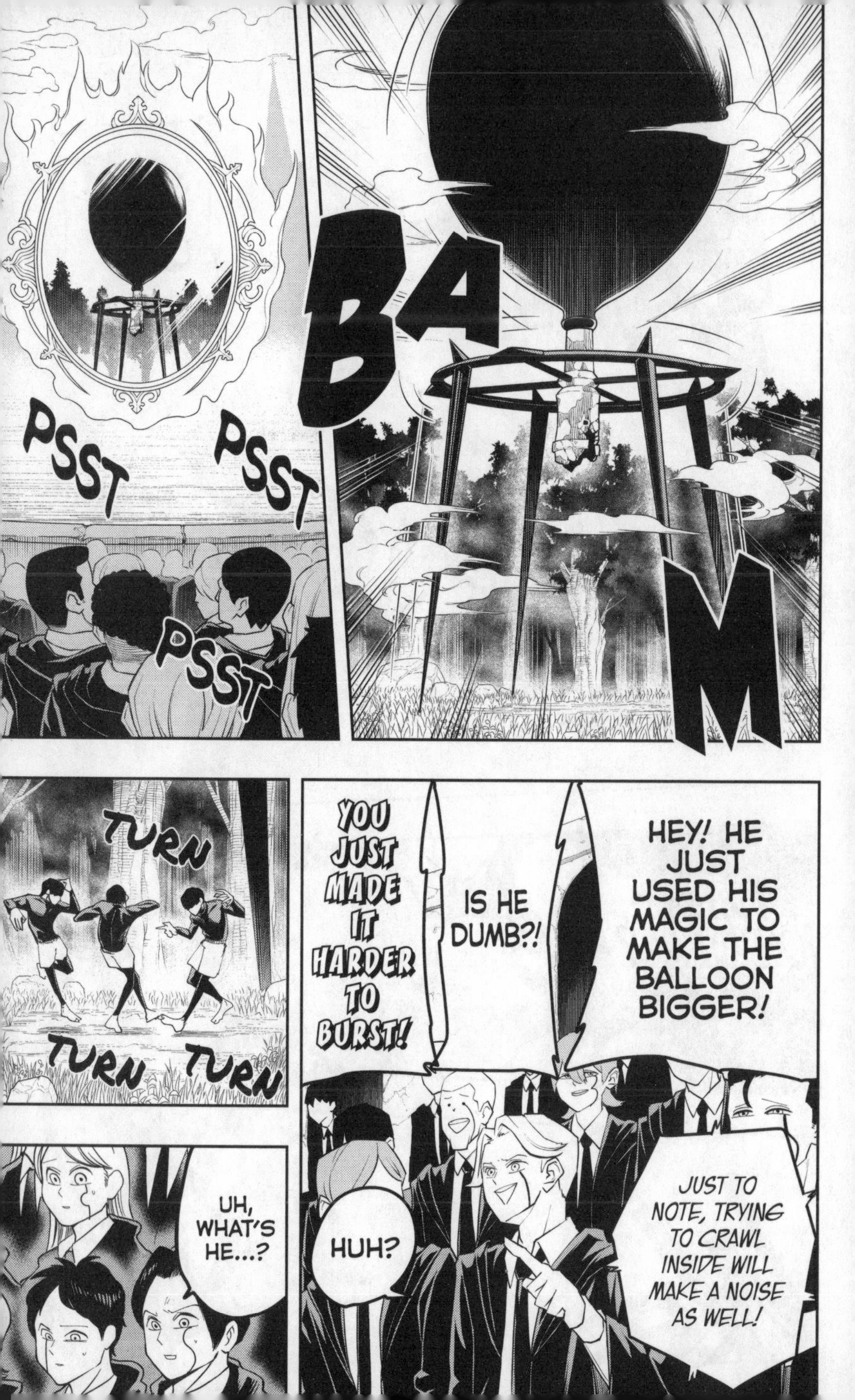
BAM
PSST PSST
PSST
HEY! HE JUST USED HIS MAGIC TO MAKE THE BALLOON BIGGER!
IS HE DUMB?!
YOU JUST MADE IT HARDER TO BURST!
JUST TO NOTE, TRYING TO CRAWL INSIDE WILL MAKE A NOISE AS WELL!
HUH?
TURN
TURN TURN
UH, WHAT'S HE...?

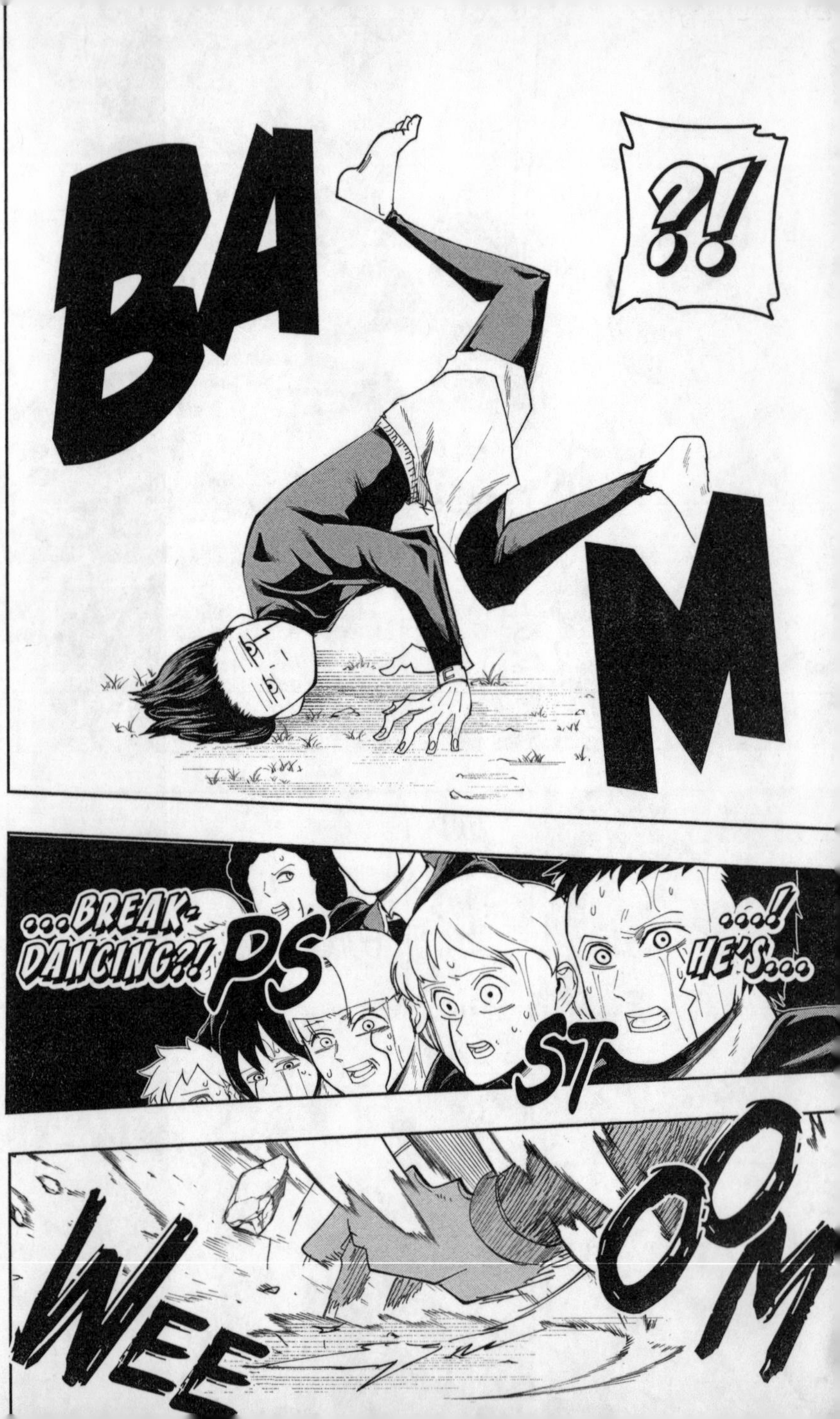
?!
BA
M
...! HE'S...
...BREAK-DANCING?!
PS
ST
WEE
OOM

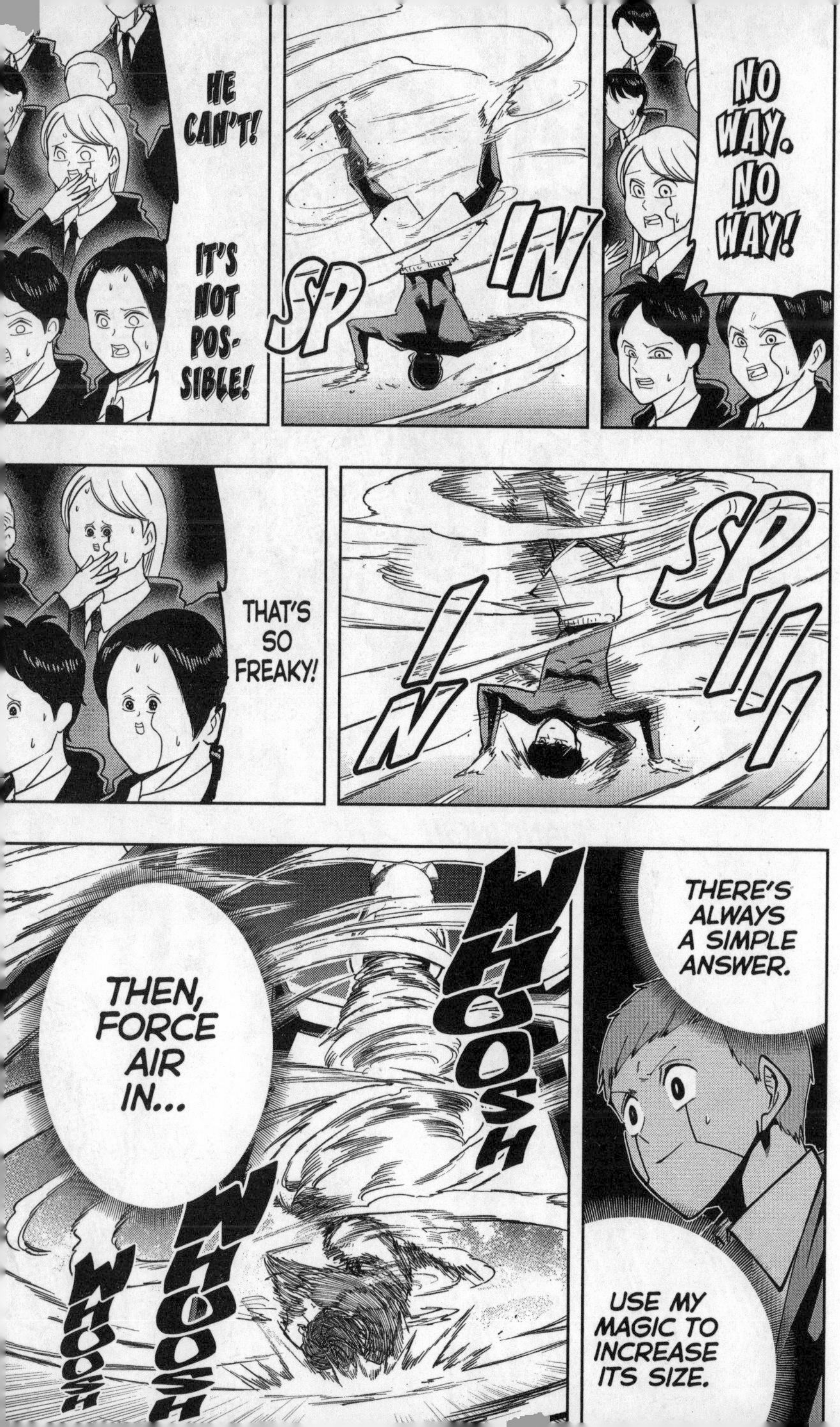
NO WAY. NO WAY!
SPIN
HE CAN'T!
IT'S NOT POS-SIBLE!
SPIIIN
THAT'S SO FREAKY!
THERE'S ALWAYS A SIMPLE ANSWER.
USE MY MAGIC TO INCREASE ITS SIZE.
WHOOSH
THEN, FORCE AIR IN...
WHOOSH
WHOOSH

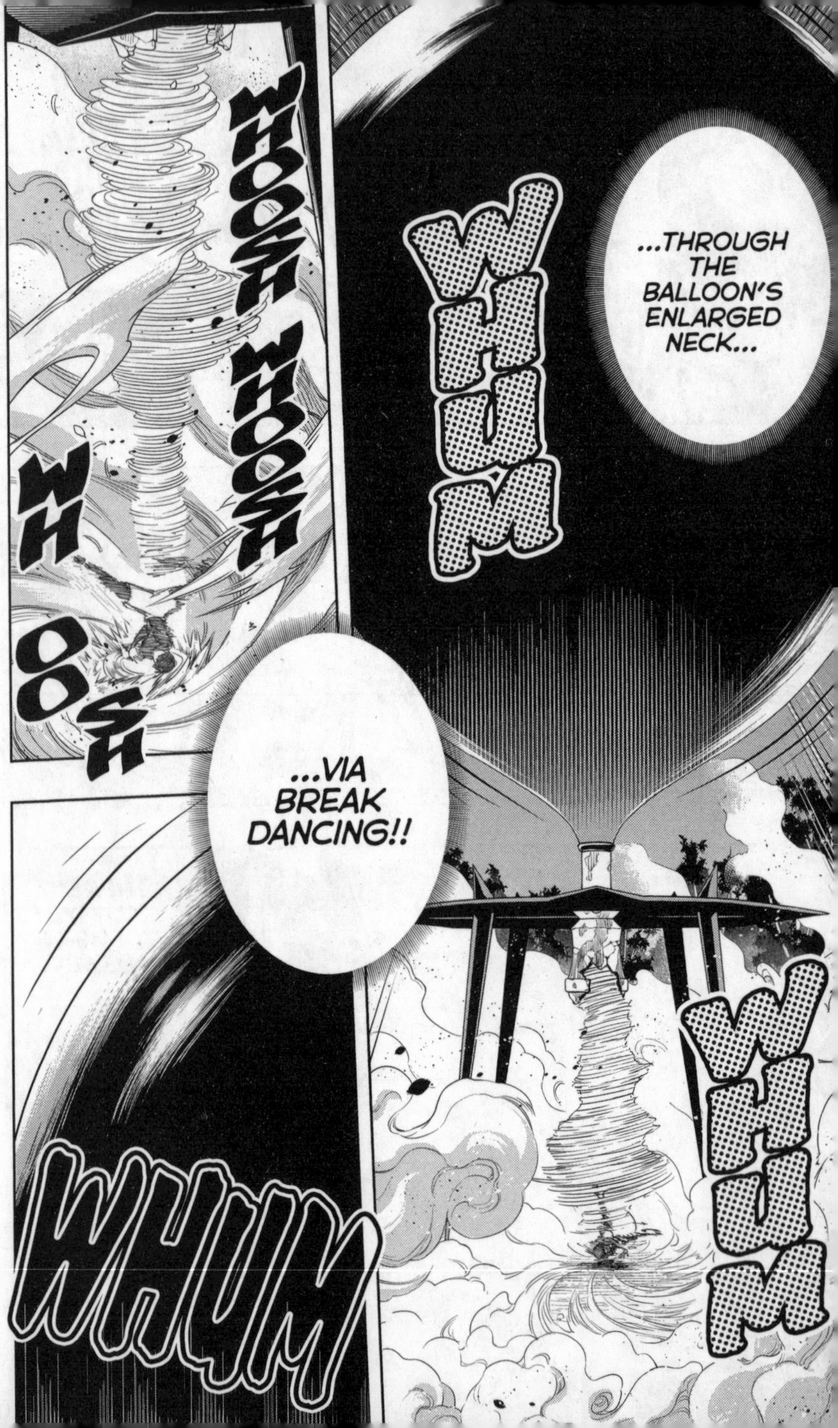
...THROUGH THE BALLOON'S ENLARGED NECK...
WHUM
...VIA BREAK DANCING!!
WHUM
WHOOSH WHOOSH
WH OOSH
WHUM

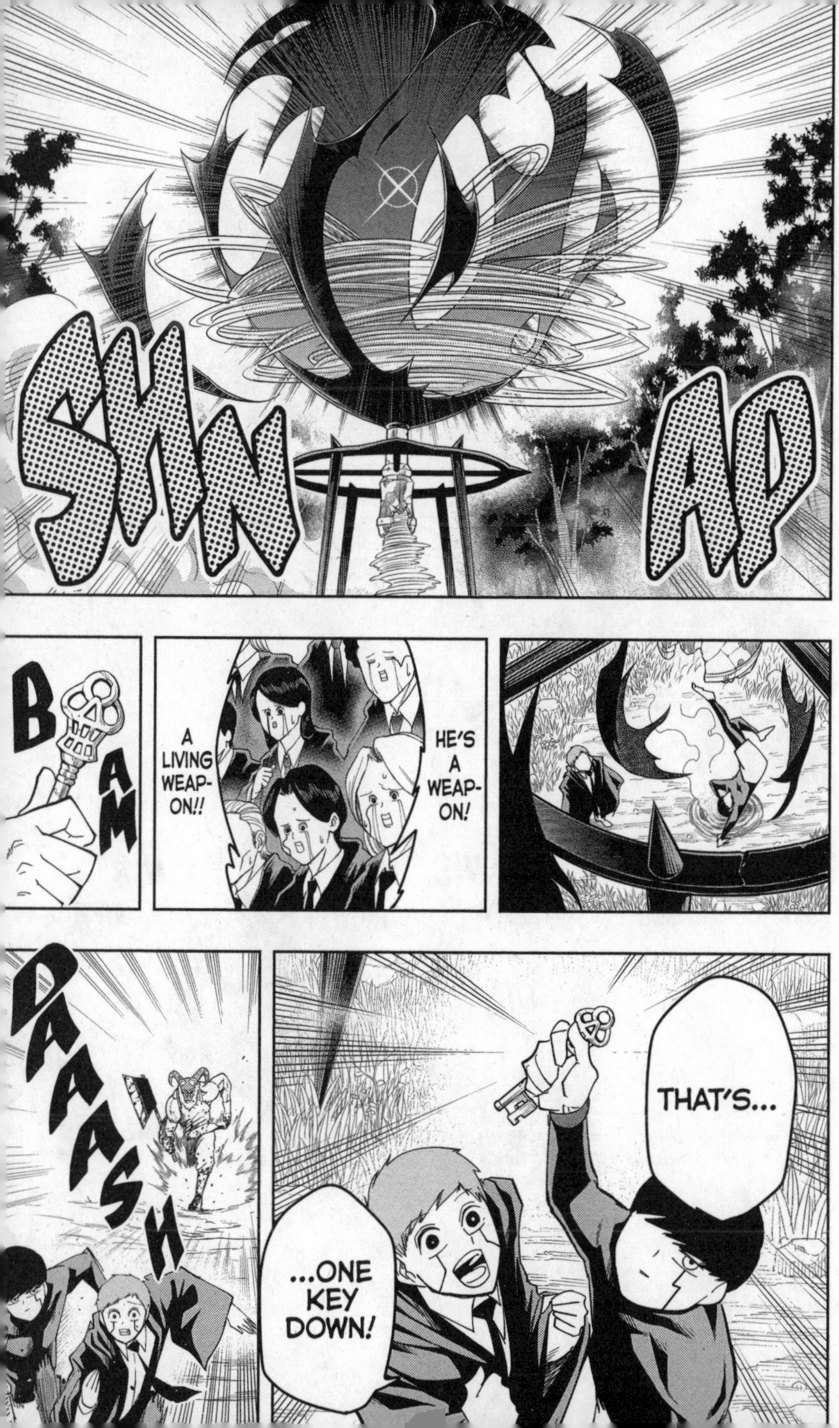
SNAP
HE'S A WEAP-ON!
A LIVING WEAP-ON!!
BAM
THAT'S...
...ONE KEY DOWN!
DAAASH

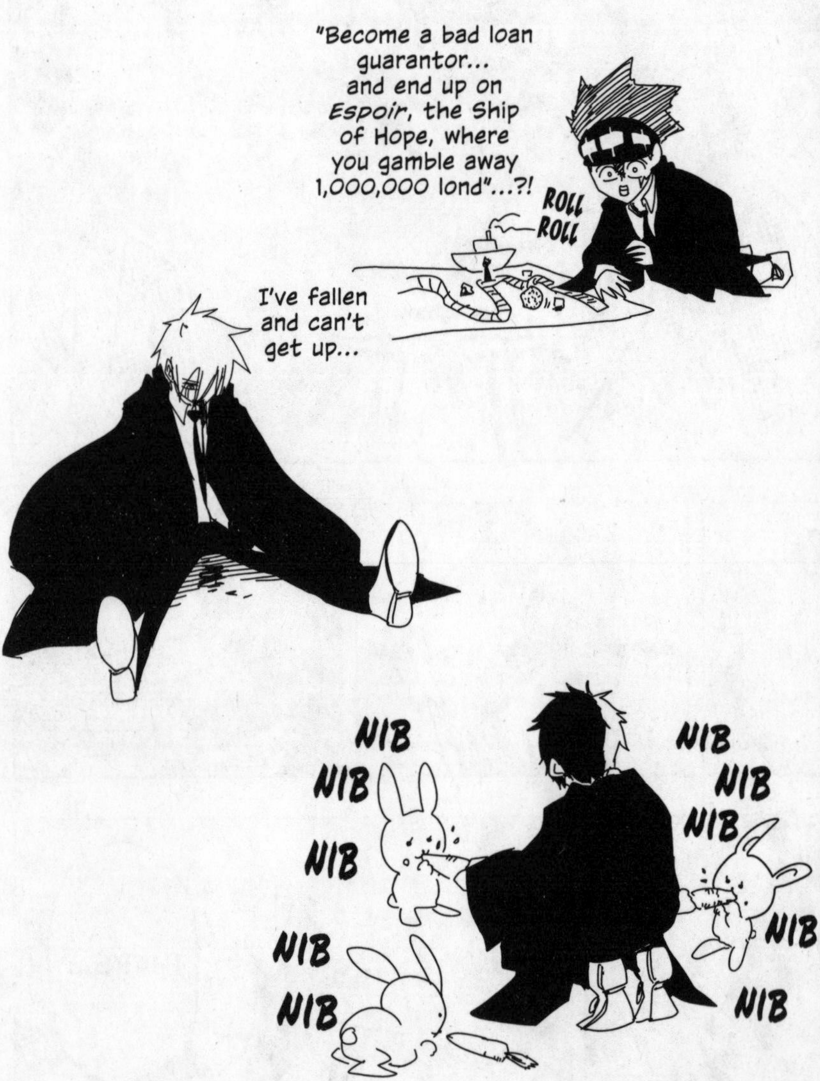
"Become a bad loan guarantor... and end up on *Espoir*, the Ship of Hope, where you gamble away 1,000,000 lond"...?!
ROLL ROLL
I've fallen and can't get up...
NIB NIB NIB
NIB NIB
NIB NIB NIB
NIB NIB

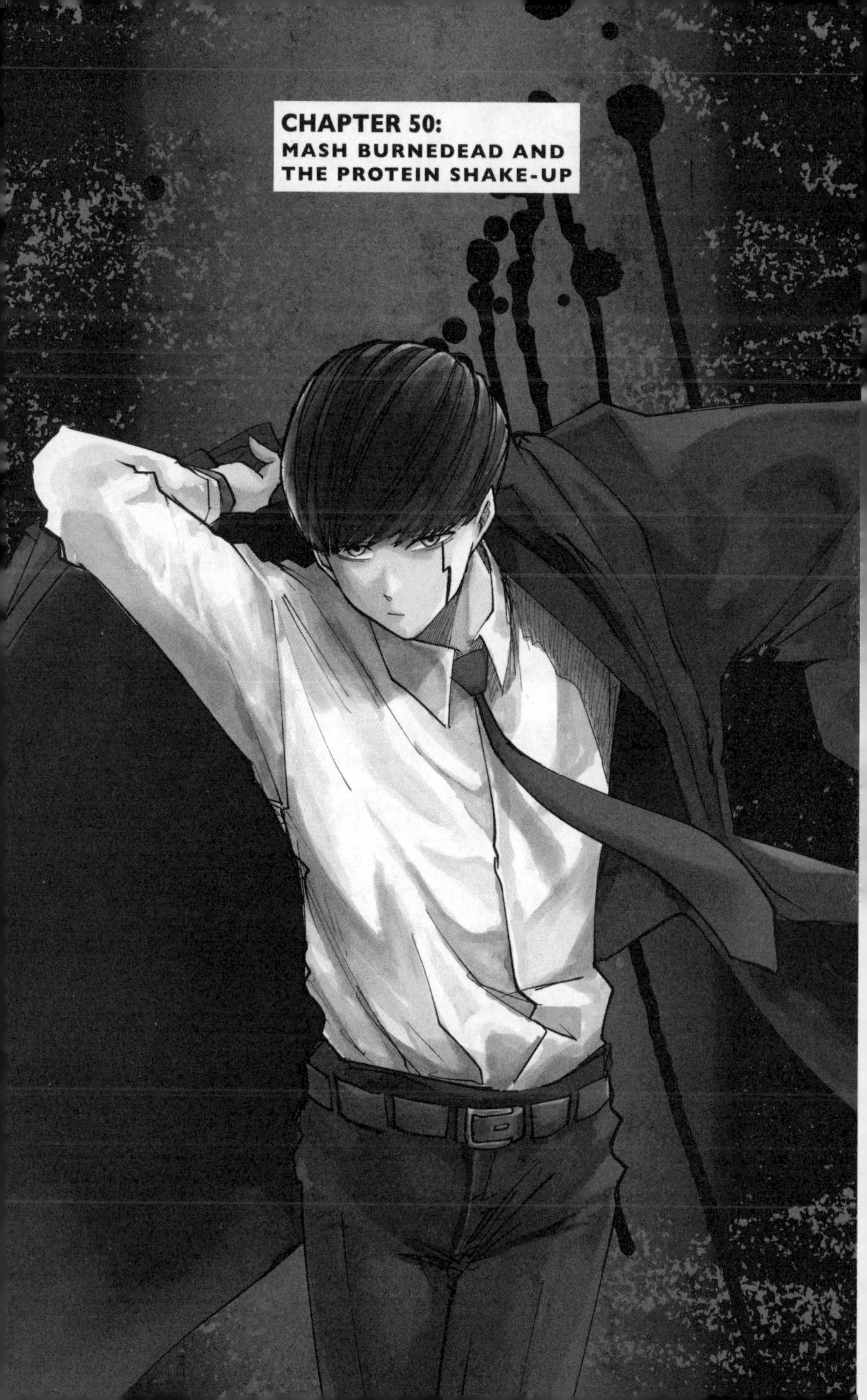
CHAPTER 50:
MASH BURNEDEAD AND
THE PROTEIN SHAKE-UP

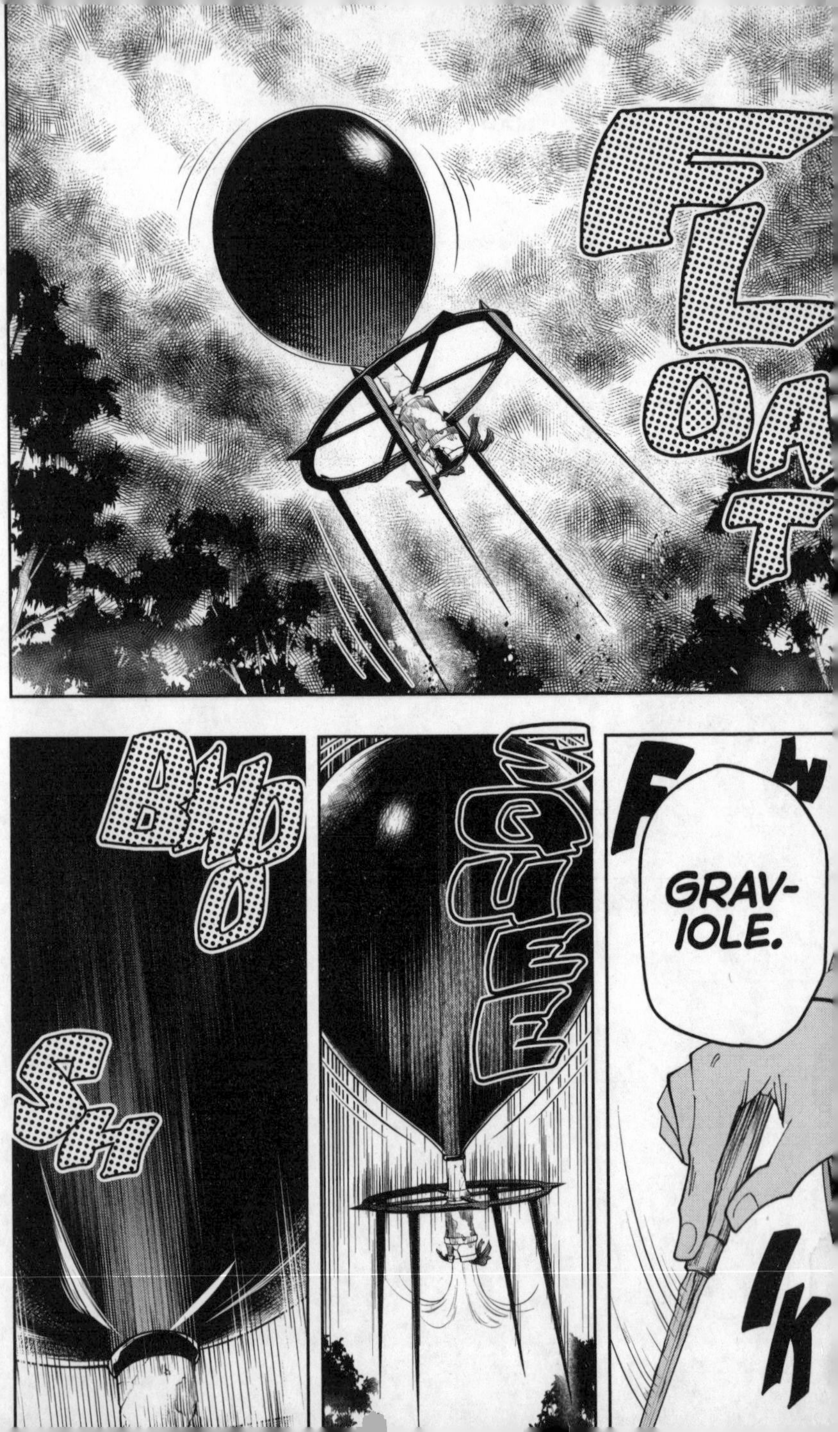
FLOAT
FW
GRAV-IOLE.
IK
SQUEEE
BWOO
SH

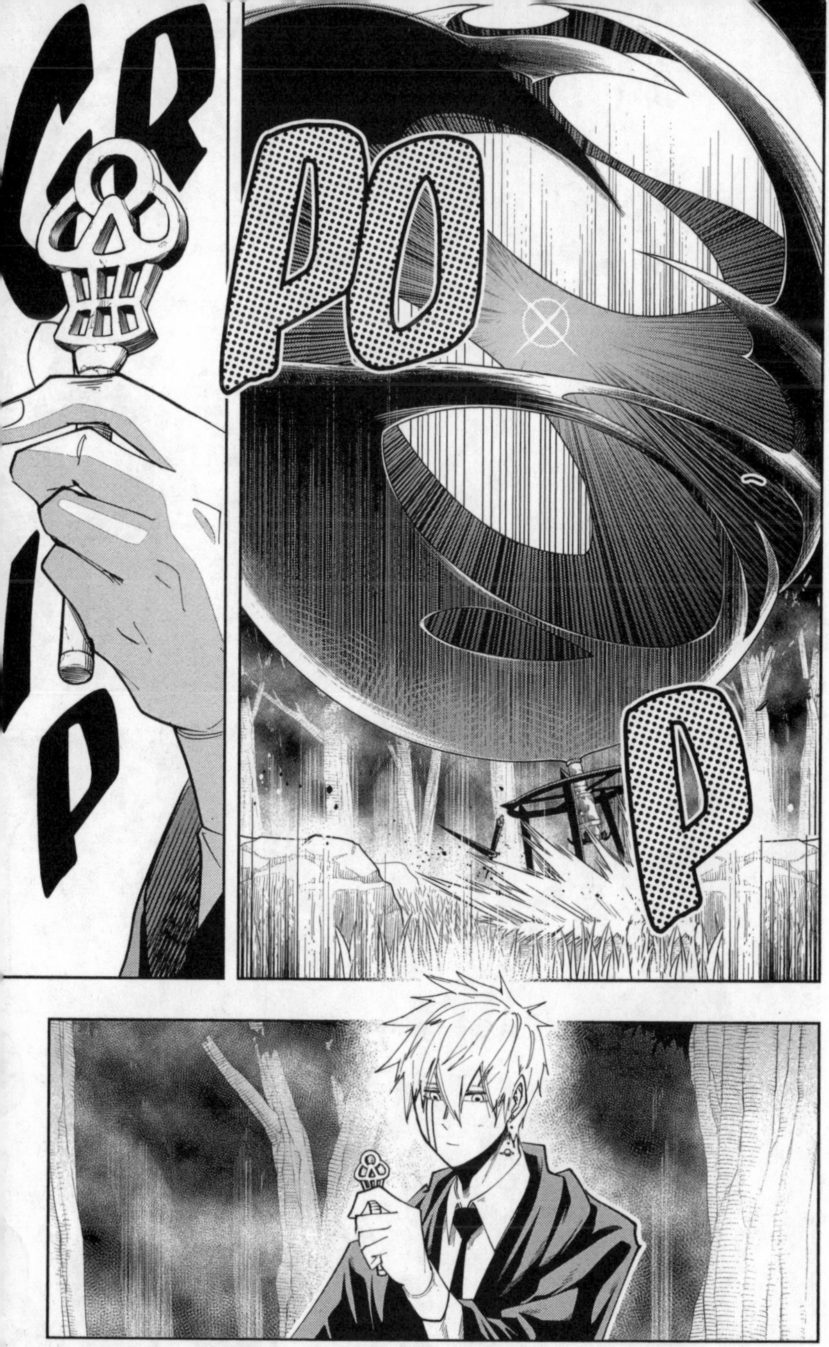
POP
GRIP

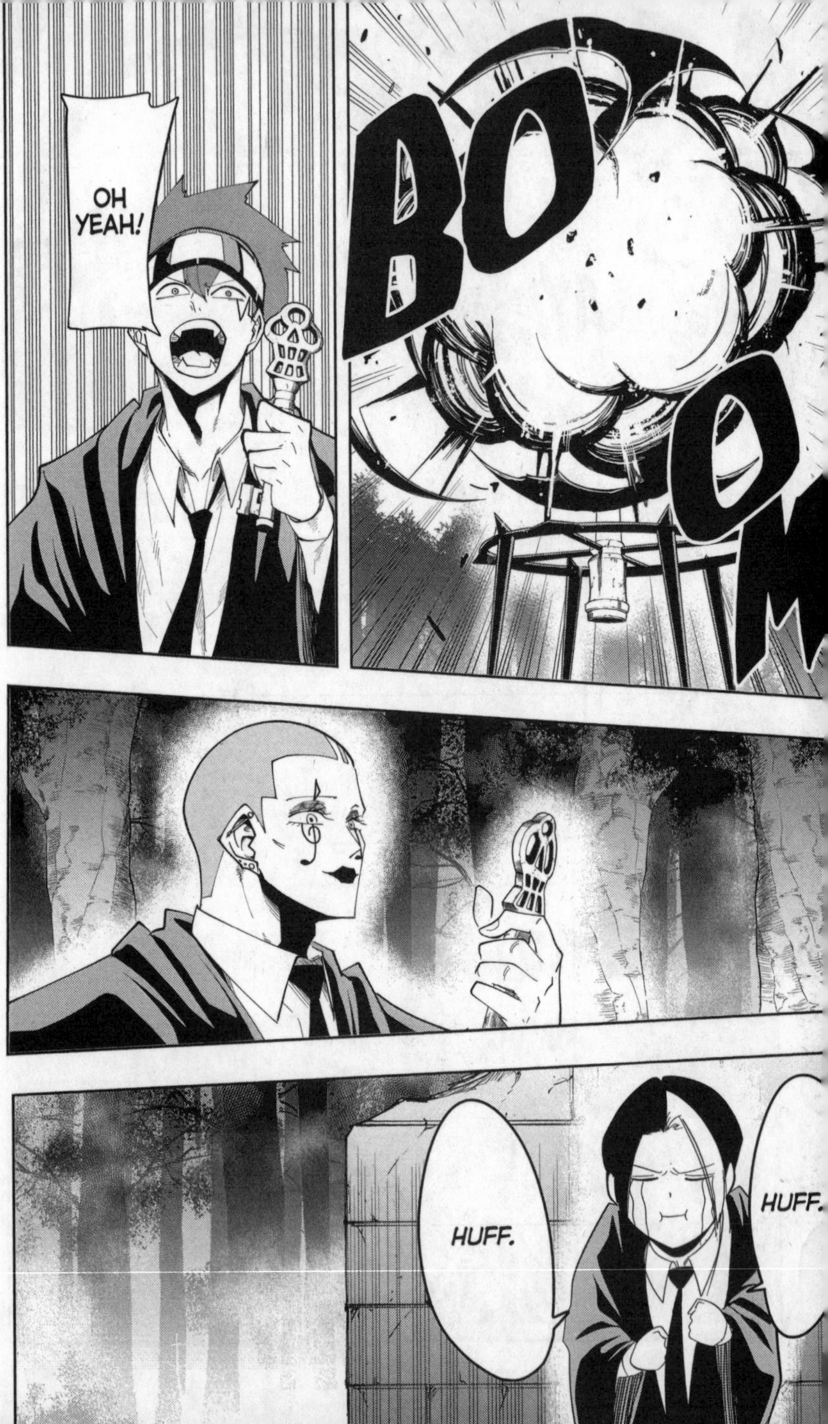

BOOM
OH YEAH!
HUFF.
HUFF.

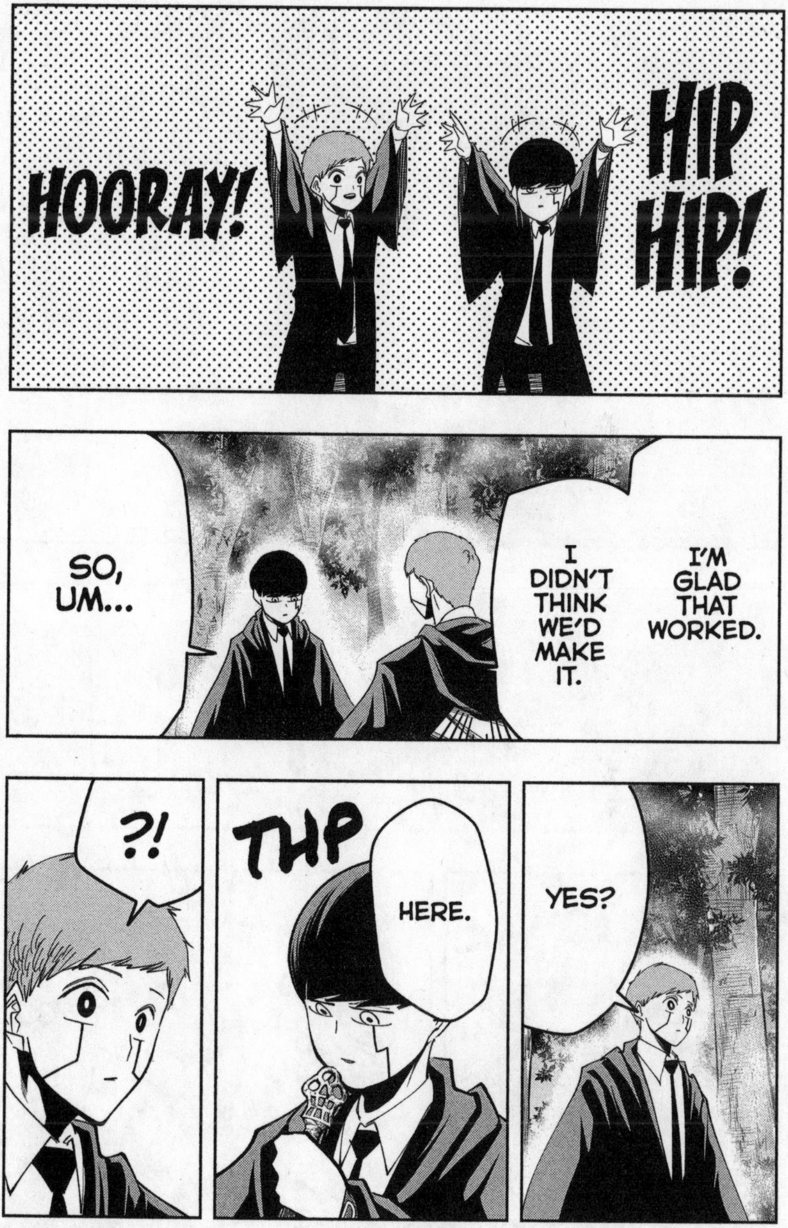
HIP HIP!
HOORAY!
I'M GLAD THAT WORKED.
I DIDN'T THINK WE'D MAKE IT.
SO, UM...
YES?
HERE.
THP
?!

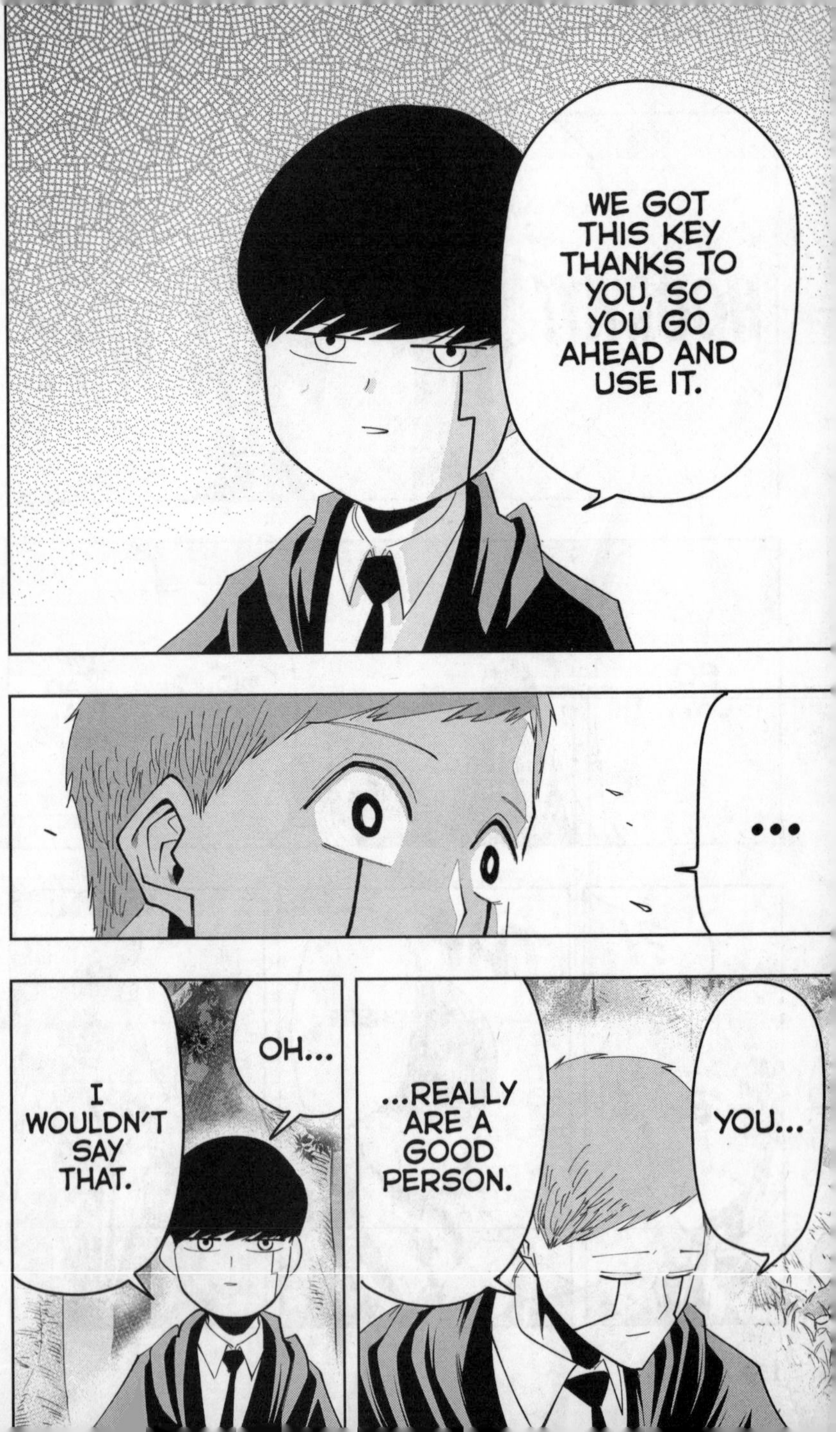
WE GOT THIS KEY THANKS TO YOU, SO YOU GO AHEAD AND USE IT.
...
YOU...
...REALLY ARE A GOOD PERSON.
OH...
I WOULDN'T SAY THAT.

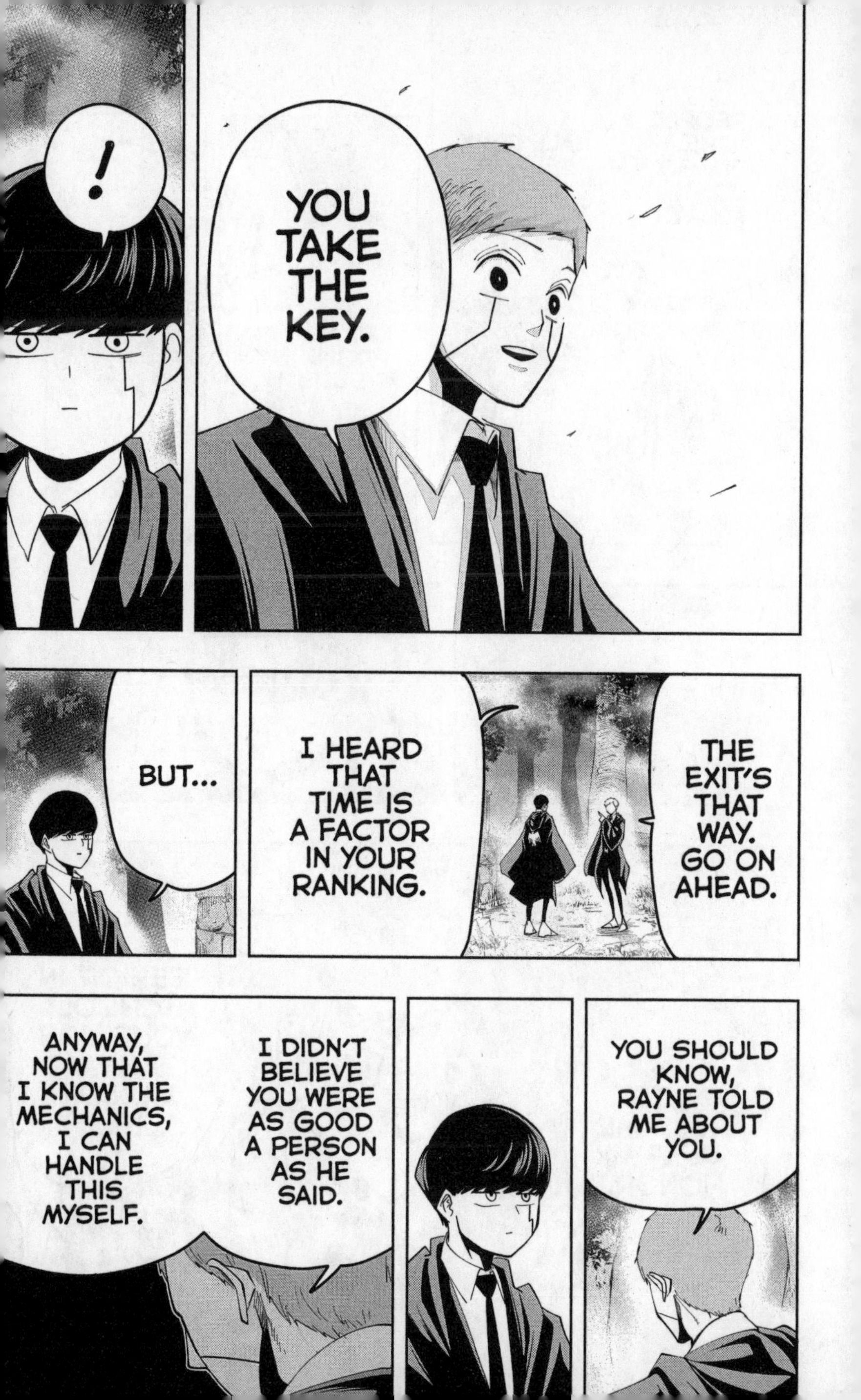
YOU TAKE THE KEY.
!
THE EXIT'S THAT WAY. GO ON AHEAD.
I HEARD THAT TIME IS A FACTOR IN YOUR RANKING.
BUT...
YOU SHOULD KNOW, RAYNE TOLD ME ABOUT YOU.
I DIDN'T BELIEVE YOU WERE AS GOOD A PERSON AS HE SAID.
ANYWAY, NOW THAT I KNOW THE MECHANICS, I CAN HANDLE THIS MYSELF.

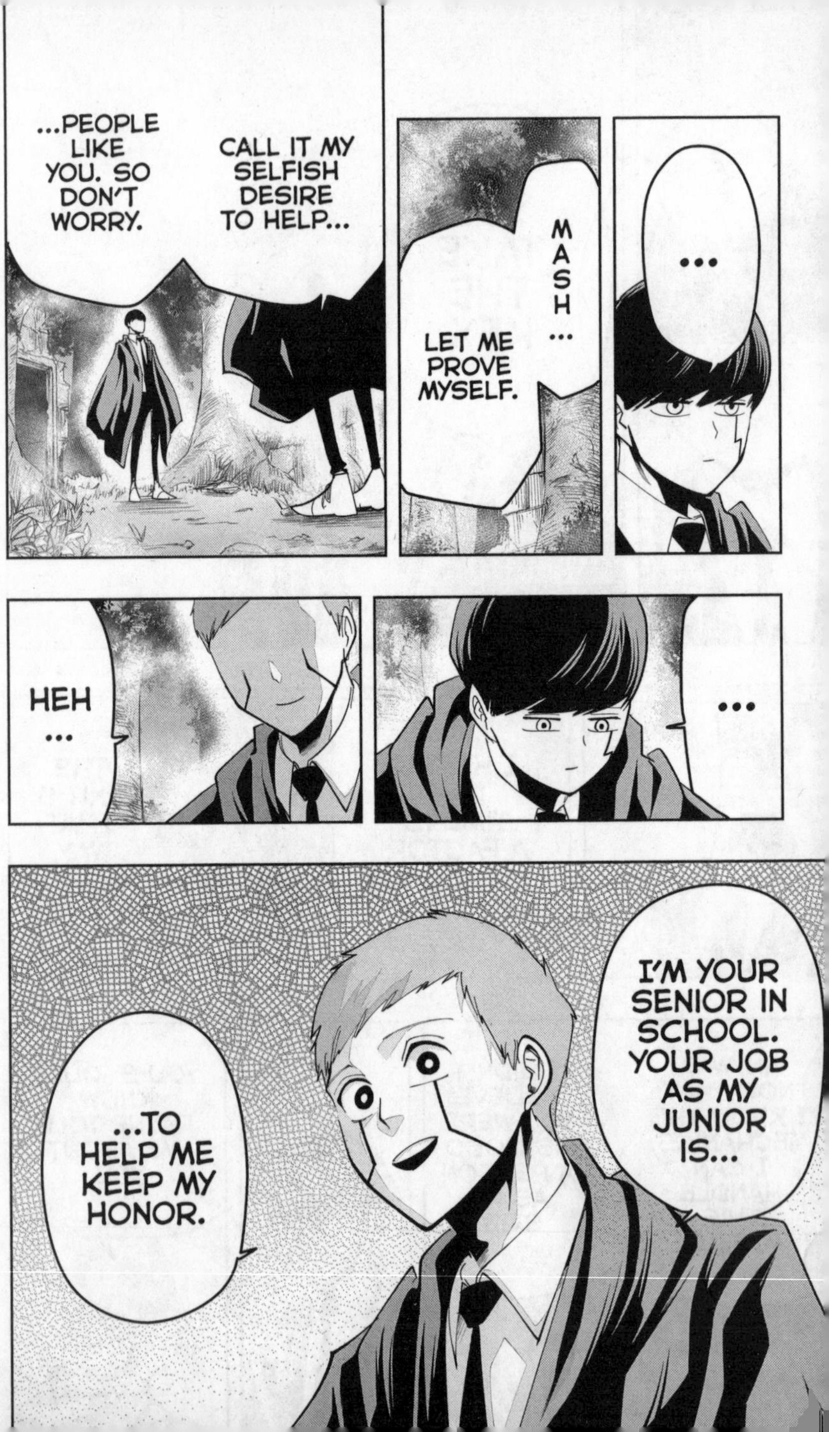
...
MASH...
LET ME PROVE MYSELF.
CALL IT MY SELFISH DESIRE TO HELP...
...PEOPLE LIKE YOU. SO DON'T WORRY.
...
HEH...
I'M YOUR SENIOR IN SCHOOL. YOUR JOB AS MY JUNIOR IS...
...TO HELP ME KEEP MY HONOR.

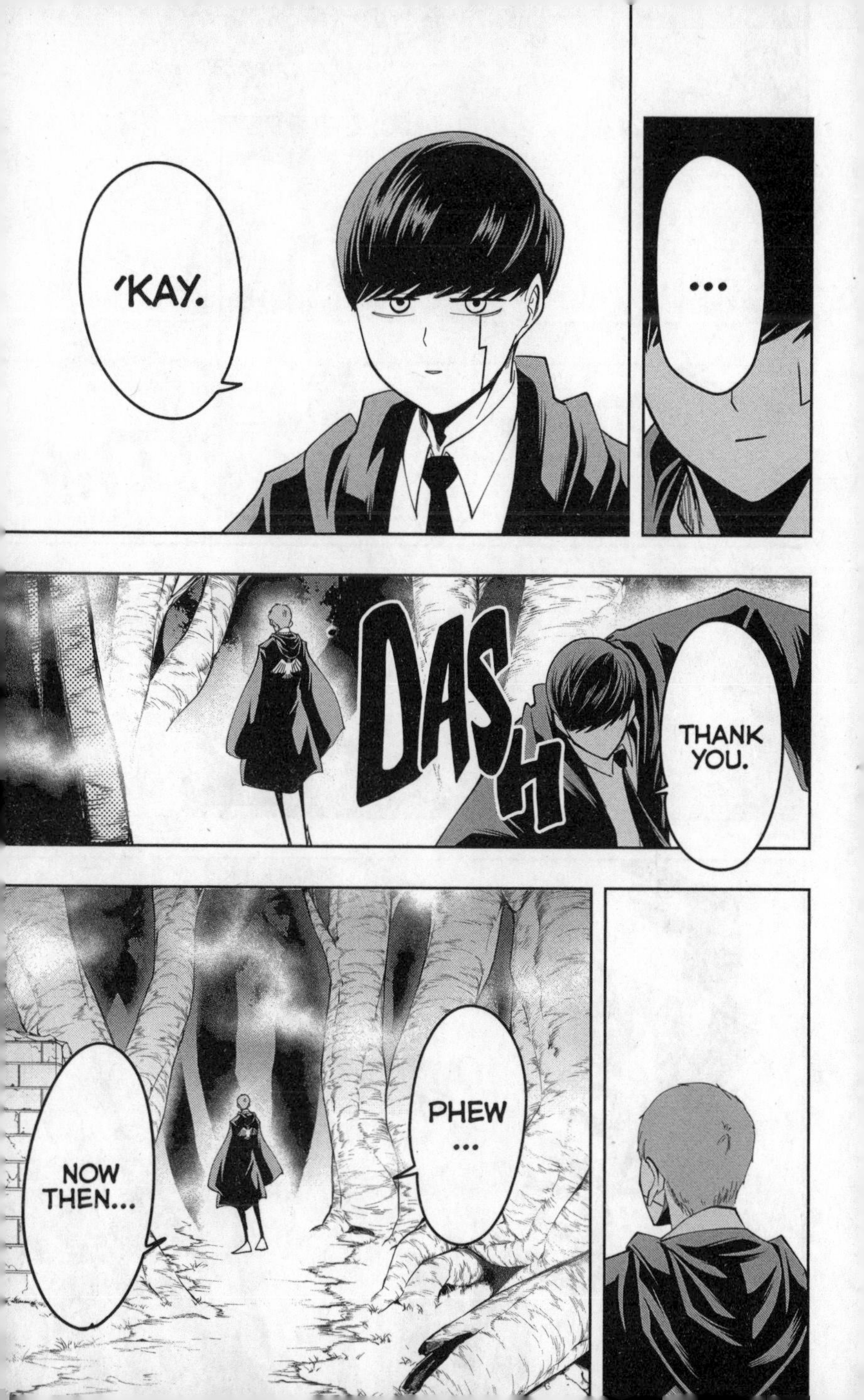
...
'KAY.
THANK YOU.
DASH
PHEW ...
NOW THEN...

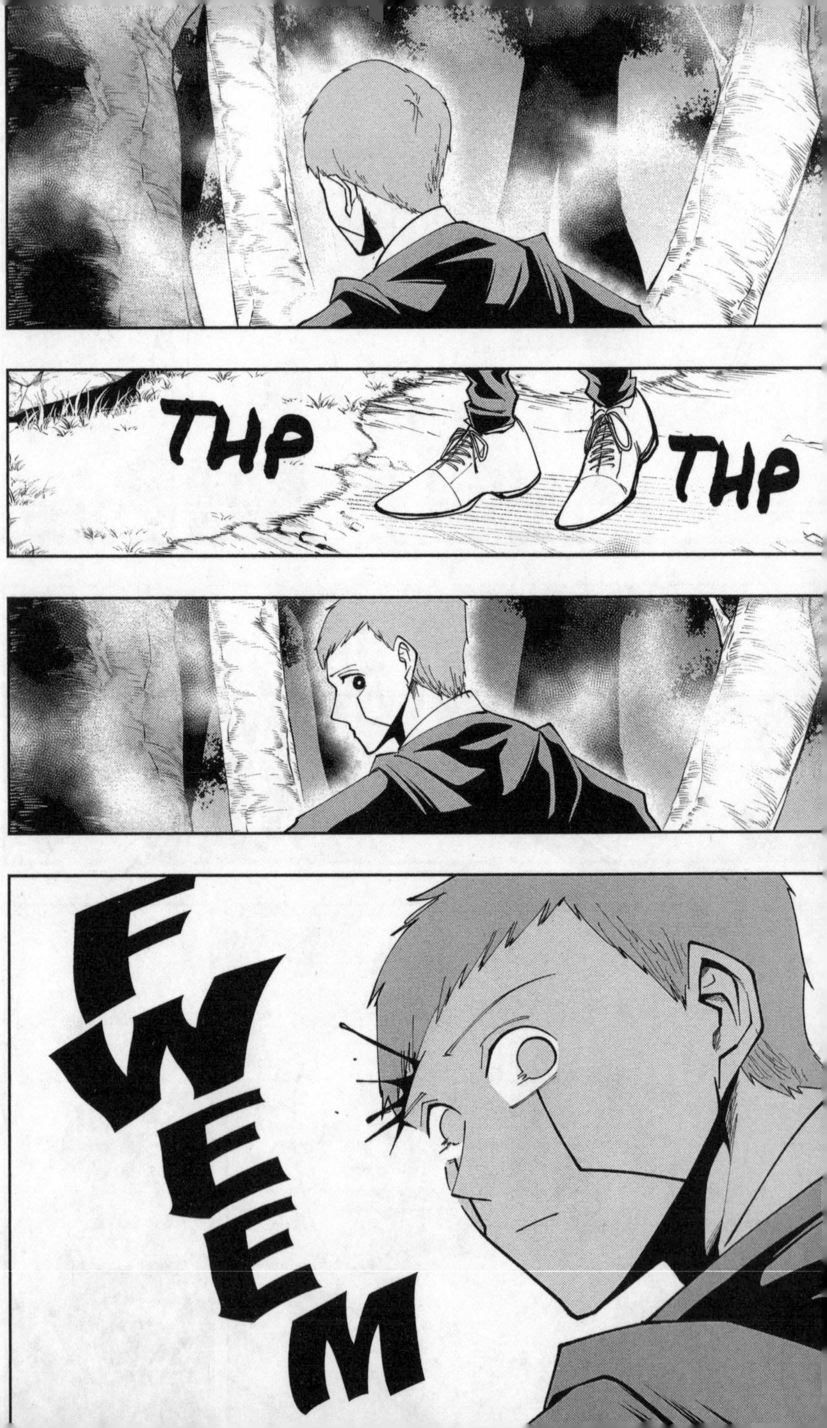
THP
THP
FWEEM

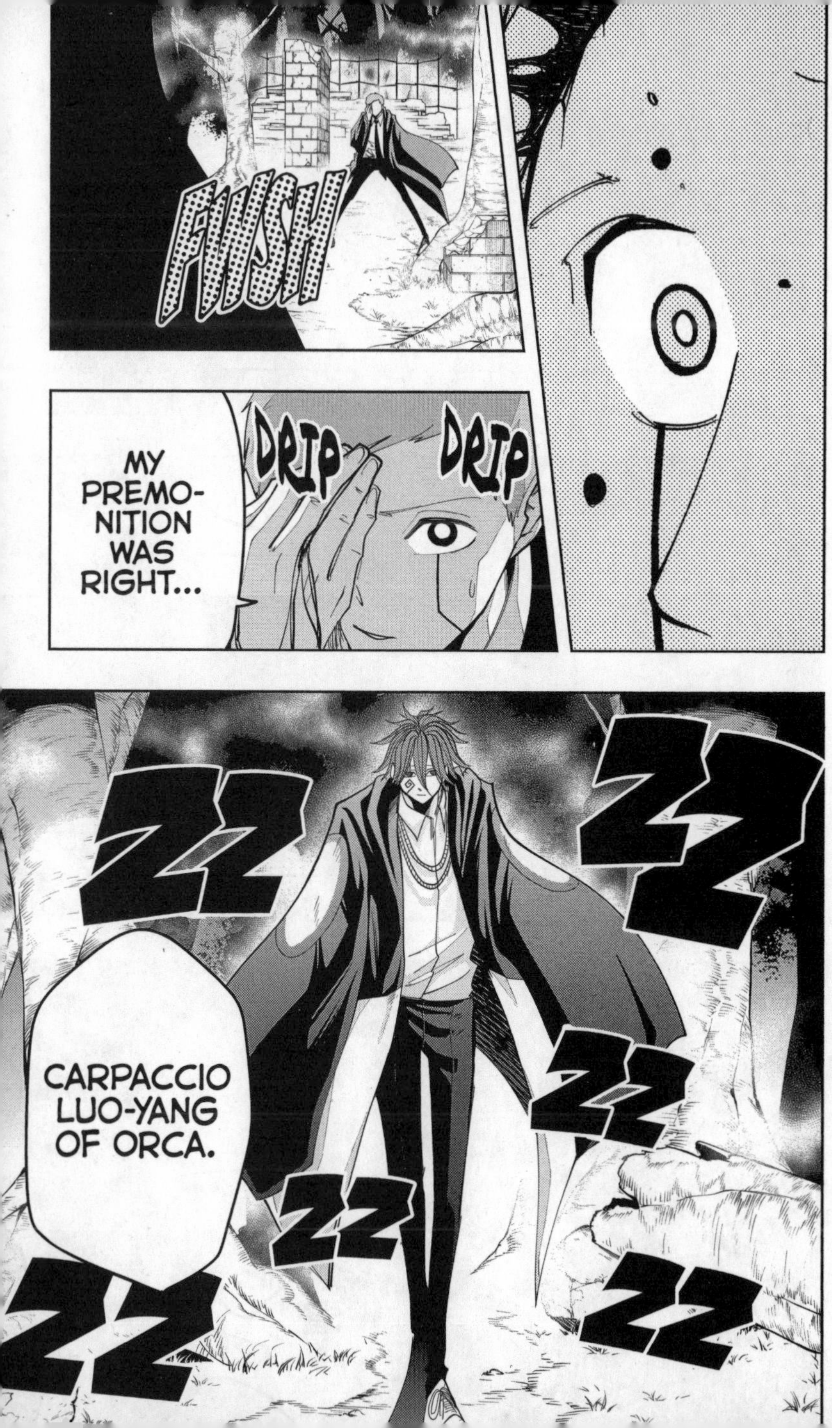
FWSH
DRIP DRIP
MY PREMO-NITION WAS RIGHT...
ZZ
ZZ
CARPACCIO LUO-YANG OF ORCA.
ZZ
ZZ
ZZ
ZZ

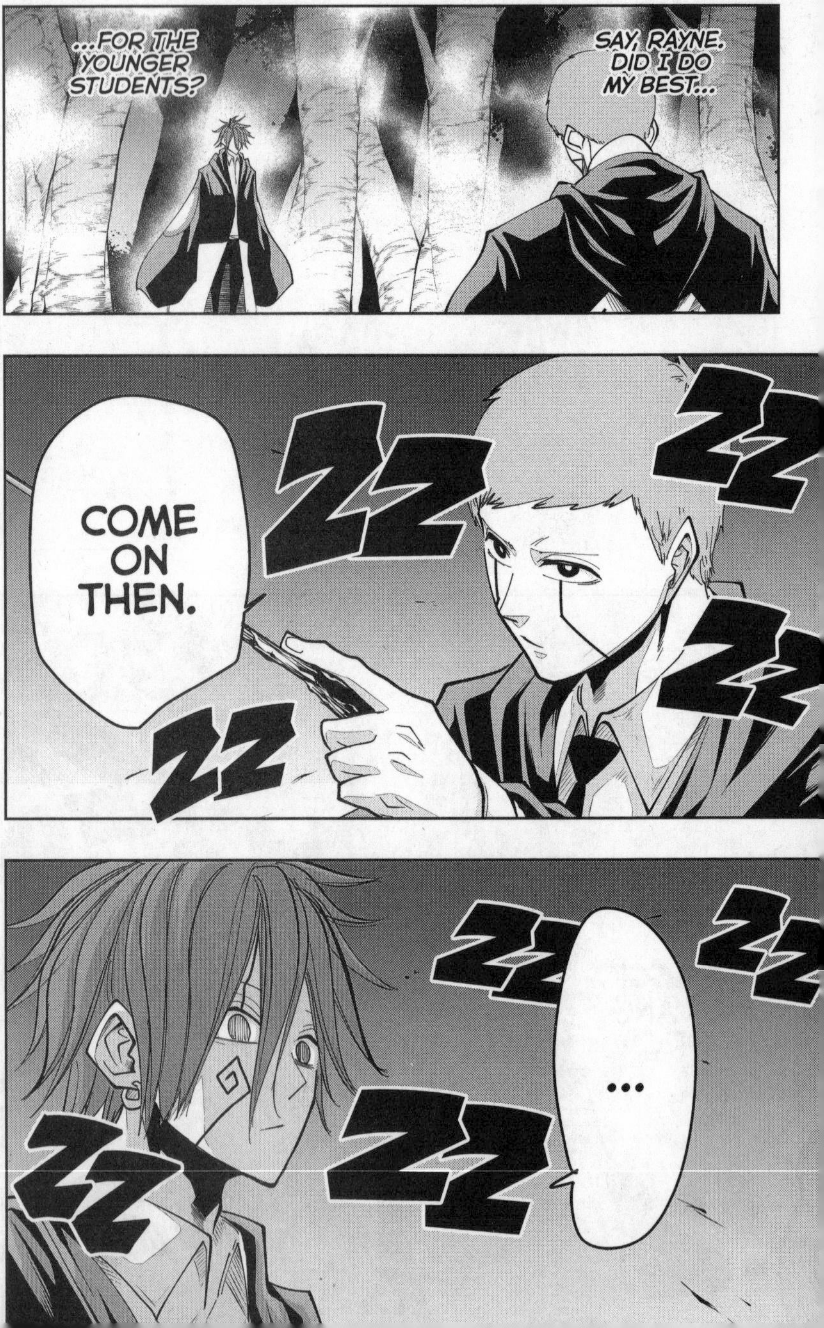
SAY, RAYNE. DID I DO MY BEST...
...FOR THE YOUNGER STUDENTS?
COME ON THEN.
...

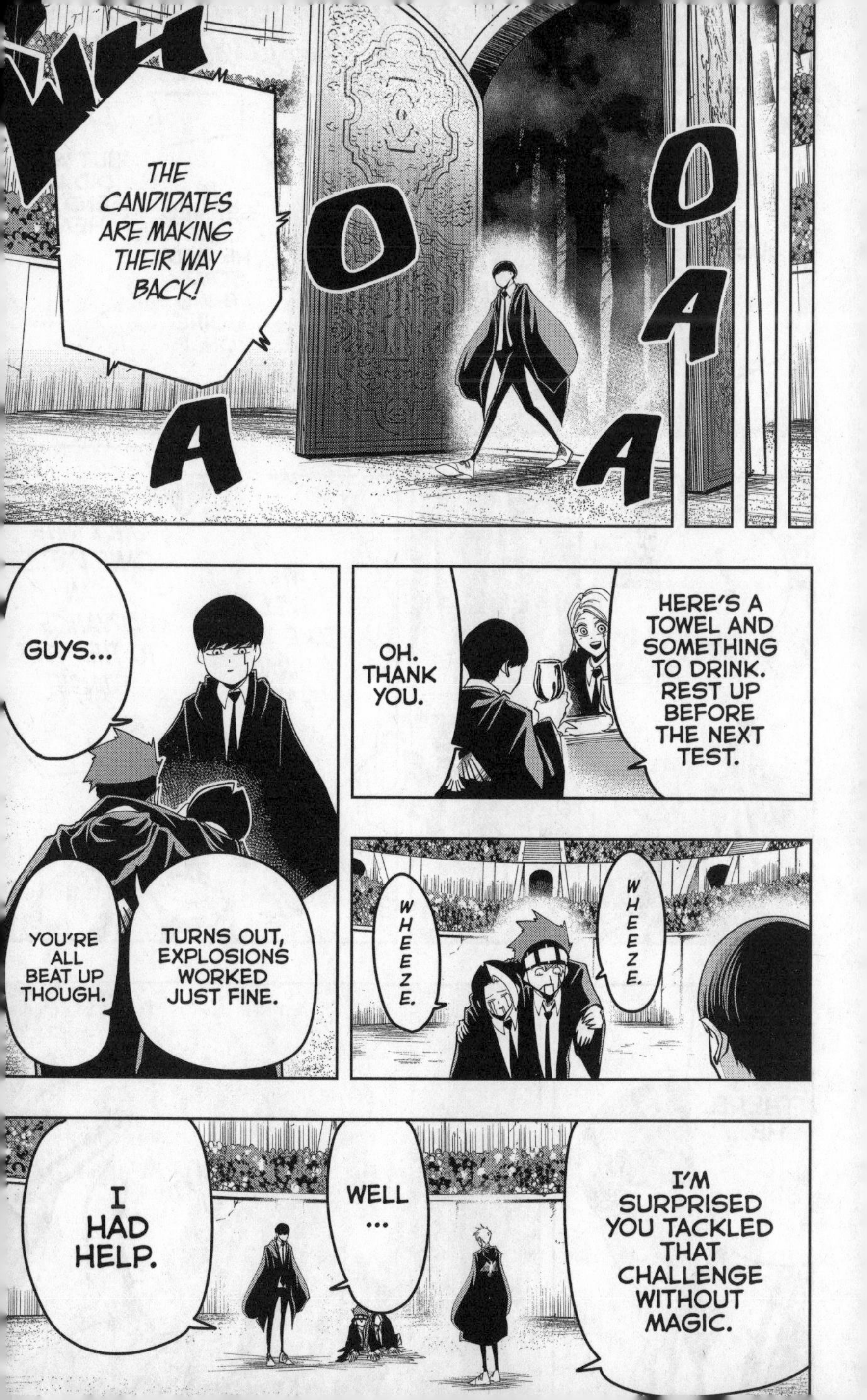
THE CANDIDATES ARE MAKING THEIR WAY BACK!
OOAAA
HERE'S A TOWEL AND SOMETHING TO DRINK. REST UP BEFORE THE NEXT TEST.
OH. THANK YOU.
WHEEZE.
WHEEZE.
GUYS...
TURNS OUT, EXPLOSIONS WORKED JUST FINE.
YOU'RE ALL BEAT UP THOUGH.
I'M SURPRISED YOU TACKLED THAT CHALLENGE WITHOUT MAGIC.
WELL...
I HAD HELP.

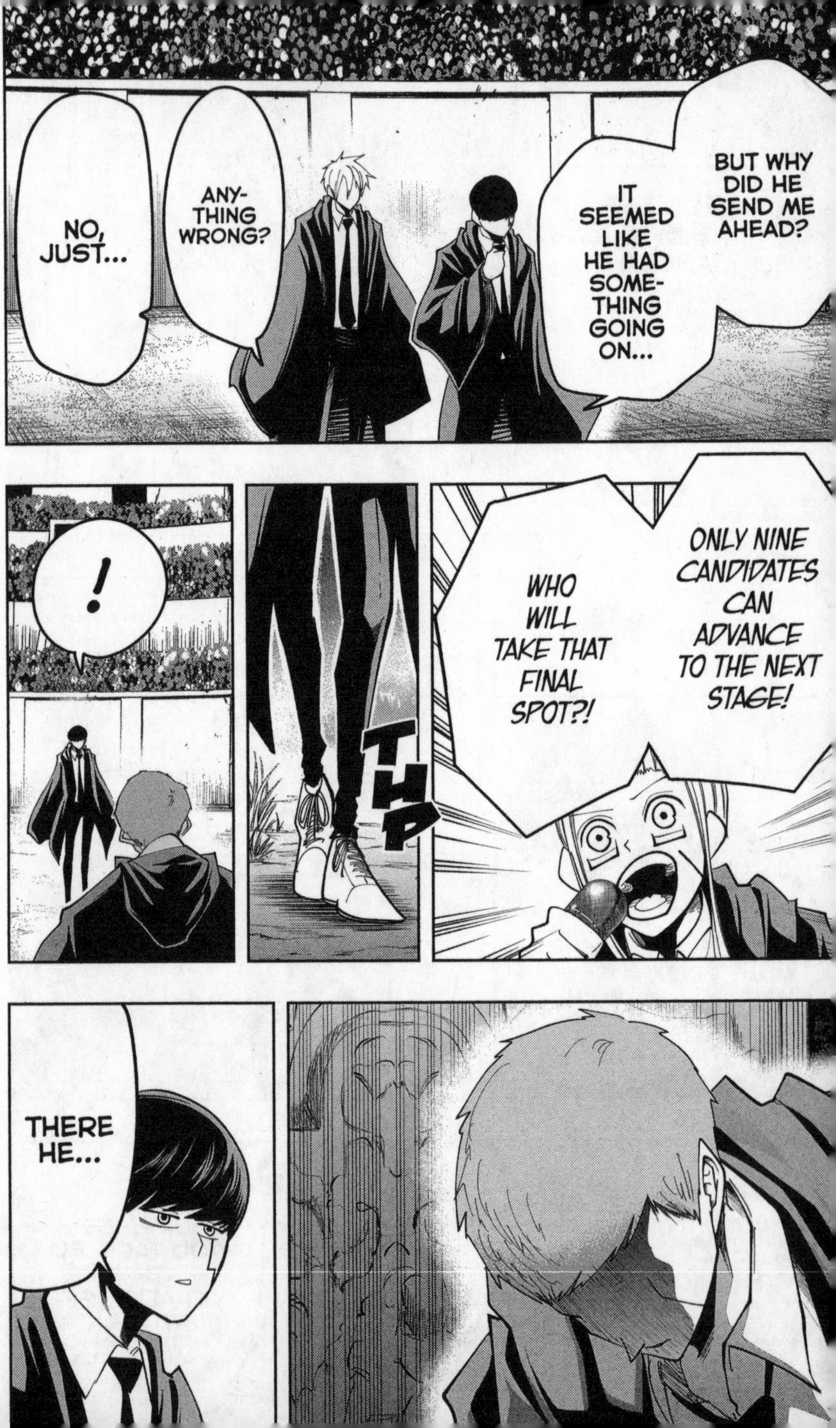
BUT WHY DID HE SEND ME AHEAD?
IT SEEMED LIKE HE HAD SOME-THING GOING ON...
ANY-THING WRONG?
NO, JUST...
ONLY NINE CANDIDATES CAN ADVANCE TO THE NEXT STAGE!
WHO WILL TAKE THAT FINAL SPOT?!
THP
!
THERE HE...

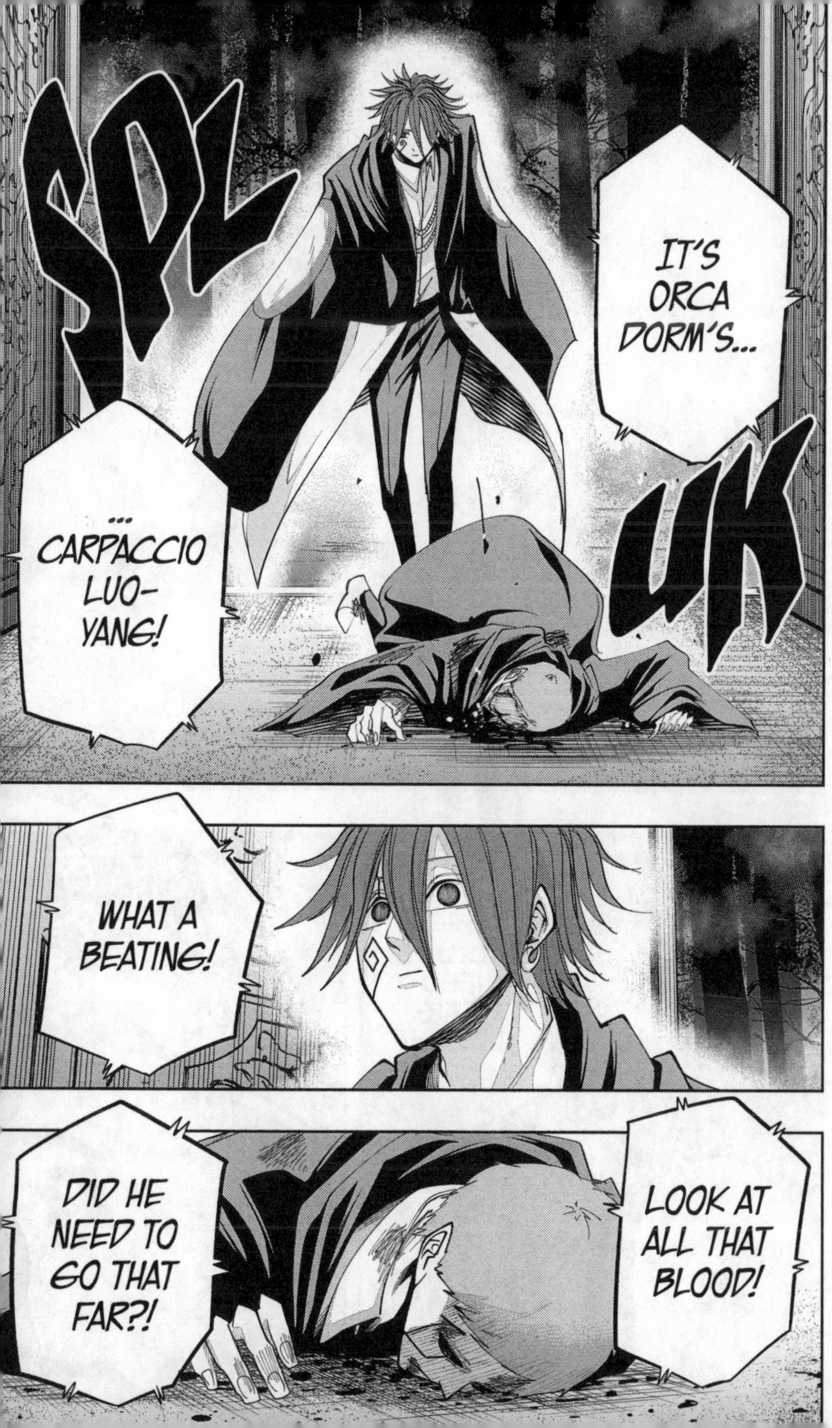
IT'S ORCA DORM'S...
SPL
UK
...CARPACCIO LUO-YANG!
WHAT A BEATING!
LOOK AT ALL THAT BLOOD!
DID HE NEED TO GO THAT FAR?!

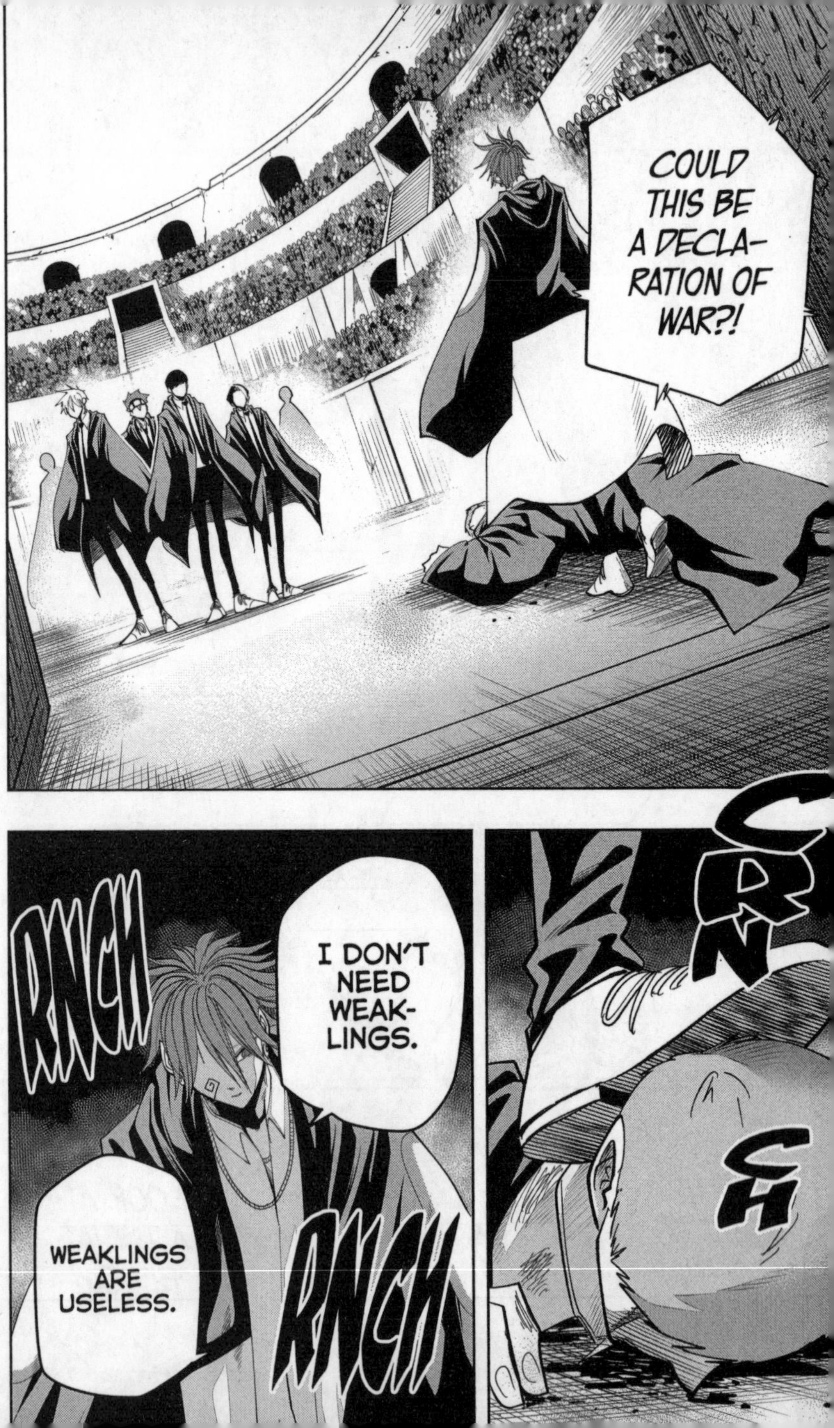
COULD THIS BE A DECLARATION OF WAR?!
CRN
CH
I DON'T NEED WEAKLINGS.
RNCH
RNCH
WEAKLINGS ARE USELESS.

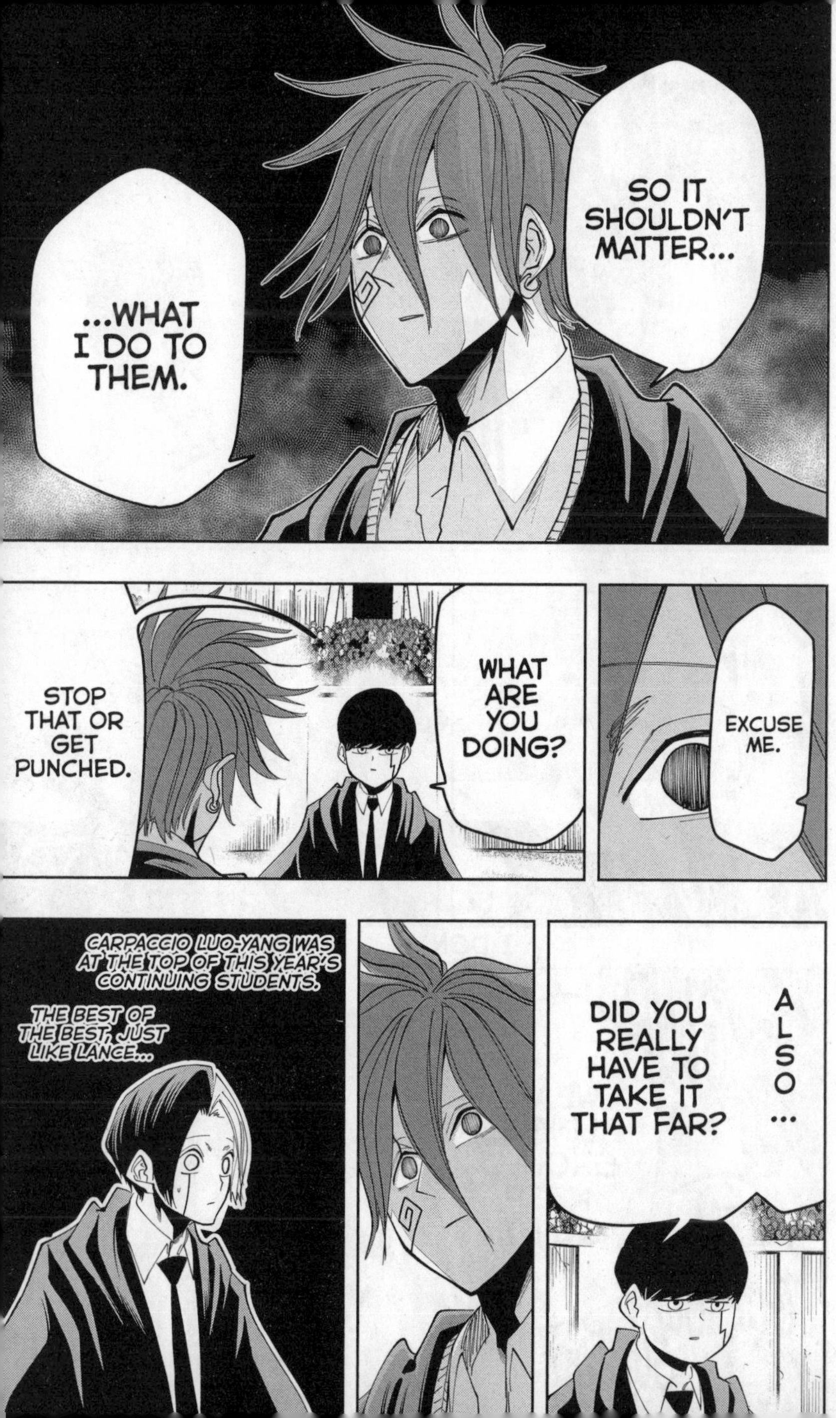
SO IT SHOULDN'T MATTER...
...WHAT I DO TO THEM.
EXCUSE ME.
WHAT ARE YOU DOING?
STOP THAT OR GET PUNCHED.
ALSO...
DID YOU REALLY HAVE TO TAKE IT THAT FAR?
CARPACCIO LUO-YANG WAS AT THE TOP OF THIS YEAR'S CONTINUING STUDENTS.
THE BEST OF THE BEST, JUST LIKE LANCE...

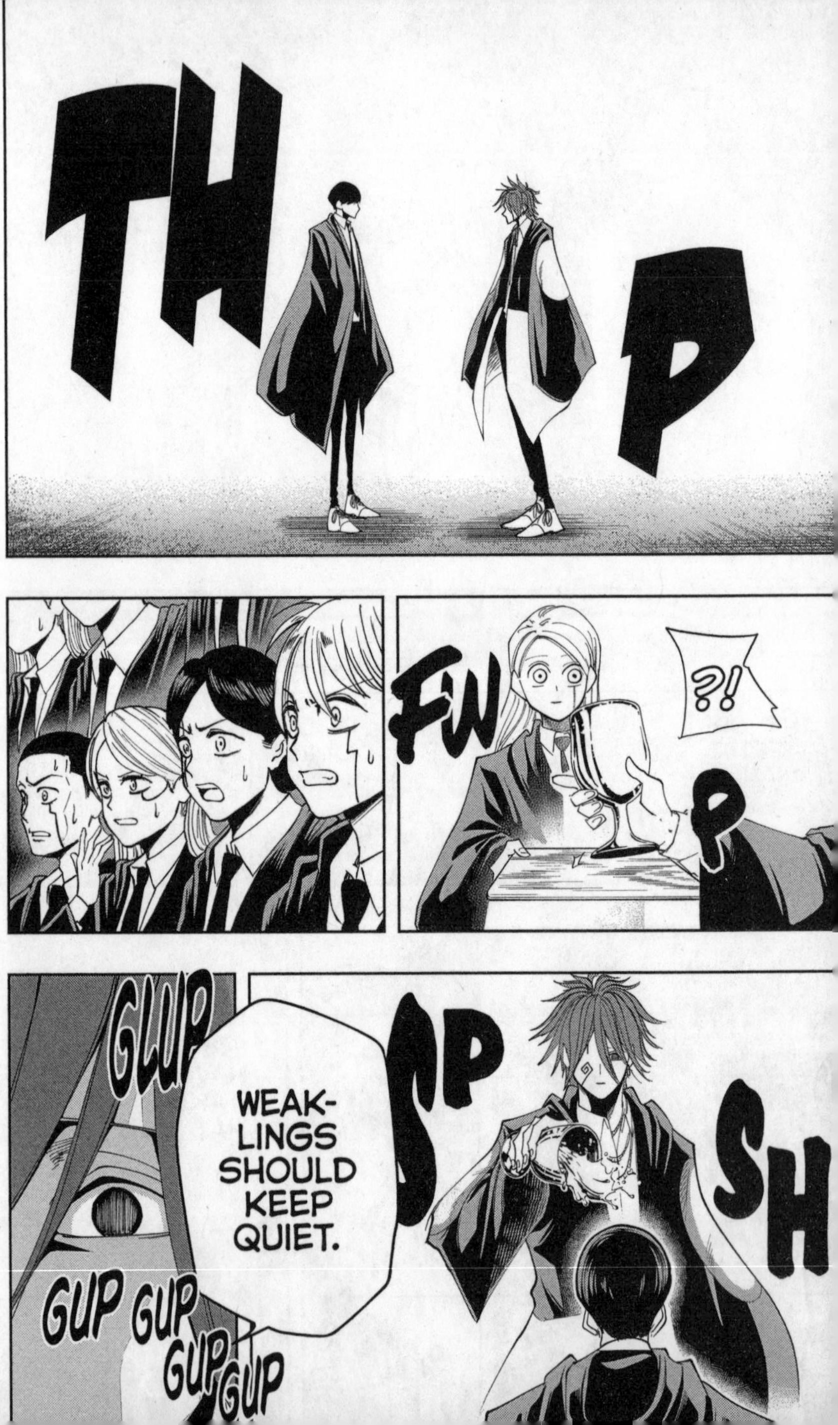
TH
P
FW
P
?!
SP
S
SH
WEAK-
LINGS
SHOULD
KEEP
QUIET.
GLUP
GUP GUP
GUP GUP

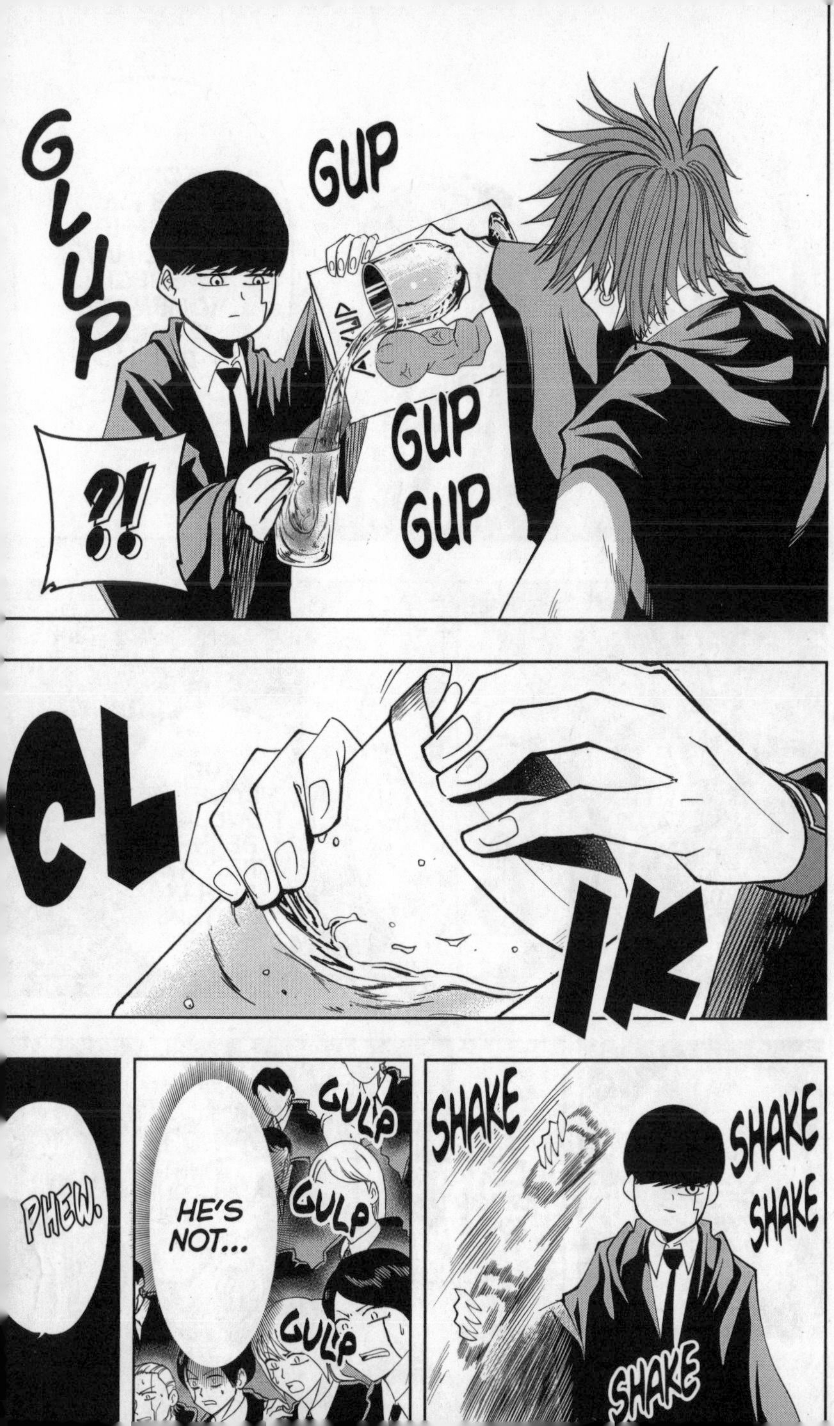
GUP
GUP GUP
GLUP
?!!
CL
IK
SHAKE
SHAKE
SHAKE
SHAKE
GULP
GULP
GULP
HE'S NOT...
PHEW.

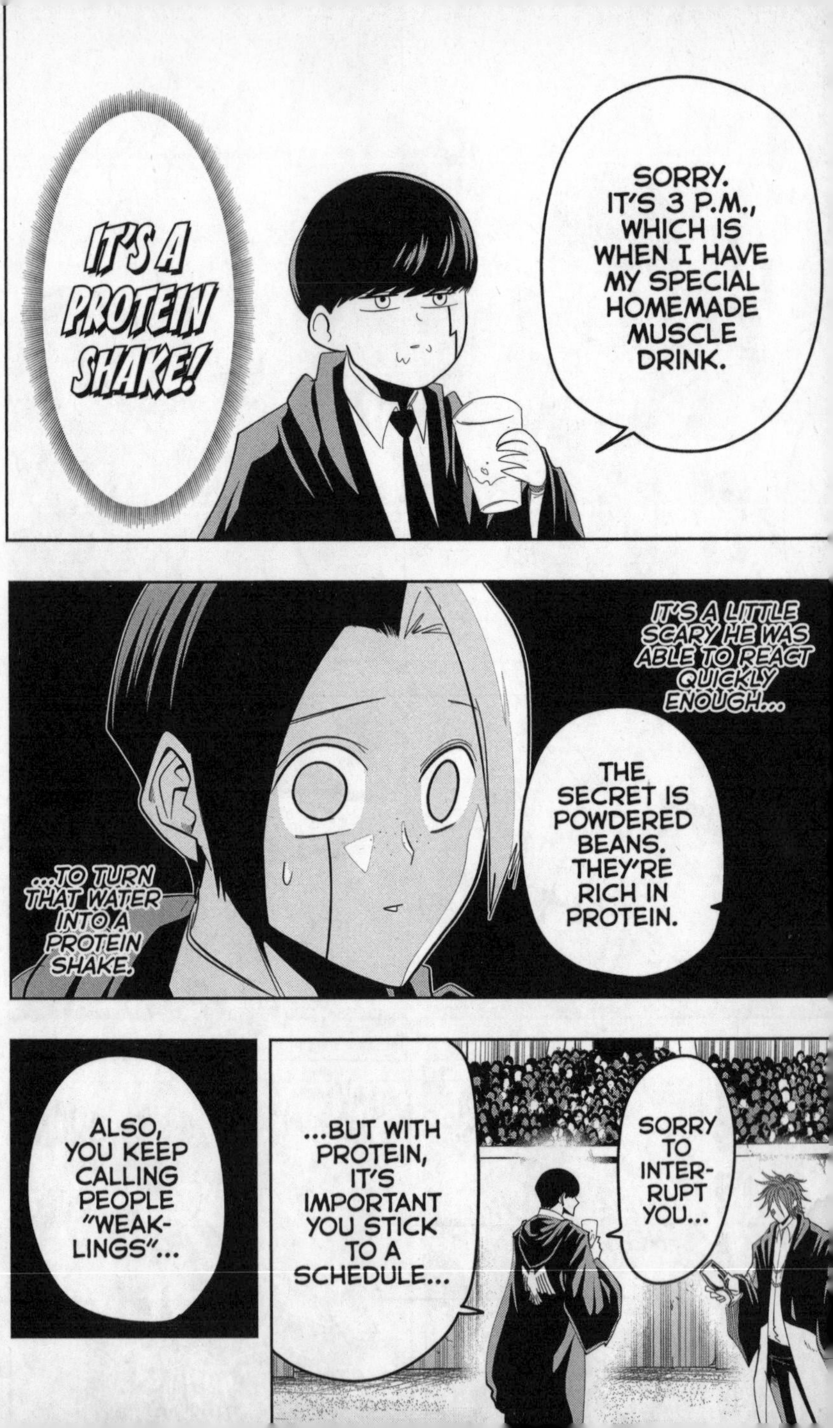
SORRY. IT'S 3 P.M., WHICH IS WHEN I HAVE MY SPECIAL HOMEMADE MUSCLE DRINK.
IT'S A PROTEIN SHAKE!
IT'S A LITTLE SCARY HE WAS ABLE TO REACT QUICKLY ENOUGH...
THE SECRET IS POWDERED BEANS. THEY'RE RICH IN PROTEIN.
...TO TURN THAT WATER INTO A PROTEIN SHAKE.
SORRY TO INTER-RUPT YOU...
...BUT WITH PROTEIN, IT'S IMPORTANT YOU STICK TO A SCHEDULE...
ALSO, YOU KEEP CALLING PEOPLE "WEAK-LINGS"...

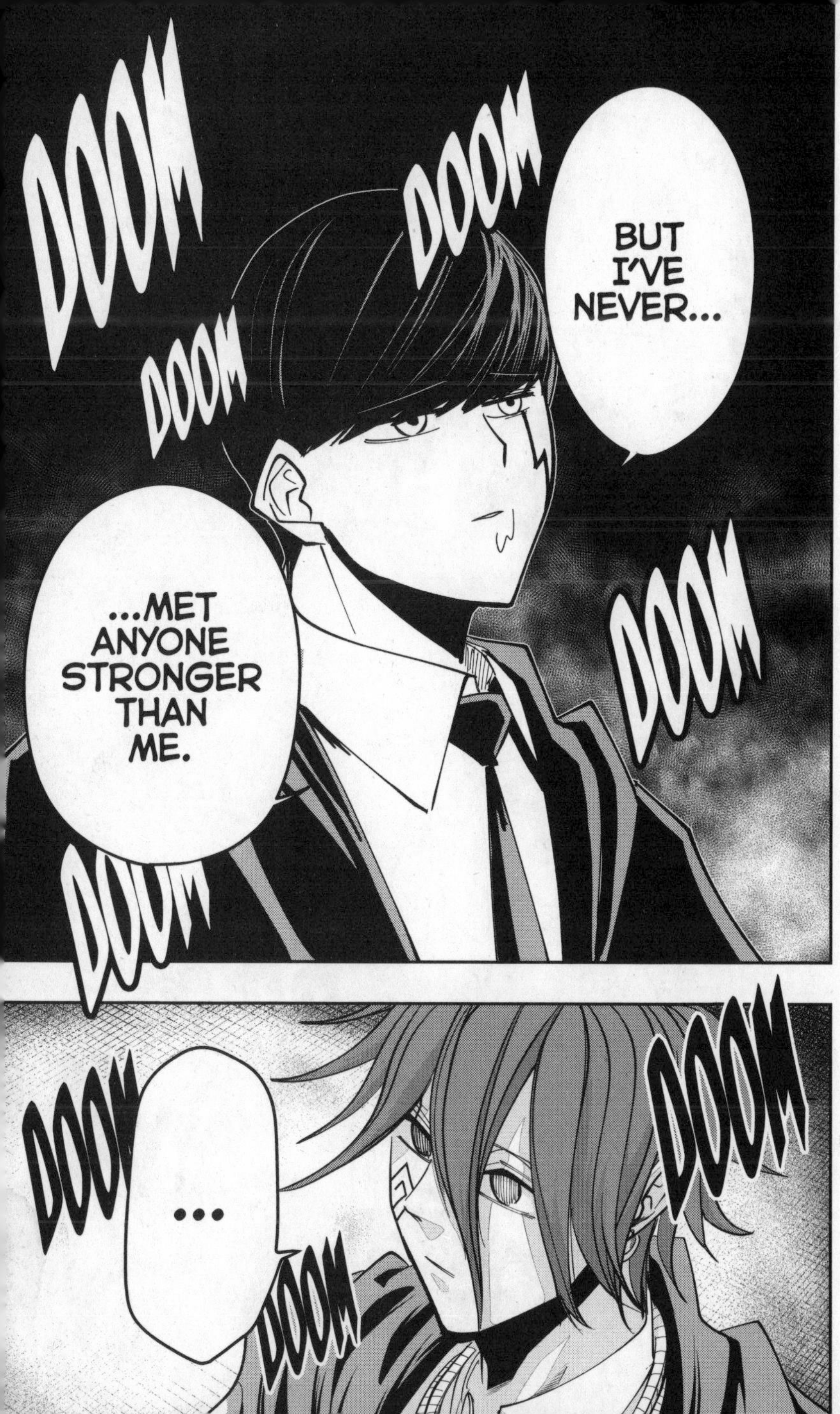
DOOM
BUT I'VE NEVER...
DOOM
DOOM
DOOM
...MET ANYONE STRONGER THAN ME.
DOOM
DOOM
DOOM
...
DOOM

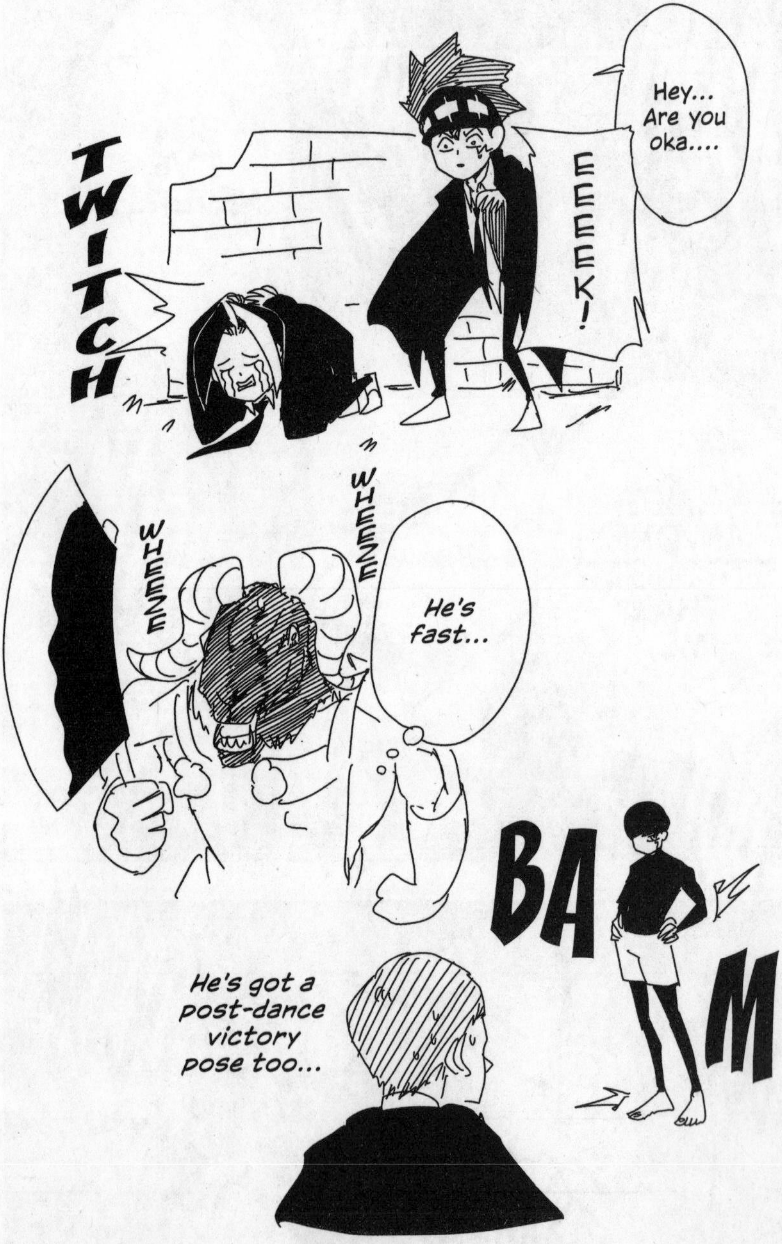
Hey... Are you oka....
EEEEK!
TWITCH
WHEEZE
He's fast...
WHEEZE
BAM
He's got a post-dance victory pose too...

CHAPTER 51:
MASH BURNEDEAD AND THE SHATTERED CRYSTAL

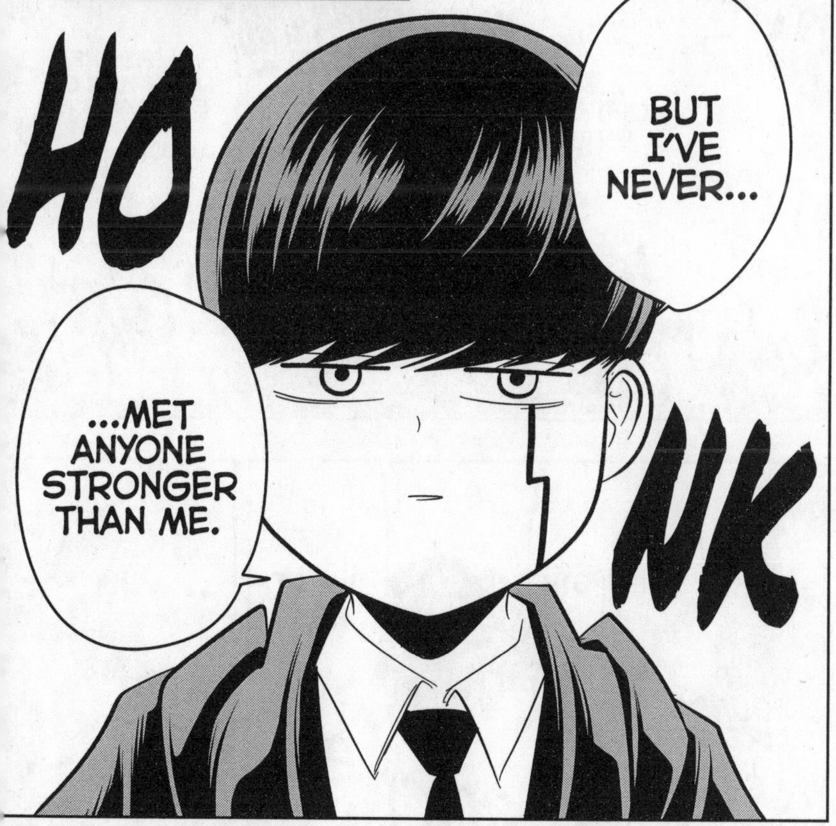
BUT I'VE NEVER...
...MET ANYONE STRONGER THAN ME.
HONK

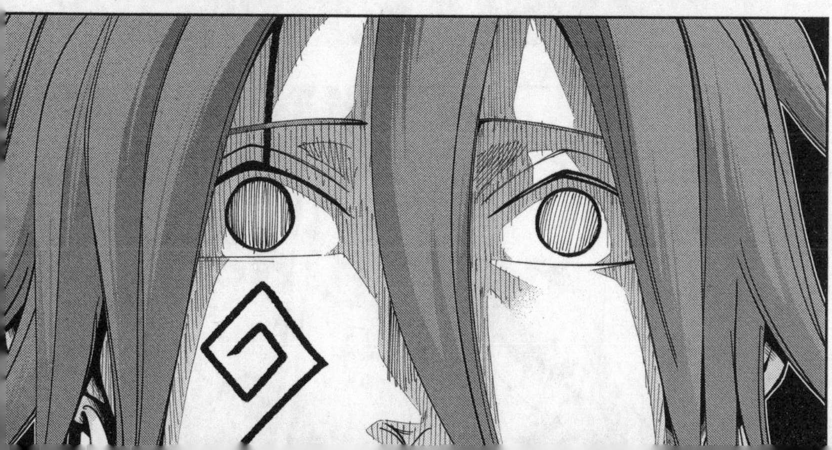

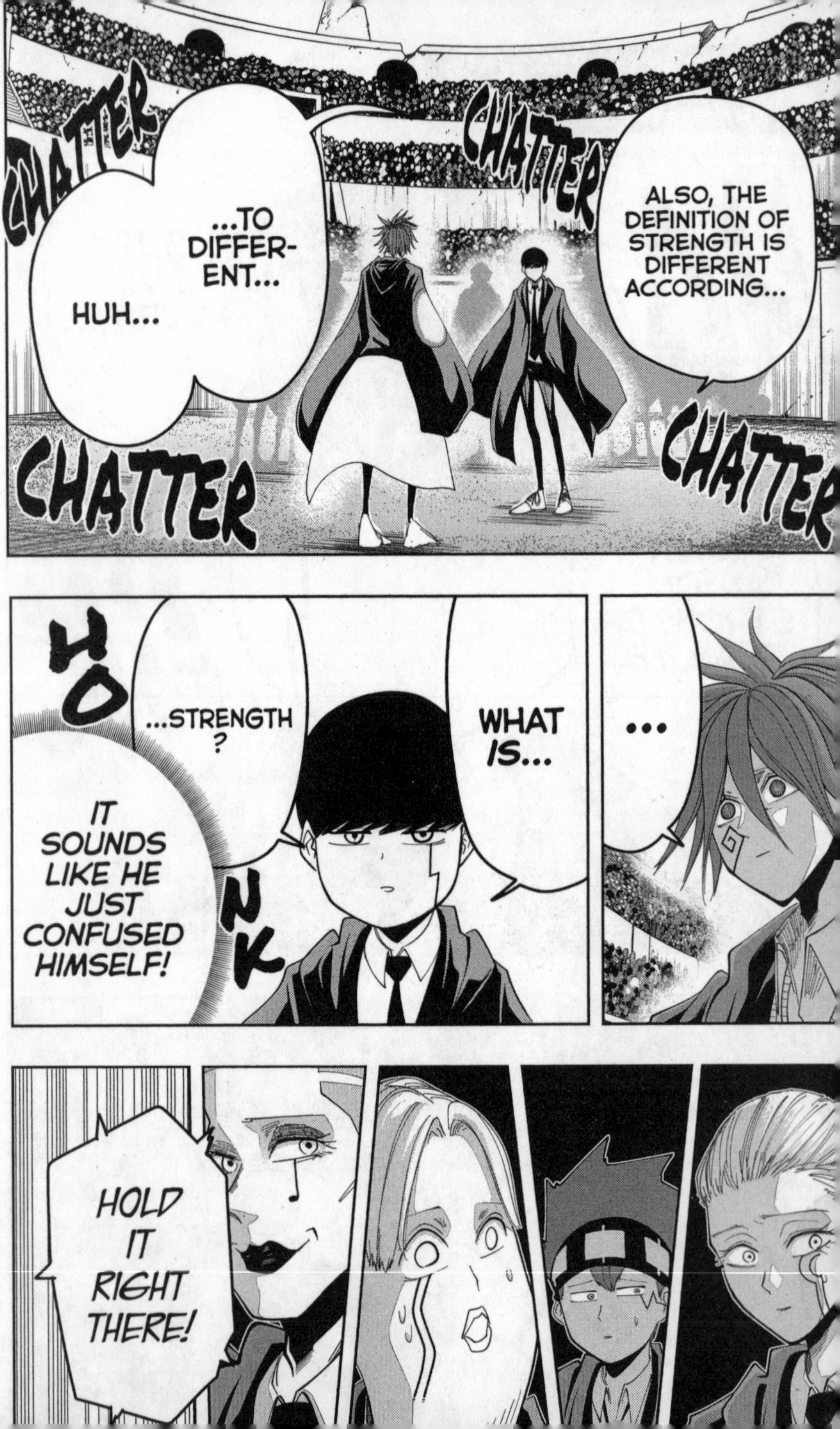
CHATTER
CHATTER
ALSO, THE DEFINITION OF STRENGTH IS DIFFERENT ACCORDING...
...TO DIFFERENT...
HUH...
CHATTER
CHATTER
...
WHAT IS...
...STRENGTH?
IT SOUNDS LIKE HE JUST CONFUSED HIMSELF!
HOLD IT RIGHT THERE!

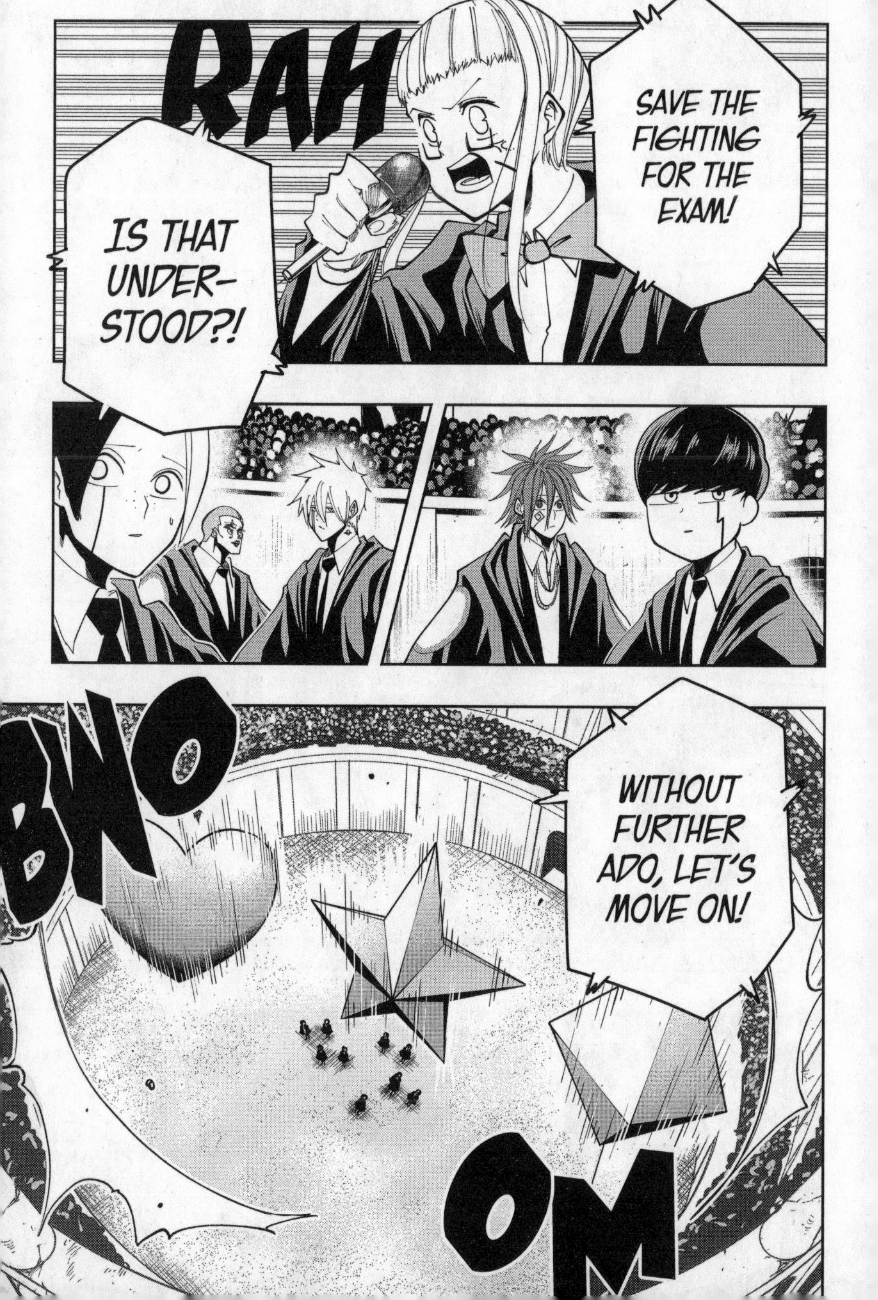
SAVE THE FIGHTING FOR THE EXAM!
RAH
IS THAT UNDER-STOOD?!
WITHOUT FURTHER ADO, LET'S MOVE ON!
BWO
OM

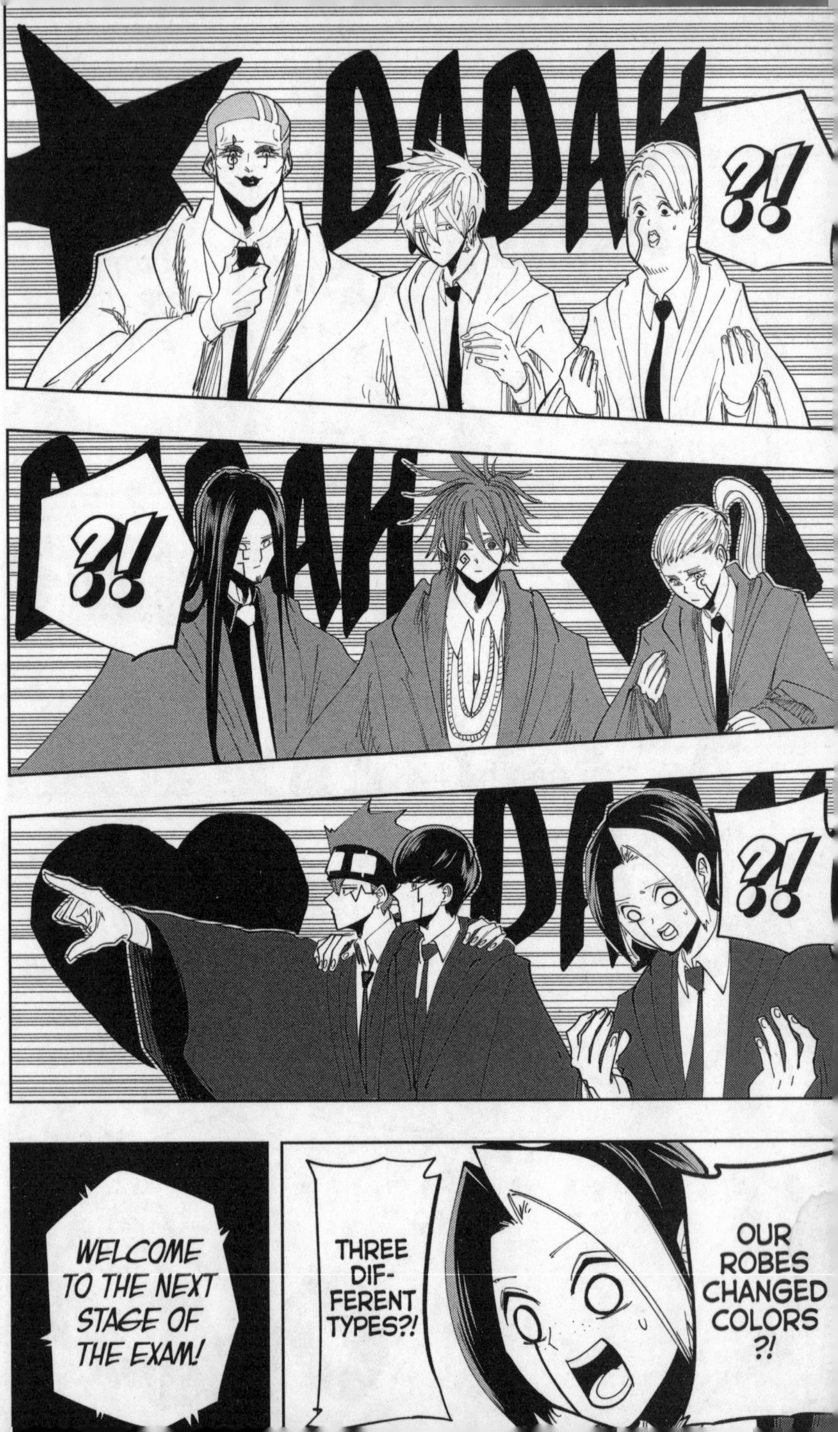
?!
DADAK
?!
?!
OUR ROBES CHANGED COLORS?!
THREE DIF-FERENT TYPES?!
WELCOME TO THE NEXT STAGE OF THE EXAM!

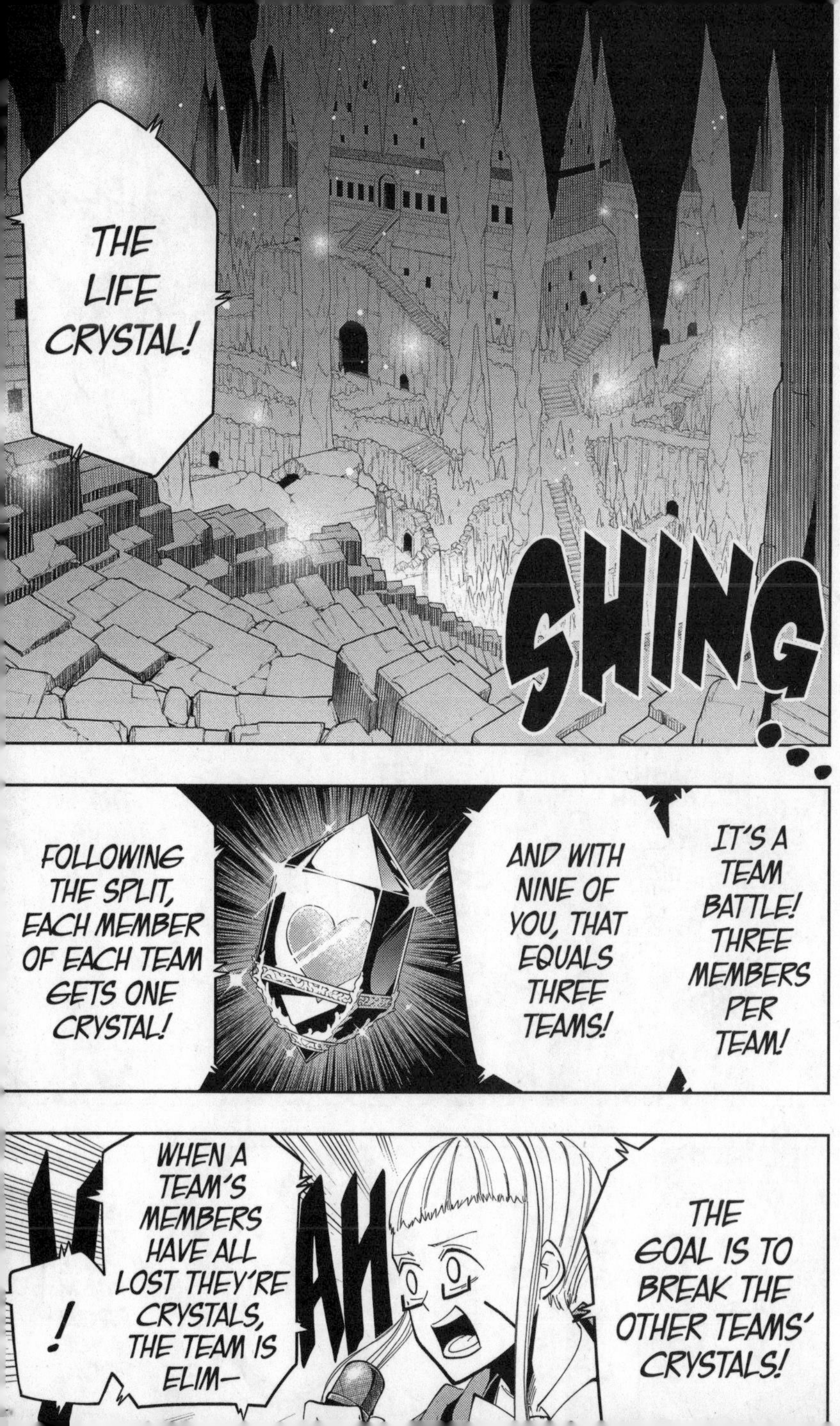
THE LIFE CRYSTAL!
SHING!
IT'S A TEAM BATTLE! THREE MEMBERS PER TEAM!
AND WITH NINE OF YOU, THAT EQUALS THREE TEAMS!
FOLLOWING THE SPLIT, EACH MEMBER OF EACH TEAM GETS ONE CRYSTAL!
THE GOAL IS TO BREAK THE OTHER TEAMS' CRYSTALS!
WHEN A TEAM'S MEMBERS HAVE ALL LOST THEY'RE CRYSTALS, THE TEAM IS ELIM-
!

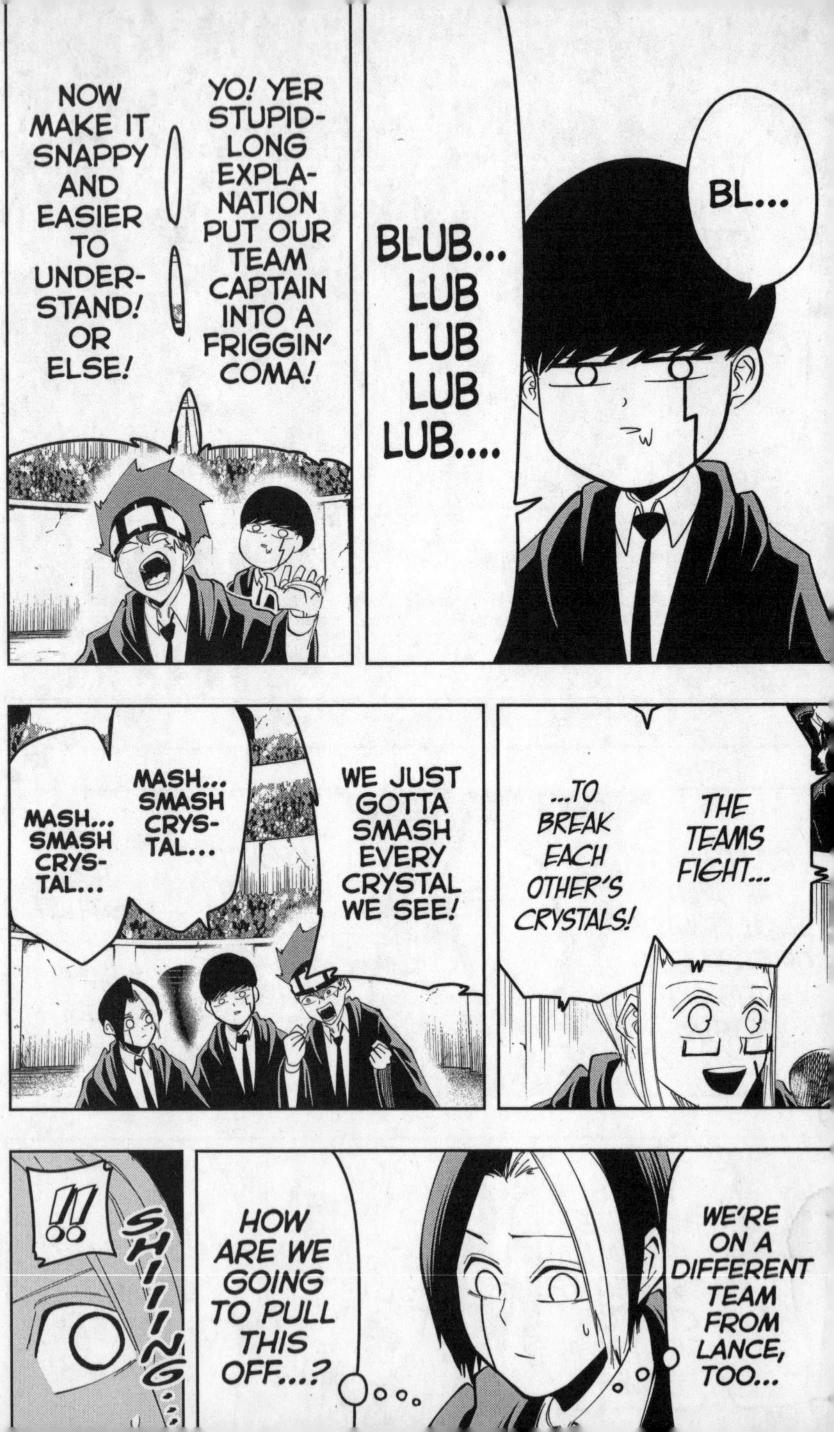
BL...
BLUB... LUB LUB LUB LUB....
YO! YER STUPID-LONG EXPLANATION PUT OUR TEAM CAPTAIN INTO A FRIGGIN' COMA!
NOW MAKE IT SNAPPY AND EASIER TO UNDERSTAND! OR ELSE!
THE TEAMS FIGHT...
...TO BREAK EACH OTHER'S CRYSTALS!
WE JUST GOTTA SMASH EVERY CRYSTAL WE SEE!
MASH... SMASH CRYS-TAL...
MASH... SMASH CRYS-TAL...
WE'RE ON A DIFFERENT TEAM FROM LANCE, TOO...
HOW ARE WE GOING TO PULL THIS OFF...?
!!
SHIIING...

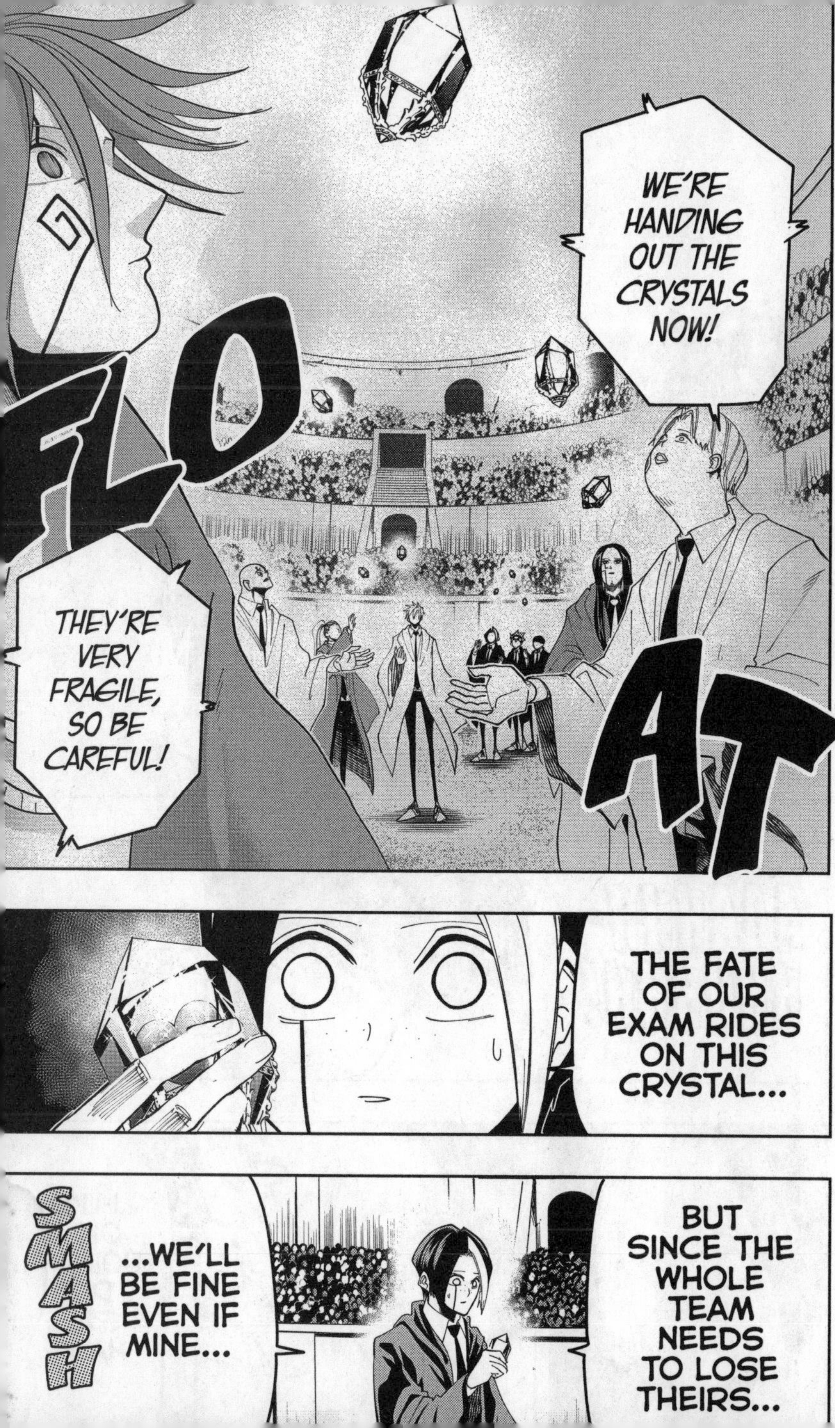
WE'RE HANDING OUT THE CRYSTALS NOW!
FLOAT
THEY'RE VERY FRAGILE, SO BE CAREFUL!
THE FATE OF OUR EXAM RIDES ON THIS CRYSTAL...
BUT SINCE THE WHOLE TEAM NEEDS TO LOSE THEIRS...
...WE'LL BE FINE EVEN IF MINE...
SMASH

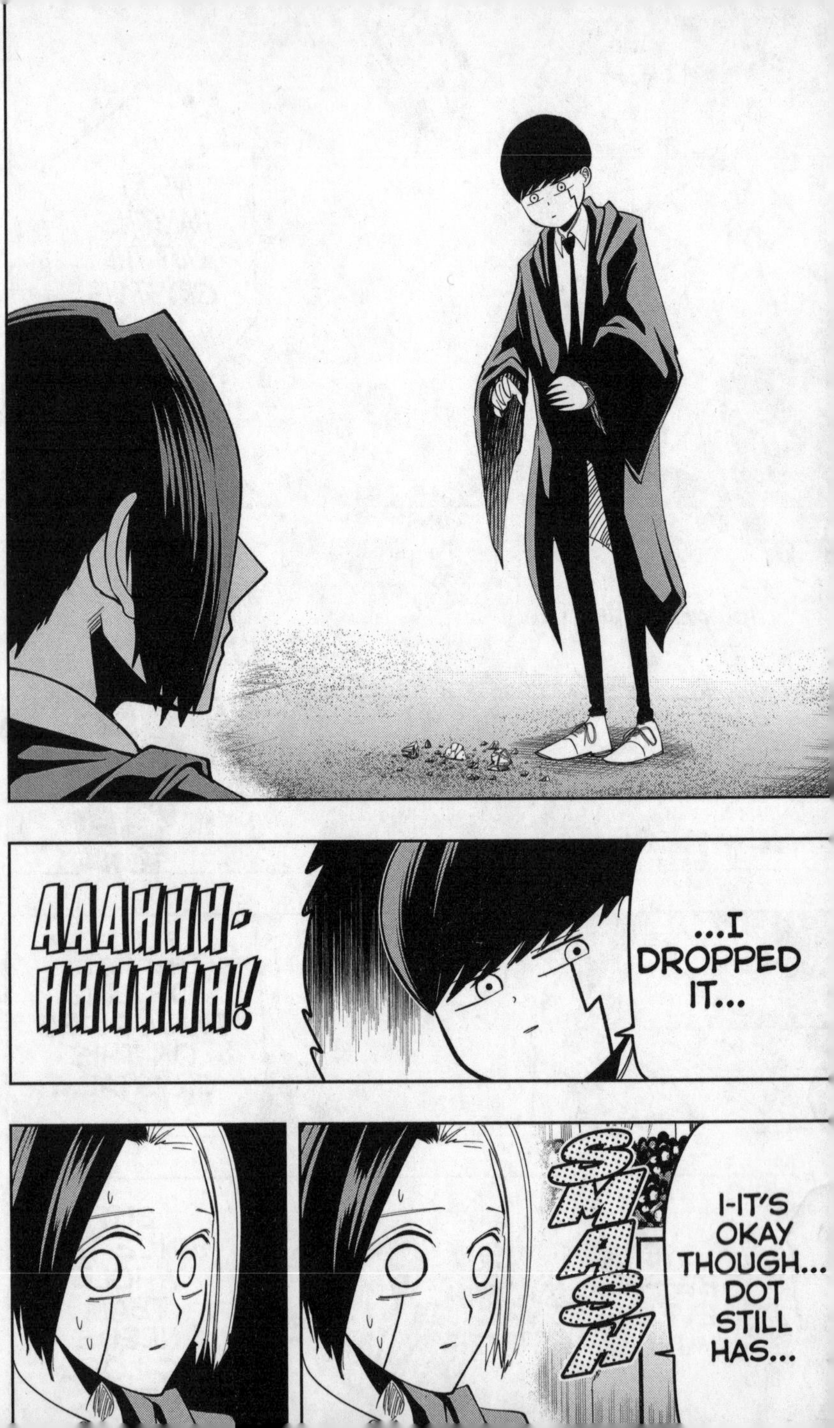
...I DROPPED IT...
AAAHHH-HHHHHH!
I-IT'S OKAY THOUGH... DOT STILL HAS...
SMASH

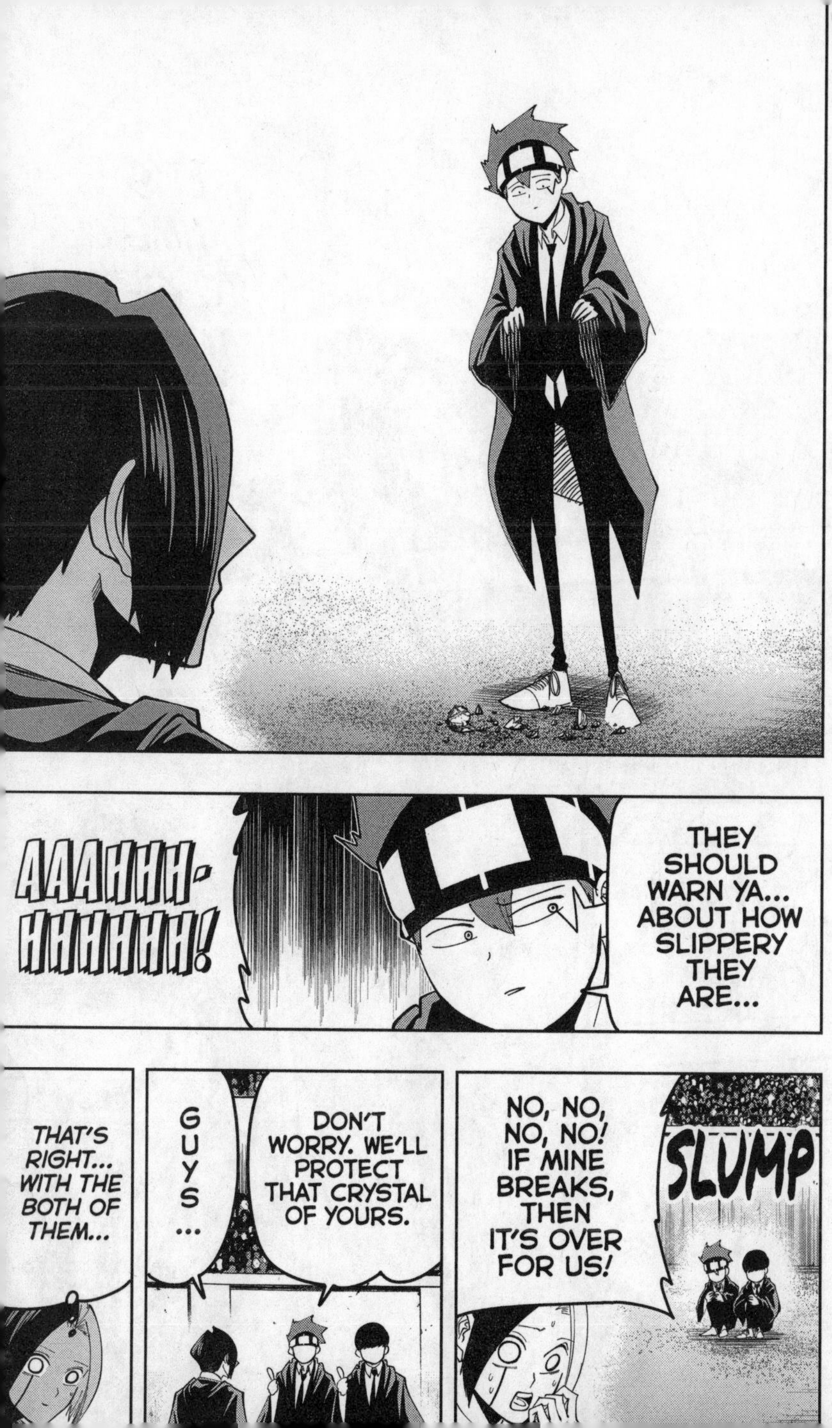
THEY SHOULD WARN YA... ABOUT HOW SLIPPERY THEY ARE...
AAAHHH-HHHHHH!
SLUMP
NO, NO, NO, NO! IF MINE BREAKS, THEN IT'S OVER FOR US!
DON'T WORRY. WE'LL PROTECT THAT CRYSTAL OF YOURS.
GUYS...
THAT'S RIGHT... WITH THE BOTH OF THEM...

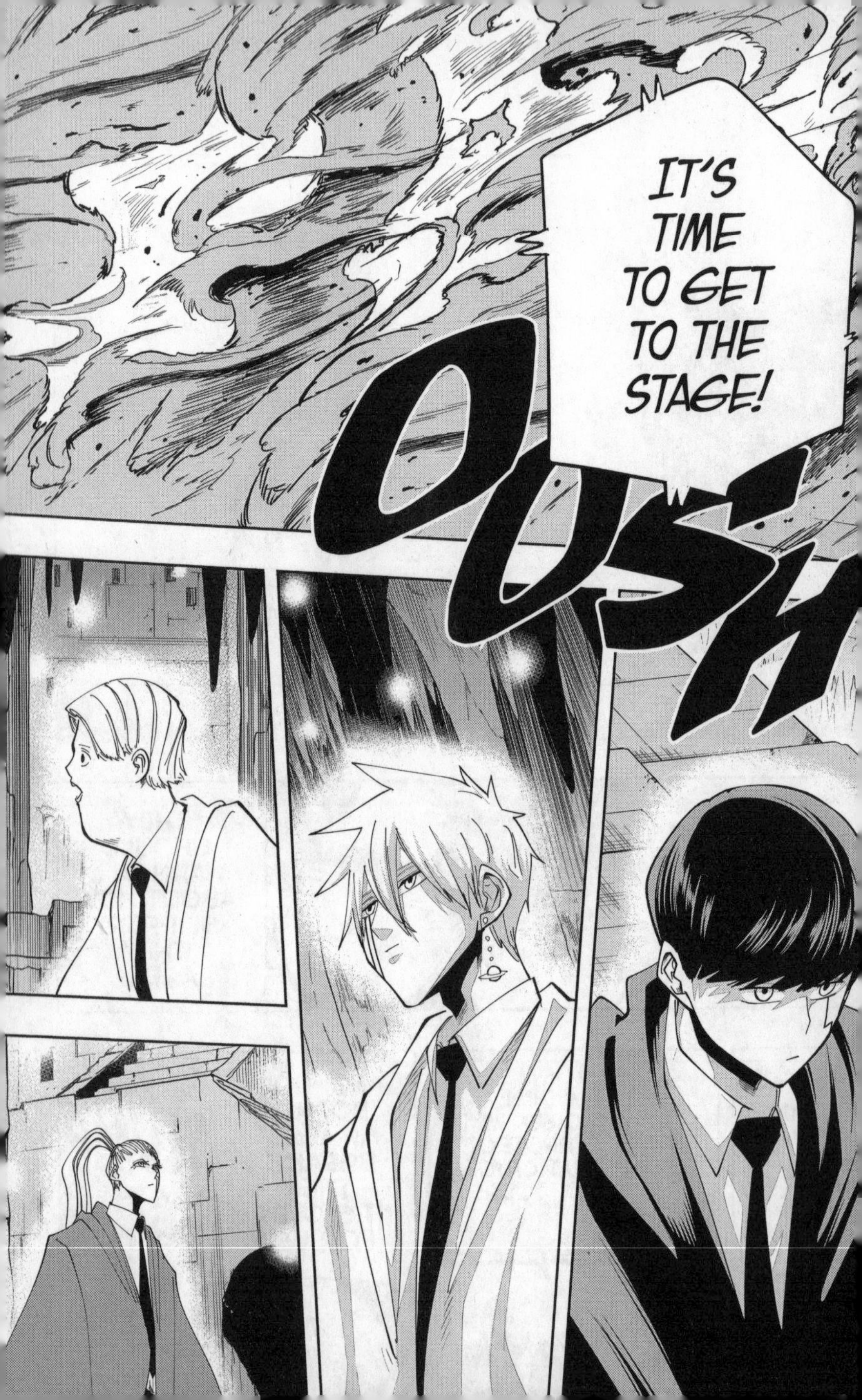
IT'S TIME TO GET TO THE STAGE!
OOSH

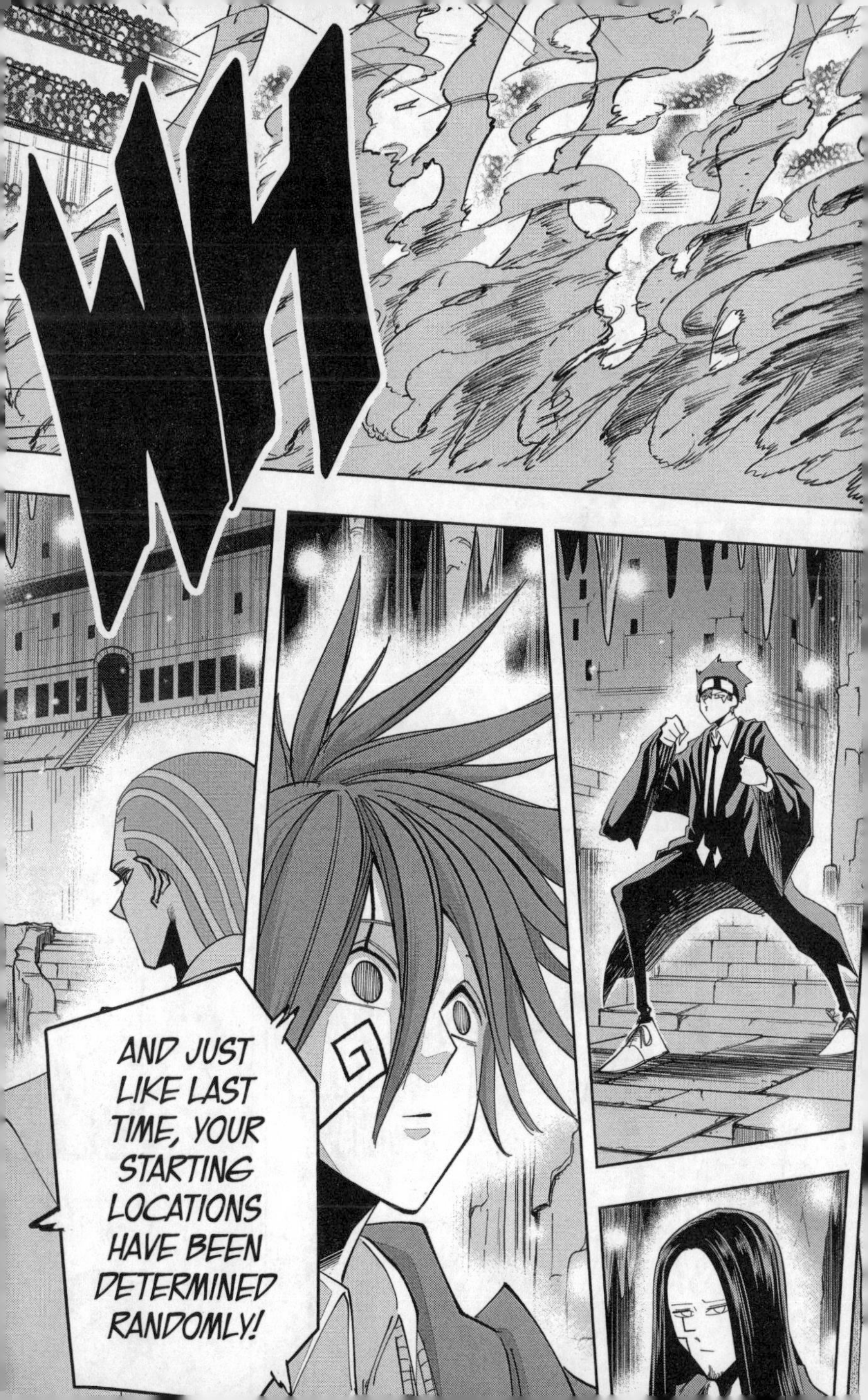

AND JUST LIKE LAST TIME, YOUR STARTING LOCATIONS HAVE BEEN DETERMINED RANDOMLY!

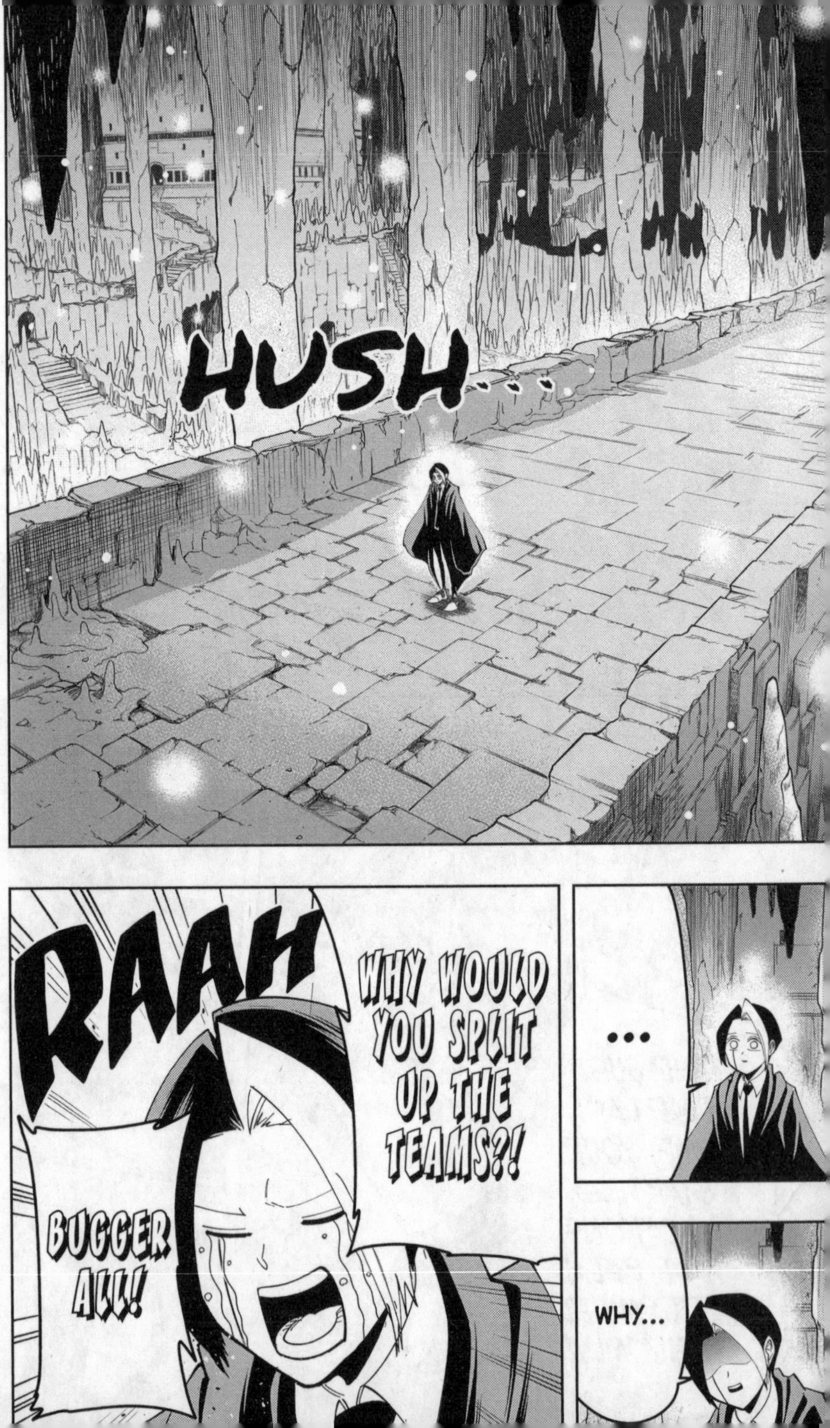
HUSH...
...
WHY...
RAAH
WHY WOULD YOU SPLIT UP THE TEAMS?!
BUGGER ALL!

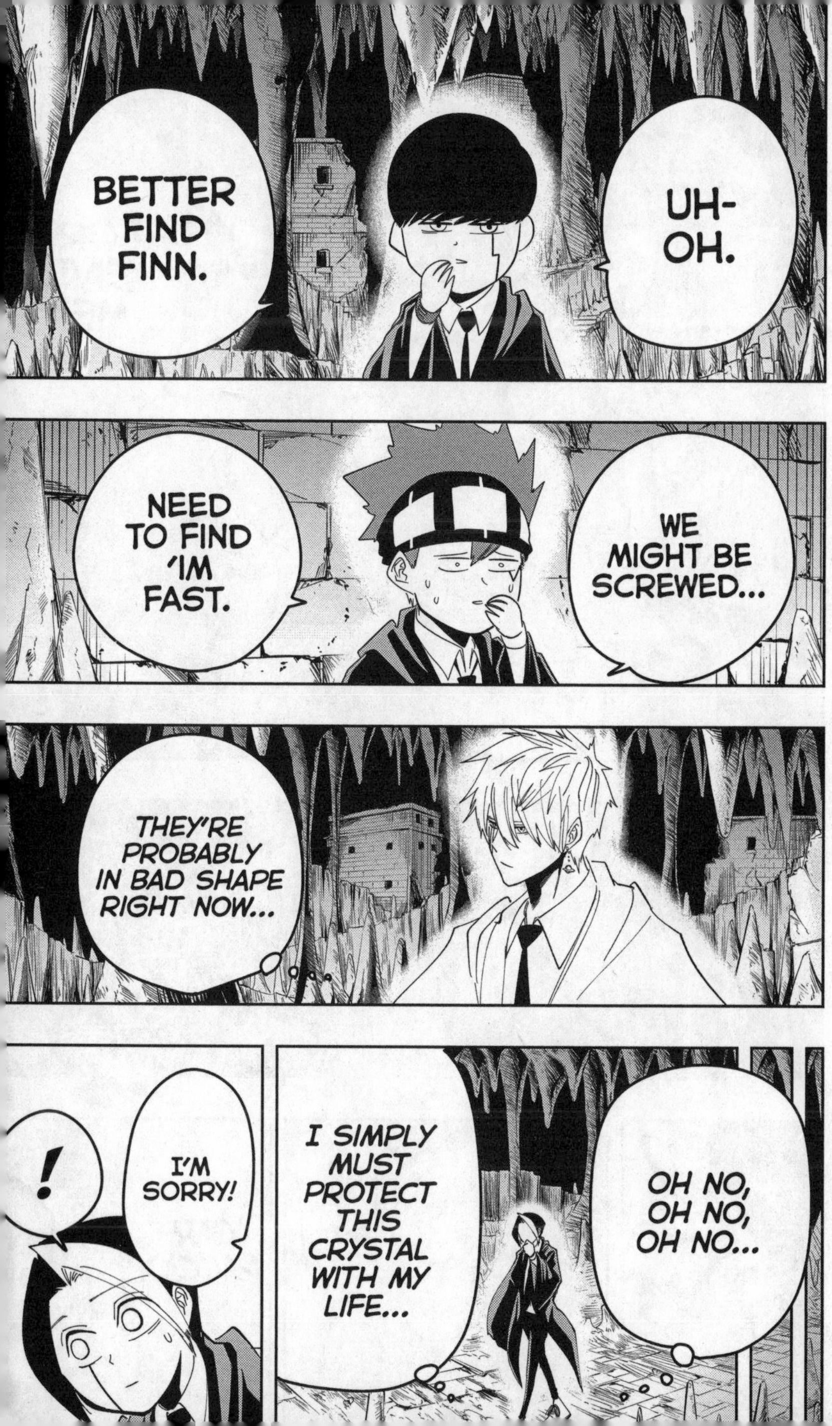
UH-OH.
BETTER FIND FINN.
WE MIGHT BE SCREWED...
NEED TO FIND 'IM FAST.
THEY'RE PROBABLY IN BAD SHAPE RIGHT NOW...
OH NO, OH NO, OH NO...
I SIMPLY MUST PROTECT THIS CRYSTAL WITH MY LIFE...
I'M SORRY!
!

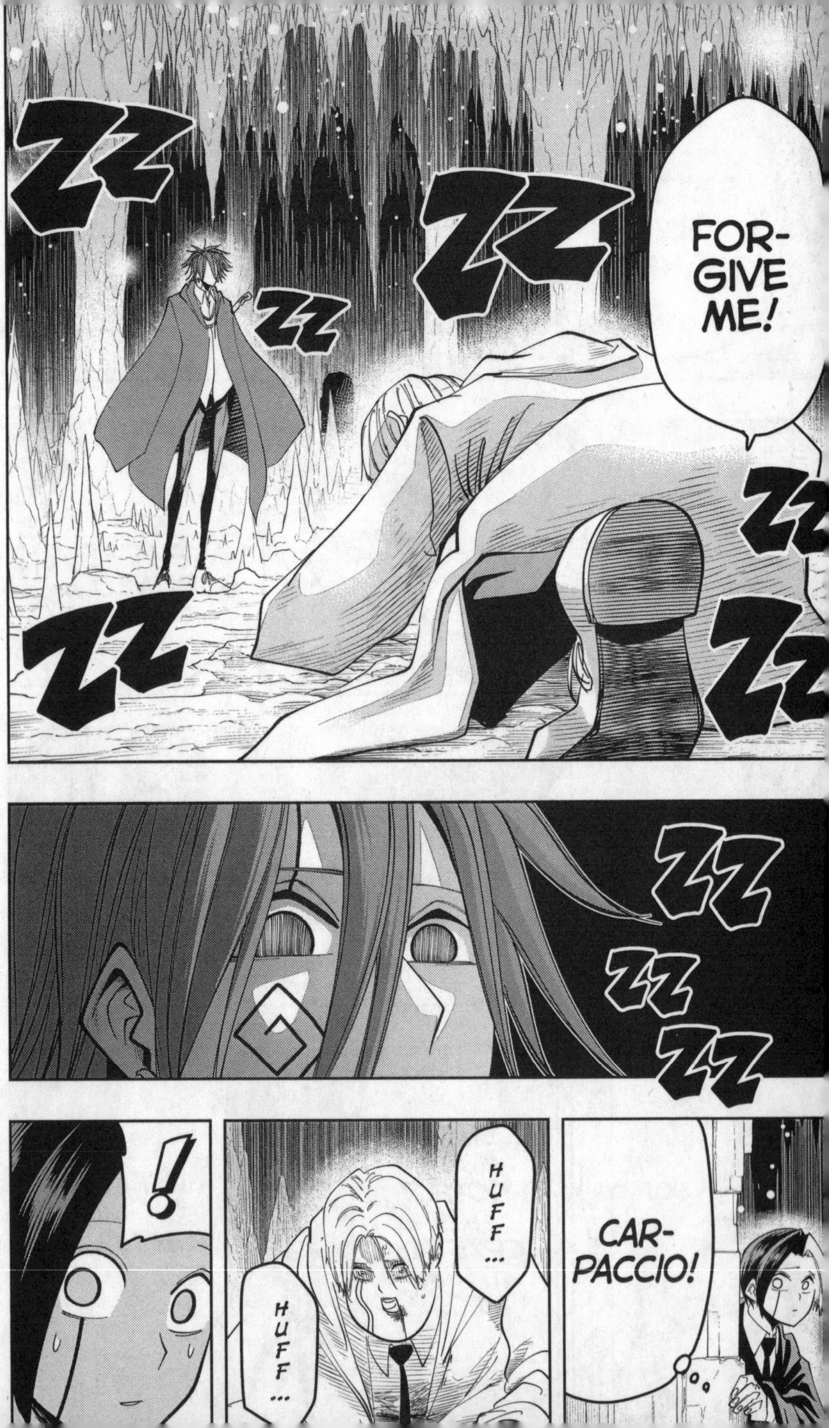
FOR-
GIVE
ME!
ZZ
ZZ
ZZ
ZZ
ZZ
ZZ
ZZ
ZZ
ZZ
ZZ
CAR-
PACCIO!
HUFF...
HUFF...
!

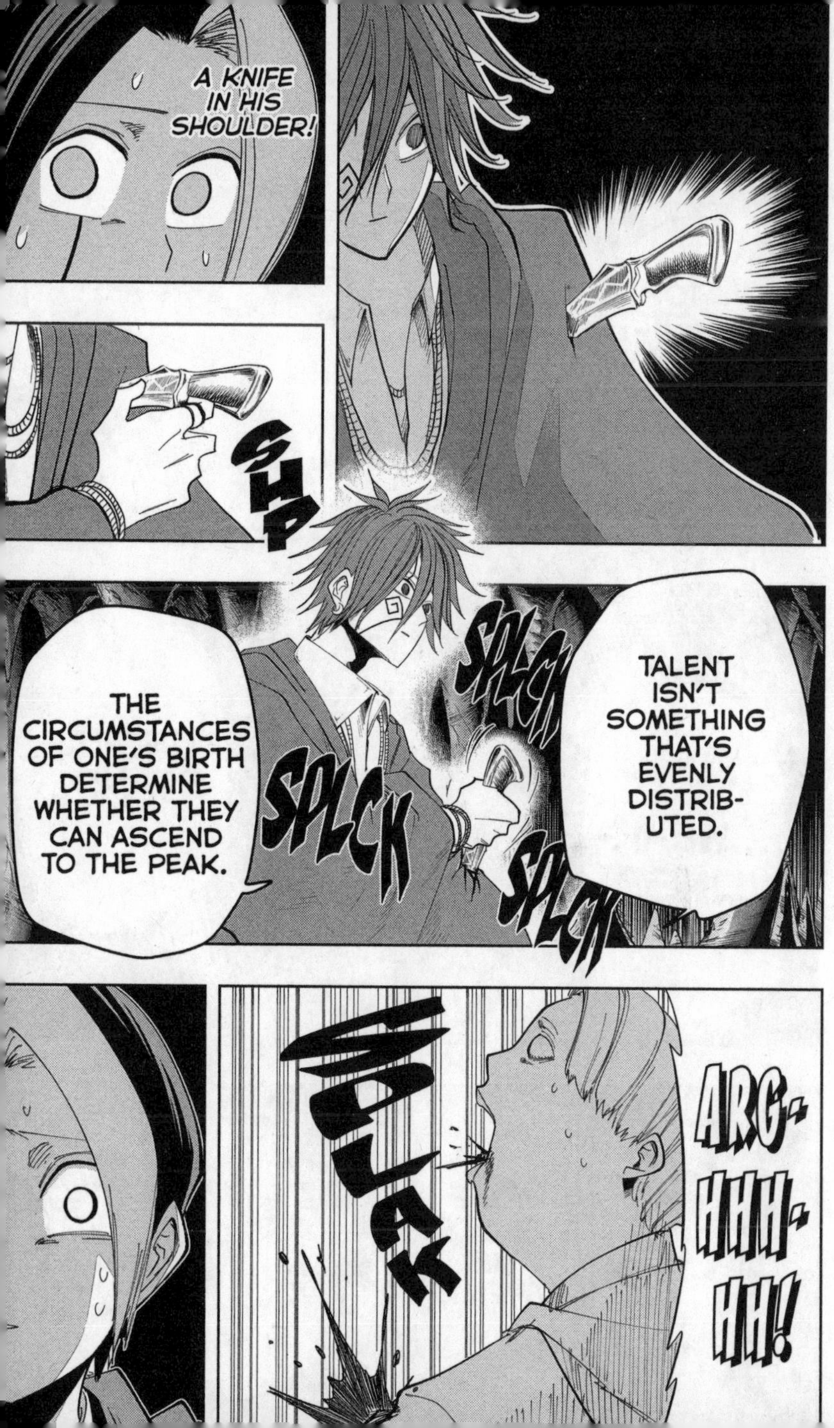
A KNIFE IN HIS SHOULDER!
SHP
TALENT ISN'T SOMETHING THAT'S EVENLY DISTRIB-UTED.
SPLCK
SPLCK
SPLCK
THE CIRCUMSTANCES OF ONE'S BIRTH DETERMINE WHETHER THEY CAN ASCEND TO THE PEAK.
ARG-HHH-HH!
SPLAK

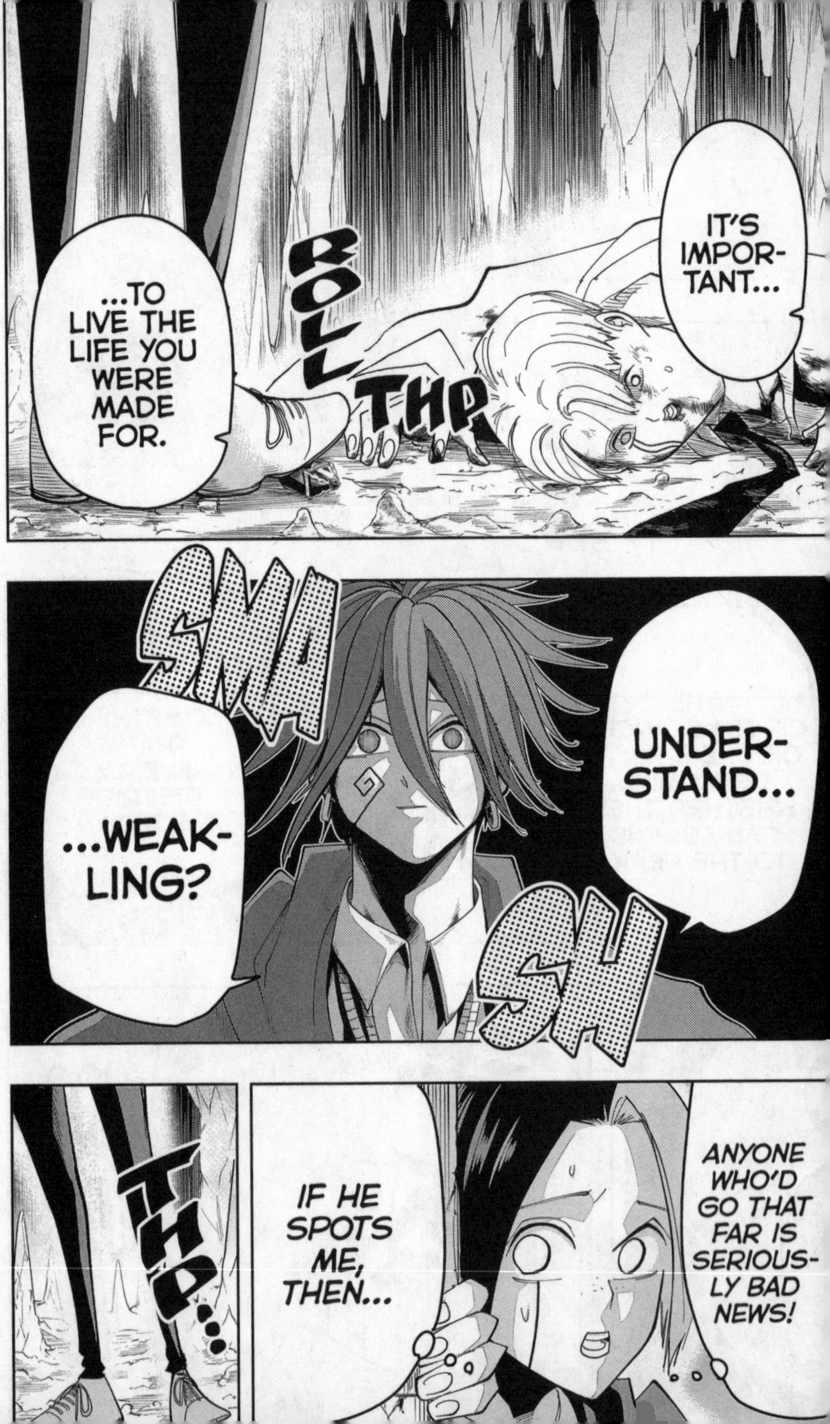
IT'S IMPORTANT...
ROLL
THP
...TO LIVE THE LIFE YOU WERE MADE FOR.
UNDERSTAND...
SMASH
...WEAKLING?
ANYONE WHO'D GO THAT FAR IS SERIOUSLY BAD NEWS!
IF HE SPOTS ME, THEN...
THP...

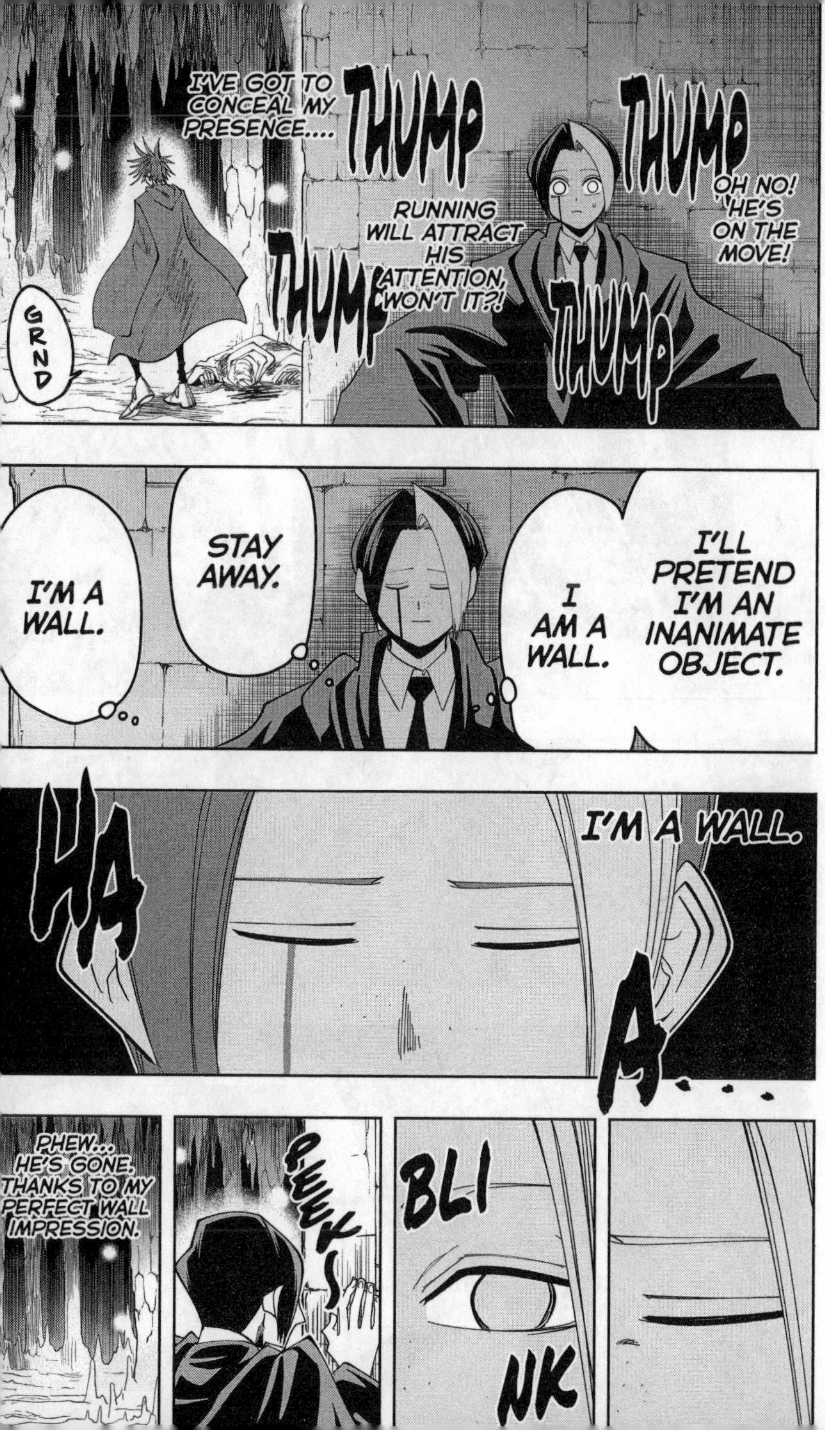
THUMP
THUMP
OH NO! HE'S ON THE MOVE!
RUNNING WILL ATTRACT HIS ATTENTION, WON'T IT?!
THUMP
THUMP
I'VE GOT TO CONCEAL MY PRESENCE....
GRND
I'LL PRETEND I'M AN INANIMATE OBJECT.
I AM A WALL.
STAY AWAY.
I'M A WALL.
I'M A WALL.
HA
A...
BLI
NK
PEEEKS
PHEW... HE'S GONE. THANKS TO MY PERFECT WALL IMPRESSION.

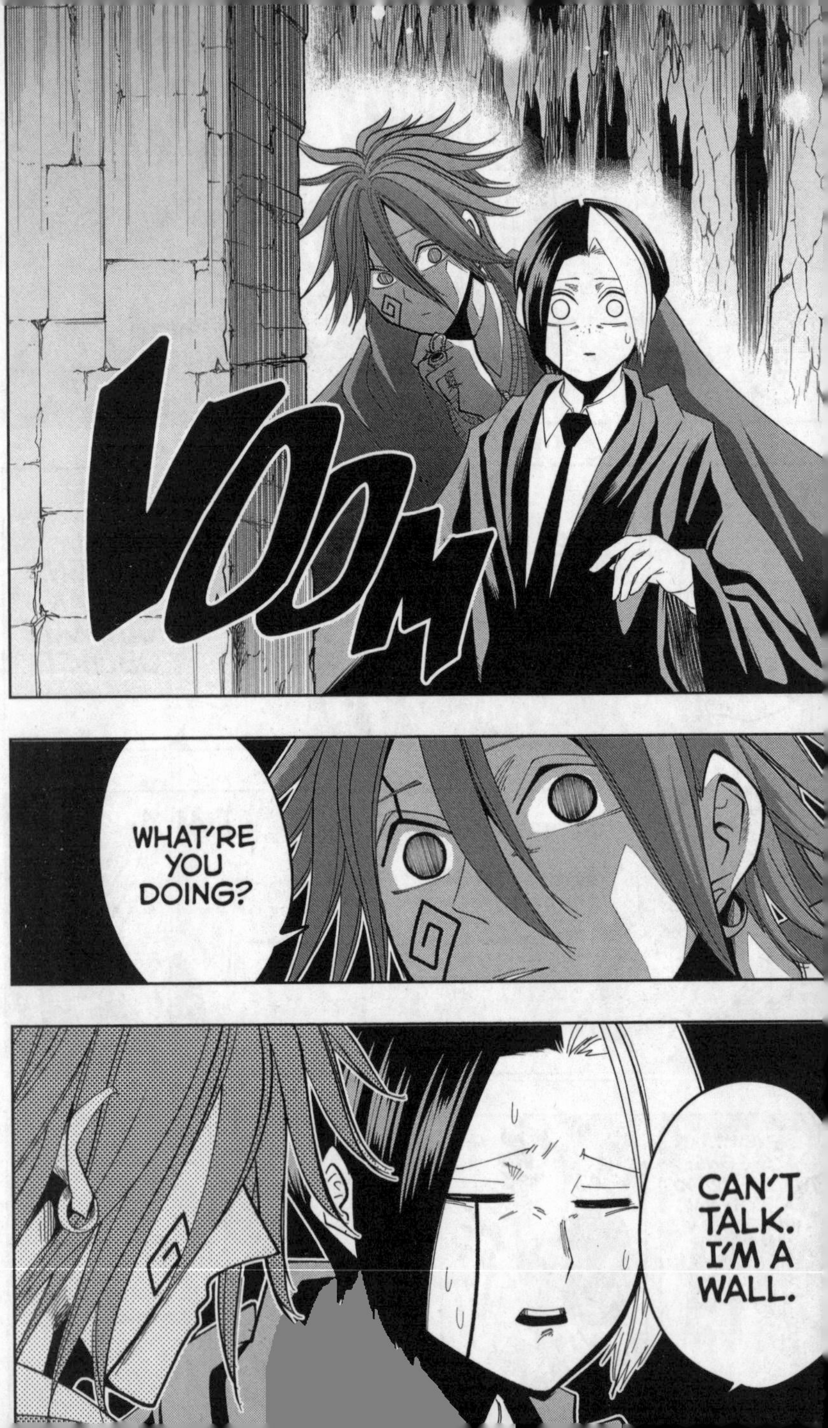
VOOM
WHAT'RE YOU DOING?
CAN'T TALK. I'M A WALL.

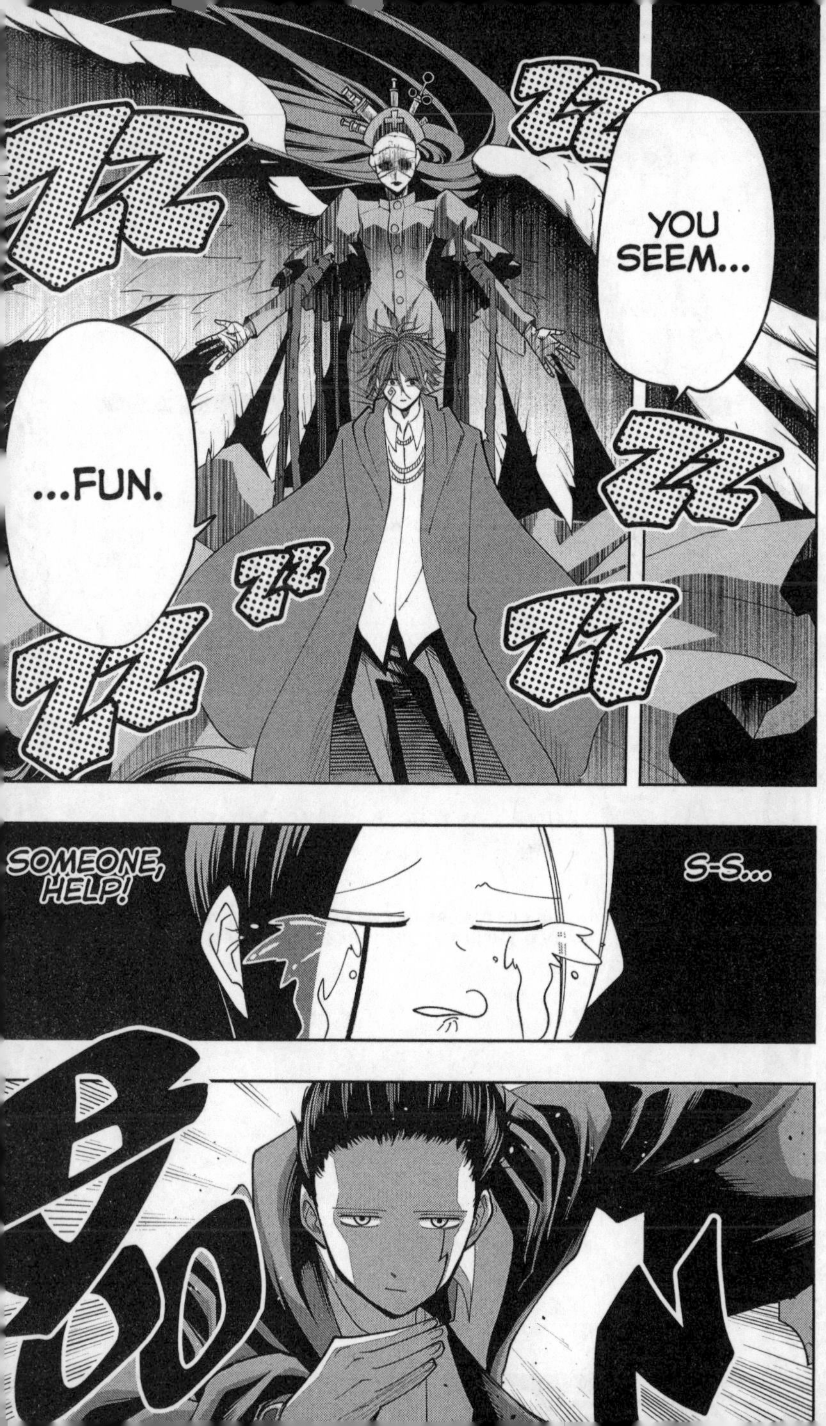
YOU SEEM...
...FUN.
S-S...
SOMEONE, HELP!

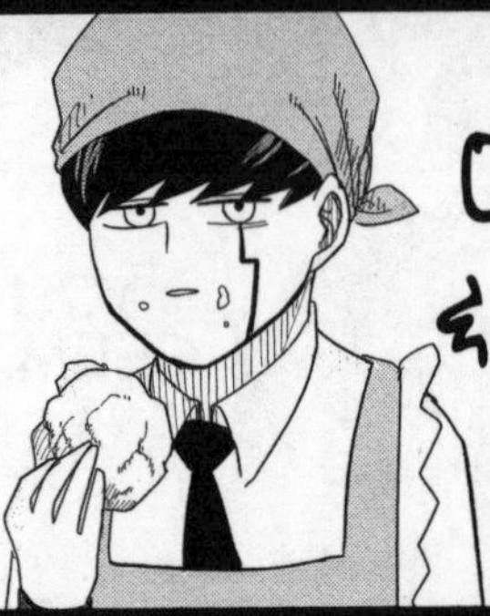

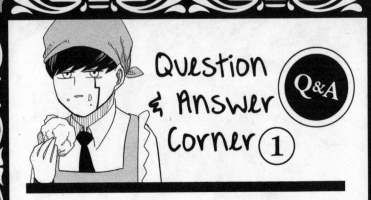

Question & Answer Corner ①

Q&A

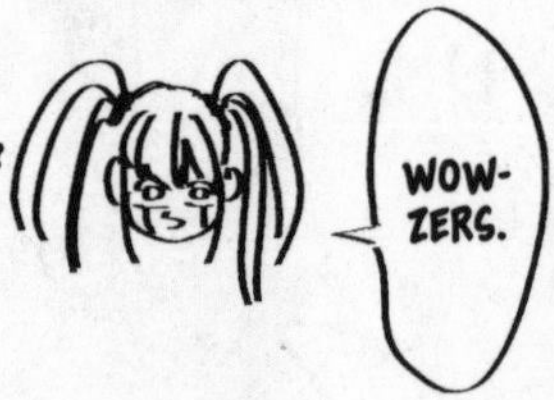
WOW-ZERS.

Q.1/ **WHAT'S LOVE'S FULL NAME? (FROM A READER)**

A.1/ Love Cute

Q.2/ **WHERE DOES MASH PICK UP HIS NEW MOVES FROM? (FROM A READER)**

A.2/ He envisions them in his head before bed.

Q.3/ **IF THE CAST WERE IN THE REAL WORLD, WHAT WOULD THEIR FUTURE JOBS BE? (FROM A READER)**

A.3/

Mash	Owner of a cream puff shop
Lance	Doctor
Finn	Civil servant
Lemon	Bookseller
Dot	Unpopular drummer

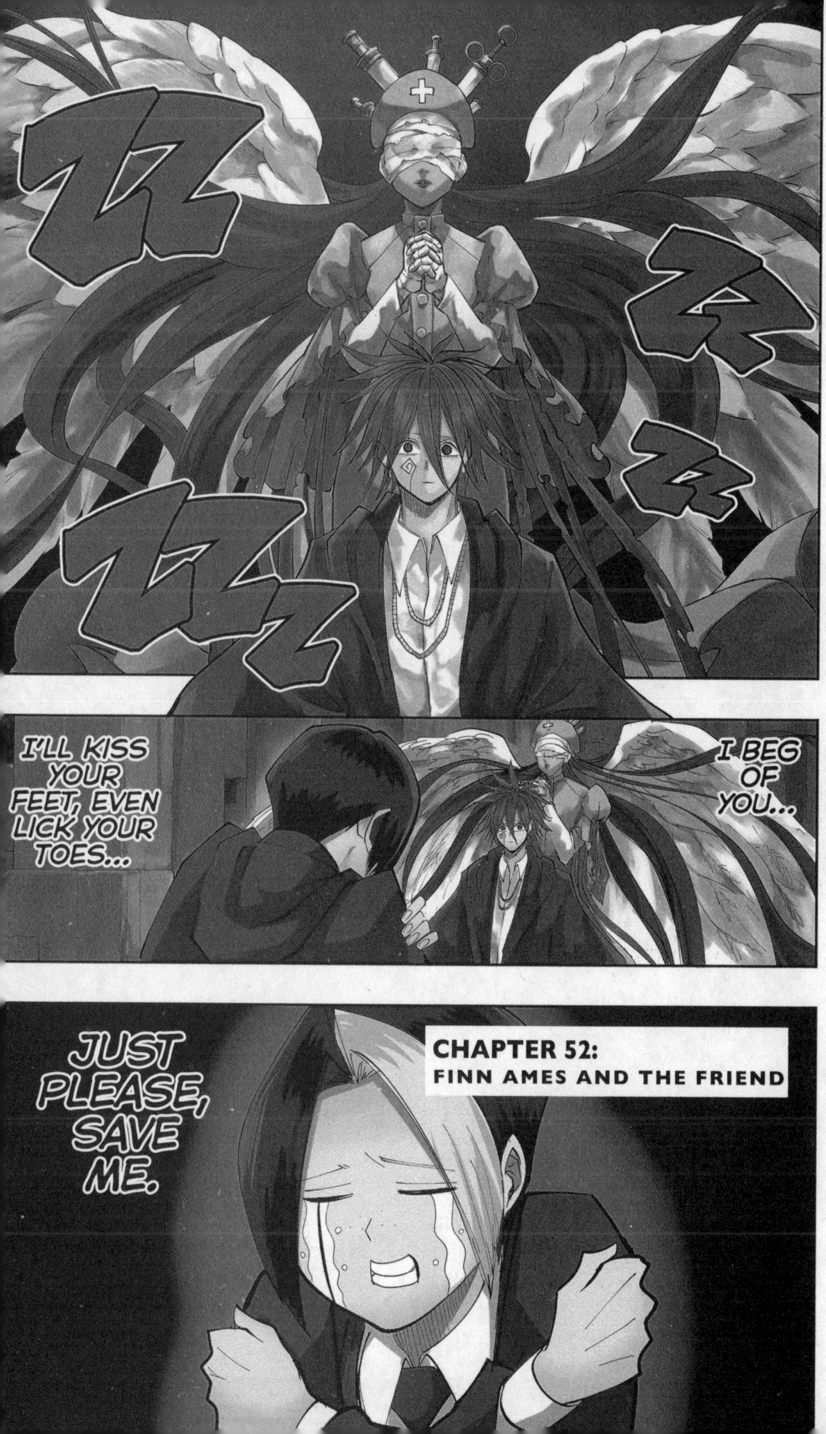
ZZ
ZZ
ZZ
ZZZZ
I BEG OF YOU...
I'LL KISS YOUR FEET, EVEN LICK YOUR TOES...
CHAPTER 52:
FINN AMES AND THE FRIEND
JUST PLEASE, SAVE ME.

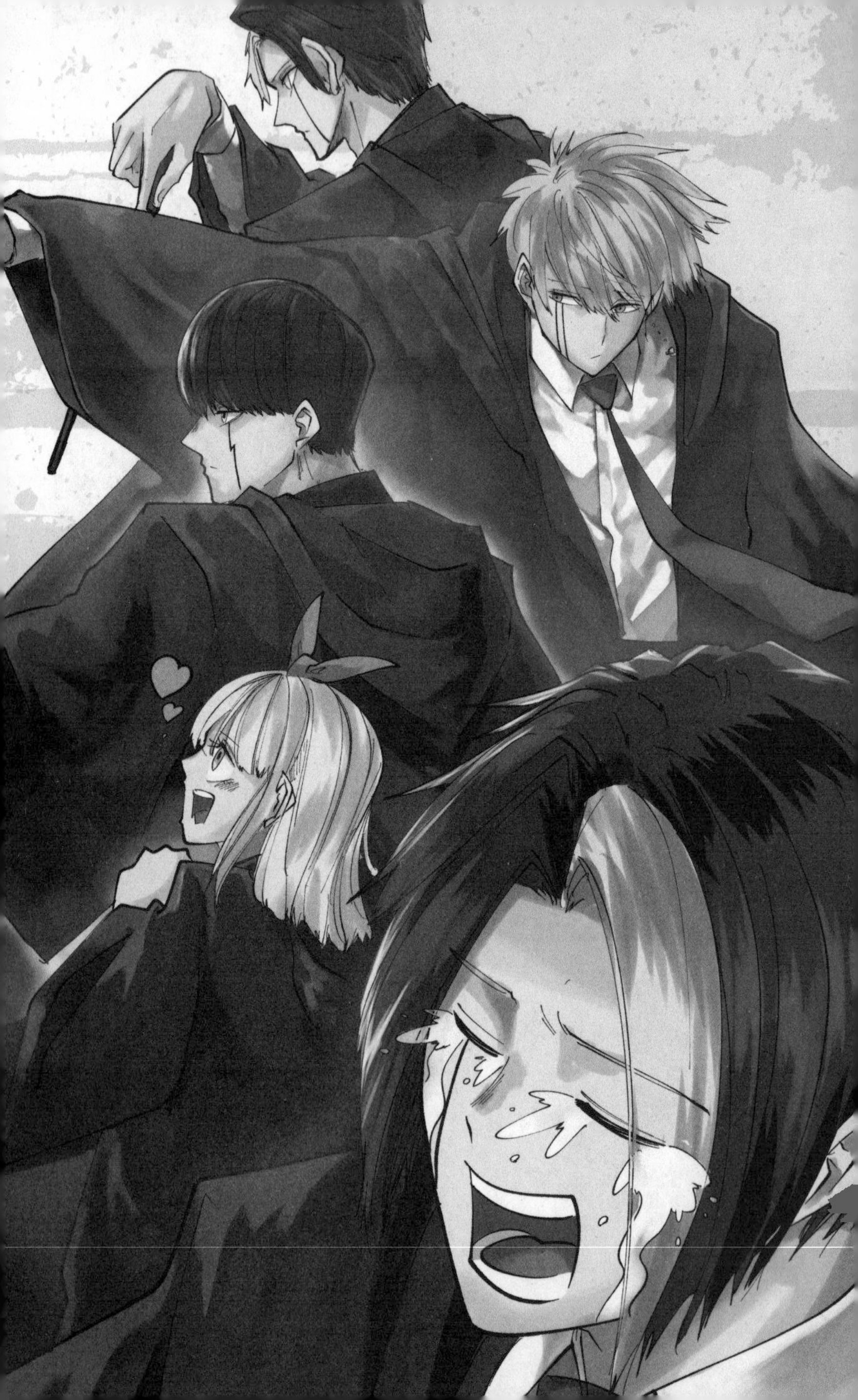

CHAPTER 52:
FINN AMES AND THE FRIEND

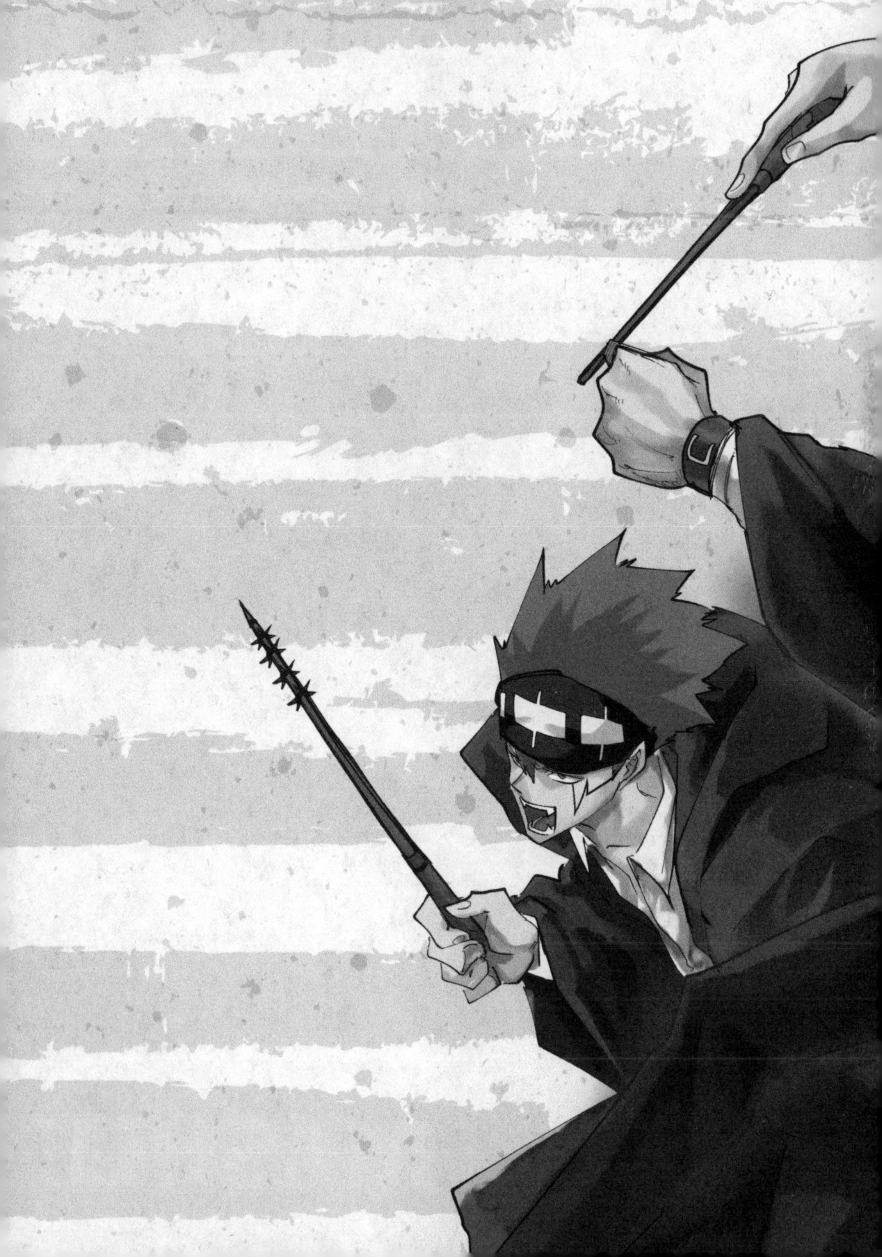

MASHLE
MAGIC AND MUSCLES

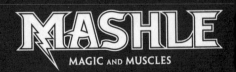

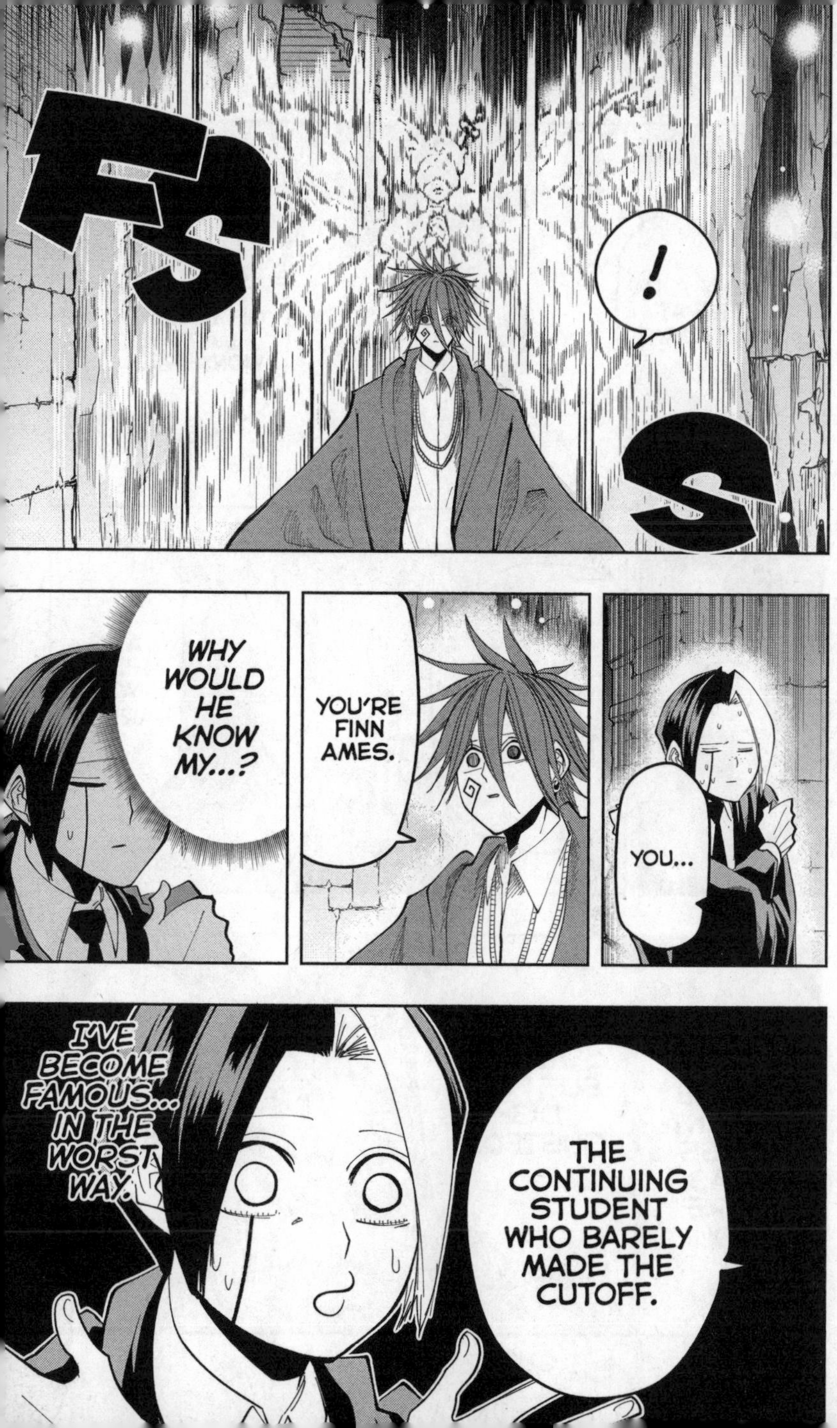
!
FS
S
YOU...
YOU'RE FINN AMES.
WHY WOULD HE KNOW MY...?
THE CONTINUING STUDENT WHO BARELY MADE THE CUTOFF.
I'VE BECOME FAMOUS... IN THE WORST WAY.

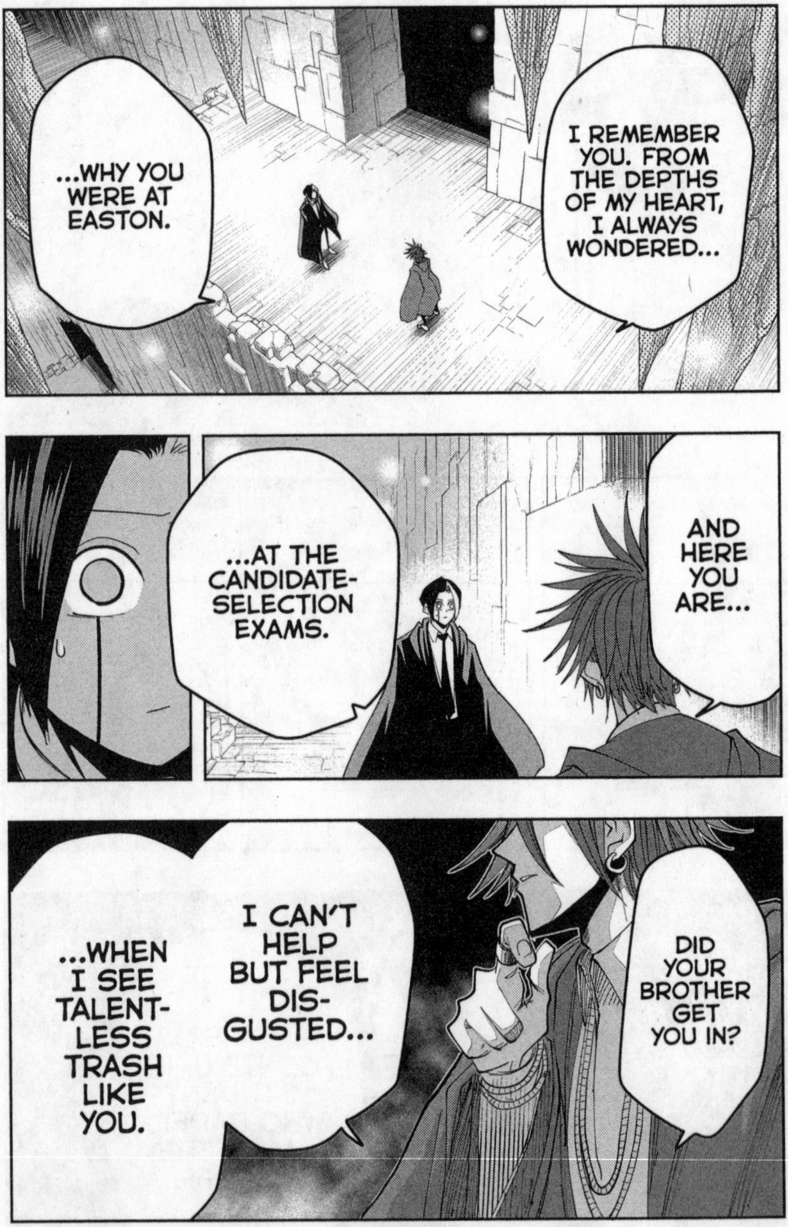
I REMEMBER YOU. FROM THE DEPTHS OF MY HEART, I ALWAYS WONDERED...
...WHY YOU WERE AT EASTON.
AND HERE YOU ARE...
...AT THE CANDIDATE-SELECTION EXAMS.
DID YOUR BROTHER GET YOU IN?
I CAN'T HELP BUT FEEL DIS-GUSTED...
...WHEN I SEE TALENT-LESS TRASH LIKE YOU.

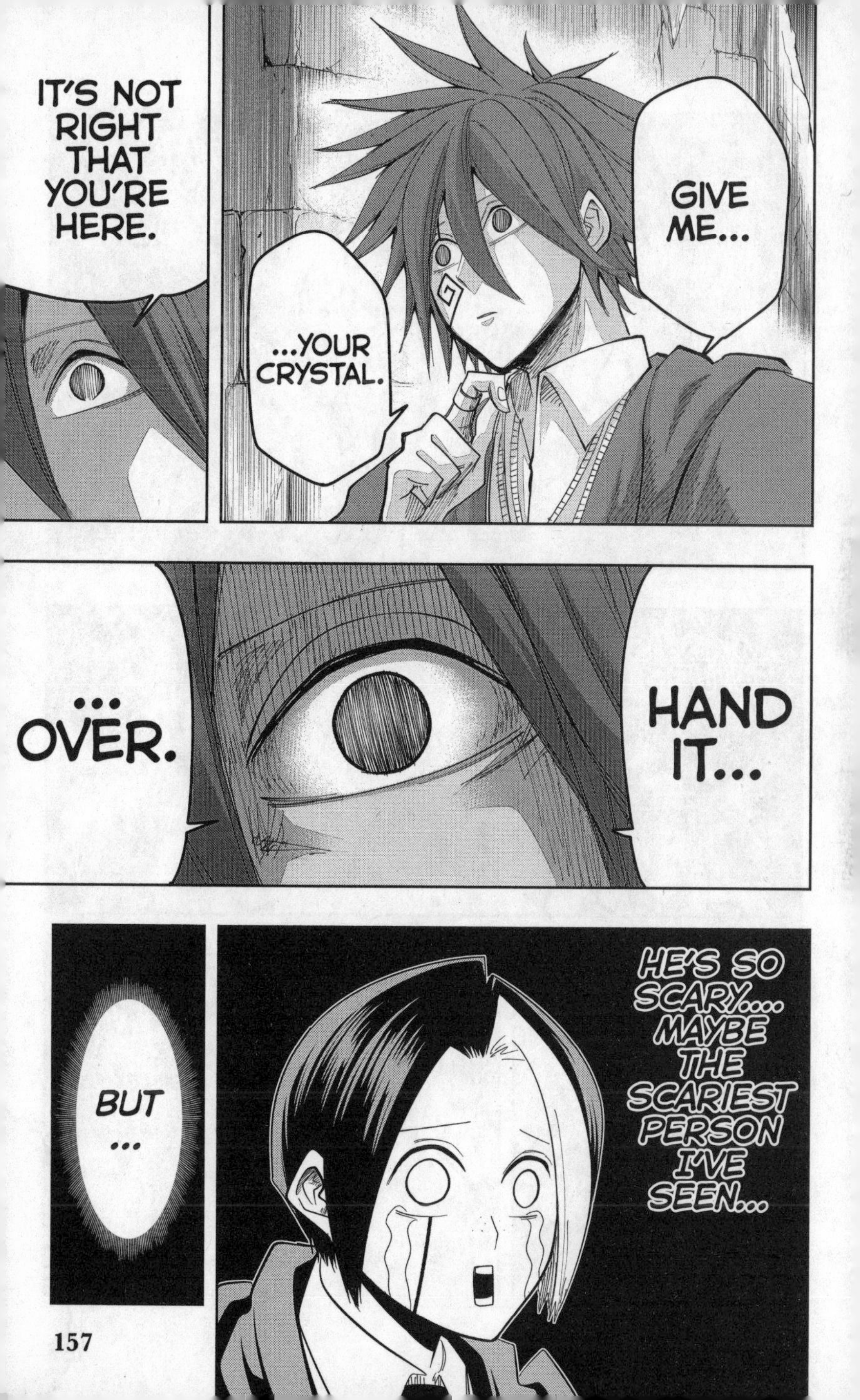
GIVE ME...
...YOUR CRYSTAL.
IT'S NOT RIGHT THAT YOU'RE HERE.
HAND IT...
... OVER.
HE'S SO SCARY... MAYBE THE SCARIEST PERSON I'VE SEEN...
BUT ...

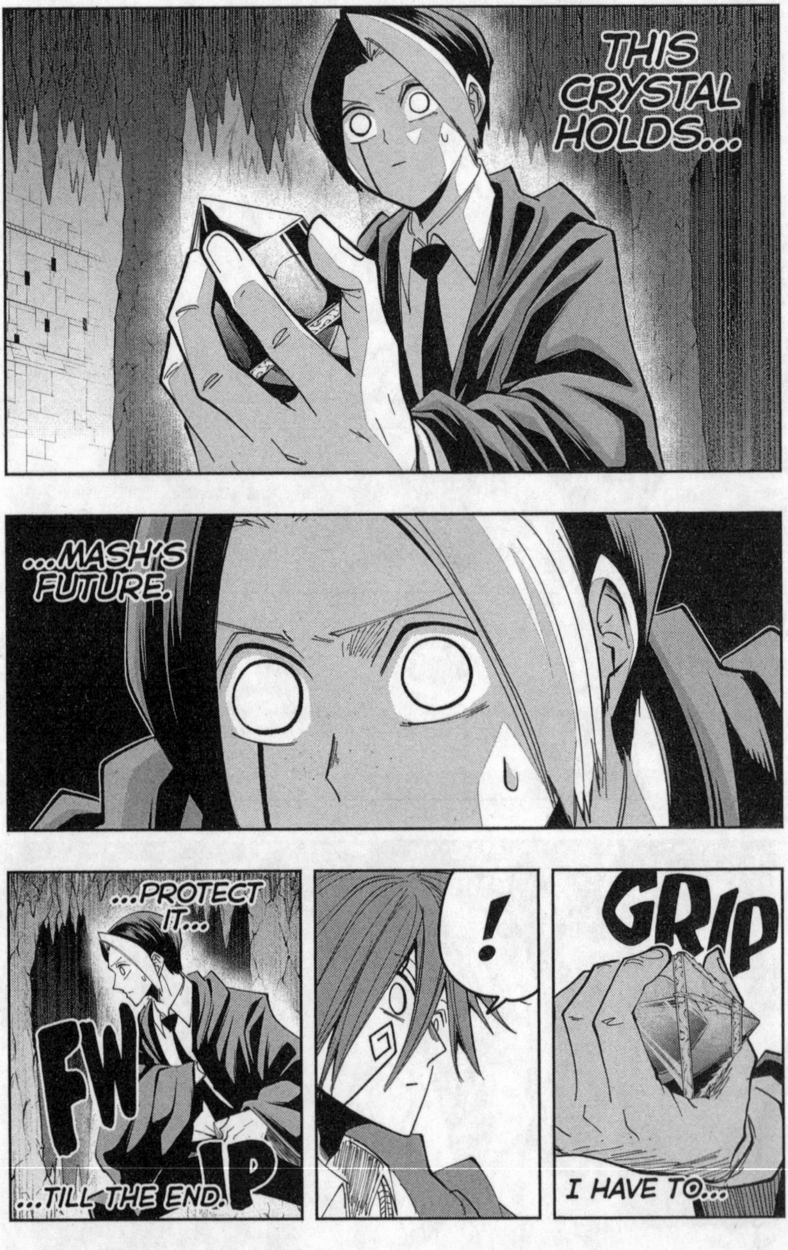
THIS CRYSTAL HOLDS...
...MASH'S FUTURE.
GRIP
I HAVE TO...
!
...PROTECT IT...
FWIP
...TILL THE END.

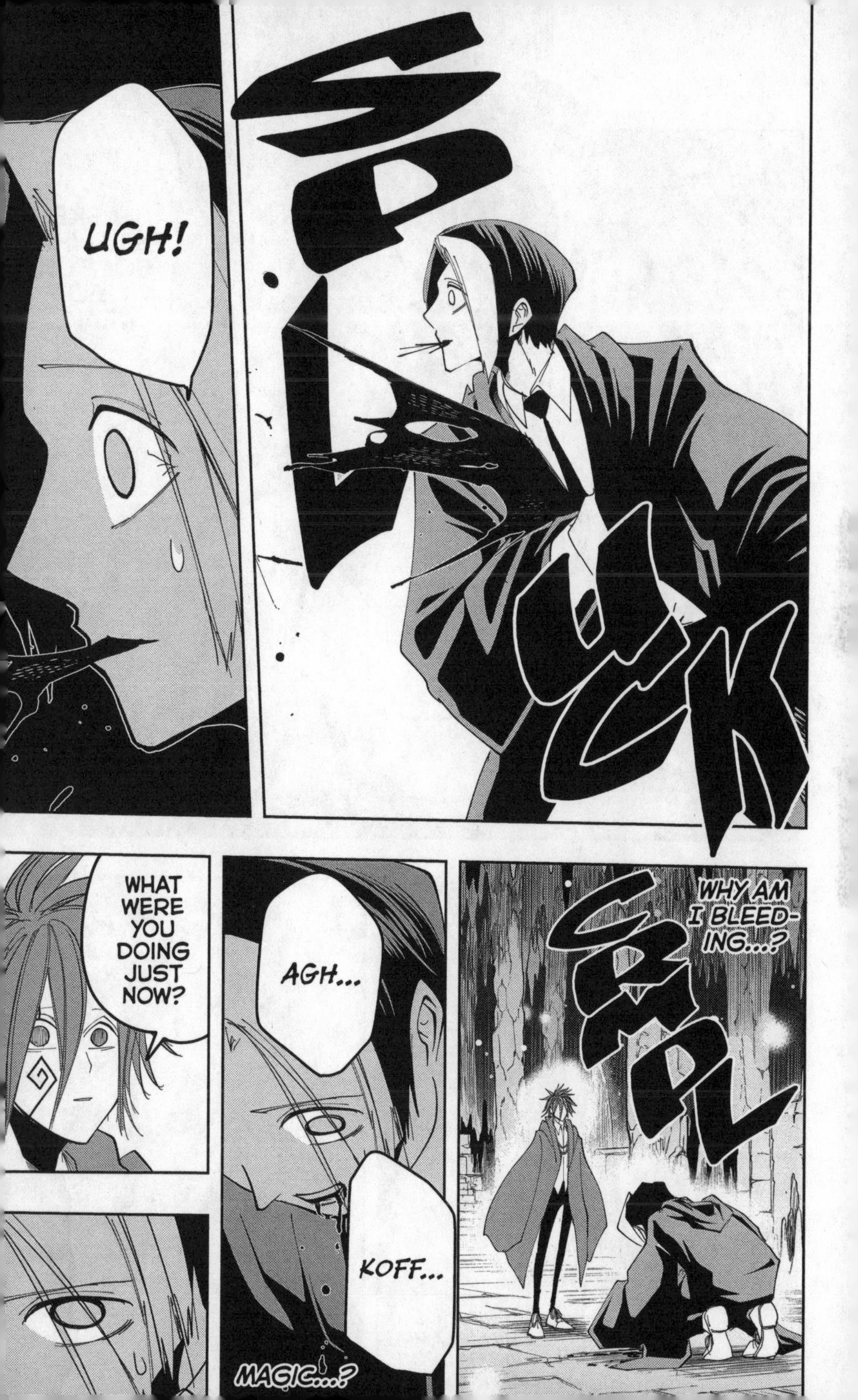
UGH!
WHY AM I BLEED-ING...?
AGH...
KOFF...
WHAT WERE YOU DOING JUST NOW?
MAGIC...?

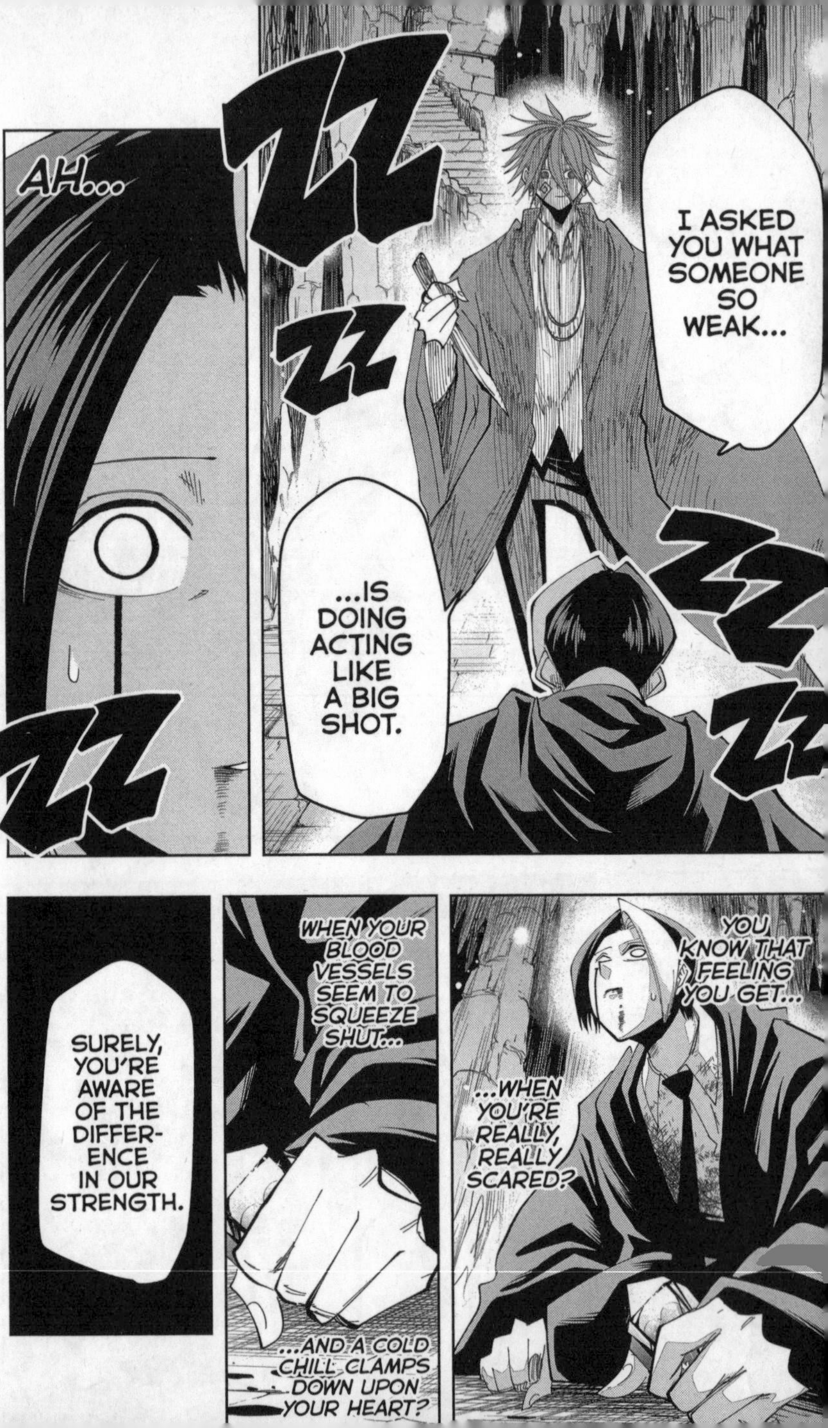
ZZ
ZZ
I ASKED YOU WHAT SOMEONE SO WEAK...
...IS DOING ACTING LIKE A BIG SHOT.
ZZ
ZZ
AH...
ZZ
YOU KNOW THAT FEELING YOU GET...
...WHEN YOU'RE REALLY, REALLY SCARED?
WHEN YOUR BLOOD VESSELS SEEM TO SQUEEZE SHUT...
...AND A COLD CHILL CLAMPS DOWN UPON YOUR HEART?
SURELY, YOU'RE AWARE OF THE DIFFERENCE IN OUR STRENGTH.

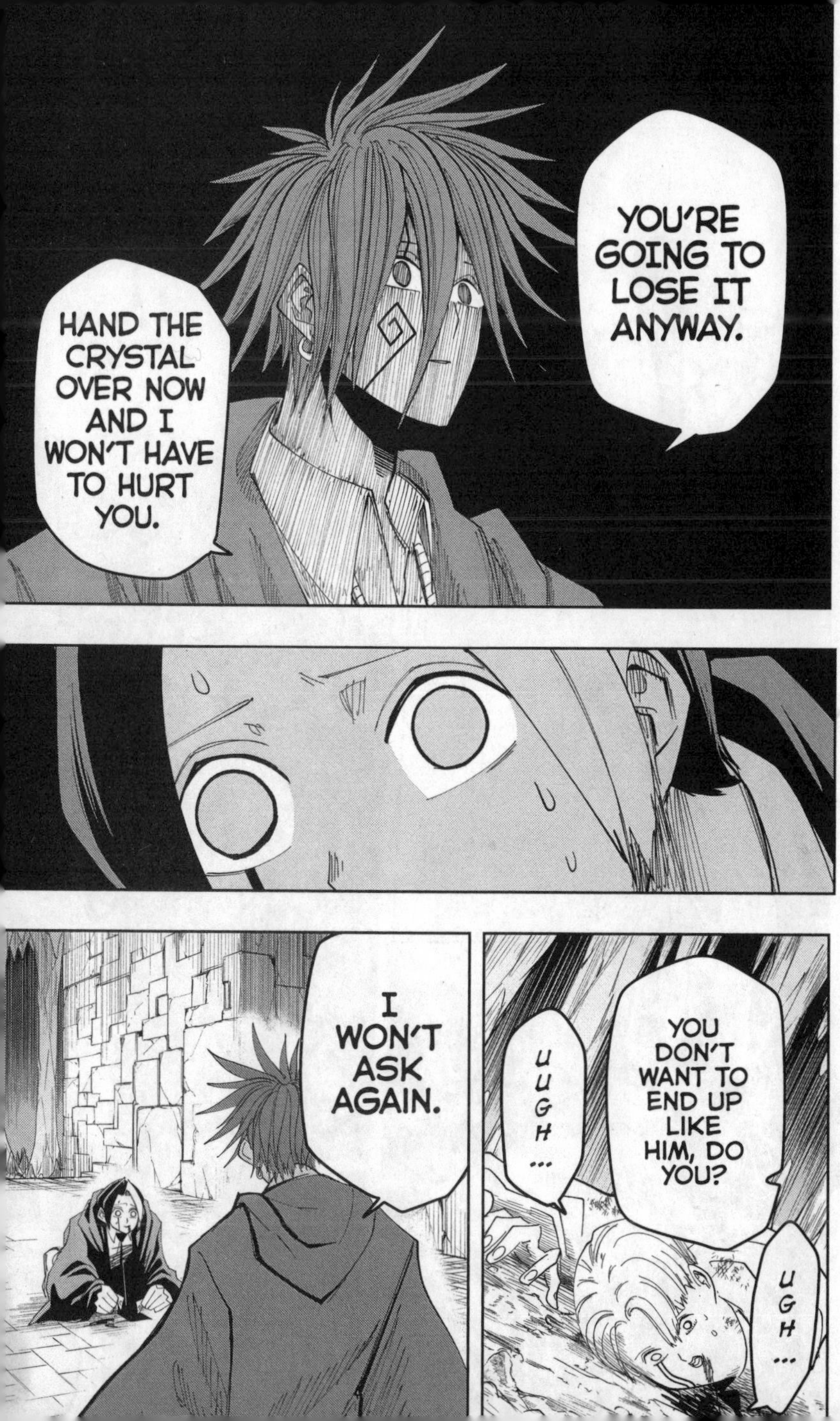
YOU'RE GOING TO LOSE IT ANYWAY.
HAND THE CRYSTAL OVER NOW AND I WON'T HAVE TO HURT YOU.
YOU DON'T WANT TO END UP LIKE HIM, DO YOU?
UUGH...
UGH...
I WON'T ASK AGAIN.

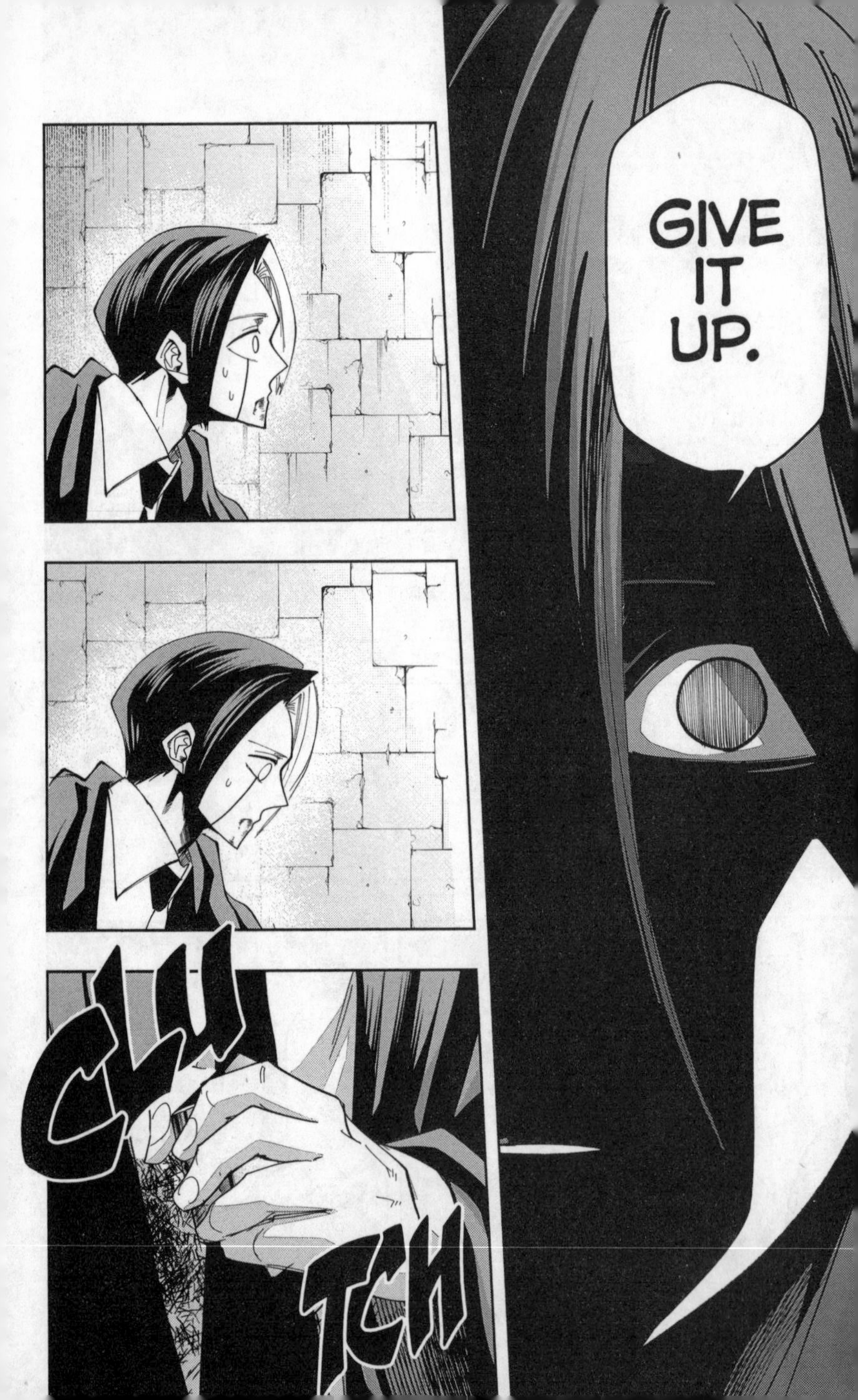
GIVE IT UP.
CLUTCH

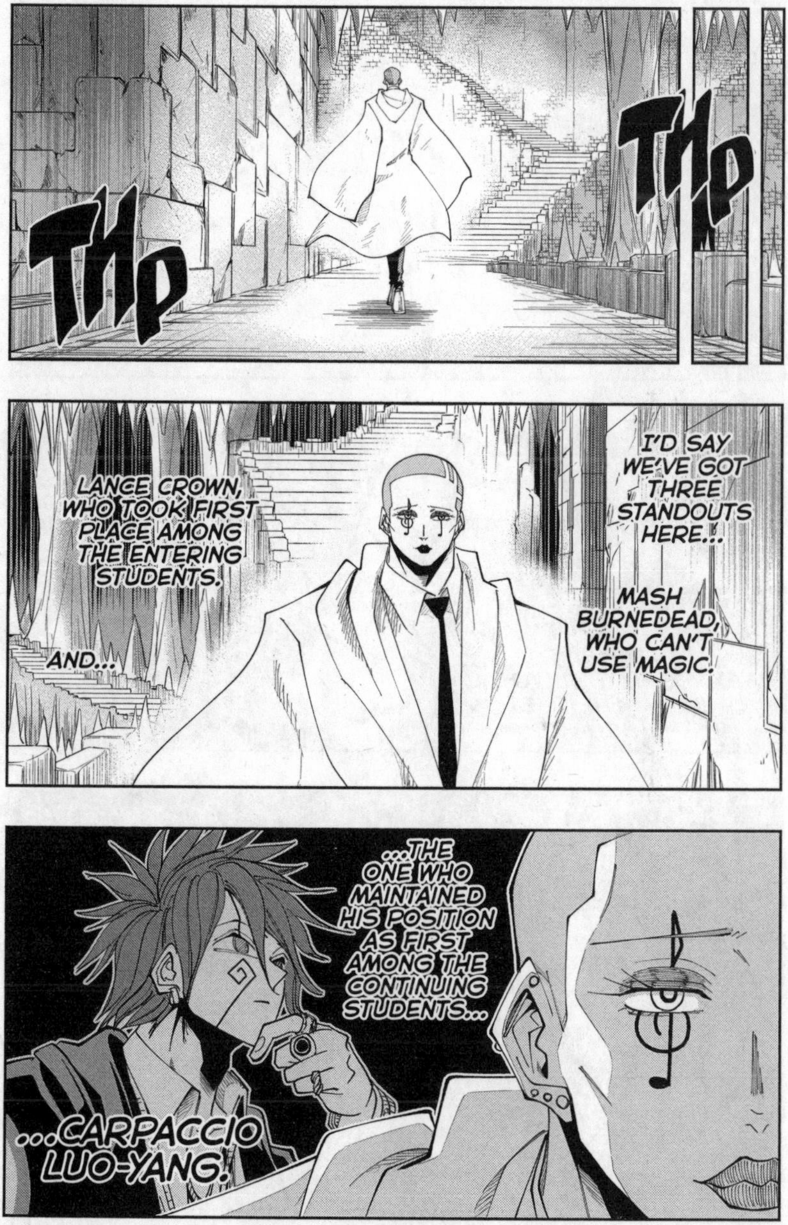
THP
THP
I'D SAY WE'VE GOT THREE STANDOUTS HERE...
MASH BURNEDEAD, WHO CAN'T USE MAGIC.
LANCE CROWN, WHO TOOK FIRST PLACE AMONG THE ENTERING STUDENTS.
AND...
...THE ONE WHO MAINTAINED HIS POSITION AS FIRST AMONG THE CONTINUING STUDENTS...
...CARPACCIO LUO-YANG!

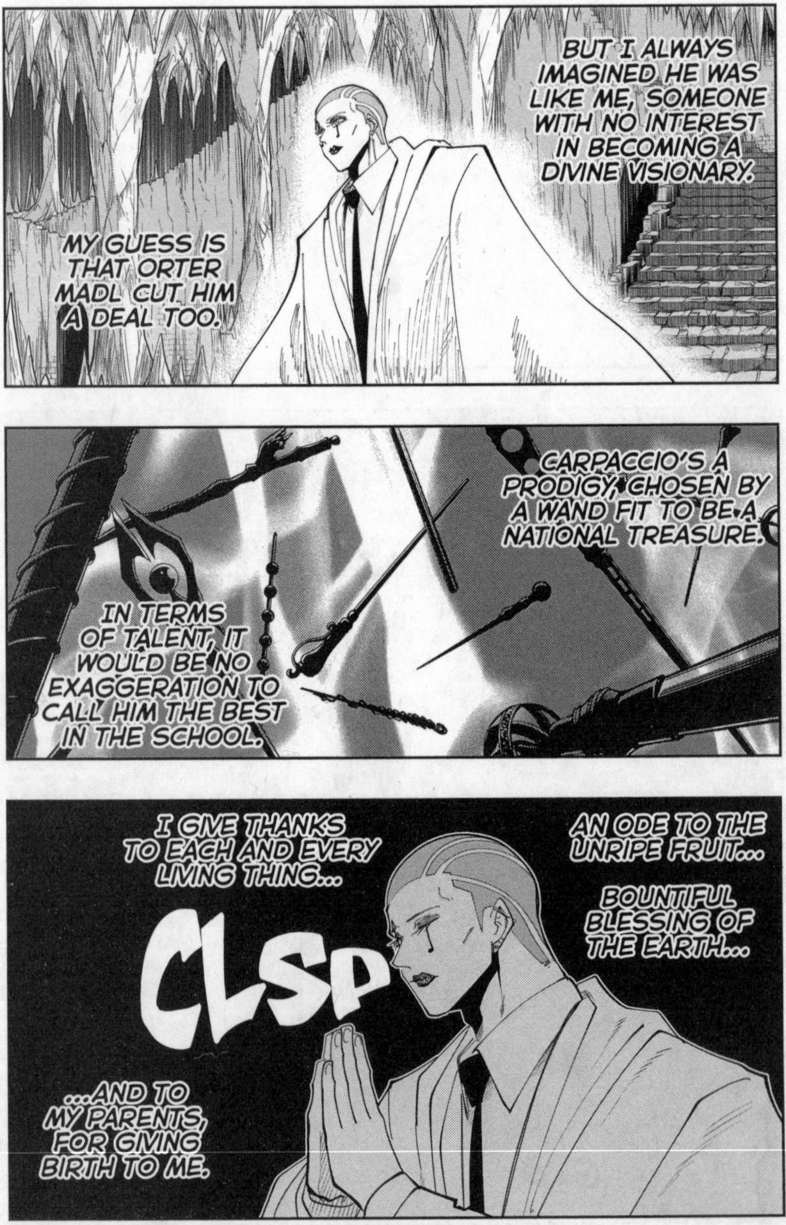
BUT I ALWAYS IMAGINED HE WAS LIKE ME, SOMEONE WITH NO INTEREST IN BECOMING A DIVINE VISIONARY.
MY GUESS IS THAT ORTER MADL CUT HIM A DEAL TOO.
CARPACCIO'S A PRODIGY, CHOSEN BY A WAND FIT TO BE A NATIONAL TREASURE.
IN TERMS OF TALENT, IT WOULD BE NO EXAGGERATION TO CALL HIM THE BEST IN THE SCHOOL.
AN ODE TO THE UNRIPE FRUIT...
BOUNTIFUL BLESSING OF THE EARTH...
I GIVE THANKS TO EACH AND EVERY LIVING THING...
CLSP
...AND TO MY PARENTS, FOR GIVING BIRTH TO ME.

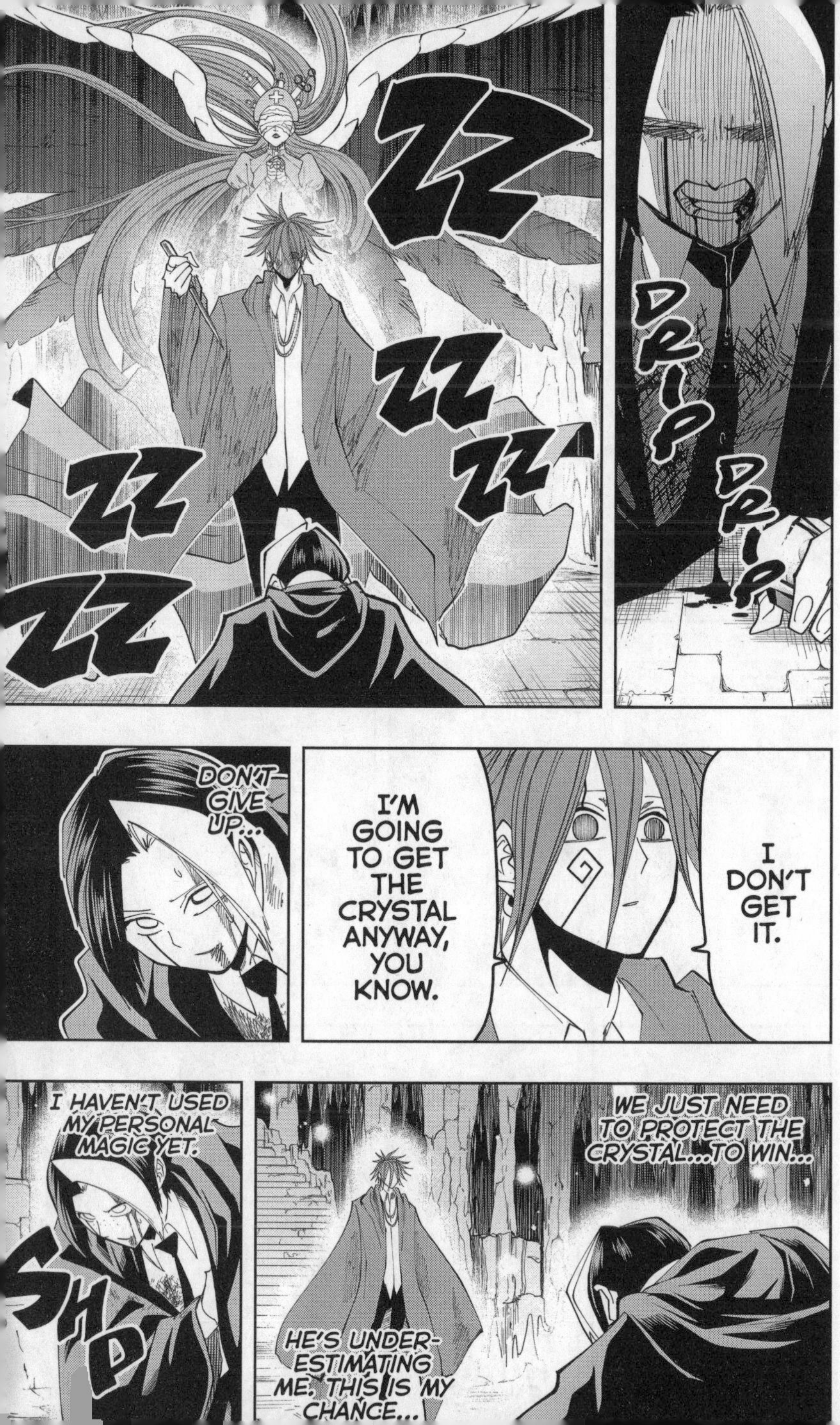
DRIP
DRIP
ZZ
ZZ
ZZ
ZZ
ZZ
I DON'T GET IT.
I'M GOING TO GET THE CRYSTAL ANYWAY, YOU KNOW.
DON'T GIVE UP...
WE JUST NEED TO PROTECT THE CRYSTAL...TO WIN...
HE'S UNDER-ESTIMATING ME. THIS IS MY CHANCE...
I HAVEN'T USED MY PERSONAL MAGIC YET.
SHP

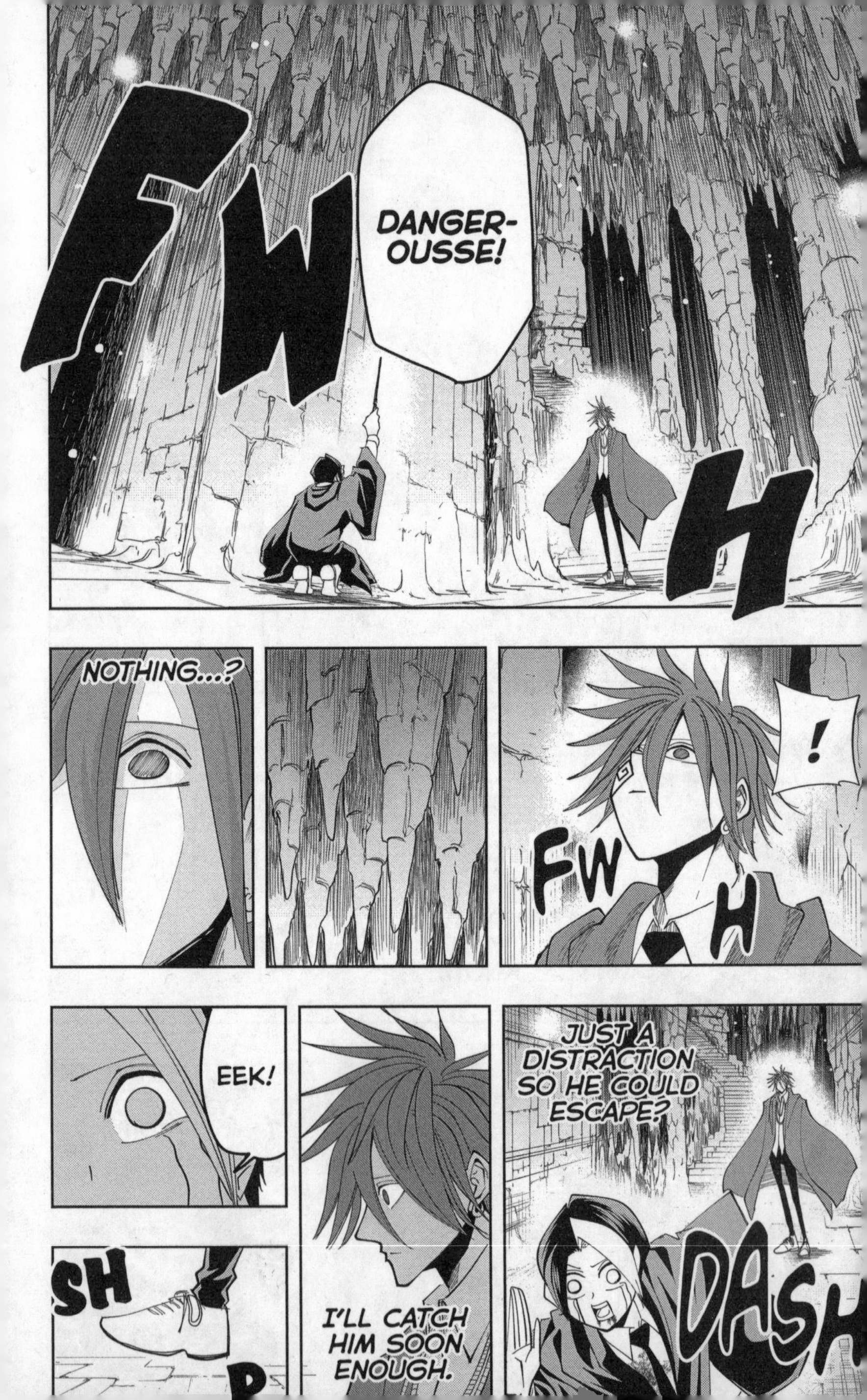
FWH
DANGER-OUSSE!
!
FWH
NOTHING...?
JUST A DISTRACTION SO HE COULD ESCAPE?
DASH
I'LL CATCH HIM SOON ENOUGH.
EEK!
SH

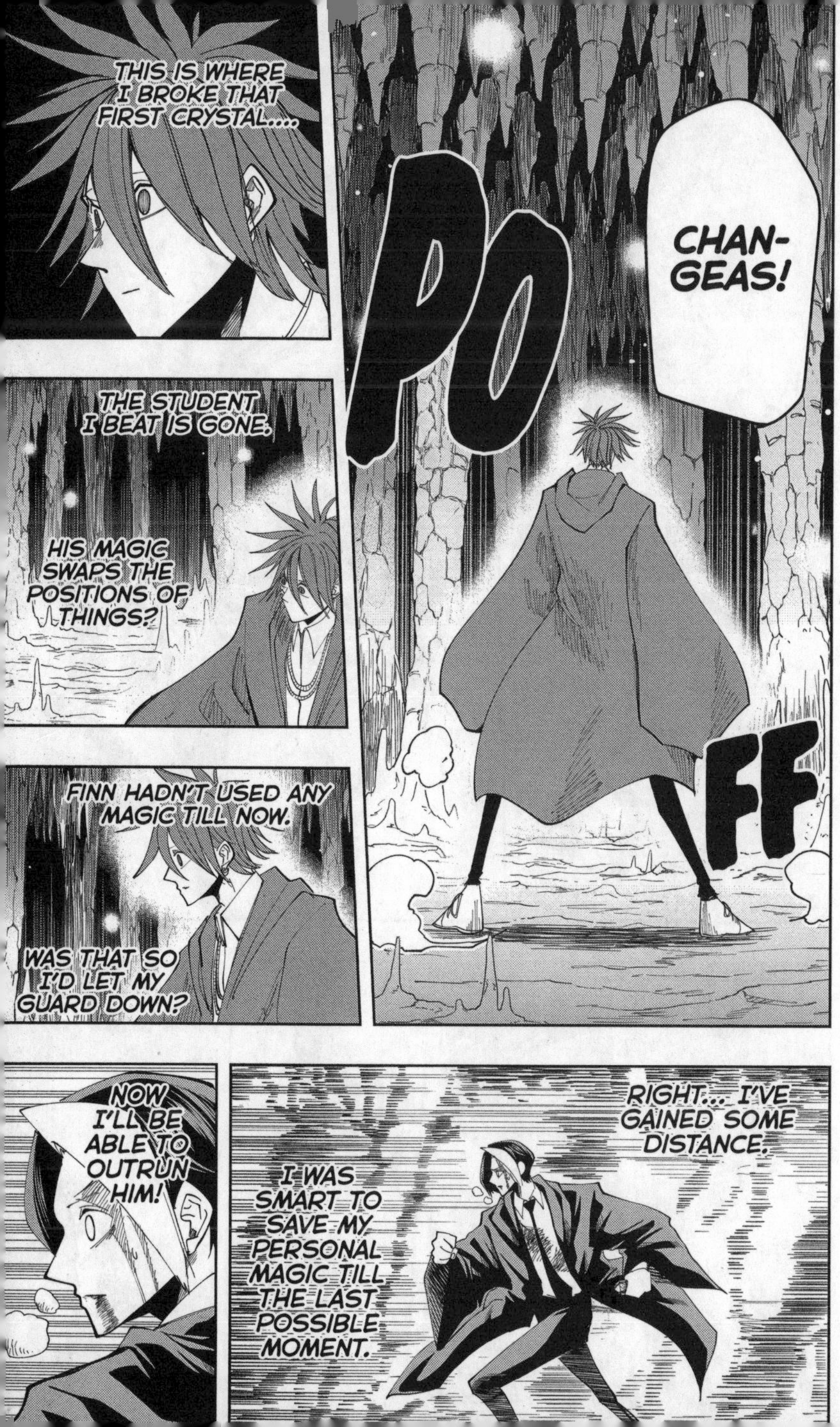
CHAN-GEAS!
POFF
THIS IS WHERE I BROKE THAT FIRST CRYSTAL....
THE STUDENT I BEAT IS GONE.
HIS MAGIC SWAPS THE POSITIONS OF THINGS?
FINN HADN'T USED ANY MAGIC TILL NOW.
WAS THAT SO I'D LET MY GUARD DOWN?
RIGHT... I'VE GAINED SOME DISTANCE.
I WAS SMART TO SAVE MY PERSONAL MAGIC TILL THE LAST POSSIBLE MOMENT.
NOW I'LL BE ABLE TO OUTRUN HIM!

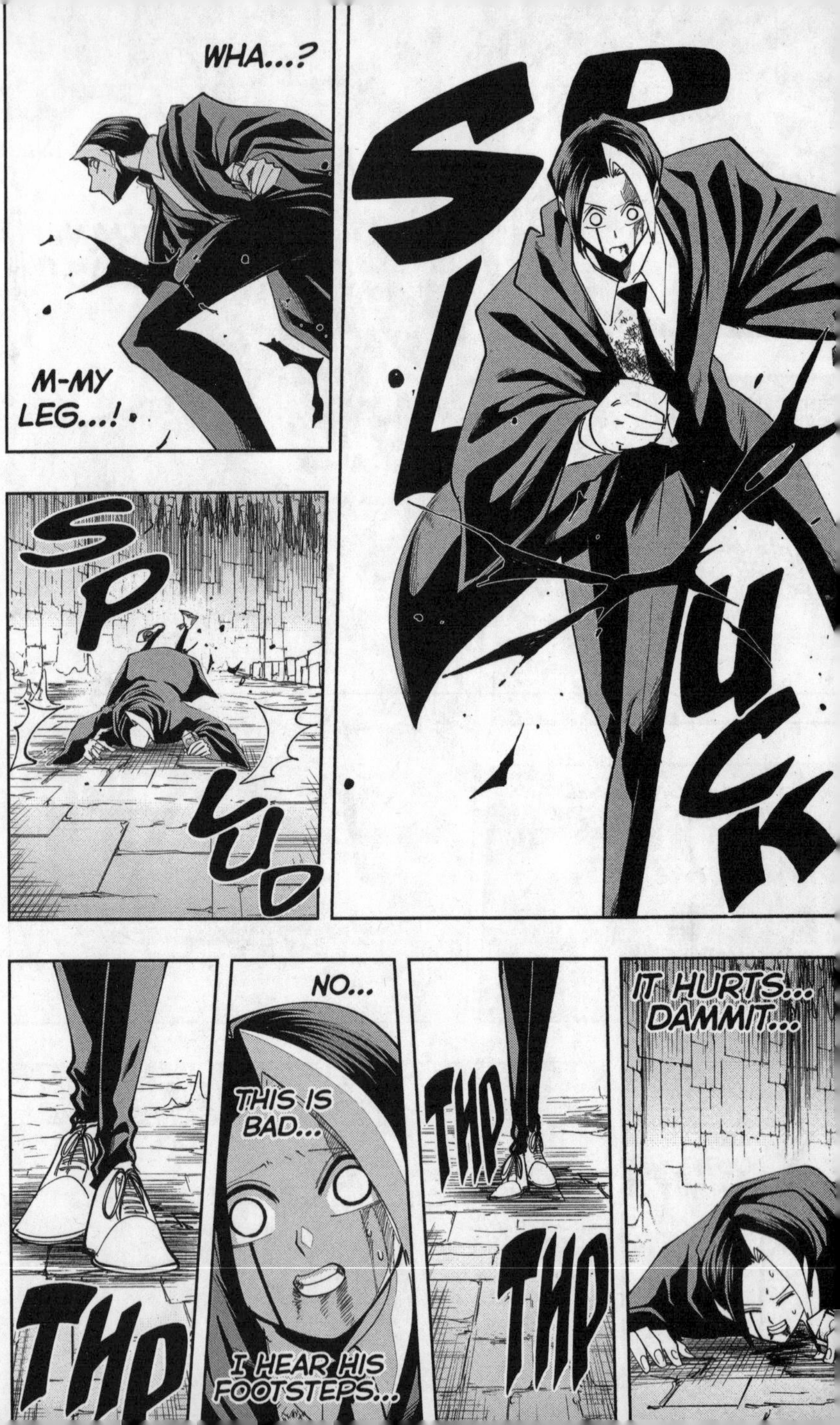
SPLUCK
WHA...?
M-MY LEG...!
SPLUD
IT HURTS... DAMMIT...
THP
THP
NO...
THIS IS BAD...
I HEAR HIS FOOTSTEPS...
THP

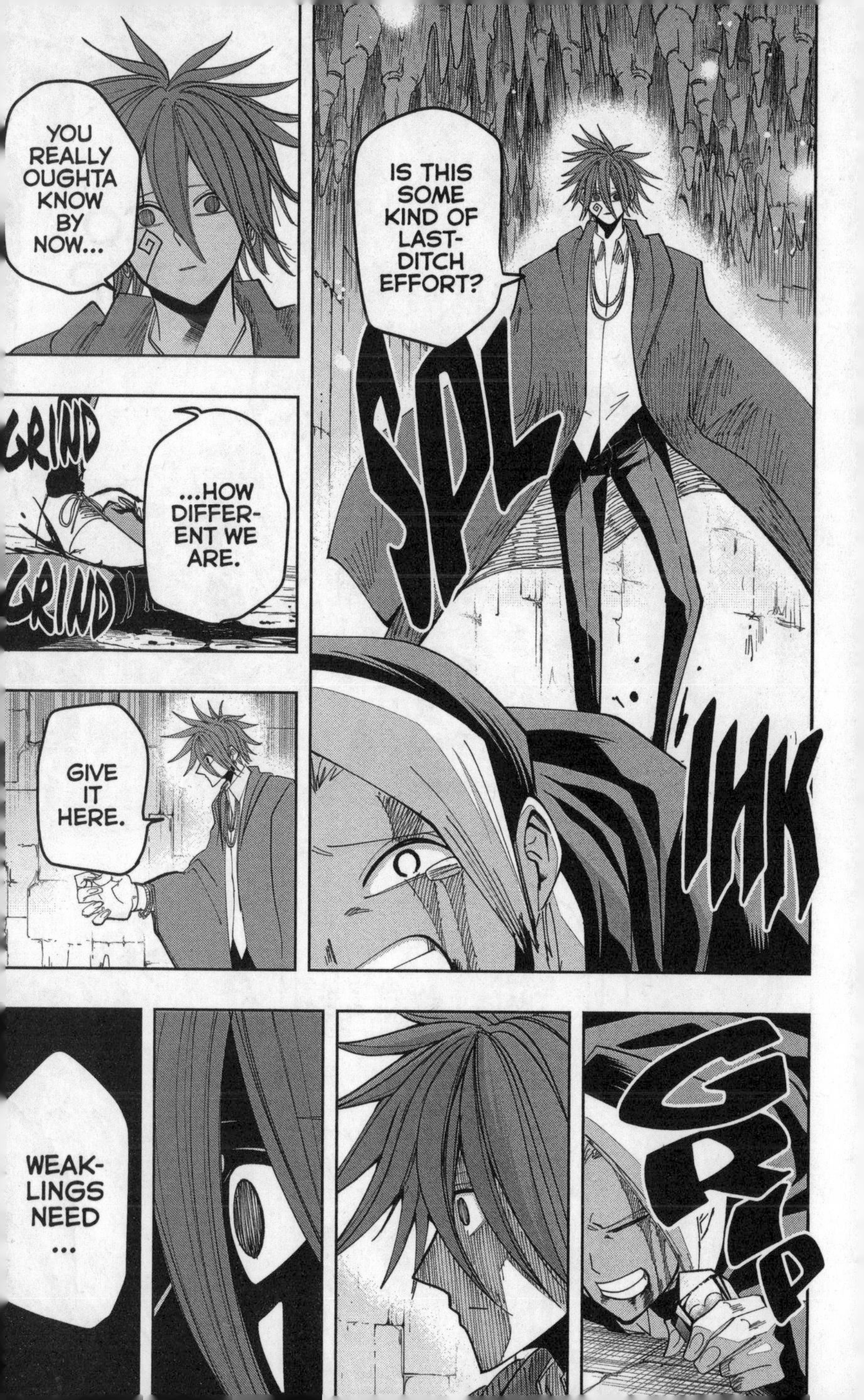
IS THIS SOME KIND OF LAST-DITCH EFFORT?
SPL
INK
YOU REALLY OUGHTA KNOW BY NOW...
GRIND
GRIND
...HOW DIFFERENT WE ARE.
GIVE IT HERE.
GRIP
WEAK-LINGS NEED ...

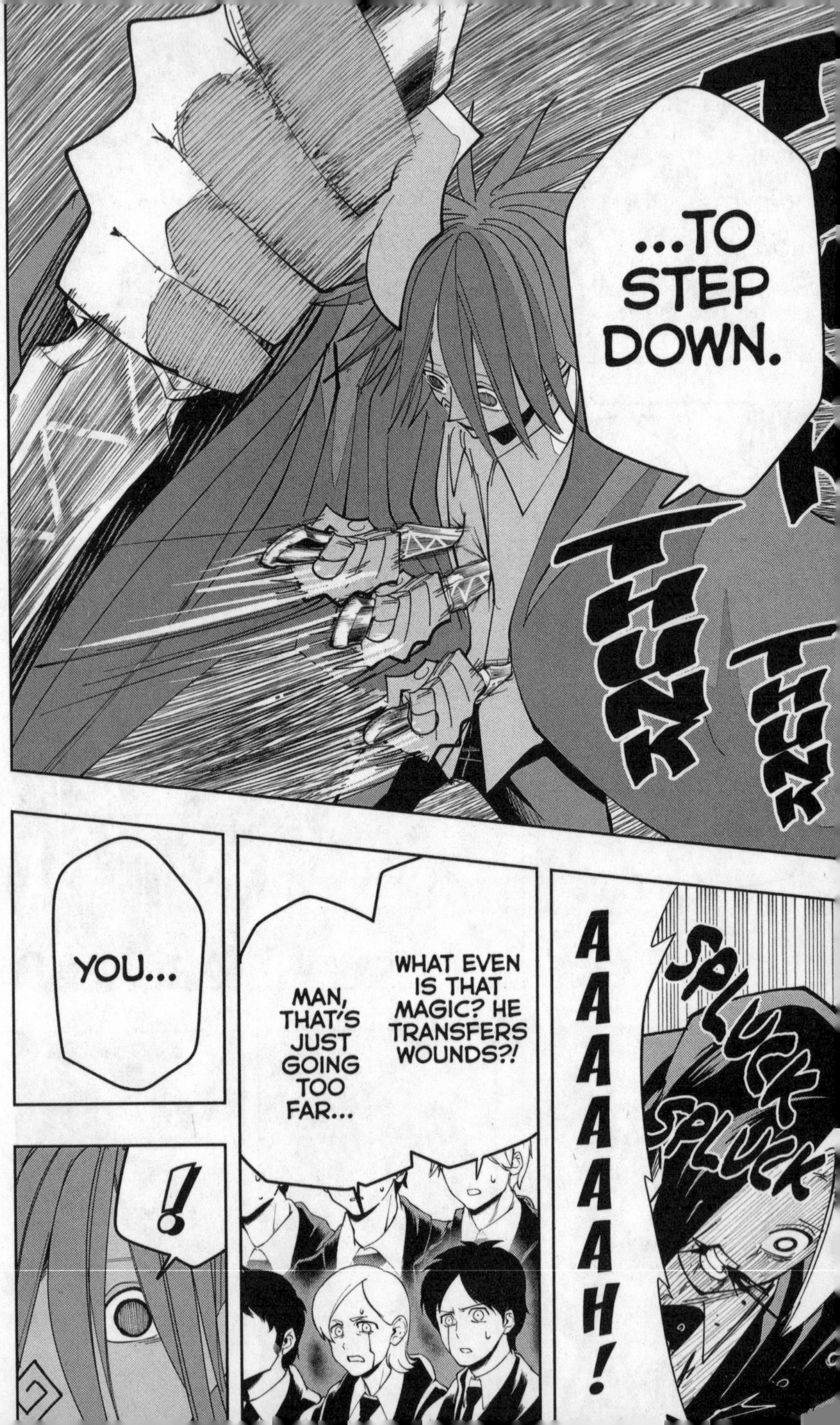
...TO STEP DOWN.
THUNK
THUNK
AAAAAAH!
SPLUCK
SPLUCK
WHAT EVEN IS THAT MAGIC? HE TRANSFERS WOUNDS?!
MAN, THAT'S JUST GOING TOO FAR...
YOU...
!

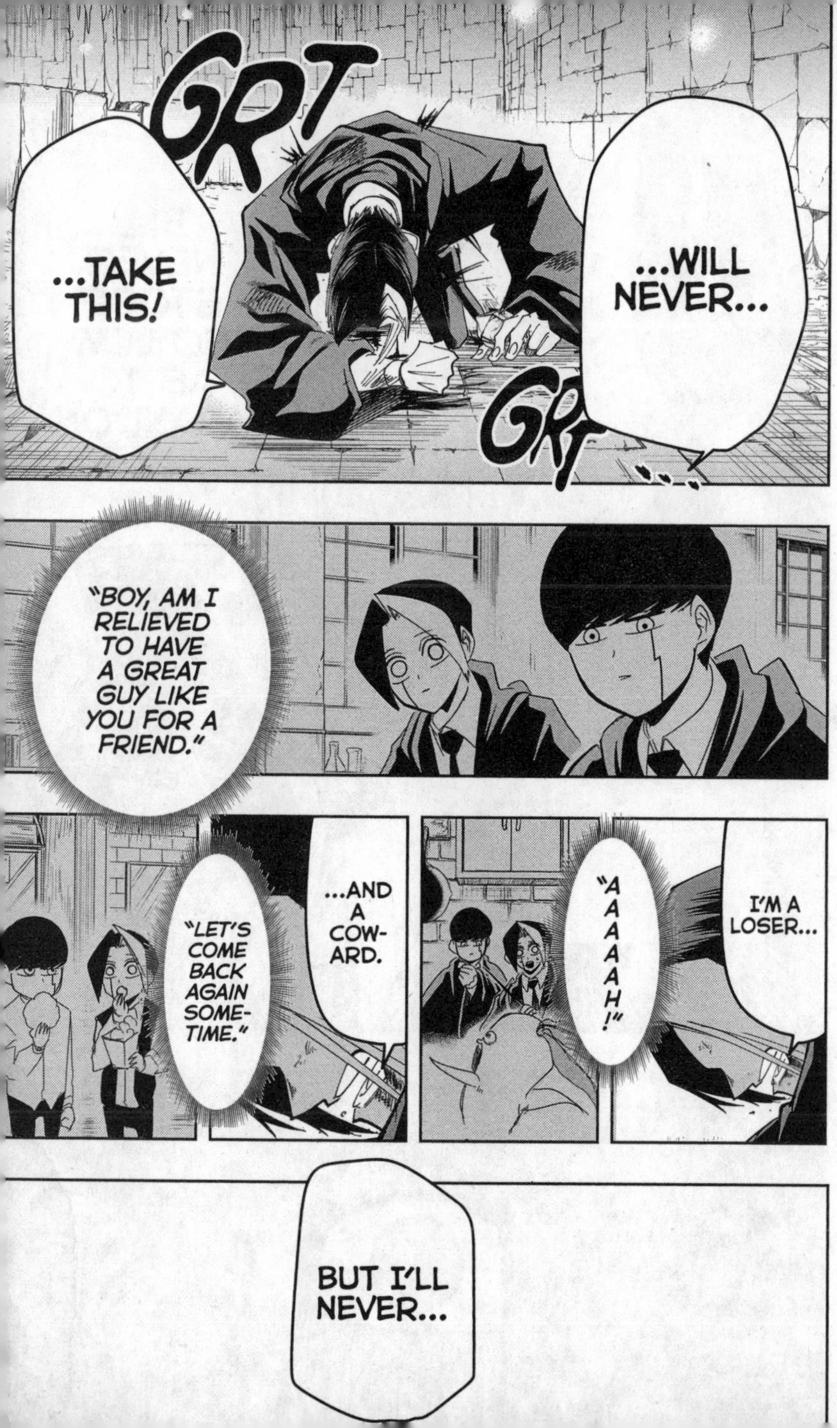
...WILL NEVER...
GRT
...TAKE THIS!
GRT
"BOY, AM I RELIEVED TO HAVE A GREAT GUY LIKE YOU FOR A FRIEND."
I'M A LOSER...
"AAAAAAH!"
...AND A COWARD.
"LET'S COME BACK AGAIN SOMETIME."
BUT I'LL NEVER...

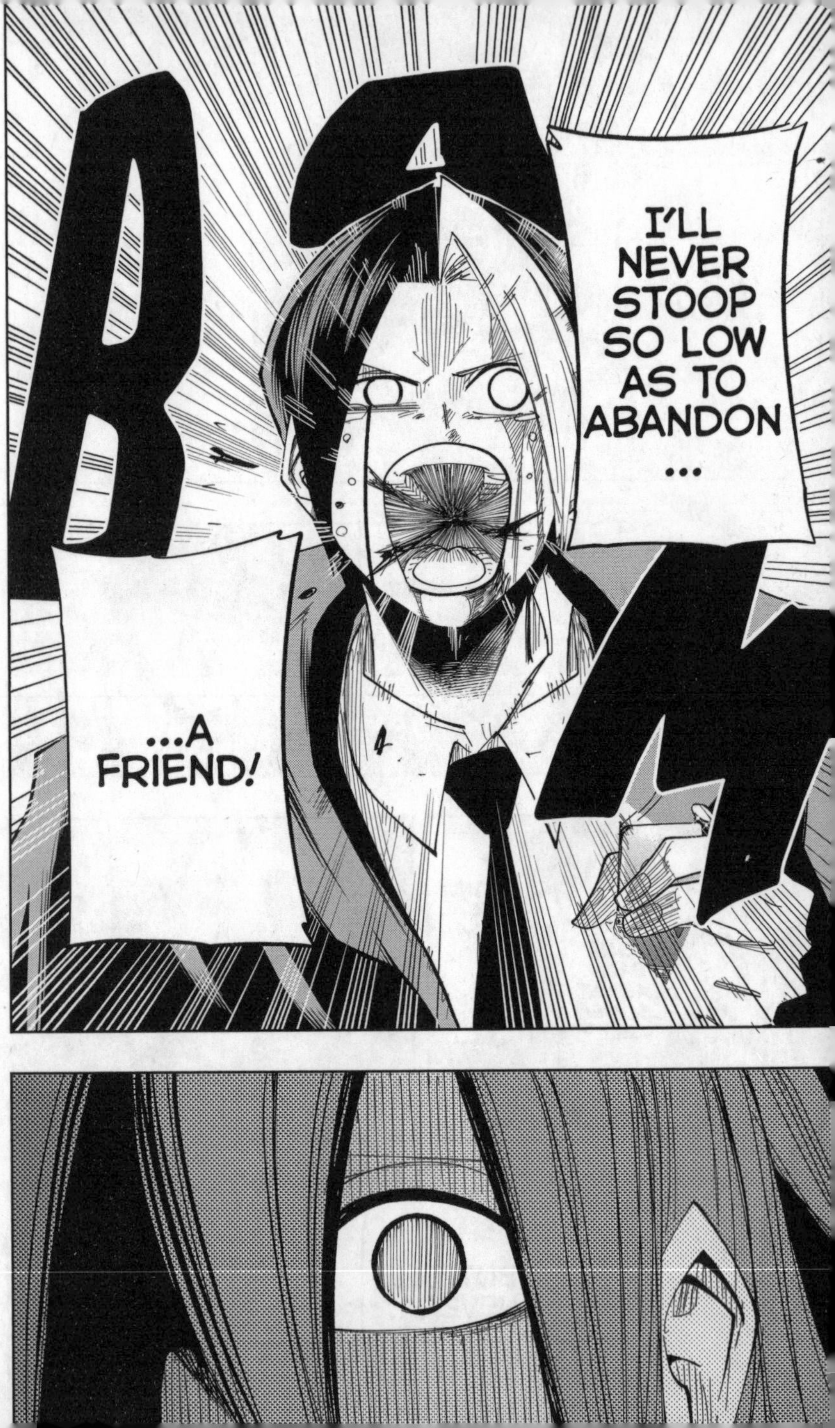
I'LL NEVER STOOP SO LOW AS TO ABANDON ...
...A FRIEND!
BAM

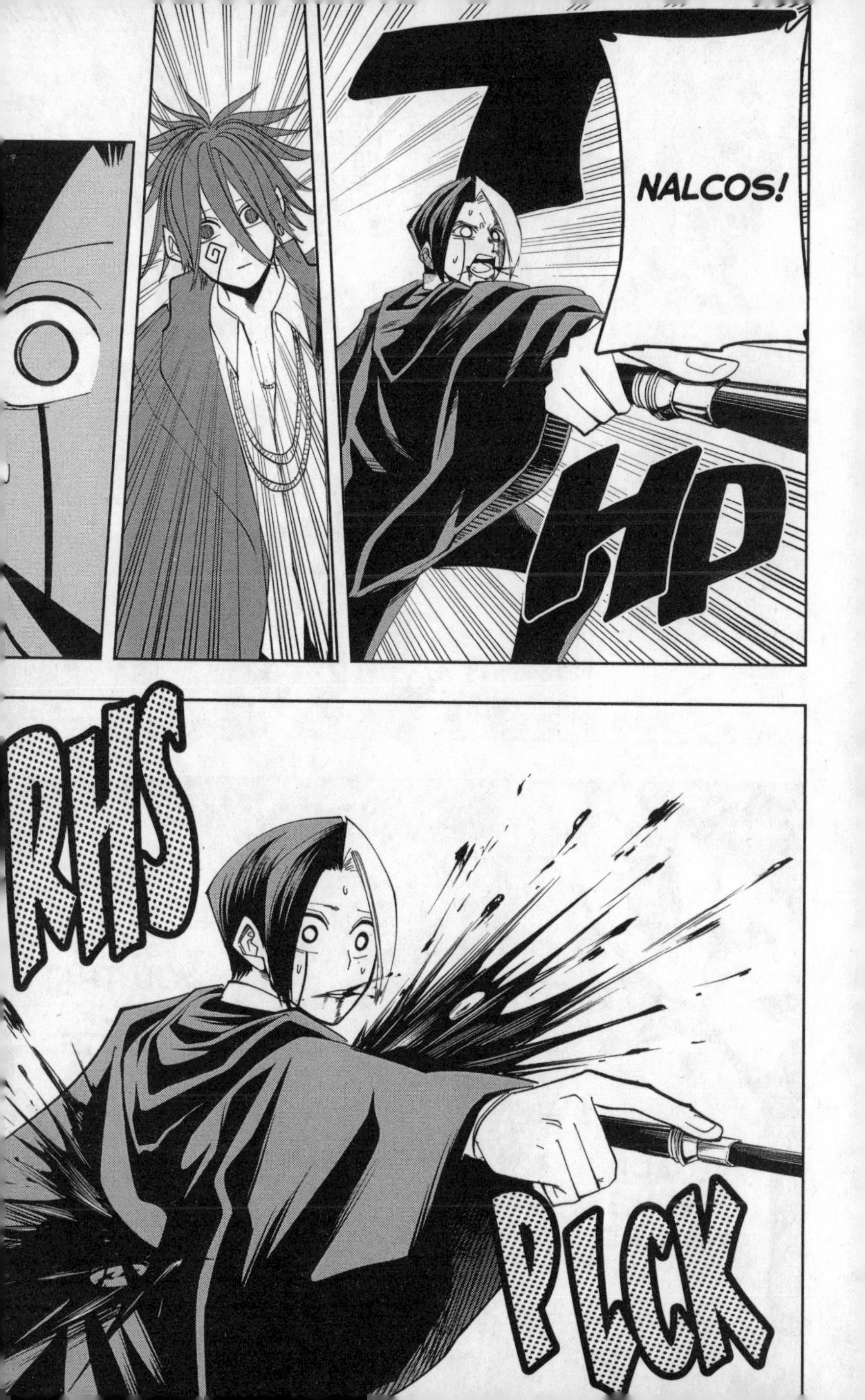
NALCOS!
PLCK

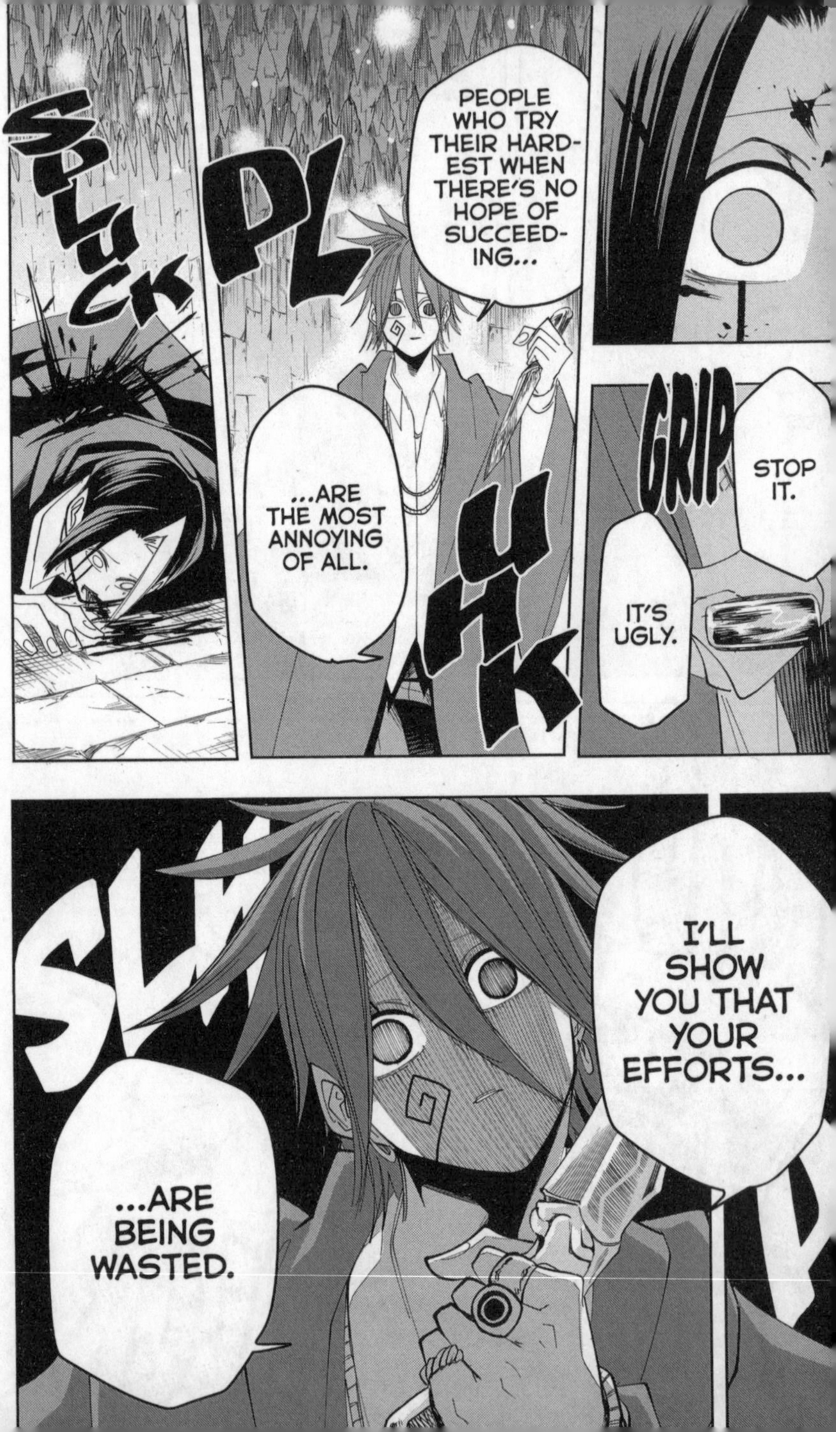
GRIP
STOP IT.
IT'S UGLY.
PEOPLE WHO TRY THEIR HARD-EST WHEN THERE'S NO HOPE OF SUCCEED-ING...
...ARE THE MOST ANNOYING OF ALL.
HUHK
PL
SPLUCK
I'LL SHOW YOU THAT YOUR EFFORTS...
...ARE BEING WASTED.

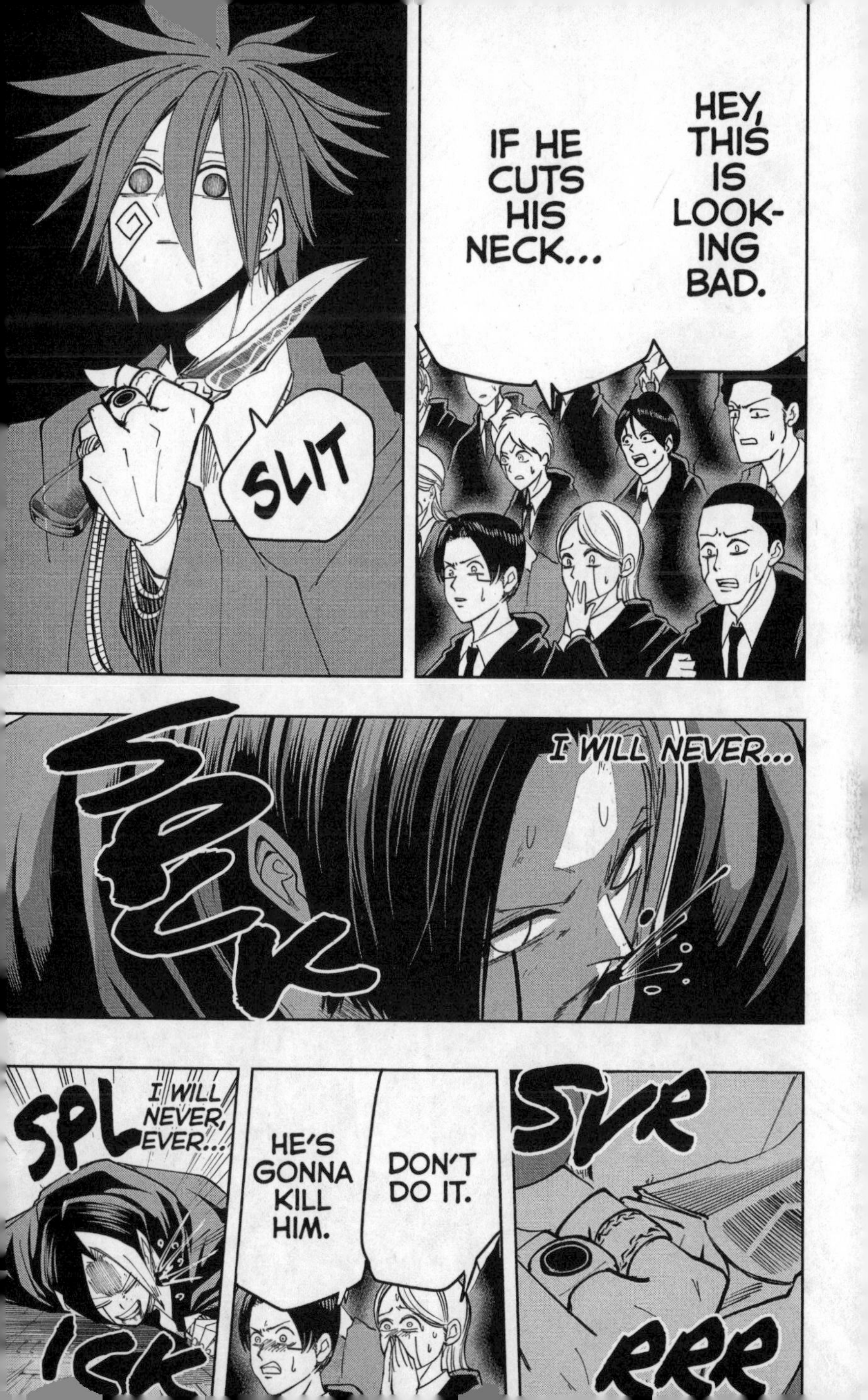
HEY, THIS IS LOOKING BAD.
IF HE CUTS HIS NECK...
SLIT
I WILL NEVER...
SVR
RRR
DON'T DO IT.
HE'S GONNA KILL HIM.
I WILL NEVER, EVER...
SPL
ICK

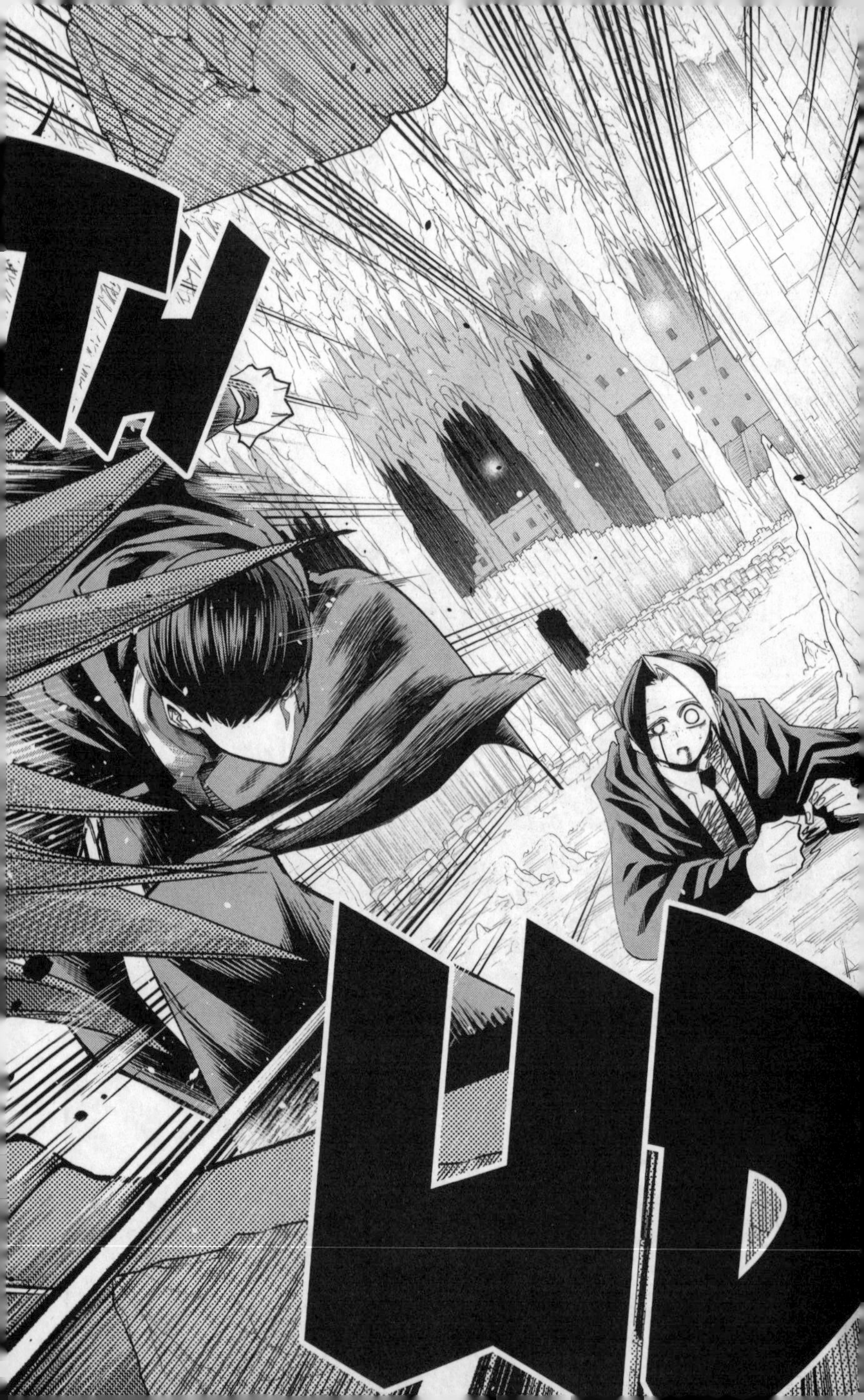
THUD

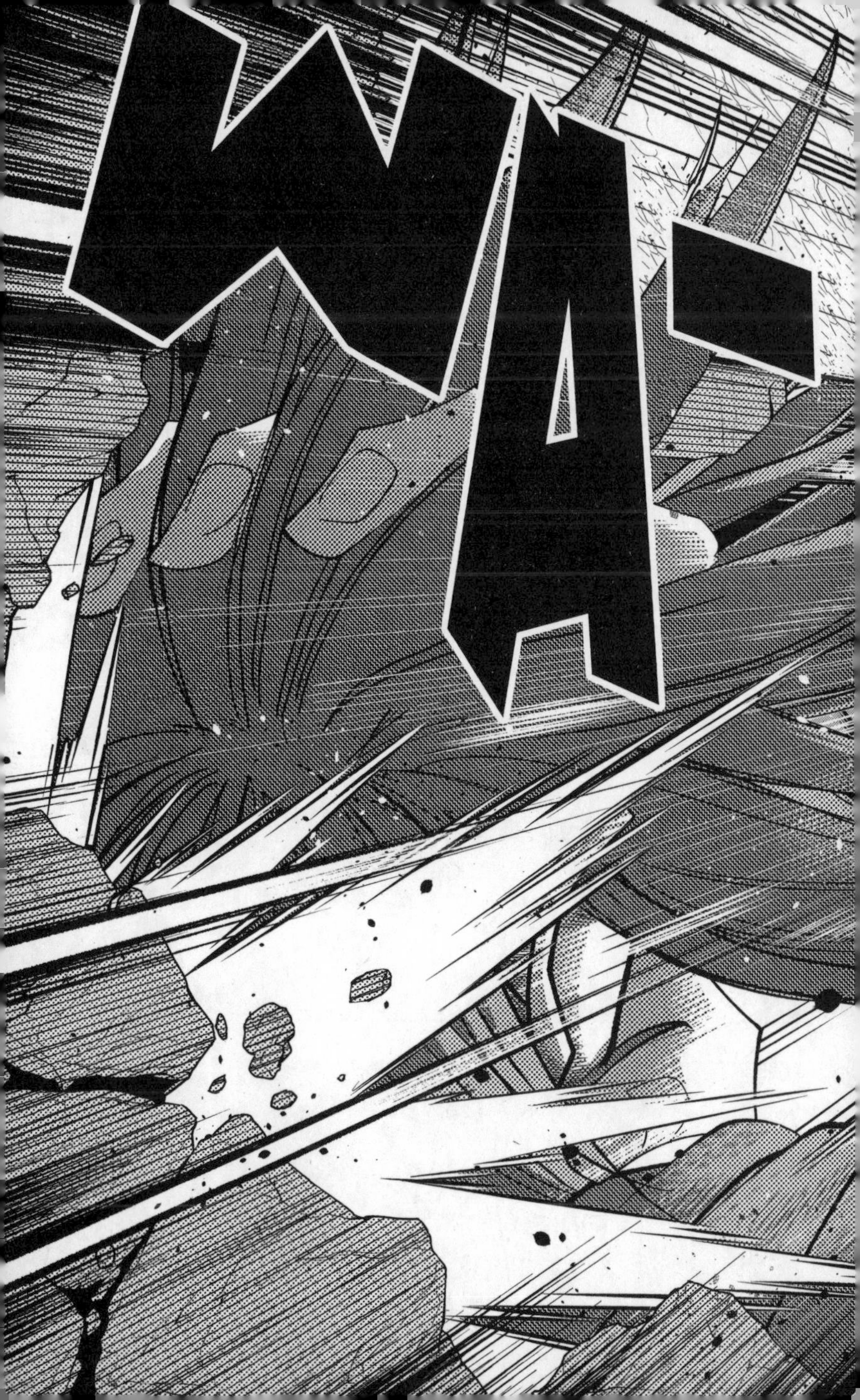
WA-

THEY'RE NOT WASTED.

CRMBLE

CRMBLE

BECAUSE I'M HERE.

FINN.

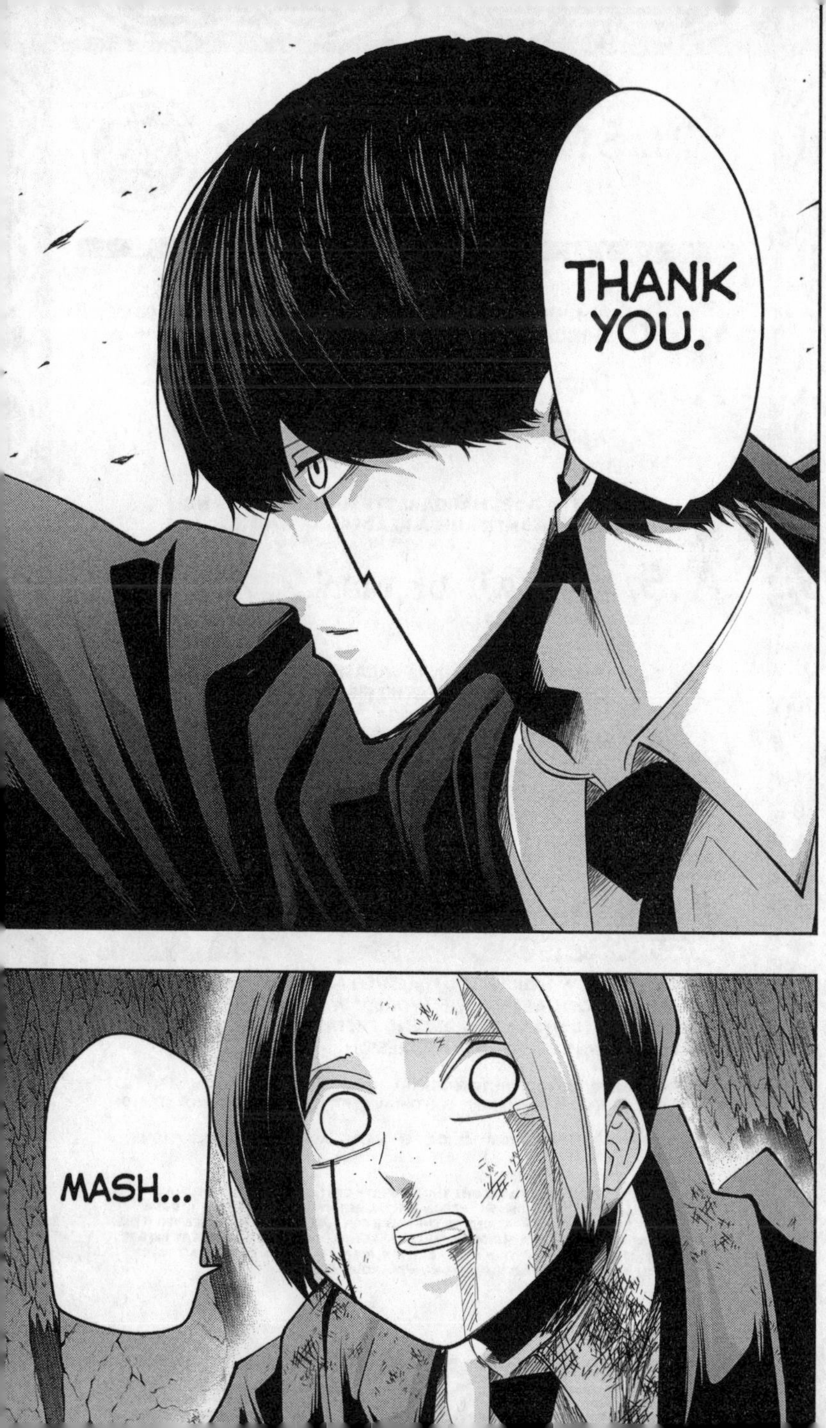
THANK YOU.
MASH...

Question & Answer Corner ②

Q&A

Q.4/ FINN'S PERSONAL MAGIC LETS HIM SWAP THE PLACE OF THINGS? (FROM A READER)

A.4/ That's right. Dangerousse was something he chanted as a bluff. And Nalcos is a basic spell anyone can use.

Q.5/ WHERE DOES MARGARETTE MACARON'S PIANO COME FROM? (FROM A READER)

A.5/ It's made of magic.

Q.6/ IF MAGIC LINES CAN INCREASE, CAN SOMEONE GO FROM ZERO LINES TO ONE LINE? (FROM A READER)

A.6/ Someone with no lines has zero potential for magic, so they can't become a single-liner.

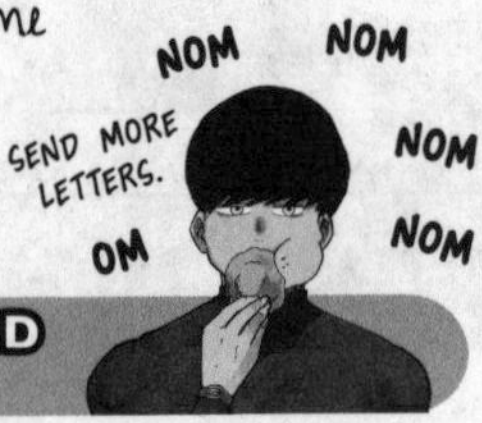
NOM
NOM
SEND MORE LETTERS.
NOM
OM
NOM

SEND US YOUR QUESTIONS AND YOUR MAGIC USERS!

WANT TO KNOW MORE ABOUT *MASHLE: MAGIC AND MUSCLES?* HAVE QUESTIONS ABOUT THE WORLD? WANT TO SEE A CERTAIN TYPE OF MAGIC USER APPEAR? SEND EVERYTHING AND ANYTHING YOU CAN THINK OF TO THIS ADDRESS!

101-8050, TOKYO, CHIYODA, HITOTSUBASHI, 2-5-10
SHUEISHA, WEEKLY SHONEN JUMP EDITORIAL DEPT. JC "MASHLE" BONUS SECTION

*BE SURE TO INCLUDE YOUR NAME (OR PEN NAME), ADDRESS, AGE AND PHONE NUMBER.

*SUBMITTED TEXT, IMAGES, ETC. BECOME THE PROPERTY OF SHUEISHA, AND SHUEISHA RESERVES ALL RIGHTS TO REPUBLISH THEM IN DIGITAL OR PHYSICAL FORM. THE EDITORIAL DEPARTMENT MAY MAKE ALTERATIONS TO THE WORK FOR PUBLICATION. ANY RECEIVED ITEMS WILL BE DISPOSED OF AFTER A PERIOD OF TIME. PLEASE MAKE A COPY OF YOUR WORK BEFORE SENDING IT IF YOU WISH TO RETAIN IT. IN ADDITION, PLEASE INDICATE IF YOU DON'T WANT YOUR NAME AND ADDRESS PUBLISHED ALONG WITH YOUR WORK.

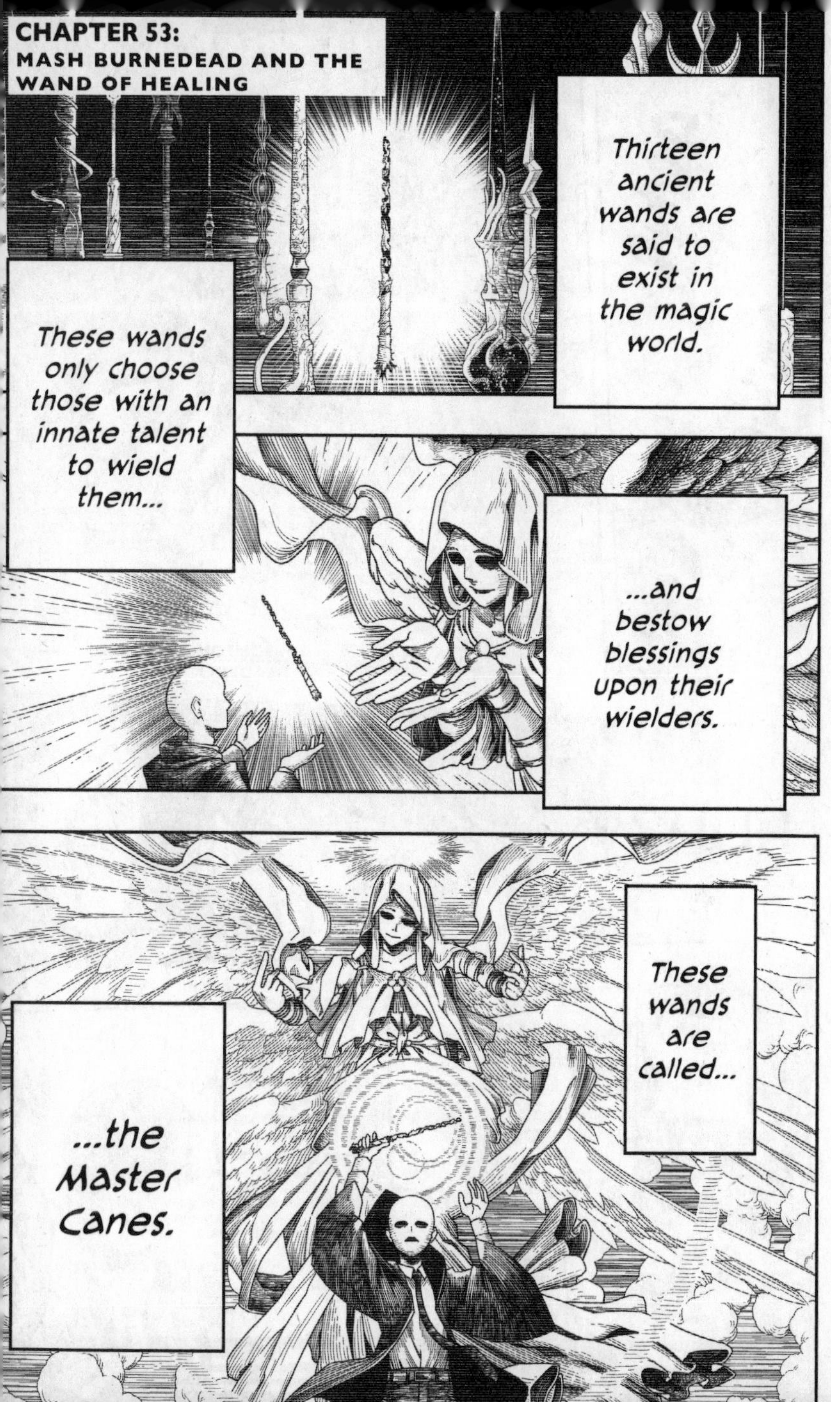
CHAPTER 53:
MASH BURNEDEAD AND THE WAND OF HEALING
Thirteen ancient wands are said to exist in the magic world.
These wands only choose those with an innate talent to wield them...
...and bestow blessings upon their wielders.
These wands are called...
...the Master Canes.

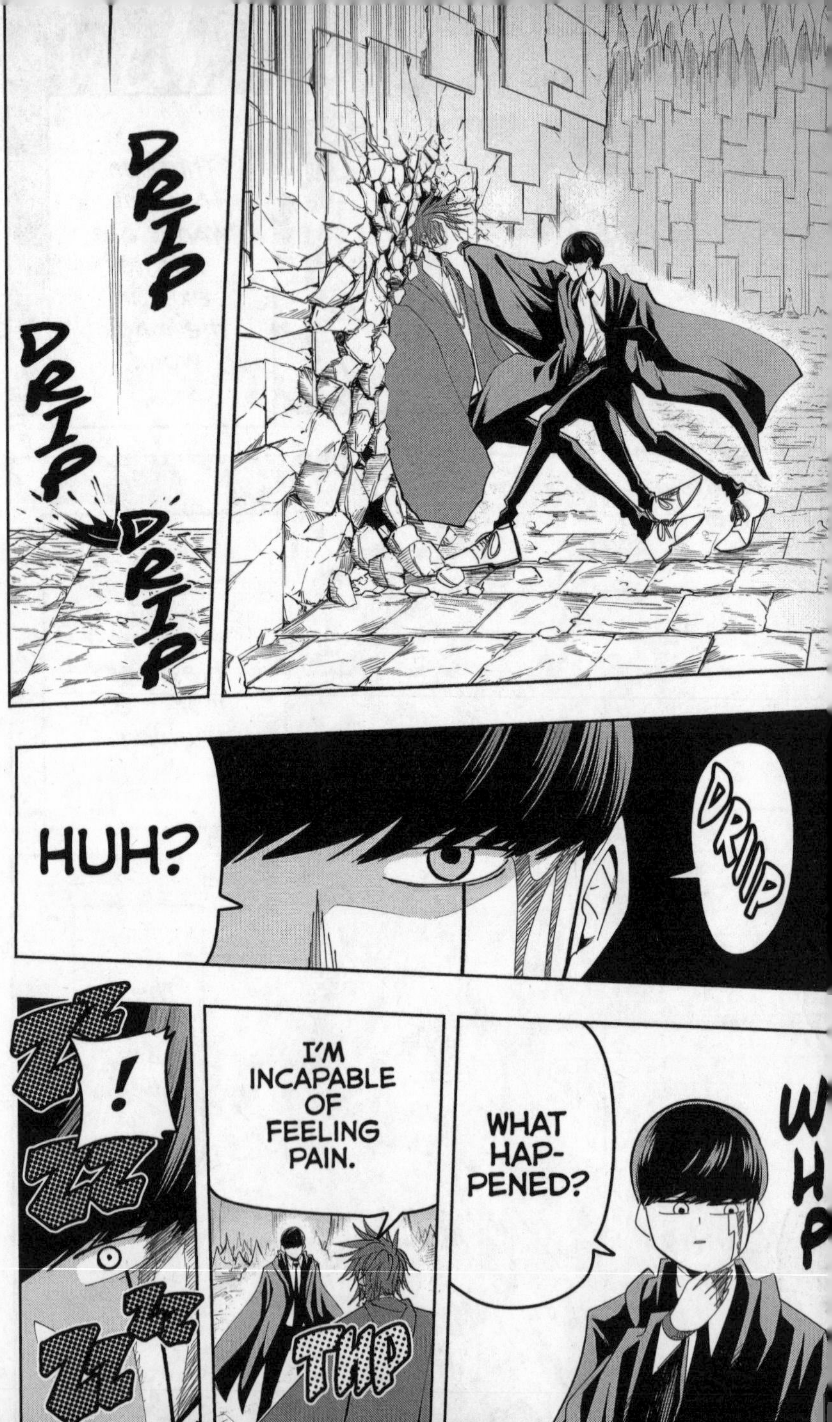
DRIP
DRIP
DRIP
DRIIP
HUH?
WHP
WHAT HAP-PENED?
I'M INCAPABLE OF FEELING PAIN.
THP
!

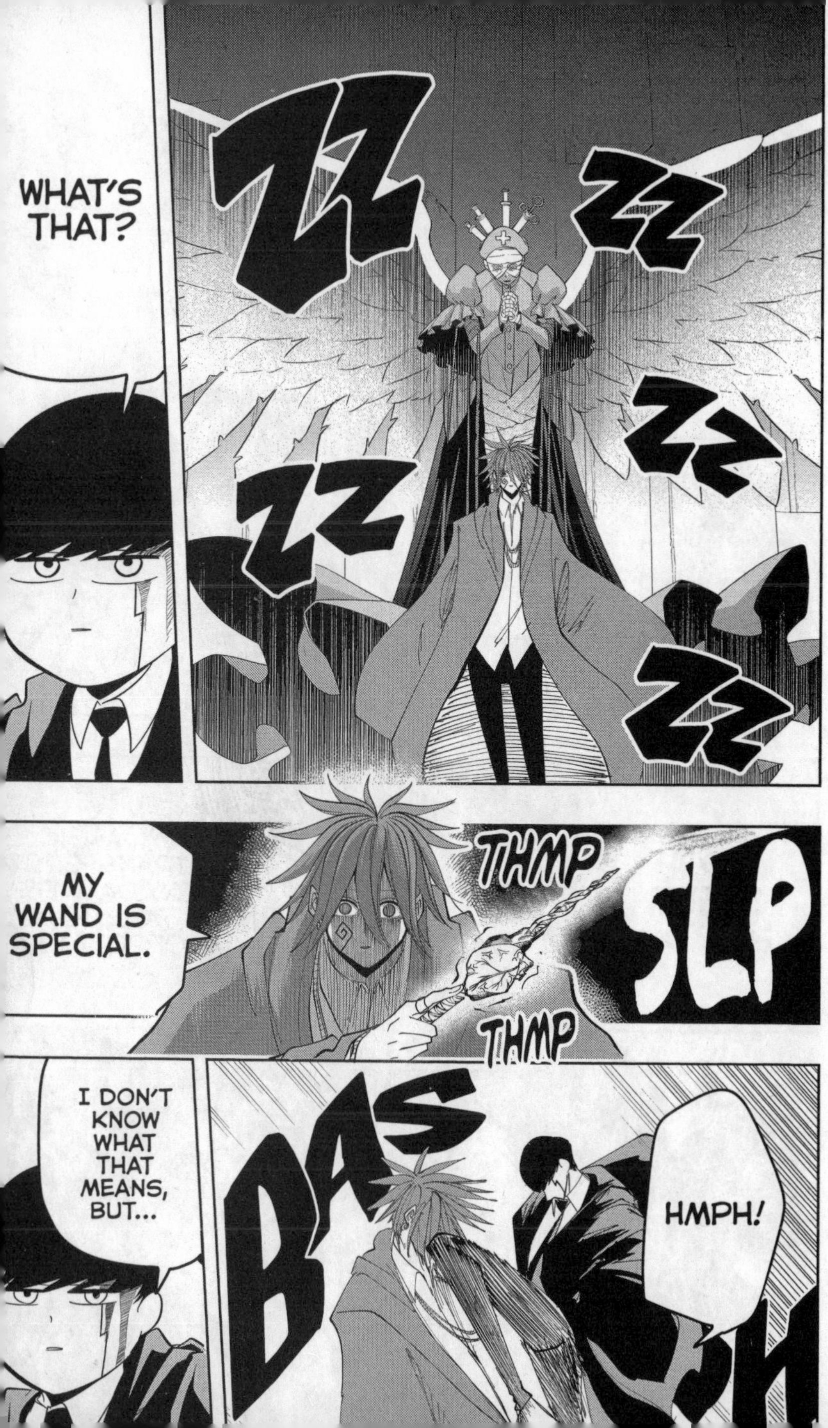
ZZ
ZZ
ZZ
ZZ
ZZ
WHAT'S THAT?
THMP
SLP
MY WAND IS SPECIAL.
THMP
HMPH!
BASH
I DON'T KNOW WHAT THAT MEANS, BUT...

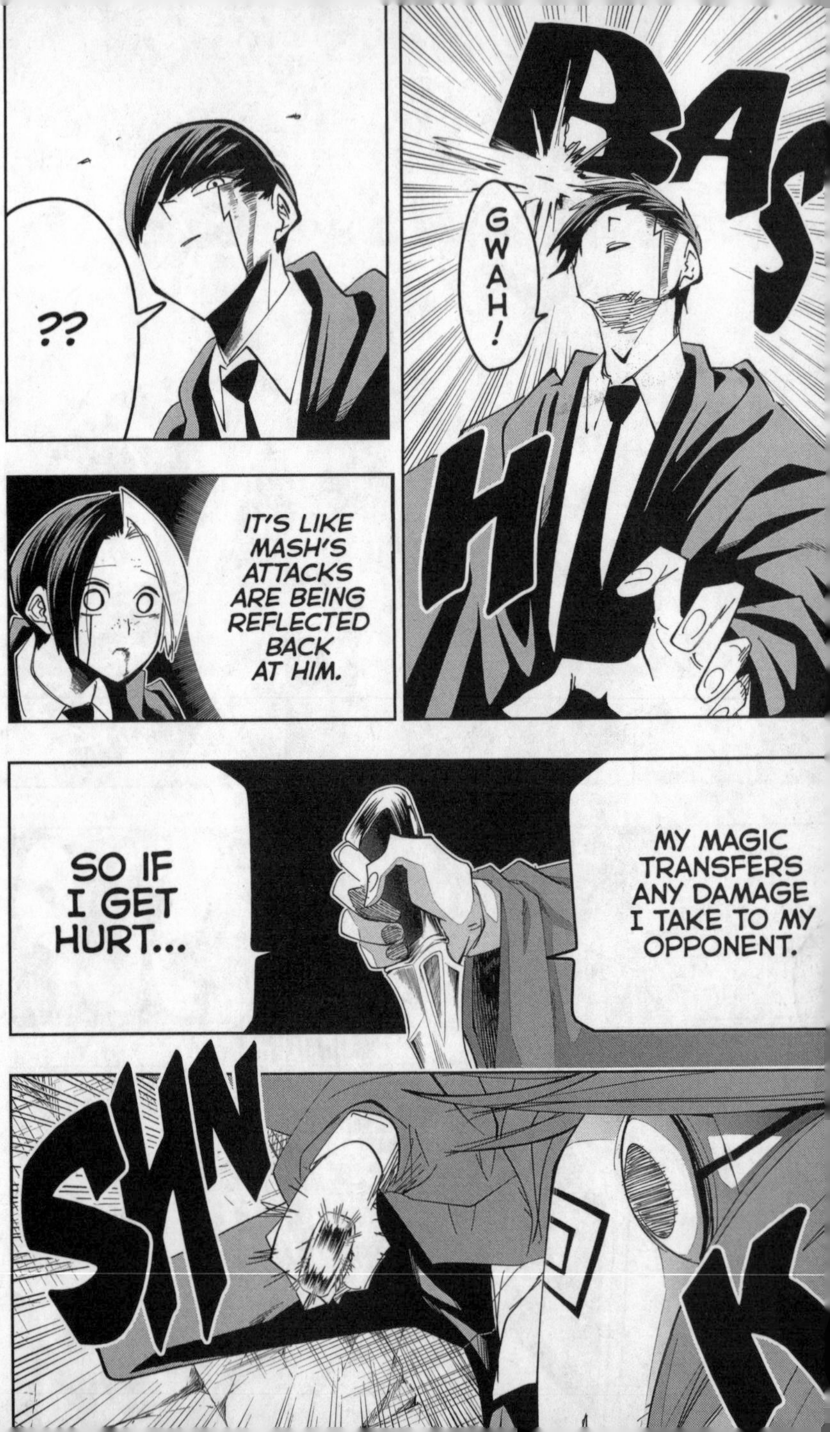
BASH
GWAH!
??
IT'S LIKE MASH'S ATTACKS ARE BEING REFLECTED BACK AT HIM.
MY MAGIC TRANSFERS ANY DAMAGE I TAKE TO MY OPPONENT.
SO IF I GET HURT...
SHNK

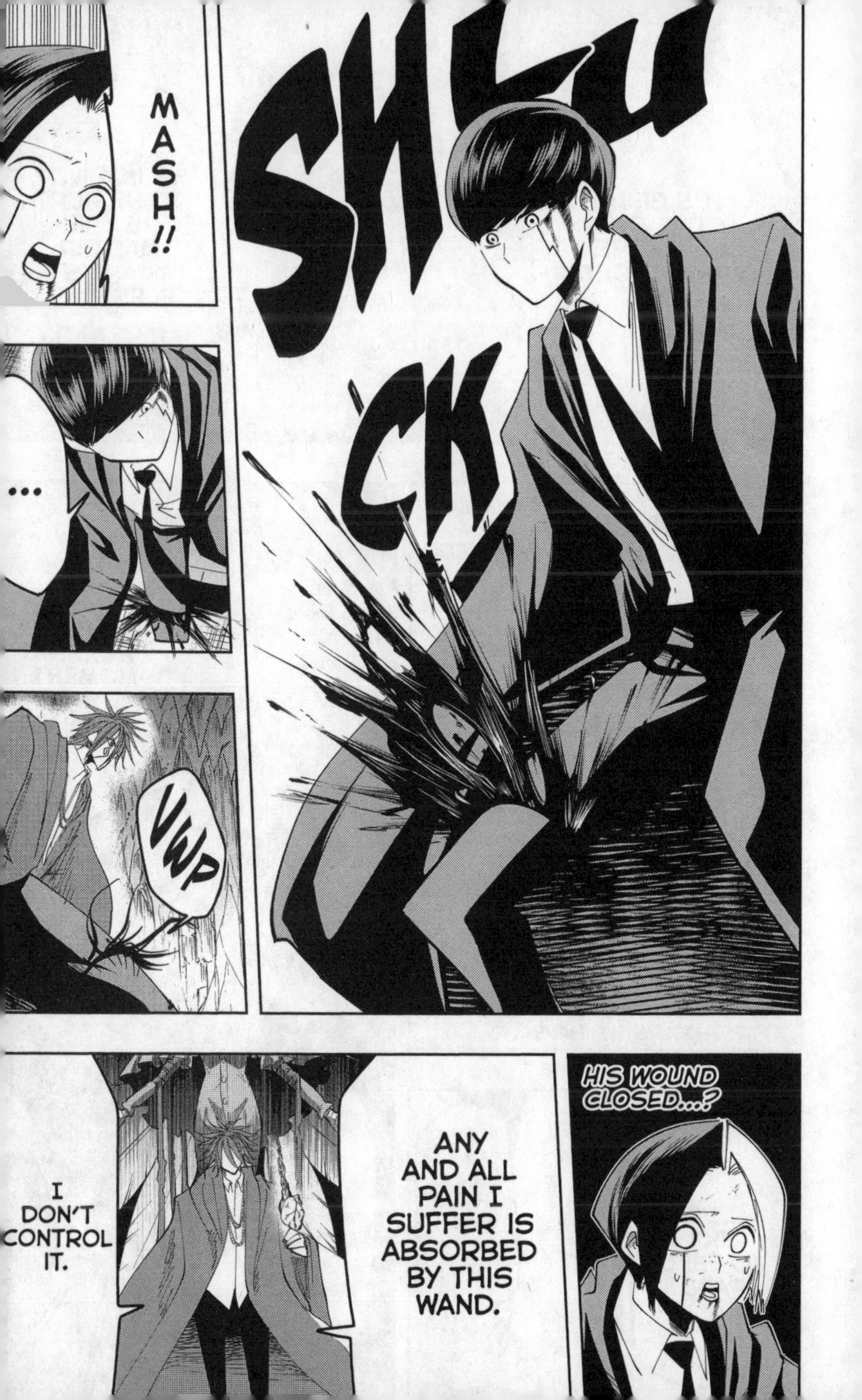
SHUCK
MASH!!
...
UWP
HIS WOUND CLOSED...?
ANY AND ALL PAIN I SUFFER IS ABSORBED BY THIS WAND.
I DON'T CONTROL IT.

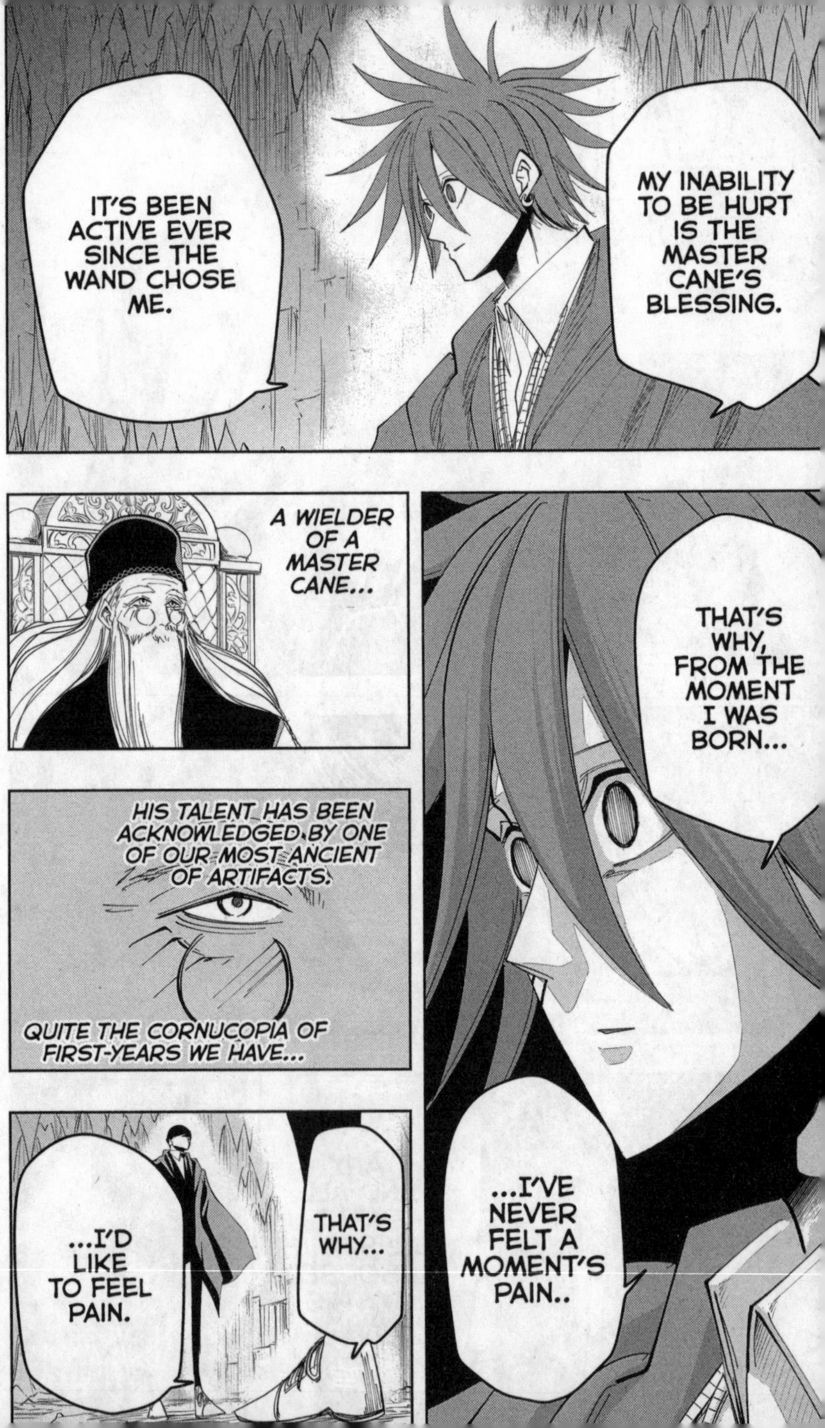
MY INABILITY TO BE HURT IS THE MASTER CANE'S BLESSING.
IT'S BEEN ACTIVE EVER SINCE THE WAND CHOSE ME.
THAT'S WHY, FROM THE MOMENT I WAS BORN...
...I'VE NEVER FELT A MOMENT'S PAIN..
A WIELDER OF A MASTER CANE...
HIS TALENT HAS BEEN ACKNOWLEDGED BY ONE OF OUR MOST ANCIENT OF ARTIFACTS.
QUITE THE CORNUCOPIA OF FIRST-YEARS WE HAVE...
THAT'S WHY...
...I'D LIKE TO FEEL PAIN.

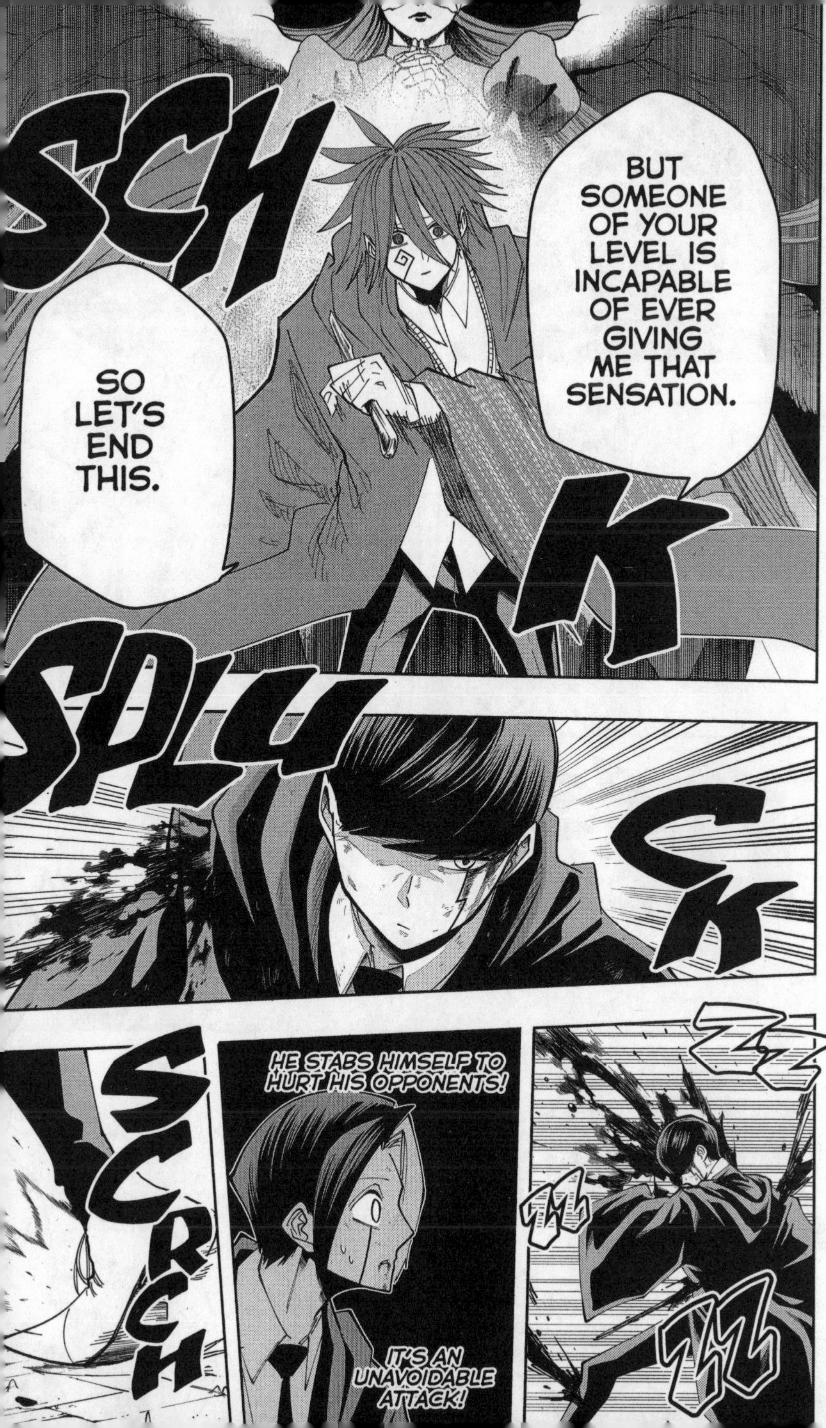
BUT SOMEONE OF YOUR LEVEL IS INCAPABLE OF EVER GIVING ME THAT SENSATION.
SCH
K
SO LET'S END THIS.
SPLU
CK
ZZZ
HE STABS HIMSELF TO HURT HIS OPPONENTS!
IT'S AN UNAVOIDABLE ATTACK!
SCRCH

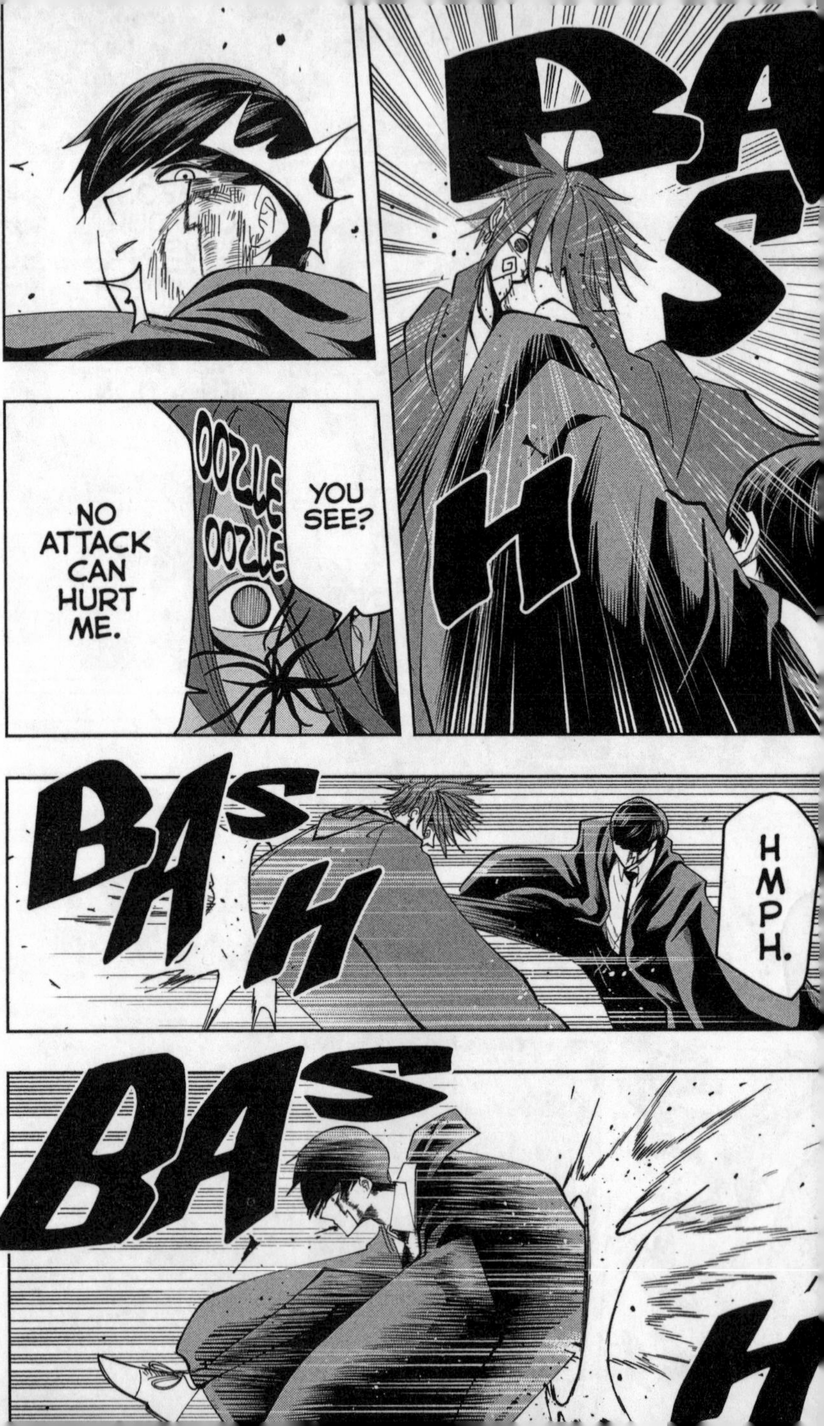
BASH
YOU SEE?
OOZLE
OOZLE
NO ATTACK CAN HURT ME.
HMPH.
BASH
BASH

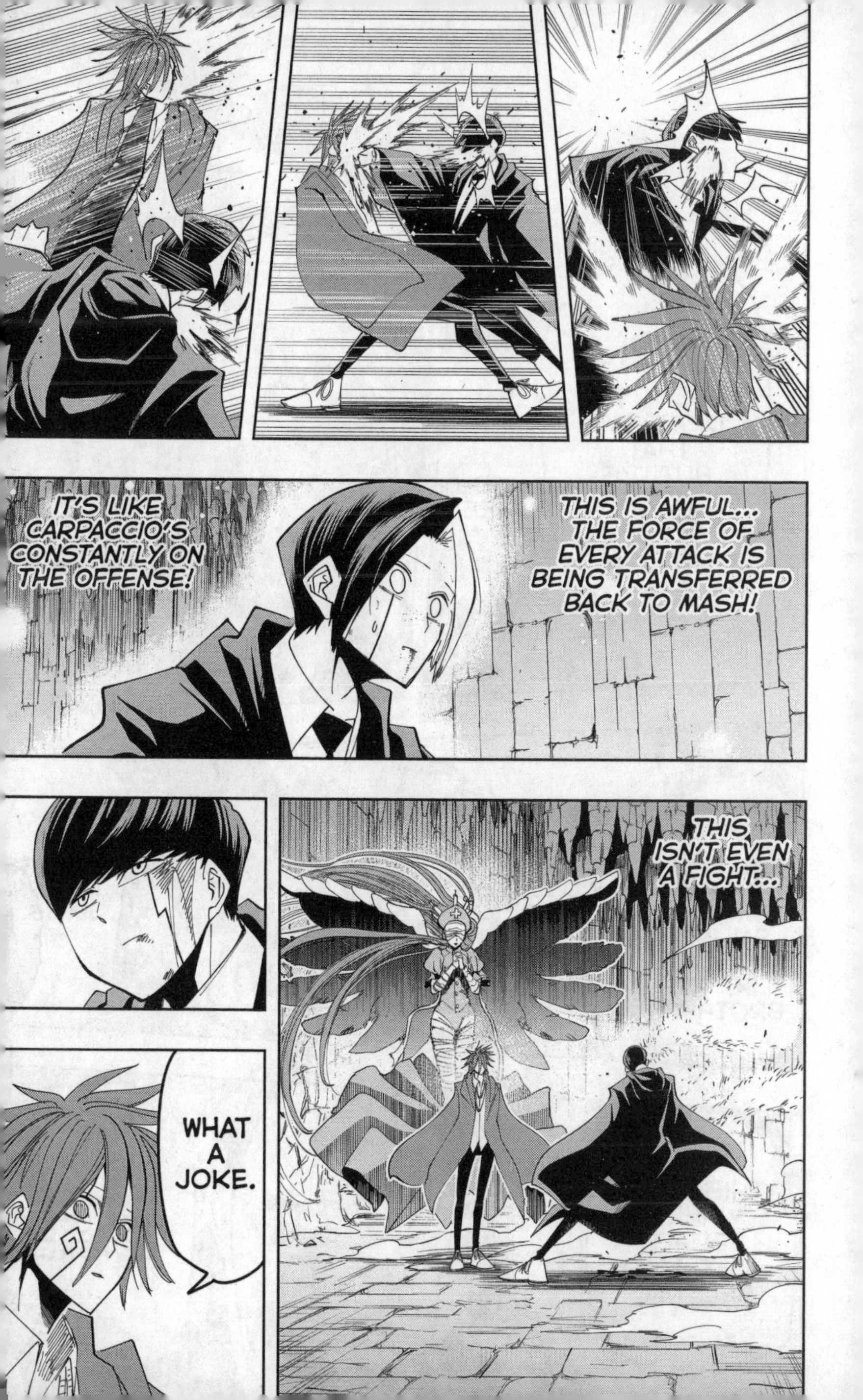
THIS IS AWFUL... THE FORCE OF EVERY ATTACK IS BEING TRANSFERRED BACK TO MASH!
IT'S LIKE CARPACCIO'S CONSTANTLY ON THE OFFENSE!
THIS ISN'T EVEN A FIGHT...
WHAT A JOKE.

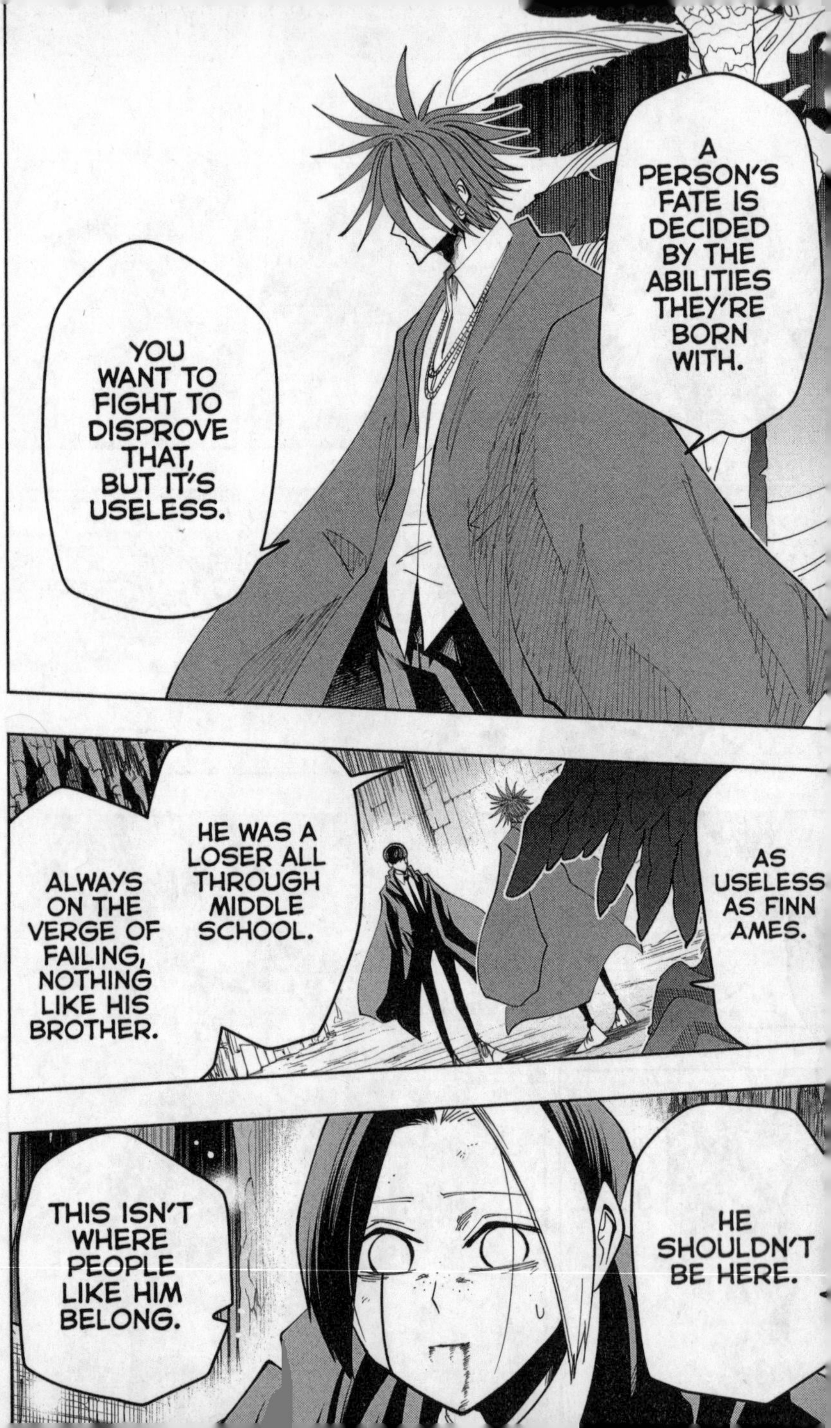
A PERSON'S FATE IS DECIDED BY THE ABILITIES THEY'RE BORN WITH.
YOU WANT TO FIGHT TO DISPROVE THAT, BUT IT'S USELESS.
AS USELESS AS FINN AMES.
HE WAS A LOSER ALL THROUGH MIDDLE SCHOOL.
ALWAYS ON THE VERGE OF FAILING, NOTHING LIKE HIS BROTHER.
HE SHOULDN'T BE HERE.
THIS ISN'T WHERE PEOPLE LIKE HIM BELONG.

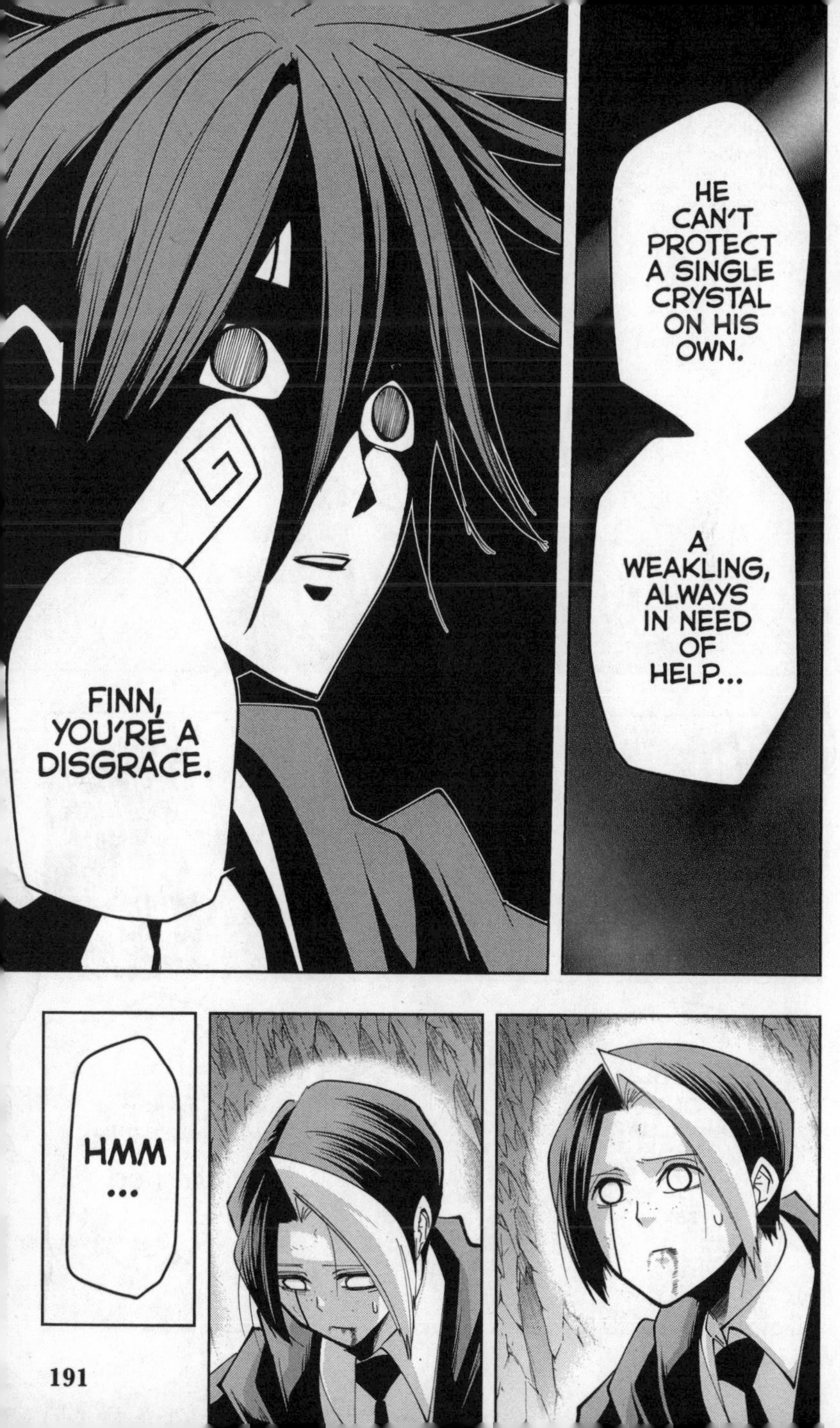
HE CAN'T PROTECT A SINGLE CRYSTAL ON HIS OWN.
A WEAKLING, ALWAYS IN NEED OF HELP...
FINN, YOU'RE A DISGRACE.
HMM ...

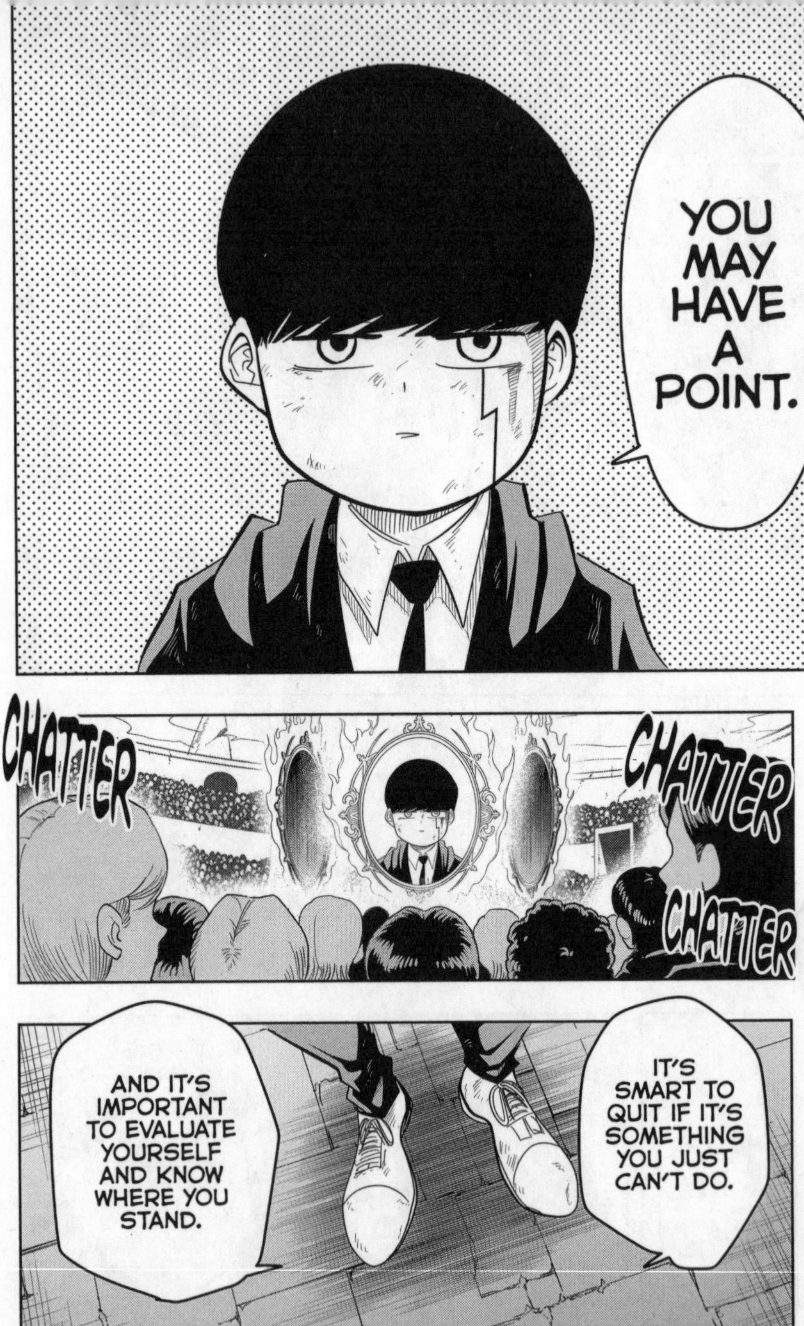
YOU MAY HAVE A POINT.
CHATTER
CHATTER
CHATTER
IT'S SMART TO QUIT IF IT'S SOMETHING YOU JUST CAN'T DO.
AND IT'S IMPORTANT TO EVALUATE YOURSELF AND KNOW WHERE YOU STAND.

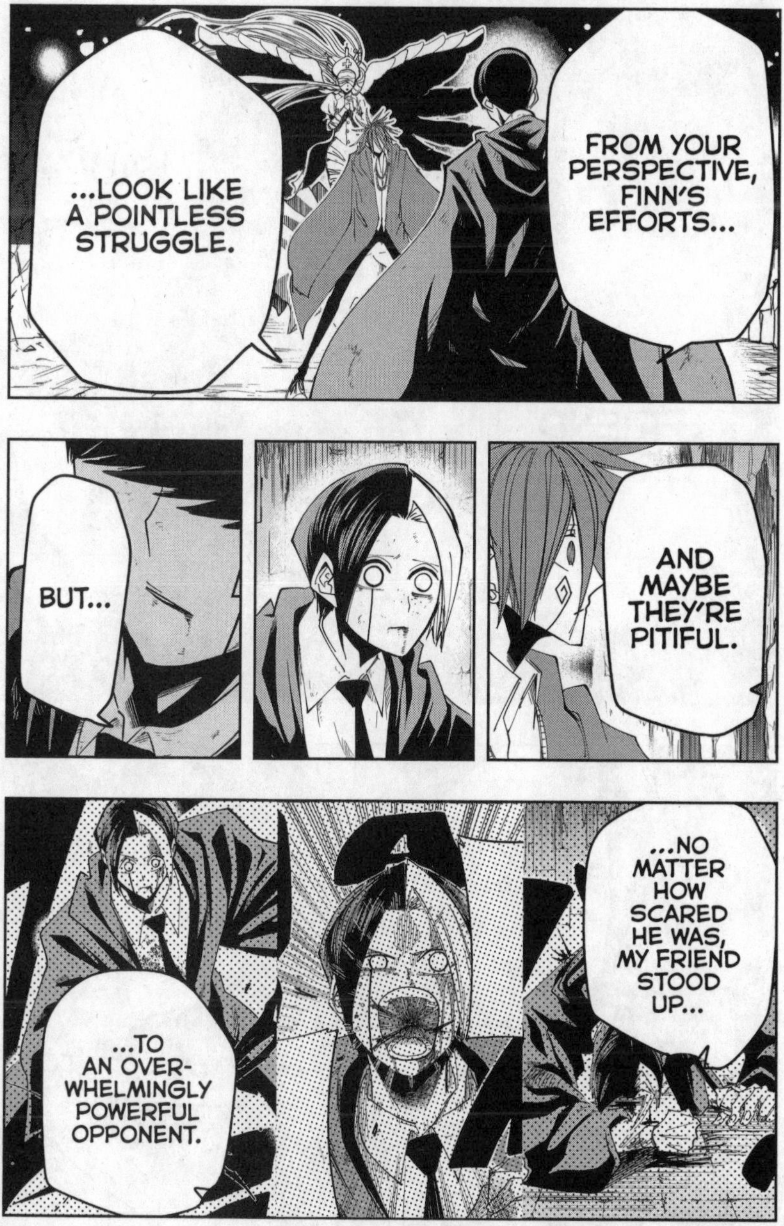
FROM YOUR PERSPECTIVE, FINN'S EFFORTS...
...LOOK LIKE A POINTLESS STRUGGLE.
AND MAYBE THEY'RE PITIFUL.
BUT...
...NO MATTER HOW SCARED HE WAS, MY FRIEND STOOD UP...
...TO AN OVER-WHELMINGLY POWERFUL OPPONENT.

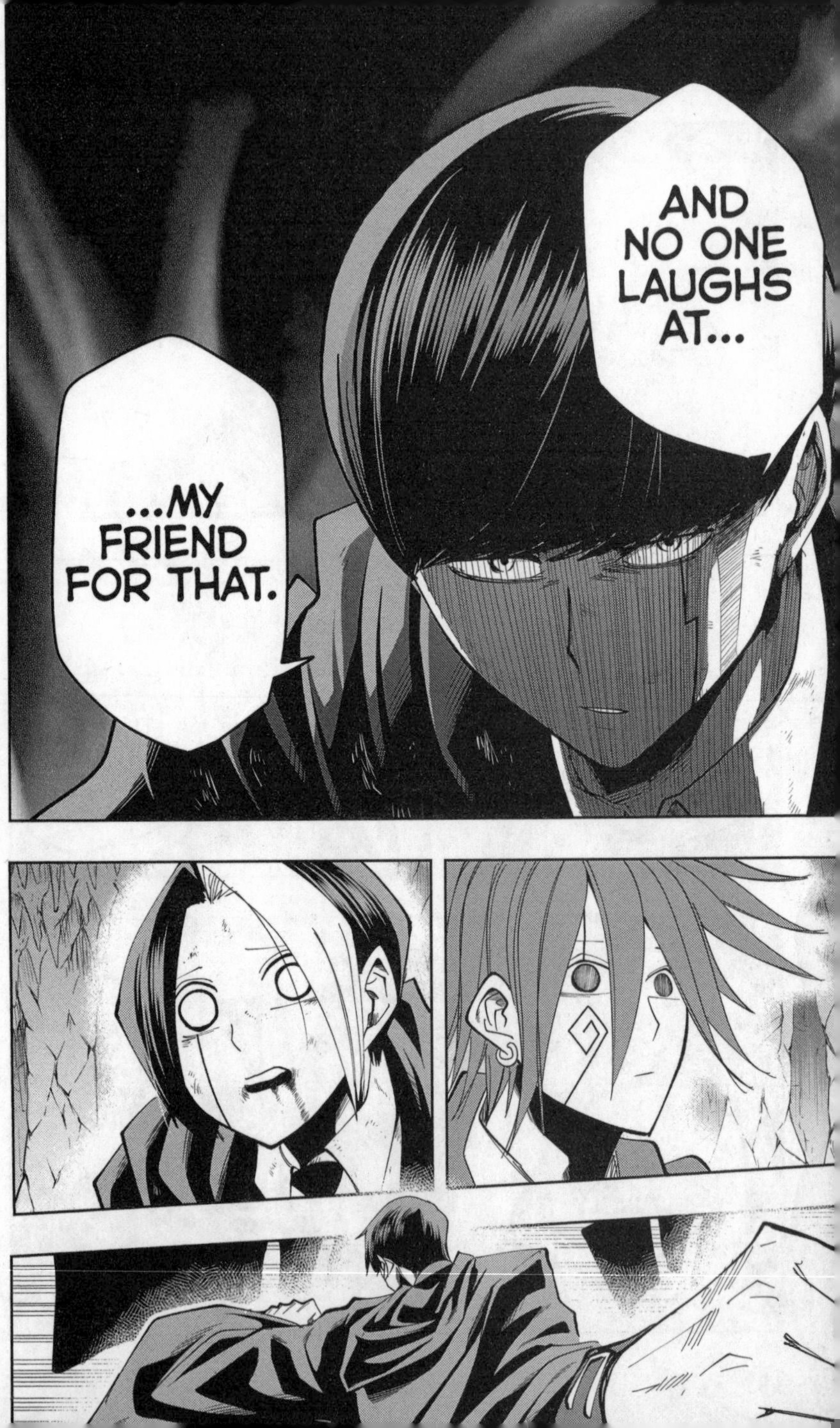
AND NO ONE LAUGHS AT...
...MY FRIEND FOR THAT.

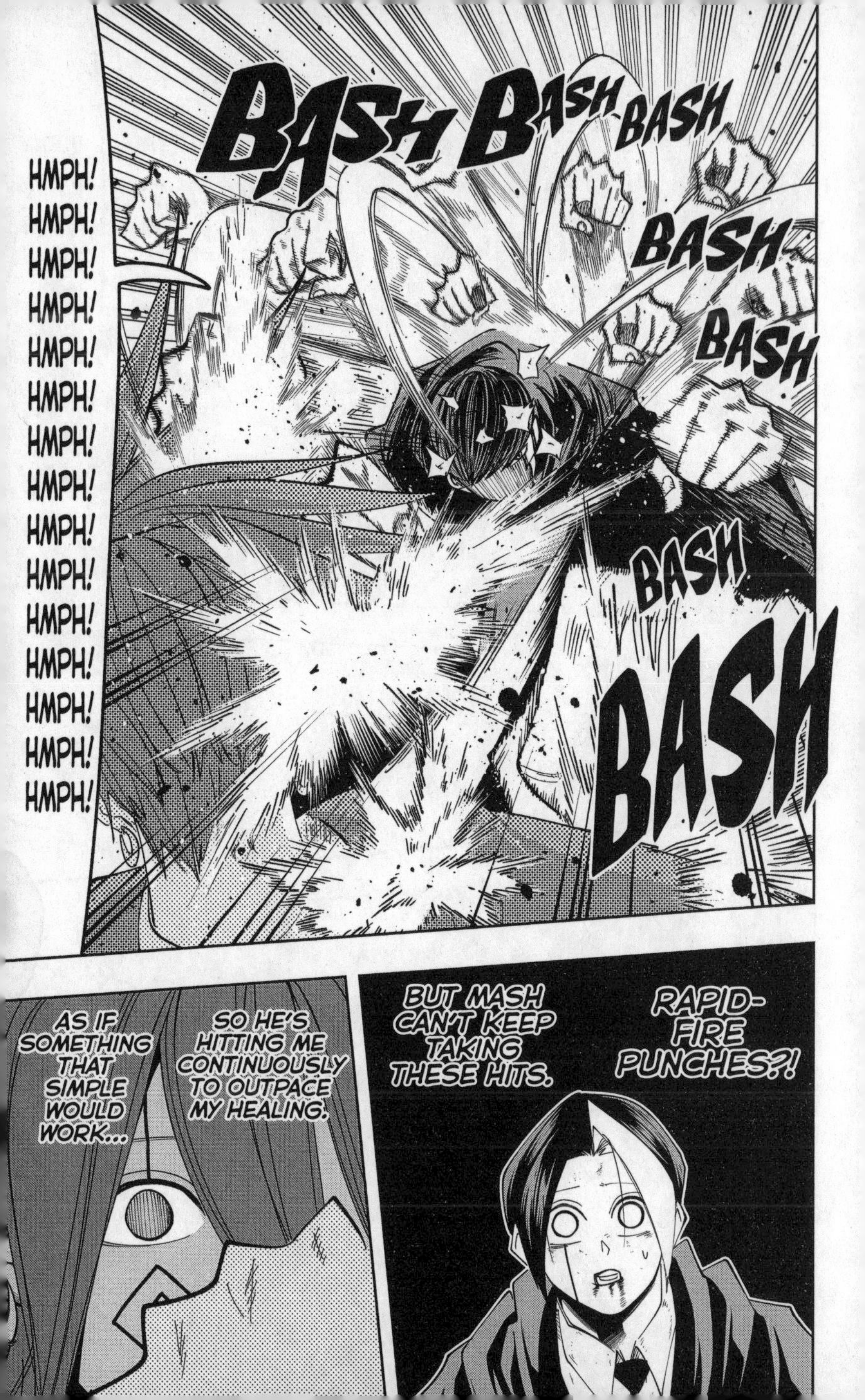
BASH BASH BASH
BASH
BASH
BASH
BASH
HMPH!
HMPH!
HMPH!
HMPH!
HMPH!
HMPH!
HMPH!
HMPH!
HMPH!
HMPH!
HMPH!
HMPH!
HMPH!
HMPH!
HMPH!
RAPID-FIRE PUNCHES?!
BUT MASH CAN'T KEEP TAKING THESE HITS.
SO HE'S HITTING ME CONTINUOUSLY TO OUTPACE MY HEALING.
AS IF SOMETHING THAT SIMPLE WOULD WORK...

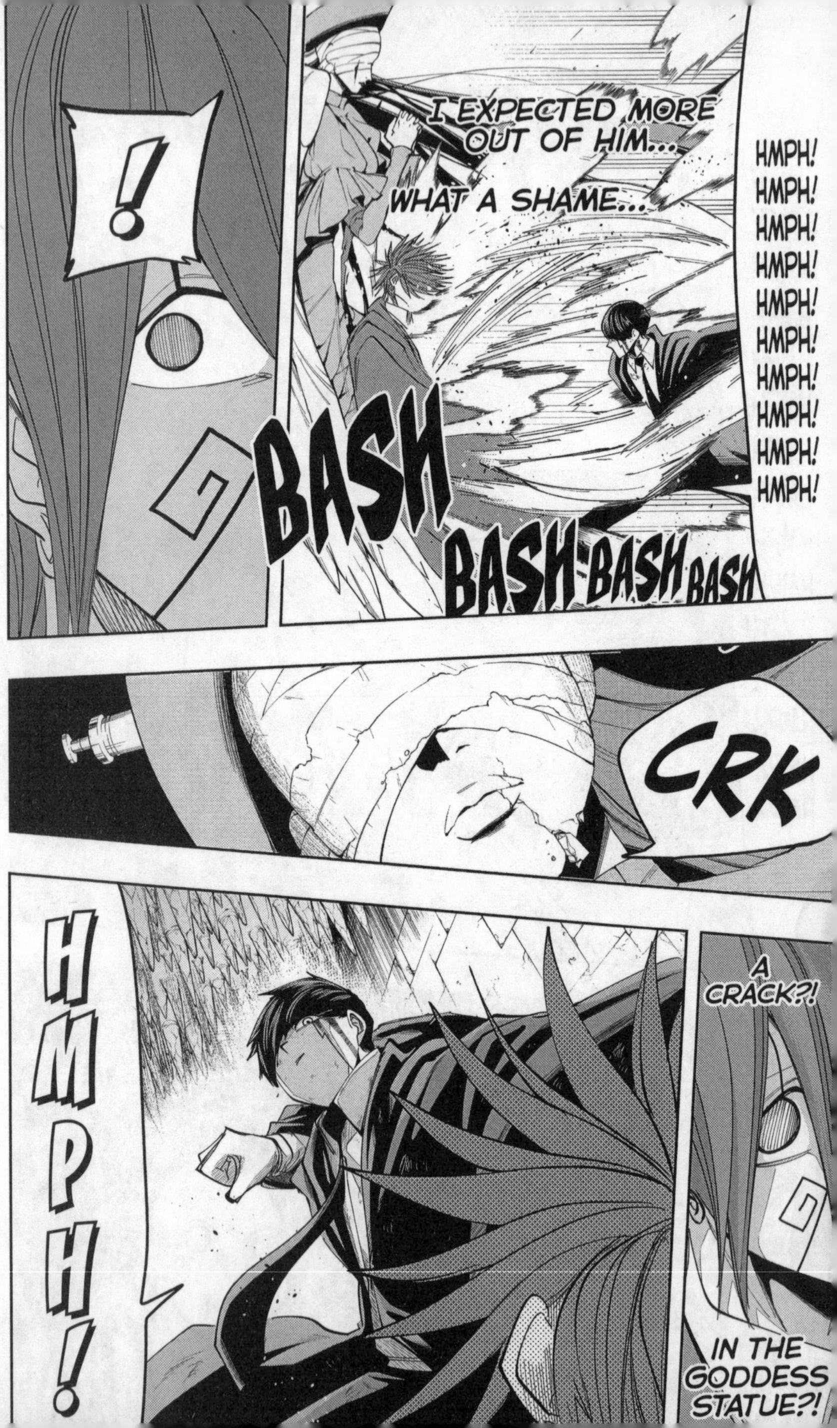
HMPH! HMPH! HMPH! HMPH! HMPH! HMPH! HMPH! HMPH! HMPH! HMPH!
I EXPECTED MORE OUT OF HIM...
WHAT A SHAME...
BASH
BASH BASH BASH
!
CRK
A CRACK?!
IN THE GODDESS STATUE?!
HMPH!

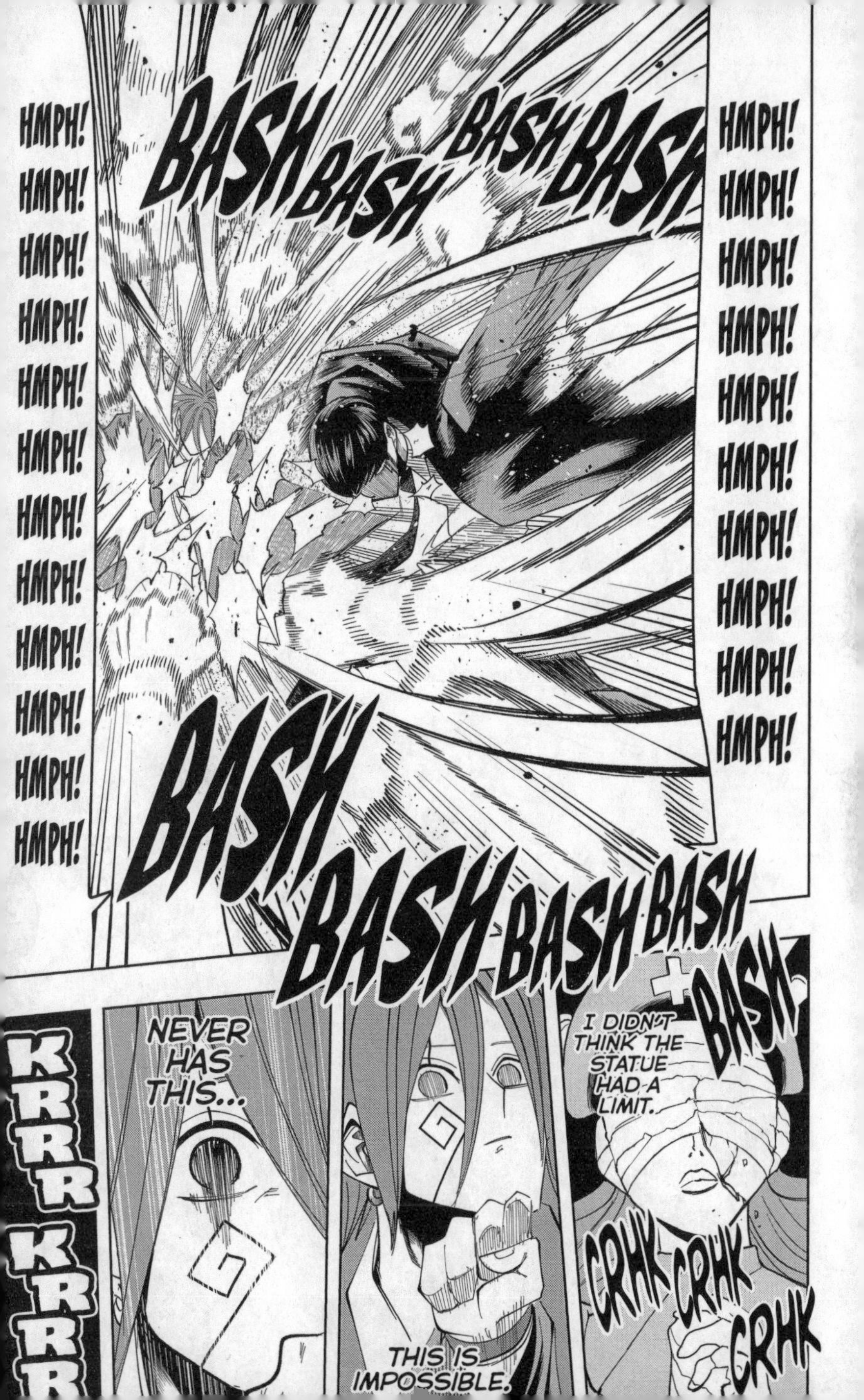
HMPH! HMPH! HMPH! HMPH! HMPH! HMPH! HMPH! HMPH! HMPH! HMPH!
BASH BASH BASH BASH
HMPH! HMPH! HMPH! HMPH! HMPH! HMPH! HMPH! HMPH! HMPH! HMPH! HMPH! HMPH!
BASH BASH BASH BASH
BASH
I DIDN'T THINK THE STATUE HAD A LIMIT.
CRHK CRHK CRHK
THIS IS IMPOSSIBLE.
NEVER HAS THIS...
KRRR KRRR

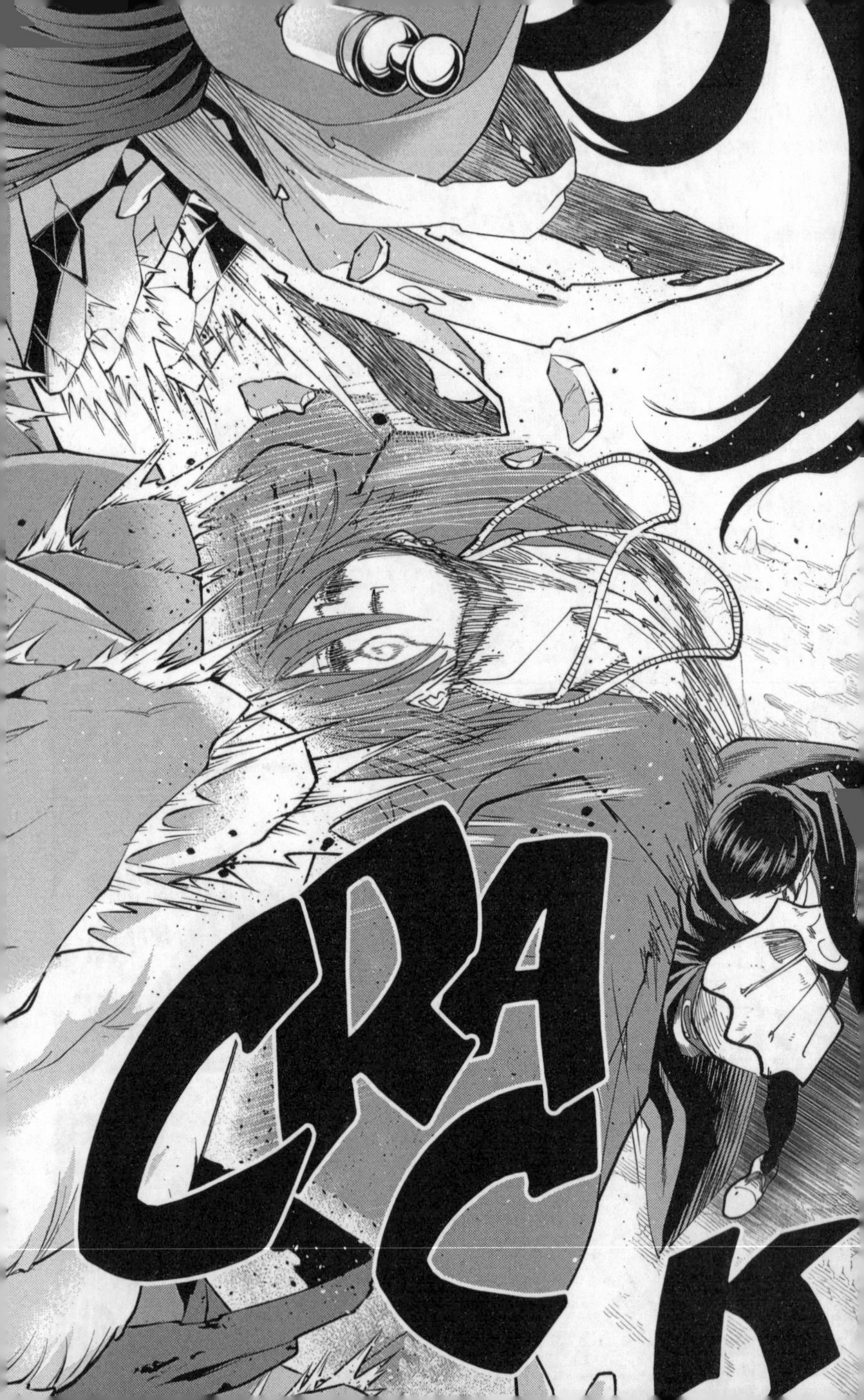
CRACK

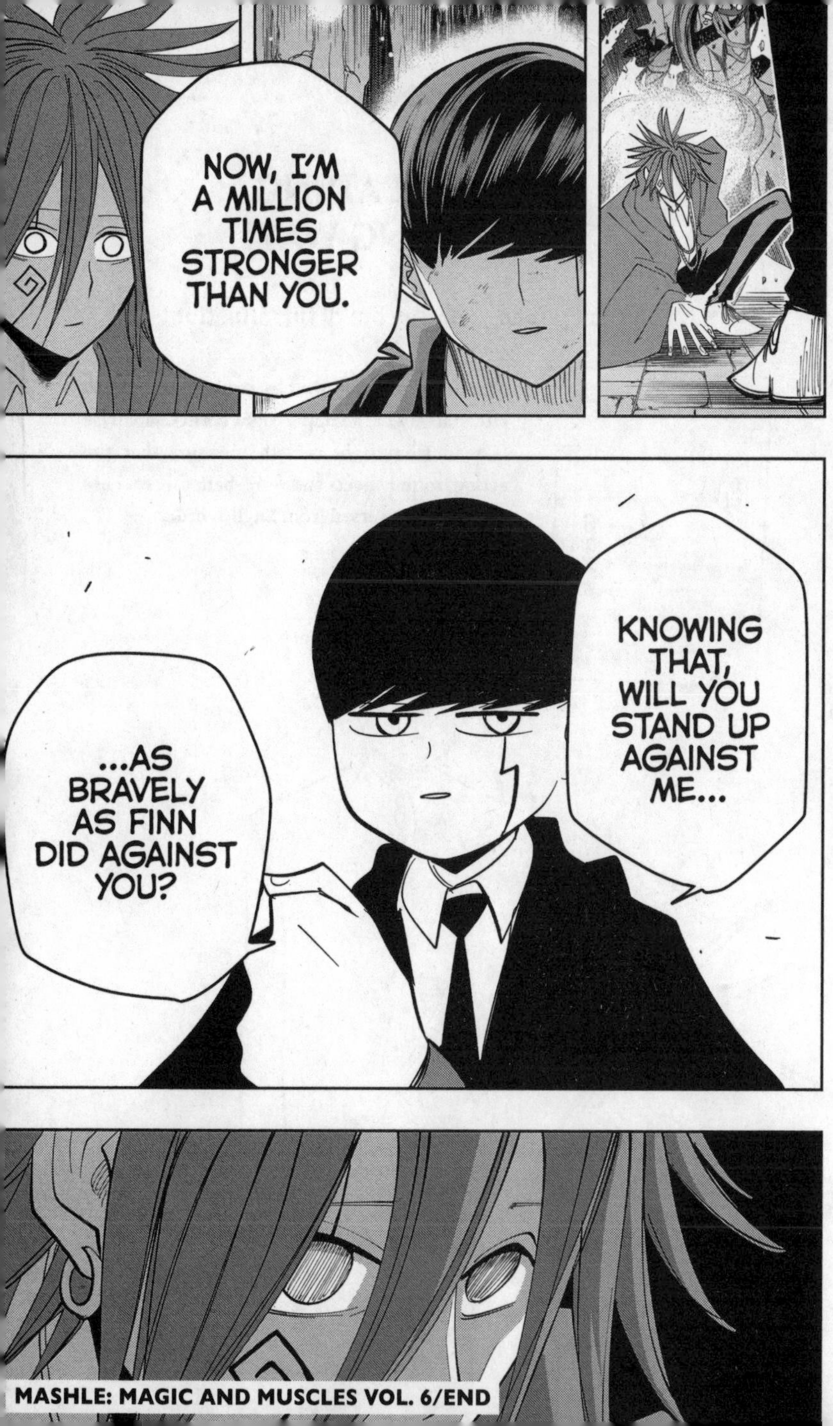
NOW, I'M A MILLION TIMES STRONGER THAN YOU.
KNOWING THAT, WILL YOU STAND UP AGAINST ME...
...AS BRAVELY AS FINN DID AGAINST YOU?
MASHLE: MAGIC AND MUSCLES VOL. 6/END

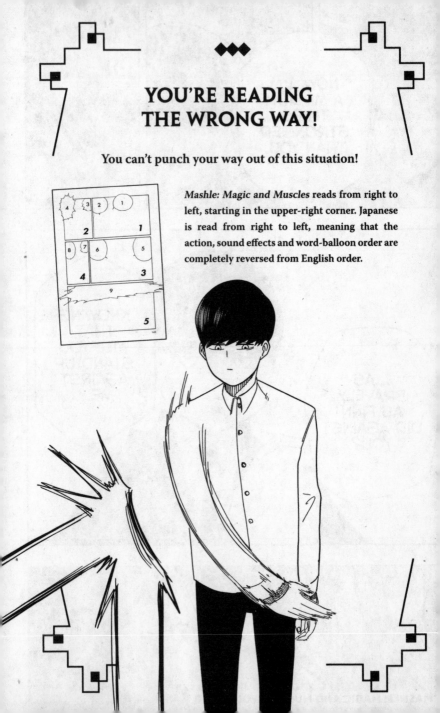

YOU'RE READING THE WRONG WAY!

You can't punch your way out of this situation!

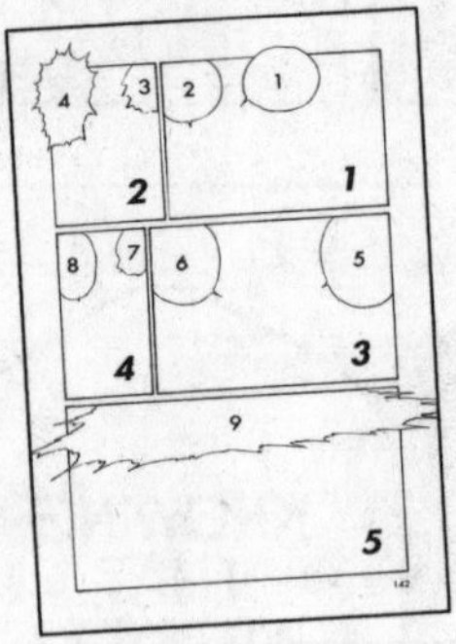
1
2
3
4
1
2
5
6
7
8
3
4
9
5
142

Mashle: Magic and Muscles **reads from right to left, starting in the upper-right corner. Japanese is read from right to left, meaning that the action, sound effects and word-balloon order are completely reversed from English order.**

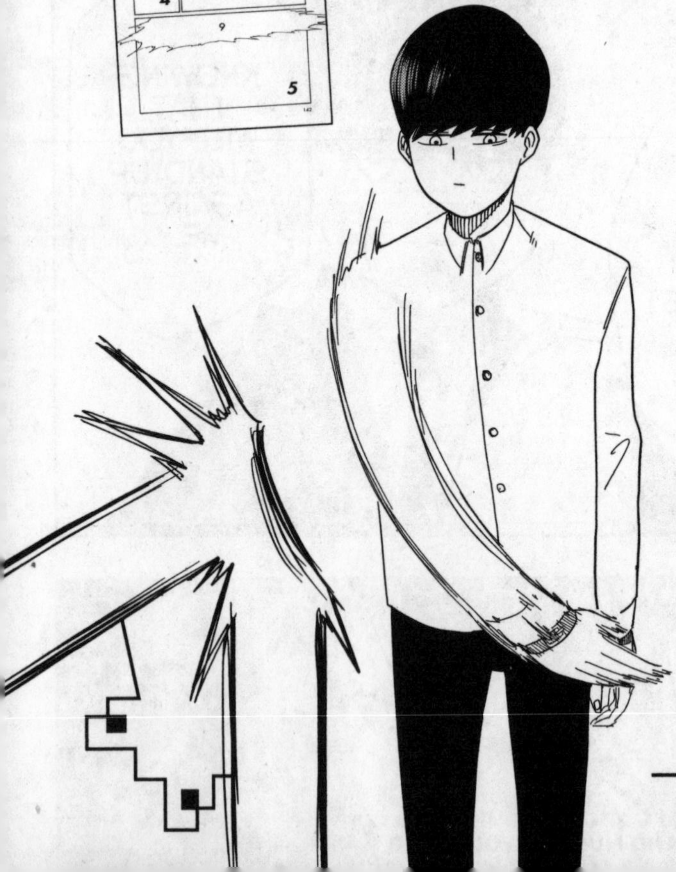